Better Homes and Gardens®

the *ultimate* soups & stews book

More than **400** satisfying meals in a bowl

Houghton Mifflin Harcourt
Boston New York

Cover image: Blaine Moats

Cover design: Suzanne Sunwoo

Published by Houghton Mifflin Harcourt Publishing Company

Published simultaneously in Canada

For information about permission to reproduce selections from this book, write to Permissions, Houghton Mifflin Harcourt Publishing Company, 215 Park Avenue South, New York, New York 10003.

Meredith Corporation

Editor: Jan Miller

Contributing Editor: Lois White

Recipe Development and Testing: Better Homes and Gardens® Test Kitchen

Publisher: Natalie Chapman

Executive Editor: Anne Ficklen

Senior Editor: Linda Ingroia

Senior Editorial Assistant: Heather Dabah

Senior Production Editor: Jacqueline Beach

Production Director: Diana Cisek

Interior Design: Jill Budden

Layout: Holly Wittenberg

Manufacturing Manager: Tom Hyland

Our seal assures you that every recipe in *The Ultimate Soups & Stews Book* has been tested in the Better Homes and Gardens Test Kitchen®. This means that each recipe is practical and reliable and meets our high standards of taste appeal. We guarantee your satisfaction with this book for as long as you own it.

Library of Congress Cataloging-in-Publication Data

Better homes and gardens the ultimate soups and stews book : more than 400 satisfying meals in a bowl.

    p. cm.

Includes index.

  ISBN 978-1-118-33561-1 (pbk.); 9781118335567 (ebk.); 9781118335628 (ebk.); 9781118335635 (ebk.)

  1. Soups. 2. Stews. 3. One-dish meals. I. Better homes and gardens. II. Title: Ultimate soups and stews book.

  TX757.B433 2013

  641.81'3—dc23

                2012011968

Printed in the United States of America

DOC 10 9 8 7 6 5 4 3

4500579365

Cover photos

Upper left on gold: Creamy Chicken Noodle Soup (page 41); Upper middle on purple: Spiced Fruit Soup (page 467); Upper right on orange: French Onion and Beef Soup (page 26); Middle row left on green: San Francisco Seafood Stew (page 345); Middle row middle on purple: Curried Pumpkin Soup (page 440); Middle row right on orange: Sweet Potato-Black Bean Stew (page 369); Bottom row left on orange: Spring Greens Soup (page 434); Bottom row middle on gold: Pork and Hominy Soup (page 113); Bottom row right on green: Chipotle Steak Chili (page 180)

390

4

134

62

table of
contents

91

344

slowcooker

lowfat

◄ Recipes that include
   slow cooker directions

◄ Recipes with 10 grams
   of fat or less per main-
   dish serving

Look for these tabs
throughout to guide
your recipe choices

6

introduction

soups for every season!

No matter the time of year, nothing can be more satisfying than
a bowl of soup. Much of the appeal of this comfort food comes
from its glorious aromas and so many distinctive flavors and
styles, whether creamy or clear, casual or elegant, brimming
with seafood or thick with vegetables. But more than ever,
soups and stews are a way to bring fresh, seasonal flavors to
the table.

Dish up any one of the extraordinary recipes in this collection
and you'll be sure to draw rave reviews every time. From the
timeless classics to soups with innovative ingredient pairings,
the recipes cover every course—from appetizers to desserts.
What's more, you can easily adapt many of the recipes to
incorporate ingredients you have on hand or leftovers you want
to use. Look for icons that identify our best slow-cooker recipes
as well as low-fat soups. Another bonus: You'll find basics on
making homemade stock, customizing your own soups, and tips
that show you how to master soups of all kinds. Making soup
has never been so easy!

Creamy Chicken Noodle Soup
page 41

soup-making ba

If you know how to boil water and have a few essential ingredients on hand—vegetables, meat, beans, and/or grains—you can make soup. To help you get started, here are a few basics on making rich soup stocks, plus techniques for cooking and freezing soups and stews. You'll also find oodles of ideas for customizing your own tasty soups.

sics

soup terms

Not all soups are alike. Texture, consistency, and ingredients are what differentiate one soup from another. Here are several types of soups you'll run across in this book.

Bisque: a rich, thick, smooth soup that's often made with shellfish, such as lobster or shrimp. It is usually thickened by pureeing ingredients or adding cream.

Chowder: a thick, chunky soup. Traditionally, a chowder is made with seafood or fish, but chowders made with poultry, vegetables, and cheeses have become popular.

Stock: a strained, thin, clear liquid in which meat, poultry, or fish has been simmered with vegetables and herbs. While normally used as an ingredient in other soups, it can be enjoyed as a light course on its own.

Gazpacho: a vegetable soup served cold, often made with tomatoes as the key ingredient.

Gumbo: hearty bowls of seafood, vegetables, and/or meat chunks that have thick broths and Creole seasonings.

Stew: a very thick soup based on chunks of meat or occasionally fish and vegetables. The thick souplike broth is a combination of the stewing liquid and the natural juices of the food being stewed.

HOT or COLD

To keep soup piping hot, serve it in warm bowls. Cold soups are more refreshing and stay cold longer when served in chilled bowls. Follow these guidelines to enjoy your soup at the right temperature.

To warm bowls: Preheat your oven to the lowest setting; then turn it off. Place bowls in the oven for 5 to 10 minutes before serving time.

To chill bowls: Place bowls in the refrigerator for 10 to 15 minutes before serving time.

Reheating soups: When reheating soup on the stove top, use high heat for broth-based soups and low heat for purees or cream soups. Bring soup to a gentle simmer until heated through. Stir as often as necessary to keep it from burning. Watch bean, potato, or flour-thickened soups closely, as they can burn easily.

Stock your pantry with canned broth, stewed tomatoes, dried pasta, and herbs and seasonings. Combine with fresh veggies or leftover meat for a quick soup supper that offers home-cooked comfort.

stock up

Rich, velvety homemade stocks are the building blocks for many soups and stews. Simmer chicken or meat, vegetables, seasonings, and water for a few hours to make your own pot of liquid gold.

Stock your pantry

When a recipe calls for broth, use one of the following convenient options to impart rich, distinctive flavor to your soups:

✳ **Canned broth:** Use chicken, beef, or vegetable broth straight from the can or resealable carton. If you prefer lower-sodium varieties, use reduced-sodium or even unsalted chicken or beef broth.

✳ **Bouillon:** Instant bouillon granules or cubes are available in chicken, beef, and vegetable flavors. Mix 1 teaspoon or 1 small cube with 1 cup water. These also come in low-sodium varieties.

✳ **Condensed broth:** Cans of condensed chicken or beef broth, which are stronger than regular-strength broth, are also a quick-fix option. Dilute them for use according to the label directions.

‹chicken stock

prep: 25 minutes   cook: 2½ hours
makes: 6 servings

3   pounds bony chicken
    pieces (wings,
    backs, and/or necks)
3   stalks celery with
    leaves, cut up
2   medium carrots,
    unpeeled and cut up
1   large onion, unpeeled
    and cut up
4   sprigs fresh parsley
2   bay leaves
2   cloves garlic, unpeeled
    and halved
1   teaspoon salt
1   teaspoon dried
    thyme, sage, or
    basil, crushed
½   teaspoon whole black
    peppercorns or
    ¼ teaspoon ground
    black pepper
6   cups cold water

1 If using wings, cut each wing at joints into three pieces. Place chicken pieces in a 6-quart Dutch oven. Add celery, carrots, onion, parsley, bay leaves, garlic, salt, thyme, and peppercorns. Add the water. Bring to boiling; reduce heat. Simmer, covered, for 2½ hours. Remove chicken pieces from Dutch oven.

2 Strain stock into a large bowl through two layers of 100-percent-cotton cheesecloth placed in a colander. Discard vegetables and seasonings. If desired, clarify stock.*

3 If using the stock while hot, skim off fat. Or chill for 6 hours; lift off fat with a spoon. If desired, cool chicken; remove meat from bones, discarding bones and skin. Reserve chicken for another use. Place stock and reserved chicken in separate airtight storage containers. Cover and chill for up to 3 days or freeze for up to 6 months.

nutrition facts per serving: 30 cal., 2 g total fat (1 g sat. fat), 5 mg chol., 435 mg sodium, 1 g carb., 0 g dietary fiber, 0 g sugar, 2 g protein.

Simmer slowly For chicken stock, simmer the meat and vegetables on the stove top for 2½ hours. Gelatin from the bones helps thicken the stock.

Strain the stock Strain the stock through two layers of 100-percent-cotton cheesecloth layered in a colander set over a large bowl. Discard chicken and vegetables. If desired, clarify broth.

*To *clarify hot strained broth,* return broth to Dutch oven. In a small bowl, combine ¼ cup cold water and 1 beaten egg white. Stir water mixture into broth. Bring to boiling. Remove from heat and let stand for 5 minutes. Strain the broth again.

beef stock

prep: 30 minutes cook: 3½ hours roast: 30 minutes
makes: 6 to 7 servings

4 pounds meaty beef
   soup bones (beef
   shank crosscuts
   or short ribs)
½ cup water
3 medium carrots,
   cut up
2 medium onions,
   unpeeled and cut up
2 stalks celery with
   leaves, cut up
1 tablespoon dried basil
   or thyme, crushed
1½ teaspoons salt
10 whole black
   peppercorns
8 sprigs fresh parsley
4 bay leaves
2 cloves garlic,
   unpeeled and
   halved
8 cups water

1 Preheat oven to 450°F. Place soup bones in a large, shallow roasting pan. Roast about 30 minutes or until brown, turning once.

2 Place soup bones in a large pot. Pour the ½ cup water into the roasting pan and scrape up browned bits; add water mixture to large pot. Stir in carrots, onions, celery, basil, salt, peppercorns, parsley, bay leaves, and garlic. Add the 8 cups water. Bring to boiling; reduce heat. Simmer, covered, for 3½ hours. Remove soup bones from broth; set aside.

3 Strain broth. Discard vegetables and seasonings.

4 If using the broth while hot, skim fat. If storing broth for later use, chill broth in a bowl for 6 hours; lift off fat with a spoon. Place broth in airtight containers. Cover and chill for up to 3 days or freeze for up to 6 months.

5 If desired, when bones are cool enough to handle, remove meat. Chop meat; discard bones. Place meat in airtight containers. Cover and chill for up to 3 days or freeze for up to 3 months.

nutrition facts per serving: 17 cal., 0 g total fat (0 g sat. fat), 3 mg chol., 595 mg sodium, 2 g carb., 1 g dietary fiber, 1 g sugar, 1 g protein.

Just a handful of ingredients can yield an ultraflavorful broth. Fill the pot with cool water and slowly bring it to a simmer. This gradual heating allows a more gentle infusion of flavors.

vegetable stock

prep: 25 minutes cook: 2 hours
makes: 6 servings

4 medium yellow
   onions
4 medium carrots
3 stalks celery with
   leaves
2 medium parsnips
   or carrots
2 medium potatoes
1 medium sweet potato
1 pound fresh button
   mushrooms
8 cups water
1½ teaspoons salt
1 teaspoon dried dill,
   basil, rosemary, or
   marjoram, crushed
½ teaspoon whole black
   peppercorns or
   ¼ teaspoon ground
   black pepper

1 Do not peel vegetables unless coated with wax. Cut onions into wedges. Cut carrots, celery, parsnips, and potatoes into about 2-inch pieces.

2 Place cut-up vegetables and mushrooms in a 6-quart Dutch oven. Add the water, salt, dill, and peppercorns. Bring to boiling; reduce heat. Simmer, covered, for 2 hours.

3 Strain stock into a large bowl through two layers of 100-percent-cotton cheesecloth placed in a colander. Discard vegetables and seasonings. Place stock in airtight storage containers. Cover and chill for up to 3 days or freeze for up to 6 months.

nutrition facts per serving: 12 cal., 0 g total fat (0 g sat. fat), 0 mg chol., 599 mg sodium, 3 g carb., 1 g dietary fiber, 1 g sugar, 0 g protein.

soups on hand

Soups can often be made in large batches—simply double a recipe that makes four to six servings and you'll likely have leftovers for future meals.

love leftovers

Leftovers from big-batch soups make great last-minute lunches. Follow these tips to store your soups and stews short term or long term.

1 To cool hot soup quickly for storage, place the soup pot in the kitchen sink. Fill the sink with cold water and ice, making sure the water level isn't high enough to splash into the pot or cause the pot to float. Stir several times while the soup is cooling. Add more ice to the water as necessary.

2 To refrigerate soup, ladle cool soup into a shallow storage container. Cover and refrigerate for 2 to 3 days.

3 To freeze soup, ladle individual servings of soup into freezer-safe containers, leaving ½ to 1 inch of space at the top of the container. Cover and freeze for up to 2 months.

4 Thaw frozen soup overnight in the refrigerator or thaw soup using the defrost setting on the microwave.

5 Avoid freezing soups with cubed potatoes (they may become mealy after thawing) and soups or stews thickened with cornstarch or flour (they may lose their thickening capacities during freezing).

a fine kettle **for soup**

The selection of pans and cookware suitable for soup-making has never been greater. Consider the following when choosing the pot that's right for you.

cookware	capacity	features	uses
Large Saucepan	3- to 4-quart capacity	Consider a pan with a short helping handle opposite the usual long handle.	Smaller batches of soup, stew, or chili.
Dutch Oven	4- to 6-quart capacity (for family-size servings)	Heavy pot with handles and a tight-fitting lid; traditionally made of cast iron. Retains heat very well and cooks evenly on the stove top or in the oven.	For simmering soups or stews on the stove top or in the oven.
Slow Cooker	3½ to 5-quart capacity (for family-size servings)	Stove top–safe inserts allow for browning meats. Cooks on high and low settings.	Great for long simmering of well-exercised cuts of meat, which become fork-tender.
Stockpot	6- to 8-quart capacity	Large, deep pot with handles and straight sides; the limited surface area minimizes evaporation during simmering. During cooking, liquid bubbles up through layers of ingredients, developing maximum flavor.	Large batches of soup, stew, or chili.

Learn to taste soups as you cook, especially nearing the end, and adjust the seasoning to your liking.

converting to the crock

Most of our soups, stews, and chilis can easily be adapted for the slow cooker. Adjust amounts to fill your cooker half to three-fourths full and follow these rules.

vegetables

Cut veggies—such as carrots, potatoes, and root vegetables—into small uniform pieces so they will cook evenly and completely.

liquids

Because the liquid doesn't boil away in a slow cooker like it does from a pot, you may not need quite as much as you would for stove-top cooking. Start with less—you can always add more later, if necessary.

meat & poultry

Long, slow cooking times are great for tougher cuts of meat, such as pork shoulder or beef chuck. Thaw your meat and poultry completely, and if you choose to brown the meat, do so right before adding to the slow cooker. Always remove skin from poultry.

beans

Dried beans require precooking. First, rinse the beans; place in a saucepan. Add enough water to cover beans by 2 inches. Bring to boiling; reduce heat. Simmer uncovered for 10 minutes. Remove from heat; cover. Let stand for 1 hour. Drain and rinse.

tasty **toppers**

Every soup—whether brothy, creamy, or chunky—gets a punch of pizzazz from a creative topper. Give one or more of these a try or come up with one of your own.

bacon
Crumbled bacon is good on cheesy, creamy soups.

nuts & seeds
Try salted, roasted pumpkin seeds, sunflower kernels, peanuts, or cashews.

fresh herbs
Try snipped basil, thyme, chives, or parsley.

rich crackers
Crumble rich round or rectangular crackers into any soup.

seasoned croutons
Reach for store-bought croutons for a quick topping.

oyster crackers
Add a handful of these bite-size soup crackers or crushed saltine crackers.

cheese
Shredded cheese of any sort adds richness and flavor.

potato chips
Why eat chips on the side when you can add them to your soup?

cheese crackers
Fish-shape cheese crackers are the perfect size to fit on your spoon.

veggie chips
These colorful chips add flavor and visual interest.

make-it-mine soup

Soups are the most forgiving of dishes and willingly accept almost any ingredient. Based on what's in season or your tastes, make up a clever new concoction.

start to finish: 30 minutes
makes: 4 servings

2 tablespoons
    vegetable oil
8 ounces Meat
    (opposite)
3 cups chopped
    Vegetables
    (opposite)
1 32-ounce carton beef
    broth or chicken
    broth
½ of a 6-ounce can
    tomato paste
    (⅓ cup)
1 1-ounce envelope
    onion soup mix
½ teaspoon Dried Herb
    (or ¼ teaspoon
    crushed red pepper)
    (opposite)
1 cup cooked Beans or
    Other (opposite)
    Salt and ground
    black pepper

1 In a 4- to 5-quart Dutch oven heat 1 tablespoon of the oil over medium-high heat. Add Meat; cook and stir until meat is brown and cooked through. If necessary, drain off fat. Remove meat from pan; set aside.

2 In the same Dutch oven heat the remaining 1 tablespoon oil over medium-high heat. Add Vegetables; cook and stir for 3 to 5 minutes or until vegetables are crisp-tender. Return meat to Dutch oven.

3 Stir in broth, tomato paste, onion soup mix, and Dried Herb. Bring to boiling over high heat; reduce heat. Simmer, covered, for 15 minutes. Stir in Beans or Other. Season to taste with salt and pepper.

meat
(pick one):
boneless chicken, turkey, beef, or
lean pork, cut into 1-inch pieces •
ground meat, such as beef, turkey,
chicken, or sausage

vegetables
(use assorted or pick one):
onion • green peas • small broccoli
florets • celery • carrots • potatoes •
corn kernels • tomatoes • zucchini •
sweet peppers

dried herb
(pick one):
rosemary • oregano • basil •
Italian seasoning • crushed red pepper

beans or other
(pick one):
canned beans, such as kidney, black,
Great Northern, or navy, rinsed and
drained • cooked barley • cooked rice •
cooked pasta

make-it-mine chili

With so many possibilities for making great chili, why limit yourself to the usual formula? With this recipe you can mix and match your way to your own one-bowl wonder.

prep: 25 minutes   cook: 20 minutes
makes: 8 servings

1½   pounds Meat
       (opposite)
3   cups chopped
       Vegetables
       (page 21)
4   cloves garlic, minced
1   tablespoon vegetable
       oil
2   15-ounce cans Beans,
       rinsed and drained
       (opposite)
2   14.5-ounce cans
       diced tomatoes,
       undrained
1   15-ounce can tomato
       sauce
1   cup Liquid (opposite)
2   tablespoons chili
       powder
1   teaspoon Dried Herb,
       crushed (opposite)
½   teaspoon ground
       black pepper or
       crushed red pepper
       Desired toppings
       (page 19)

1 In a large Dutch oven cook Meat, Vegetables, and garlic in hot oil over medium-high heat until meat is brown and vegetables are tender. Drain fat. Stir in Beans, tomatoes, tomato sauce, Liquid, chili powder, Dried Herb, and pepper.

2 Bring to boiling; reduce heat. Simmer, covered, about 20 minutes for ground meat (about 1 hour for cubed meat) or until meat is tender, stirring occasionally.

3 Ladle chili into bowls. Serve with desired toppings.

meat
(pick one):
boneless beef chuck top blade (flat-iron)
steak or pork shoulder, trimmed and cut
into ¾-inch cubes • beef stew meat •
ground beef or pork

beans
(pick one):
black • pinto • garbanzo (chickpeas) •
cannellini (white kidney •
red kidney

liquid
(pick one):
beer • water • beef broth •
apple juice • chicken broth

dried herb
(pick one):
thyme • oregano •
Italian seasoning • basil

2

bubbling-hot

Some of your favorite soups may be the ones you're most familiar with. Whether it's traditional French onion soup topped with a blanket of nutty Gruyère or an old-fashioned ham and bean soup that simmers all day, nothing satisfies like these steaming bowls of comfort.

clas

sics

The addition of beef transforms a traditional French onion soup into a satisfying main dish. Take your pick—use leftover roast beef or buy something from the deli.

french onion and beef soup

start to finish: 25 minutes

makes: 4 servings

3 tablespoons butter

1 medium onion, thinly sliced and separated into rings

2 10.5-ounce cans condensed French onion soup

2½ cups water

8 ounces cooked roast beef, cubed

4 1-inch slices French bread

½ cup shredded Gruyère cheese or Swiss cheese (2 ounces)

1 In a large skillet heat butter over medium heat until melted. Add onion; cook for 5 to 7 minutes or until very tender. Stir in French onion soup, the water, and beef. Bring to boiling, stirring mixture occasionally.

2 Meanwhile, preheat broiler. Place bread slices on a baking sheet. Broil about 4 inches from the heat about 1 minute or until toasted on one side. Top the toasted sides of bread slices with cheese. Broil about 1 minute more or until cheese is melted.

3 Top each serving with cheese bread slices.

nutrition facts per serving: 465 cal., 21 g total fat (10 g sat. fat), 82 mg chol., 1701 mg sodium, 40 g carb., 3 g dietary fiber, 28 g protein.

Here's a fun and tasty soup recipe the whole family can enjoy. For the full cheeseburger effect, serve on toasted buns with all the fixings.

all-american cheeseburger soup

prep: 20 minutes cook: 20 minutes broil: 1 minute
makes: 6 servings

1   pound ground beef
½   cup chopped onion
     (1 medium)
½   cup chopped celery
     (1 stalk)
2   cloves garlic, minced
2   tablespoons all-
     purpose flour
2   14-ounce cans
     reduced-sodium
     beef broth
2   medium potatoes,
     scrubbed and
     coarsely chopped
1   14.5-ounce can diced
     tomatoes, drained
1   8-ounce package
     shredded cheddar
     and American
     cheese blend (2 cups)
1   6-ounce can tomato
     paste
¼   cup ketchup
2   tablespoons Dijon-
     style mustard
1   cup whole milk
6   cocktail buns or
     brown-and-serve
     rolls, split and
     toasted*
     Assorted condiments
     (pickles, onions,
     lettuce, mustard,
     and/or ketchup)
     (optional)

1 In a large pot cook beef, onion, celery, and garlic over medium heat until meat is browned and vegetables are tender; drain fat. Sprinkle flour on beef mixture; cook and stir for 2 minutes. Stir in broth and potatoes. Bring to boiling, stirring occasionally. Reduce heat. Simmer, covered, for 10 minutes or until potatoes are tender.

2 Stir in tomatoes, cheese, tomato paste, ketchup, and mustard; cook and stir until soup comes to a gentle boil. Stir in milk; heat through. Serve with toasted buns and top with condiments.

nutrition facts per serving: 528 cal., 27 g total fat (13 g sat. fat), 94 mg chol., 1461 mg sodium, 39 g carb., 4 g dietary fiber, 32 g protein.

*note: To toast buns, preheat the broiler. Place split buns, split sides up, on a broiler pan. Brush with 1 tablespoon melted butter or olive oil. Broil 4 to 5 inches from heat for about 1 minute or until golden.

To peel pearl onions easily, place them in boiling water for 30 seconds; drain and rinse with cold water. Cut off the root end and squeeze from the other end.

beef bourguignon

prep: 40 minutes cook: 1¼ hours
makes: 6 servings

1 pound boneless beef chuck roast, cut into ¾-inch cubes
2 tablespoons vegetable oil
1 cup chopped onion (1 large)
1 clove garlic, minced
1½ cups Burgundy
¾ cup beef broth
1 teaspoon dried thyme, crushed
¾ teaspoon dried marjoram, crushed
½ teaspoon salt
¼ teaspoon ground black pepper
2 bay leaves
3 cups whole fresh mushrooms
4 medium carrots, cut into ¾-inch pieces
8 ounces pearl onions or 2 cups frozen small whole onions
2 tablespoons all-purpose flour
¼ cup water
3 cups hot cooked noodles or mashed potatoes
2 slices bacon, crisp-cooked, drained, and crumbled
1 tablespoon chopped fresh parsley

1 In a large pot cook half of the meat in 1 tablespoon of the hot oil until meat is brown; remove meat from pan. Add remaining oil and meat, chopped onion, and garlic to pot; cook until meat is brown and onion is tender. Drain fat. Return all meat to pot.

2 Stir in wine, beef broth, thyme, marjoram, salt, pepper, and bay leaves. Bring to boiling; reduce heat. Simmer, covered, about 45 minutes, stirring occasionally. Add mushrooms, carrots, and pearl onions. Return to boiling; reduce heat. Simmer, covered, for 25 to 30 minutes more or until vegetables are tender, stirring occasionally. Discard bay leaves.

3 Combine flour and the water; stir into meat mixture. Cook and stir until thickened and bubbly. Cook and stir for 1 minute more. Serve with noodles. Top with bacon and parsley.

nutrition facts per serving: 430 cal., 19 g total fat (6 g sat. fat), 66 mg chol., 444 mg sodium, 35 g carb., 4 g dietary fiber, 19 g protein.

slow cooker directions: Brown meat, chopped onion, and garlic as directed. In a 3½- or 4-quart slow cooker layer mushrooms, carrots, and pearl onions. Sprinkle with 3 tablespoons quick-cooking tapioca. Place meat mixture on vegetables. Add thyme, marjoram, salt, pepper, and bay leaves. Pour 1¼ cups wine and ½ cup beef broth over all. Cover and cook on low-heat setting for 10 to 12 hours or on high-heat setting for 5 to 6 hours or until tender. Discard bay leaves. Continue as directed.

Pork stew meat and boneless lamb are equally as good in this colorful stew. For pork, only simmer about 30 minutes in Step 1. If using a slow cooker, prepare as directed with the times given below.

old-fashioned beef stew

prep: 20 minutes cook: 1½ hours
makes: 5 servings

2   tablespoons all-purpose flour
12 ounces beef stew meat, cut into ¾-inch cubes
2   tablespoons vegetable oil
3   cups vegetable juice
1   cup beef broth
1   medium onion, cut into thin wedges
1   tablespoon Worcestershire sauce
1   teaspoon dried oregano, crushed
½   teaspoon dried marjoram, crushed
¼   teaspoon ground black pepper
1   bay leaf
3   cups cubed potato (about 3 medium)
1½ cups frozen cut green beans
1   cup frozen whole-kernel corn
1   cup sliced carrot (2 medium)

1 Place flour in a resealable plastic bag. Add meat cubes, a few at a time, shaking to coat. In a large saucepan or pot brown meat in hot oil; drain fat. Stir in vegetable juice, broth, onion, Worcestershire sauce, oregano, marjoram, pepper, and bay leaf. Bring to boiling; reduce heat. Simmer, covered, for 1 to 1¼ hours or until meat is nearly tender.

2 Stir in potato, green beans, corn, and carrot. Return to boiling; reduce heat. Simmer, covered, about 30 minutes more or until meat and vegetables are tender. Discard bay leaf.

nutrition facts per serving: 362 cal., 17 g total fat (5 g sat. fat), 39 mg chol., 664 mg sodium, 39 g carb., 6 g dietary fiber, 16 g protein.

slow cooker directions: Prepare and brown meat as directed. In a 3½- or 4-quart slow cooker layer meat, onion, potato, green beans, corn, and carrot. Combine 2 cups vegetable juice, the broth, Worcestershire sauce, oregano, marjoram, pepper, and bay leaf. Pour over meat and vegetables in slow cooker. Cover and cook on low-heat setting for 10 to 12 hours or on high-heat setting for 5 to 6 hours or until meat and vegetables are tender.

This hearty French-style stew is the perfect dish for a leisurely Sunday supper. Serve it with a full-bodied red wine and crusty bread to soak up the gravy.

beef ragout with gravy

prep: 45 minutes   cook: 1 hour 50 minutes
makes: 6 to 8 servings

¼ cup all-purpose flour
2 pounds boneless beef chuck roast, cut into 1-inch cubes
3 tablespoons vegetable oil
4 cups water
½ cup chopped onion (1 medium)
1 clove garlic, minced
2 bay leaves
2 teaspoons Worcestershire sauce
1 teaspoon sugar
1 teaspoon lemon juice
½ teaspoon salt
½ teaspoon ground black pepper
½ teaspoon paprika
  Pinch ground allspice
6 tiny new potatoes, halved
6 medium carrots, quartered
1 pound boiling onions, peeled
2 tablespoons water
1 tablespoon all-purpose flour
¼ cup dry sherry (optional)
  Snipped fresh parsley

1 Place ¼ cup flour in a resealable plastic bag. Add meat cubes, a few at a time, shaking to coat. In a 4-quart Dutch oven heat oil over medium-high heat. Add beef cubes, one-third at a time; cook and stir until beef is brown. Drain fat. Return all beef to Dutch oven. Add the 4 cups water, chopped onion, garlic, and bay leaves. Stir in Worcestershire sauce, sugar, lemon juice, salt, black pepper, paprika, and allspice. Bring to boiling; reduce heat. Simmer, covered, for 1½ to 2 hours or until meat is nearly tender.

2 Add potatoes, carrots, and boiling onions. Return to boiling; reduce heat. Simmer, covered, for 20 to 30 minutes more or until vegetables are tender. Remove and discard bay leaves. Using a slotted spoon, transfer meat and vegetables to a serving dish. Cover and keep warm.

3 For gravy, in a small bowl combine 2 tablespoons water and 1 tablespoon flour; stir into liquid in Dutch oven. Cook and stir until thickened and bubbly. Cook and stir for 1 minute more. If desired, stir in sherry. Pour gravy over meat and vegetables. Sprinkle with parsley.

nutrition facts per serving: 320 cal., 8 g total fat (2 g sat. fat), 89 mg chol., 348 mg sodium, 26 g carb., 4 g dietary fiber, 35 g protein.

Smoky chipotle chiles add deep, rich flavor to this chunky Mexican-style stew. The dried smoked jalapenos bring on a direct hit of heat, while the piquant adobo sauce lends a slow burn.

beef and red bean chili

prep: 45 minutes stand: 1 hour slow cook: 10 to 12 hours (low) or 5 to 6 hours (high)
makes: 8 servings

1 cup dry red beans or dry red kidney beans
1 tablespoon olive oil
2 pounds boneless beef chuck pot roast, cut into 1-inch pieces
1 cup coarsely chopped onion (1 large)
1 15-ounce can tomato sauce
1 14.5-ounce can diced tomatoes with green chiles, undrained
1 14-ounce can reduced-sodium beef broth
2 to 3 chipotle peppers in adobo sauce, finely chopped, plus 2 teaspoons adobo sauce*
2 teaspoons dried oregano, crushed
1 teaspoon ground cumin
¾ cup finely chopped red sweet pepper (1 medium)
¼ cup snipped fresh cilantro

1 Rinse beans. Place beans in a large saucepan or Dutch oven. Add enough water to cover beans by 2 inches. Bring to boiling; reduce heat. Simmer, uncovered, for 10 minutes. Remove from heat. Cover and let stand for 1 hour. (Or place beans in a large saucepan. Add water to cover beans by 2 inches. Cover and let soak in a cool place for 6 to 8 hours or overnight.)

2 Meanwhile, in a large skillet heat oil over medium-high heat. Add half of the meat and the onion; cook and stir until meat is brown. Using a slotted spoon, transfer meat-onion mixture to a 3½- or 4-quart slow cooker. Repeat with remaining meat. Stir tomato sauce, undrained tomatoes, broth, chipotle chiles and adobo sauce, oregano, and cumin into mixture in slow cooker. Drain and rinse the beans; stir into mixture in cooker.

3 Cover and cook on low-heat setting for 10 to 12 hours or on high-heat setting for 5 to 6 hours. Top each serving with sweet pepper and cilantro.

nutrition facts per serving: 288 cal., 7 g total fat (2 g sat. fat), 67 mg chol., 702 mg sodium, 24 g carb., 6 g dietary fiber, 31 g protein

*note: Fresh chile peppers and canned chipotle chile peppers contain volatile oils that can burn your skin and eyes, so avoid direct contact with them as much as possible. When working with the chiles, wear disposable plastic or rubber gloves. If your bare hands do touch the chiles, wash your hands and nails thoroughly with soap and hot water. If you get chile oil in your eyes, flush them with cool water.

Roasting the vegetables before adding them to the soup gives them an extra flavor boost.

beef and barley stew with roasted winter vegetables

prep: 45 minutes cook: 1 hour 35 minutes bake: 35 minutes oven: at 375°F
makes: 6 to 8 servings

¼ cup all-purpose flour
½ teaspoon salt
½ teaspoon ground
     black pepper
2 to 2½ pounds
     boneless beef chuck
     roast, trimmed of
     excess fat and cut
     into 1-inch pieces
¼ cup olive oil
½ cup chopped onion
     (1 medium)
2 cloves garlic, minced
½ teaspoon dried
     thyme, crushed
1 14.5-ounce can beef
     broth
2 cups water
1 cup dry red wine
4 medium red or yellow
     potatoes, cut into
     1-inch chunks
4 medium carrots,
     peeled and cut into
     1-inch chunks
½ cup regular barley
2 tablespoons snipped
     fresh parsley
     (optional)

1 In a large bowl combine flour, ¼ teaspoon of the salt, and ¼ teaspoon of the pepper. Add meat; toss to coat. In a Dutch oven heat 1 tablespoon of the oil over medium heat. Add half of the meat; cook until brown, stirring occasionally. Remove meat from Dutch oven; set aside. Repeat with another 1 tablespoon of the oil and remaining meat.

2 Add onion, garlic, and thyme to Dutch oven; cook and stir for 3 minutes. Add broth, stirring to scrape up any browned bits from bottom of the Dutch oven. Add the water and wine. Bring to boiling; reduce heat to low. Simmer, covered, for 1 hour.

3 Meanwhile, preheat oven to 375°F. In a shallow roasting pan combine potatoes and carrots. Drizzle with the remaining 2 tablespoons olive oil; sprinkle with remaining ¼ teaspoon salt and remaining ¼ teaspoon pepper. Toss to coat. Roast, uncovered, for 35 to 45 minutes or until vegetables are tender and lightly browned, stirring once or twice.

4 Stir barley into beef mixture; cook about 35 minutes more or until barley is tender. Stir in roasted vegetables. If desired, stir in fresh parsley.

nutrition facts per serving: 455 cal., 24 g total fat (8 g sat. fat), 71 mg chol., 436 mg sodium, 27 g carb., 5 g dietary fiber, 26 g protein.

Start this quick-to-assemble recipe before you head out and supper will be ready and waiting when you return after a busy day. It features common ingredients you're likely to find in the pantry or fridge.

busy-day beef-vegetable soup

prep: 20 minutes slow cook: 8 to 10 hours (low) or 4 to 5 hours (high)
makes: 4 servings

1 pound boneless
   beef chuck roast,
   trimmed and cut
   into bite-size pieces
3 medium carrots, cut
   into ½-inch-thick
   slices
2 small potatoes,
   peeled, if desired,
   and cut into ½-inch
   cubes
½ cup chopped onion
   (1 medium)
½ teaspoon salt
½ teaspoon dried
   thyme, crushed
1 bay leaf
2 14.5-ounce cans
   diced tomatoes,
   undrained
1 cup water
½ cup frozen peas
   Fresh parsley sprigs
   (optional)

1 In a 3½- or 4-quart slow cooker combine beef, carrots, potatoes, and onion. Sprinkle with salt and thyme. Add bay leaf. Pour undrained tomatoes and water over all.

2 Cover and cook on low-heat setting for 8 to 10 hours or on high-heat setting for 4 to 5 hours. Discard bay leaf. Stir in frozen peas. If desired, garnish each serving with parsley.

nutrition facts per serving: 279 cal., 8 g total fat (3 g sat. fat), 72 mg chol., 860 mg sodium, 26 g carb., 7 g dietary fiber, 26 g protein.

You can't go wrong with this flavorful soup—it's colorful, good for you, and takes just 30 minutes to whip up. Serve immediately so the pasta doesn't overcook.

meatball and vegetable soup with pasta

start to finish: 30 minutes
makes: 6 to 8 servings

3   14.5-ounce cans beef broth
1   15-ounce can Great Northern or cannellini (white kidney) beans, rinsed and drained
1   14.5-ounce can diced tomatoes with basil, garlic, and oregano, undrained
1   12- to 16-ounce package frozen cooked meatballs
1   10-ounce package frozen mixed vegetables
1   cup dried small pasta (such as elbow macaroni, small shells, mini penne, or rotini)
    Snipped fresh parsley (optional)

In a 4-quart Dutch oven combine broth, beans, undrained tomatoes, meatballs, and frozen vegetables. Bring to boiling; stir in pasta. Return to boiling; reduce heat. Simmer, uncovered, about 10 minutes or until pasta is tender. Ladle soup into bowls. If desired, sprinkle with parsley.

nutrition facts per serving: 319 cal., 5 g total fat (2 g sat. fat), 32 mg chol., 1552 mg sodium, 45 g carb., 7 g dietary fiber, 24 g protein.

beef and vegetable soup with pasta: Prepare as above, except substitute one 17-ounce package refrigerated cooked beef tips with gravy for the frozen cooked meatballs.

Beef round steak or chuck roast are good cuts to use for this savory country-style stew. Remove and discard any fat from the meat before cutting it into cubes.

hearty mexican beef stew

prep: 30 minutes cook: 1¼ hours stand: 30 minutes
makes: 4 servings

1   tablespoon vegetable oil
12   ounces beef stew meat
1   14-ounce can beef broth
½   teaspoon salt
¼   teaspoon ground black pepper
2   or 3 dried ancho peppers
2   cups chopped, peeled tomatoes (2 large) or one 14.5-ounce can diced tomatoes, undrained
1   medium onion, cut up
3   cloves garlic, minced
½   teaspoon ground cumin
2   medium potatoes, cut into 1-inch cubes
1   large fresh ear of corn, shucked and cut crosswise into 1-inch slices, or 1 cup frozen whole kernel corn
1   medium zucchini or yellow summer squash, halved lengthwise and cut into 1-inch slices

1 In a 4-quart Dutch oven heat oil over medium heat. Add meat; cook and stir until brown. Drain fat. Add broth, salt, and black pepper. Bring to boiling; reduce heat. Simmer, covered, for 45 minutes.

2 Meanwhile, cut chile peppers open; discard stems and seeds. Place peppers in a small bowl and cover with boiling water. Let stand at room temperature for 30 minutes to soften. Drain well; coarsely chop peppers.

3 In a blender or food processor combine chopped peppers, tomatoes, onion, garlic, and cumin. Cover and blend or process until nearly smooth. Stir into beef mixture.

4 Add potatoes and corn. Bring to boiling; reduce heat. Simmer, covered, for 20 minutes. Stir in zucchini. Return to boiling; reduce heat. Simmer, covered, for 10 to 15 minutes more or until meat and vegetables are tender.

nutrition facts per serving: 291 cal., 8 g total fat (2 g sat. fat), 50 mg chol., 741 mg sodium, 32 g carb., 6 g dietary fiber, 25 g protein.

Hungarian paprika, featured in this hearty stew, is the finest in the world. In Hungary, paprika comes in six classes, ranging from sweet (mild) to hot.

goulash

prep: 25 minutes   cook: 1 hour 25 minutes
makes: 6 to 8 servings

1 In a 4- to 5-quart Dutch oven heat oil over medium-high heat. Add meat and onion; cook about 5 minutes or until meat is brown and onion is tender.

2 Add flour, paprika, and garlic; cook for 3 minutes, stirring constantly. Stir in broth, undrained tomatoes, carrots, tomato paste, bay leaf, marjoram, caraway seeds, and black pepper. Bring to boiling; reduce heat. Simmer, covered, for 50 minutes, stirring occasionally.

3 Add potatoes. Simmer, covered, for 25 to 30 minutes more or until meat and potatoes are tender. Remove and discard bay leaf. If desired, top each serving with sour cream.

nutrition facts per serving: 235 cal., 7 g total fat (1 g sat. fat), 39 mg chol., 1074 mg sodium, 22 g carb., 3 g dietary fiber, 21 g protein.

2	tablespoons vegetable oil
1	pound beef top round steak, cut into ½-inch cubes
½	cup chopped onion (1 medium)
2	tablespoons all-purpose flour
1	tablespoon Hungarian paprika
2	cloves garlic, minced
3	14.5-ounce cans chicken broth
1	14.5-ounce can diced tomatoes, undrained
1½	cups sliced carrot (3 medium)
2	tablespoons tomato paste
1	bay leaf
½	teaspoon dried marjoram, crushed
½	teaspoon caraway seeds, crushed
½	teaspoon ground black pepper
2	cups cubed peeled potatoes (2 medium)
	Sour cream (optional)

Tougher cuts of meat, such as short ribs, and fibrous root vegetables are ideal candidates for braising. The long-simmering cooking method where browned meat and cut-up veggies cook in a tightly covered pot results in tender, flavorful bites.

chipotle-braised short ribs and cheesy polenta

prep: 50 minutes   cook: 3 hours
makes: 6 servings

3 pounds boneless beef
   short ribs or 12 bone-
   in beef short ribs
1 teaspoon kosher salt
   or ¾ teaspoon salt
½ teaspoon ground
   black pepper
⅓ cup all-purpose flour
1 tablespoon vegetable
   oil
2 cups dry red wine
   or cranberry juice
1 14-ounce can beef
   broth or 1¾ cups
   beef stock
1 tablespoon snipped
   fresh thyme or
   1 teaspoon dried
   thyme, crushed
3 cloves garlic, peeled
1 bay leaf
2 tablespoons sugar
8 ounces carrots,
   cut into chunks
2 parsnips, peeled and
   sliced
1 10-ounce package
   red pearl onions,
   peeled (15 to 20)
1 cup chopped, seeded
   tomato (1 large)
1 or 2 chipotle peppers
   in adobo sauce,
   drained and chopped
1 recipe Cheesy Polenta

1 Trim fat from meat. Sprinkle with salt and black pepper. Dredge meat in flour, coating well on all sides. In a 6- to 8-quart Dutch oven heat oil over medium-high heat. Brown meat, half at a time. Add wine, beef broth, dried thyme (if using), garlic, and bay leaf. Bring to boiling; reduce heat. Simmer, covered, for 2 hours.

2 Meanwhile, in a saucepan bring lightly salted water to boiling. Add sugar; stir until sugar is dissolved. Add carrots, parsnips, and onions. Cook, uncovered, for 5 to 7 minutes or until tender. Drain. Submerge vegetables in a bowl of ice water. Let stand 5 minutes. Drain; cover and chill until ready to use.

3 Add tomato, fresh thyme (if using), and chipotle pepper to meat mixture. Simmer, covered, for 30 minutes. Add chilled vegetables; return to boiling. Simmer, covered, for 30 minutes more or until meat is very tender. Remove and discard bay leaf.

4 To serve, remove beef and vegetables with a slotted spoon. Arrange in shallow bowls. Spoon Cheesy Polenta alongside the beef and vegetable mixture. Skim fat from cooking juices; spoon some of the juices over all.

nutrition facts per serving: 463 cal., 15 g total fat (6 g sat. fat), 60 mg chol., 1100 mg sodium, 43 g carb., 5 g dietary fiber, 25 g protein.

cheesy polenta: In a large saucepan bring 2½ cups water to boiling. Meanwhile, combine 1 cup yellow cornmeal, 1 cup cold water, and ½ teaspoon salt. Slowly add cornmeal mixture to boiling water, stirring constantly. Cook and stir until mixture returns to boiling. Reduce heat to low. Cook, uncovered, for 10 to 15 minutes or until mixture is very thick, stirring occasionally. Stir in ¼ cup milk. Gently stir in ½ cup finely shredded Parmesan cheese (2 ounces) until melted.

lighten up

A few simple changes can make any soup healthier.

- fat-free thickener: *Use an immersion blender to puree potatoes, beans, and other root veggies in soups to add thickness and body.*

- swap ingredients: *Replace full-fat dairy products with reduced-fat milk, cheese, sour cream, and/or yogurt. Replace part of the whipping cream or heavy cream with half-and-half or milk.*

Some folks say homemade chicken noodle soup helps battle a cold or the flu, but even doubters agree its comforting flavor has great appeal. This version serves a crowd and is creamy and rich without added cream.

creamy chicken noodle soup

prep: 25 minutes slow cook: 6 to 8 hours (low) or 3 to 4 hours (high)
+ 20 minutes (high)
makes: 8 servings

1	32-ounce container reduced-sodium chicken broth
3	cups water
2½	cups chopped cooked chicken (about 12 ounces)
1½	cups sliced carrot (3 medium)
1½	cups sliced celery (3 stalks)
1½	cups fresh mushrooms, sliced (4 ounces)
¼	cup chopped onion
1½	teaspoons dried thyme, crushed
¾	teaspoon garlic pepper
3	ounces reduced-fat cream cheese (Neufchâtel), cut up
2	cups dried egg noodles

1 In a 5- to 6-quart slow cooker combine chicken broth, the water, chicken, carrot, celery, mushrooms, onion, thyme, and garlic pepper.

2 Cover and cook on low-heat setting for 6 to 8 hours or on high-heat setting for 3 to 4 hours.

3 If using low-heat setting, turn cooker to high-heat setting. Stir in cream cheese until combined. Stir in uncooked noodles. Cover and cook for 20 to 30 minutes more or until noodles are just tender.

nutrition facts per serving: 170 cal., 6 g total fat (2 g sat. fat), 54 mg chol., 401 mg sodium, 11 g carb., 2 g dietary fiber, 17 g protein.

On a chilly night, enjoy the ultimate in comfort food—a nourishing, steaming hot bowl of chicken, vegetables, and egg noodles.

chicken noodle–vegetable soup

prep: 30 minutes cook: 35 minutes
makes: 6 servings

2   14-ounce cans
     chicken broth
1   cup water
1   10.75-ounce can
     condensed cream of
     chicken soup
½   teaspoon dried
     thyme, crushed
⅛   teaspoon salt
⅛   teaspoon ground
     black pepper
2   medium skinless
     chicken legs with
     thigh portions
     (1¼ pounds total)
1   cup sliced carrot
     (2 medium)
¾   cup chopped onion
½   cup sliced celery
     (1 stalk)
1   bay leaf
4   ounces dried wide
     noodles (about 2 cups)
½   cup frozen peas

1 In a 4-quart pot combine broth, the water, cream of chicken soup, thyme, salt, and pepper. Add chicken legs, carrot, onion, celery, and bay leaf. Bring to boiling; reduce heat. Simmer, covered, for 30 to 40 minutes or until chicken is no longer pink and vegetables are tender.

2 Remove chicken from pot; cool slightly. Discard bay leaf. Return broth mixture to boiling. Add noodles and frozen peas; cook for 5 to 7 minutes or until noodles are tender and peas are heated through, stirring occasionally. Remove chicken from bones; discard bones. Shred or chop meat; stir into soup. Heat through.

nutrition facts per serving: 223 cal., 7 g total fat (2 g sat. fat), 64 mg chol., 1063 mg sodium, 24 g carb., 2 g dietary fiber, 16 g protein.

This beloved Italian soup is both hearty and healthy and can easily be adapted according to the veggies you have in your pantry or refrigerator. Customize your own, swapping kidney beans or chickpeas for cannollini beans, yellow summer squash for zucchini, or peas for green beans.

chicken minestrone soup

start to finish: 45 minutes
makes: 8 servings

1   cup sliced carrot
    (2 medium)
½   cup chopped celery
    (1 stalk)
½   cup chopped onion
    (1 medium)
1   tablespoon olive oil
3   14-ounce cans
    chicken broth
2   15- to 19-ounce cans
    cannellini (white
    kidney) beans,
    rinsed and drained
8   to 10 ounces skinless,
    boneless chicken
    breasts, cut into
    bite-size pieces
4   ounces fresh green
    beans, cut into
    ½-inch pieces
    (1 cup)
¼   teaspoon ground
    black pepper
1   cup dried bow tie
    pasta
1   medium zucchini,
    quartered
    lengthwise and cut
    into ½-inch-thick
    slices
1   14.5-ounce can diced
    tomatoes with basil,
    garlic, and oregano,
    undrained

1 In a 5- to 6-quart Dutch oven, cook the carrot, celery, and onion in hot oil over medium heat for 5 minutes, stirring frequently. Add broth, cannellini beans, chicken, green beans, and pepper. Bring to boiling; add pasta. Reduce heat. Simmer, uncovered, for 5 minutes.

2 Stir in zucchini. Return to boiling; reduce heat. Simmer, uncovered, for 8 to 10 minutes more or until pasta is tender and green beans are crisp-tender. Stir in undrained tomatoes; heat through.

nutrition facts per serving: 183 cal., 4 g total fat (1 g sat. fat), 16 mg chol., 1115 mg sodium, 27 g carb., 7 g dietary fiber, 16 g protein.

Wild rice brings a chewy texture and a nutty, earthy flavor to this simple soup while cream and dry sherry add richness. This is a great way to use up leftover Thanksgiving turkey.

wild rice and turkey soup

prep: 25 minutes   cook: 20 minutes
makes: 6 servings

1 6.2-ounce package quick-cooking long-grain and wild rice mix
2 tablespoons butter or margarine
4 ounces fresh shiitake mushrooms, stems removed and sliced (about 1½ cups)
2 stalks celery, sliced (1 cup)
2 14-ounce cans reduced-sodium chicken broth or 3½ cups chicken stock
¼ teaspoon ground black pepper
2 cups chopped smoked turkey or chopped cooked turkey or chicken (about 10 ounces)
1 cup whipping cream
2 tablespoons dry sherry (optional)

1 Prepare the rice mix (using the seasoning packet) according to package directions, except omit any butter or margarine.

2 In a large saucepan melt butter over medium heat. Add mushrooms and celery; cook about 5 minutes or until vegetables are almost tender and most of the mushroom liquid has evaporated, stirring occasionally. Add chicken broth and pepper. Bring to boiling; reduce heat. Simmer, covered, for 5 minutes. Stir in cooked rice mix, turkey, whipping cream and, if desired, dry sherry. Heat through.

nutrition facts per serving: 347 cal., 21 g total fat (12 g sat. fat), 90 mg chol., 1301 mg sodium, 28 g carb., 1 g dietary fiber, 15 g protein.

This recipe calls for browning the pork hocks in butter. Browning adds flavor to the meat as well as browned bits to the pan, which lend richness to the finished soup.

split pea soup

prep: 20 minutes   cook: 1 hour 20 minutes
makes: 4 servings

2¾   cups water
1½   cups dry split peas,
        rinsed and drained
1   14-ounce can
        reduced-sodium
        chicken broth
1   to 1½ pounds meaty
        smoked pork
        hocks or one 1- to
        1½-pound meaty
        ham bone
¼   teaspoon dried
        marjoram, crushed
        Pinch ground black
        pepper
1   bay leaf
½   cup chopped carrot
        (1 medium)
½   cup chopped celery
        (1 stalk)
½   cup chopped onion
        (1 medium)

1 In a large saucepan combine water, split peas, broth, pork hocks, marjoram, pepper, and bay leaf. Bring to boiling; reduce heat. Simmer, covered, for 1 hour, stirring occasionally. Remove pork hocks.

2 When cool enough to handle, cut meat off bones; discard bones. Coarsely chop meat. Return meat to saucepan. Stir in carrot, celery, and onion. Return to boiling; reduce heat. Simmer, covered, for 20 to 30 minutes more or until vegetables are tender. Discard bay leaf.

nutrition facts per serving: 307 cal., 3 g total fat (1 g sat. fat), 19 mg chol., 676 mg sodium, 47 g carb., 19 g dietary fiber, 25 g protein.

slow cooker directions: In a 3½- or 4-quart slow cooker combine split peas, pork hocks, marjoram, pepper, bay leaf, carrot, celery, and onion. Pour the water and chicken broth over all. Cover and cook on low-heat setting for 8 to 10 hours or on high-heat setting for 4 to 5 hours. Discard bay leaf. Remove hocks, cut off meat, and add to soup.

Roasting the corn makes it sweeter and intensifies its flavor. Puree half of the roasted corn for creaminess. Leave the other half whole for texture.

creamy corn chowder

prep: 25 minutes bake: 20 minutes oven: at 450°F cook: 20 minutes
makes: 8 servings

1   16-ounce package
    frozen whole-kernel
    corn
1   pound Yukon Gold
    potatoes, peeled
    and cut into ½-inch
    pieces
2   tablespoons olive oil
    Chicken broth
    (optional)
½   cup thinly sliced leek*
2   tablespoons finely
    chopped shallot
4   cups chicken broth
1   teaspoon dried
    marjoram, crushed
½   teaspoon salt
½   teaspoon ground
    ginger
½   teaspoon ground
    white pepper
3   cups half-and-half or
    light cream
    Salt
    Ground white pepper

1 Thaw frozen corn and pat dry with paper towels. Preheat oven to 450°F. Line a 15×10×1-inch baking pan with foil. Lightly grease the foil. Spread corn on half of the prepared pan. In a resealable plastic bag combine potatoes and 1 tablespoon of the oil. Seal and shake well to coat potatoes with oil. Spread potatoes on the other half of the prepared pan. Roast, uncovered, for 10 minutes. Stir, keeping corn and potatoes separate. Roast for 10 minutes more, stirring once or twice. Remove pan from oven. Set aside.

2 Transfer half of the roasted corn (about ¾ cup) to a food processor or blender. Cover and process or blend until smooth; if necessary, add a small amount of chicken broth to help blend corn.

3 In a 4-quart Dutch oven, heat the remaining 1 tablespoon oil over medium heat. Add leek and shallot; cook and stir for 6 to 8 minutes or until leek is very soft and golden. Add whole corn and pureed corn; cook and stir for 1 minute. Stir in roasted potatoes, 4 cups chicken broth, marjoram, salt, ginger, and white pepper. Bring to boiling; reduce heat. Cover and simmer for 10 to 12 minutes or until potatoes are tender.

4 Add half-and-half; cook and stir until heated through. Season to taste with additional salt and white pepper.

nutrition facts per serving: 588 cal., 15 g total fat (7 g sat. fat), 33 mg chol., 1342 mg sodium, 94 g carb., 2 g dietary fiber, 20 g protein.

*note: See tip on cleaning leeks, page 464.

For cheesier flavor, use cheddar (sharp, if you like) in this indulgently rich soup.

baked potato soup

prep: 20 minutes   bake: 40 minutes   oven: at 425°F   cook: 20 minutes
makes: 5 to 6 servings

2   large baking potatoes
     (about 8 ounces
     each)
3   tablespoons butter
     or margarine
6   tablespoons thinly
     sliced green onion (3)
3   tablespoons all-
     purpose flour
2   teaspoons snipped
     fresh dill or chives
     or ¼ teaspoon dried
     dill
¼   teaspoon salt
¼   teaspoon ground
     black pepper
4   cups milk
1¼ cups shredded
     American cheese
     (5 ounces)
4   slices bacon, crisp-
     cooked, drained,
     and crumbled

1 Preheat oven to 425°F. Scrub potatoes with a vegetable brush; pat dry. Prick several times with a fork. Bake for 40 to 60 minutes or until tender. Let cool. Cut potatoes in half lengthwise; gently scoop out pulp, breaking up any large pieces. Discard potato skins.

2 In a large saucepan melt butter over medium heat. Add half of the green onion; cook and stir until tender. Stir in flour, dill, salt, and pepper. Add milk all at once; cook and stir for 12 to 15 minutes or until thickened and bubbly. Add the potato pulp and 1 cup of the cheese; stir until cheese is melted.

3 Top each serving with remaining cheese, remaining green onion, and bacon.

nutrition facts per serving: 372 cal., 22 g total fat (13 g sat. fat), 68 mg chol., 821 mg sodium, 26 g carb., 1 g dietary fiber, 17 g protein.

superfast

sim

Short on time? Not to worry!
Soup's on in 30 minutes or less
with easy, delicious recipes
that call on a handful of fresh
ingredients and pantry staples.
These one-pot meals are
perfect for busy weeknights
or whenever you just don't
feel like spending much time
in the kitchen.

This brothy, vegetable-packed soup gets its zip from the rosemary-and-roasted-garlic red potatoes, which you'll find in the refrigerator case of most supermarkets.

no-fuss beef soup

start to finish: 20 minutes
makes: 4 servings

1   17-ounce package
     refrigerated cooked
     beef roast au jus
1   8-ounce package
     peeled fresh baby
     carrots, sliced
3½ cups water
½   16-ounce package
     refrigerated
     rosemary-and-
     roasted-garlic-
     seasoned diced red-
     skinned potatoes
     (about 2 cups)
1   14.5-ounce can
     diced fire-roasted
     tomatoes with
     garlic, undrained
2   tablespoons snipped
     fresh oregano
     Ground black pepper

1 Pour juices from beef roast into large saucepan or saucepan; set meat aside. Add carrots and 1 cup of the water to saucepan. Bring to boiling; reduce heat. Simmer, covered, for 3 minutes. Add remaining water, potatoes, tomatoes, and 1 tablespoon of the oregano. Return to boiling; reduce heat. Simmer, covered, for 3 minutes or until vegetables are tender. Break beef into bite-size pieces and add to stew; heat through. Season to taste with salt.

2 Top each serving with pepper and remaining oregano.

nutrition facts per serving: 253 cal., 9 g total fat (4 g sat. fat), 64 mg chol., 948 mg sodium, 20 g carb., 3 g dietary fiber, 25 g protein.

A quick simmer on the stove makes this a great soup for busy weeknights. The cook in the family will love how easily it comes together — especially using packaged precooked roast and frozen veggies.

speedy beef stew

start to finish: 25 minutes
makes: 4 servings

1   17-ounce package
    refrigerated cooked
    beef roast au jus
2   10.75-ounce cans
    condensed beefy
    mushroom soup
1   16-ounce package
    frozen mixed
    vegetables
4   teaspoons snipped
    fresh basil or
    1½ teaspoons dried
    basil, crushed
1½ cups milk

1 If necessary, cut meat into bite-size pieces. In a 4-quart Dutch oven combine meat, soup, frozen vegetables, and dried basil, if using. Bring to boiling; reduce heat. Simmer, covered, for 10 minutes.

2 Stir in milk and fresh basil, if using. Heat through.

nutrition facts per serving: 386 cal., 15 g total fat (7 g sat. fat), 80 mg chol., 1688 mg sodium, 33 g carb., 5 g dietary fiber, 33 g protein.

time-saving tip

The next time you grab a bag of budget-friendly frozen veggies, feel good about adding these time-savers to your meal. Frozen veggies are just as nutritious as fresh ones because they are frozen at their peak, locking in the freshest flavor.

This quick and easy low-calorie soup, laden with herbs, uses a mix of ground beef and ground turkey to keep the fat content low.

quick hamburger soup

start to finish: 30 minutes
makes: 6 servings

4 ounces extra-lean
    ground beef
4 ounces ground turkey
    breast
¾ cup finely chopped
    onion (1 large)
½ cup coarsely
    shredded carrot
    (1 medium)
½ cup sliced celery
    (1 stalk)
1 clove garlic, minced
3 cups reduced-sodium
    beef broth
1 14.5-ounce can
    diced tomatoes,
    undrained
½ teaspoon dried sage,
    crushed
½ teaspoon dried
    thyme, crushed
¼ teaspoon dried
    rosemary, crushed
⅛ teaspoon salt
⅛ teaspoon ground
    black pepper
1 cup chopped potato
    (1 medium)
    Fresh sage leaves
    (optional)

1 In a Dutch oven cook beef, turkey, onion, carrot, celery, and garlic until meat is brown and onion is tender; drain fat.

2 Add broth, undrained tomatoes, sage, thyme, rosemary, salt, and pepper. Bring to boiling; stir in potato and reduce heat. Simmer, covered, for 10 to 15 minutes or until vegetables are tender. If desired, garnish with fresh sage leaves.

nutrition facts per serving: 103 cal., 2 g total fat (1 g sat. fat), 19 mg chol., 418 mg sodium, 10 g carb., 1 g dietary fiber, 10 g protein.

Frozen meatballs are the secret shortcut for this quick, hearty stew. Allspice adds aromatic notes reminiscent of cloves, cinnamon, and nutmeg.

spiced meatball stew

start to finish: 30 minutes
makes: 8 servings

1 In a Dutch oven combine meatballs, beans, carrot, broth, Worcestershire sauce, allspice, and cinnamon. Bring to boiling; reduce heat. Simmer, covered, for 10 minutes.

2 Stir in undrained tomatoes. Return to boiling; reduce heat. Simmer, covered, about 5 minutes more or until vegetables are crisp-tender.

- 1 16-ounce package (32) frozen cooked Italian-style meatballs
- 3 cups green beans cut into 1-inch pieces
- 2 cups sliced carrot (4 medium)
- 1 14.5-ounce can beef broth
- 2 teaspoons Worcestershire sauce
- ½ to ¾ teaspoon ground allspice
- ½ teaspoon ground cinnamon
- 2 14.5-ounce cans diced tomatoes, undrained

nutrition facts per serving: 230 cal., 15 g total fat (7 g sat. fat), 44 mg chol., 976 mg sodium, 14 g carb., 4 g dietary fiber, 10 g protein.

20-minute noodle bowls

start to finish: 20 minutes
makes: 4 servings

In a large saucepan combine broth and peanut sauce. Bring to boiling. Stir in frozen vegetables and noodles (discard seasoning packet). Return to boiling; reduce heat. Simmer, covered, for 3 minutes or until noodles and vegetables are tender.

- 1 14-ounce can reduced-sodium chicken broth or reduced-sodium beef broth
- ½ cup bottled peanut sauce
- 2 cups frozen stir-fry or mixed vegetables
- 2 3-ounce packages ramen noodles (any flavor), broken

nutrition facts per serving: 293 cal., 12 g total fat (7 g sat. fat), 0 mg chol., 532 mg sodium, 39 g carb., 3 g dietary fiber, 8 g protein.

Refrigerated pasta products are a boon to busy cooks—unlike dry pasta, which takes at least 10 minutes to cook, these tender bites are ready in just a few minutes.

tortellini-meatball soup

start to finish: 30 minutes
makes: 4 to 6 servings

1 cup chopped sweet
  onion (1 large)
1 cup coarsely chopped
  carrot (2 medium)
3 cloves garlic, minced
1 tablespoon olive oil
  or vegetable oil
1 32-ounce carton
  reduced-sodium or
  regular chicken
  or beef broth
½ cup water
1 9-ounce package
  refrigerated four-
  cheese tortellini
½ 16-ounce package
  (16) frozen cooked
  Italian-style
  meatballs
1 teaspoon dried Italian
  seasoning, crushed
3 cups chopped fresh
  spinach or half of a
  10-ounce package
  frozen chopped
  spinach, thawed
  and drained
3 tablespoons chopped
  roasted red sweet
  pepper
  Salt
  Ground black pepper
1 tablespoon snipped
  fresh basil

1 In a Dutch oven cook onion, carrot, and garlic in hot oil over medium heat for 3 minutes, stirring occasionally. Add broth and the water. Bring to boiling. Stir in tortellini, meatballs, and Italian seasoning. Return to boiling; reduce heat. Simmer, uncovered, for 4 minutes.

2 Stir in spinach and roasted sweet pepper. Simmer, uncovered, about 3 minutes more or until tortellini are tender. Season to taste with salt and black pepper. Before serving, stir in basil.

nutrition facts per serving: 461 cal., 23 g total fat (9 g sat. fat), 68 mg chol., 1443 mg sodium, 44 g carb., 5 g dietary fiber, 22 g protein.

Bits of smoky kielbasa sausage accent the sweet flavors of tender squash and carrots in this seasonal soup. Kielbasa, a smoked Polish sausage link seasoned with garlic and marjoram, is often sold precooked for heat-and-serve convenience.

winter vegetable soup

start to finish: 30 minutes
makes: 6 servings

6 ounces kielbasa or
smoked sausage,
halved lengthwise
and sliced
⅓ cup chopped onion
(1 small)
2 14-ounce cans
chicken broth
2 cups water
½ of a small butternut
squash, peeled,
seeded, and cubed
(about 1⅓ cups)
1 cup sliced carrot
(2 medium)
⅛ to ¼ teaspoon ground
black pepper
1 15- to 16-ounce can
red kidney beans,
rinsed and drained
1 cup dried ditalini
or orzo pasta
2 cups baby spinach
leaves

1 Heat a 4-quart Dutch oven over medium heat. Add kielbasa and onion; cook about 5 minutes or until onion is tender, stirring occasionally. Add broth, the water, squash, carrot, and pepper. Bring to boiling; reduce heat. Simmer, covered, for 5 minutes.

2 Stir in beans and pasta. Return to boiling; reduce heat. Cover and boil gently about 6 minutes or until pasta and vegetables are tender, stirring occasionally. Stir in spinach. Serve immediately.

nutrition facts per serving: 259 cal., 10 g total fat (4 g sat. fat), 13 mg chol., 923 mg sodium, 32 g carb., 7 g dietary fiber, 13 g protein.

Jazz up a carton of ready-to-go broth with Asian flavors for a soup every bit as enticing as those at your favorite Chinese restaurant.

chinese dumpling soup

start to finish: 25 minutes
makes: 4 servings

1 32-ounce carton
    mushroom broth
    or vegetable broth
1 cup water
2 teaspoons grated
    fresh ginger
2 10-ounce packages
    frozen pork
    potstickers or
    dumplings with
    sauce packet*
2 medium carrots,
    cut into thin 2-inch
    strips, or 1 cup
    shredded carrots
1 small bunch green
    onion, trimmed and
    sliced diagonally

1 In a Dutch oven combine broth, the water, ginger, and the sauce packet from one package of potstickers. Bring to boiling over high heat.

2 Add potstickers, carrots, and most of the green onion. Return to simmering. Cook, covered, for 8 to 10 minutes or until potstickers are heated through.

3 Sprinkle each serving with remaining green onion.

nutrition facts per serving: 369 cal., 16 g total fat (6 g sat. fat), 18 mg chol., 1207 mg sodium, 42 g carb., 4 g dietary fiber, 14 g protein.

*tip: If no sauce packet is provided, add 2 teaspoons soy sauce and 1 teaspoon toasted sesame oil.

Broccoli and cheese always make a delicious pair. Add ham and roasted garlic and you have a sure winner. If you own an immersion blender, you can blend the soup right in the pan.

broccoli-cheese soup

prep: 15 minutes cook: 10 minutes
makes: 4 servings

2 14-ounce cans
    chicken broth
1 16-ounce package
    fresh broccoli florets
½ cup chopped onion
    (1 medium)
2 teaspoons bottled
    roasted garlic
1 cup shredded Swiss
    cheese (4 ounces)
1 cup half-and-half or
    light cream
½ cup cubed cooked
    ham
    Salt
    Ground black pepper

1 In a large saucepan, combine broth, broccoli, onion, and roasted garlic. Bring to boiling; reduce heat. Simmer, covered, about 10 minutes or until broccoli is very tender. Transfer broccoli mixture, half at a time, to a blender or food processor. Cover and blend or process until smooth. Return pureed mixture to saucepan.

2 Bring broccoli mixture to simmering. Add cheese; cook and stir until cheese is melted. Stir in half-and-half and ham. Season to taste with salt and pepper.

nutrition facts per serving: 283 cal., 18 g total fat (10 g sat. fat), 58 mg chol., 1213 mg sodium, 14 g carb., 4 g dietary fiber, 18 g protein.

With a few imaginative touches, canned soups can be super starters for quick, tasty meals. This recipe, for example, starts with ready-to-serve lentil soup and cooked chicken.

chicken and lentil soup with garlic-cheese toasts

start to finish: 20 minutes
makes: 4 servings

1   19-ounce can ready-
     to-serve lentil soup
1   cup loosely packed
     frozen crinkle-cut
     carrots
¼   teaspoon dried
     thyme, crushed
8   slices French bread
2   tablespoons
     margarine or butter
¼   teaspoon garlic
     powder
¾   cup shredded
     mozzarella or
     cheddar cheese
1   5.5-ounce can tomato
     juice (about ⅔ cup)
1   cup cubed cooked
     chicken

1 Preheat broiler. In a medium saucepan stir together soup, carrots, and thyme. Bring mixture to boiling; reduce heat. Simmer, covered, 8 to 9 minutes or until carrots are tender.

2 Meanwhile, for garlic-cheese toasts, place bread slices on unheated rack of a broiler pan. Spread with margarine; sprinkle with garlic powder. Broil 5 inches from heat for 1 minute or until golden brown. Top with cheese. Return to broiler; broil 30 to 60 seconds or until cheese melts slightly and edges are golden brown. Stir tomato juice and chicken into soup; heat through. Serve toasts with soup.

nutrition facts per serving: 349 cal., 6 g total fat, 49 mg chol., 923 mg sodium, 32 g carb., 24 g protein.

Get a head start on this comfort soup with a package of hashed brown potatoes. For blending safety, cool the soup slightly and blend in batches. Fill the blender no more than half full of soup and blend on low speed.

potato-cheddar soup

start to finish: 30 minutes
makes: 4 servings

1   28-ounce package
    frozen diced hash
    brown potatoes
    with onions and
    peppers
3   cups fat-free
    half-and-half
1   cup chopped
    miniature sweet
    peppers
1   cup water
½   teaspoon salt
½   teaspoon curry
    powder
⅛   to ¼ teaspoon
    cayenne pepper
    or ground black
    pepper
1½ cups shredded
    cheddar cheese
    (6 ounces)
    Sliced miniature
    sweet peppers
    (optional)
    Snipped fresh parsley
    (optional)

1 In a 4-quart Dutch oven combine potatoes, half-and-half, chopped sweet peppers, ½ cup of the water, salt, curry powder, and cayenne pepper. Bring just to boiling; reduce heat to medium. Cook, covered, for 10 minutes, stirring occasionally. Cool slightly.

2 Transfer 3 cups of the potato mixture to a blender; add the remaining ½ cup water. Cover and blend until nearly smooth. Return to Dutch oven; cook and stir until mixture is heated through and potatoes are tender. Stir in cheese. Cook and stir over low heat until cheese is melted.

3 If desired, top each serving with sliced sweet peppers and parsley.

nutrition facts per serving: 438 cal., 17 g total fat (11 g sat. fat), 54 mg chol., 883 mg sodium, 53 g carb., 5 g dietary fiber, 19 g protein.

This flavor-packed soup features beans, potatoes, and Italian pork sausage cooked in a garlicky tomato broth. Hearty leaves of escarole, chopped and stirred in at the end, add texture.

quick sausage minestrone

prep: 15 minutes   **cook:** 25 minutes
makes: 6 servings

1   19-ounce can
    cannellini (white
    kidney) beans,
    rinsed and drained
2   cups peeled and
    cubed potato
    (2 medium)
1   14.5-ounce can
    Italian-style stewed
    tomatoes, undrained
    and cut up
1   14.5-ounce can
    reduced-sodium
    beef broth
8   ounces cooked Italian
    sausage links, cut
    into ½-inch slices
2   teaspoons bottled
    minced garlic
¼   teaspoon crushed red
    pepper flakes
2   cups chopped
    escarole or Swiss
    chard leaves
⅓   cup shredded
    Parmesan or Asiago
    cheese

1 In a Dutch oven combine beans, potato, tomatoes, broth, sausage, garlic, and red pepper flakes. Bring to boiling; reduce heat. Simmer, covered, for 25 to 30 minutes or until potatoes are tender.

2 Before serving, stir in escarole. Sprinkle each serving with cheese.

nutrition facts per serving: 256 cal., 12 g total fat (4 g sat. fat), 25 mg chol., 942 mg sodium, 26 g carb., 6 g dietary fiber, 16 g protein.

quick chicken minestrone: Prepare as directed, except substitute two 6-ounce packages refrigerated cooked Italian-style chicken breast strips for the sausage, one 10-ounce package frozen cut green beans for the potatoes, and low-sodium chicken broth for the beef broth. Reduce cooking time to 15 minutes or until green beans are tender. Before serving, stir in 2 cups torn fresh spinach in place of the escarole.

Just a few ingredients make up this simple but hearty stew. Pureed squash from the freezer case of your supermarket forms the rich base while chipotle salsa adds extra kick.

winter squash and sage sausage chili

start to finish: 20 minutes
makes: 4 servings

1 pound bulk sage sausage or your favorite sausage
1 15-ounce can cannellini beans, rinsed and drained
1 12-ounce package frozen winter squash puree, thawed
1 cup chunky-style chipotle salsa or other salsa
1½ cups water
1 3.5-ounce package herb-flavored goat cheese, crumbled
   Fresh sage (optional)

In large saucepan cook sausage over medium heat until brown and no pink remains, stirring to break up; drain fat. Stir in beans, squash, salsa, and the water. Bring to boiling; reduce heat. Simmer, uncovered, 10 minutes, stirring occasionally. Serve in bowls; sprinkle with goat cheese and sage, if using.

nutrition facts per serving: 385 cal., 14 g total fat (7 g sat. fat), 119 mg chol., 1466 mg sodium, 34 g carb., 7 g dietary fiber, 39 g protein.

You won't even miss the pie, thanks to this warm and hearty bowl that incorporates the enticing flavors of a fully loaded pizza.

pizza soup

prep: 10 minutes   **cook:** 10 minutes
makes: 6 servings

1   cup chopped onion
    (1 large)
1   cup chopped green
    sweet pepper
    (1 large)
1   cup sliced fresh
    mushrooms
1   cup halved, sliced
    zucchini
1   14.5-ounce can beef
    broth
1   14.5-ounce can
    Italian-style
    tomatoes, undrained
    and cut up
1   8-ounce can pizza
    sauce
4   ounces fully cooked
    smoked sausage
    links, thinly sliced
½   teaspoon pizza
    seasoning
½   cup shredded
    reduced-fat
    mozzarella cheese
    (2 ounces)

1 In a medium saucepan combine onion, sweet pepper, mushrooms, zucchini, and ¼ cup of the broth. Bring to boiling; reduce heat. Simmer, covered, for 5 minutes.

2 Stir in the remaining broth, undrained tomatoes, pizza sauce, sausage, and seasoning. Simmer for 5 to 10 minutes more or until the vegetables are tender. Top each serving with cheese.

nutrition facts per serving: 163 cal., 9 g total fat (3 g sat. fat), 18 mg chol., 919 mg sodium, 12 g carb., 2 g dietary fiber, 10 g protein.

Combine cans of beef broth and cream of onion soup to form the base for this quick, satisfying soup. If you have fresh parsley, use 6 tablespoons instead of the flakes and stir it in just before serving.

easy beef and noodle soup

start to finish: 25 minutes
makes: 4 servings

1 pound lean ground beef

2½ cups water

1 10.75-ounce can condensed cream of onion soup

1 10.5-ounce can condensed beef broth

1½ cups dried medium noodles

2 tablespoons dried parsley flakes

Finely shredded Parmesan cheese (optional)

1 In a large saucepan or skillet cook meat over medium-high heat until brown. Drain fat. Stir in the water, onion soup, broth, noodles, and parsley flakes.

2 Bring to boiling; reduce heat. Simmer, covered, for about 5 minutes or until noodles are tender, stirring occasionally. If desired, sprinkle individual servings with Parmesan cheese.

nutrition facts per serving: 357 cal., 19 g total fat (7 g sat. fat), 98 mg chol., 1218 mg sodium, 19 g carb., 1 g dietary fiber, 27 g protein.

Thin golden rounds of baked Parmesan cheese make a fine accompaniment for this soup by adding satisfying richness and a pleasing crunch.

spicy sausage soup

start to finish: 25 minutes
makes: 6 servings

1   pound bulk hot or
     mild pork sausage
¼   cup chopped onion
2   cloves garlic, minced
3   14-ounce cans
     chicken broth
½   teaspoon dried Italian
     seasoning, crushed
4   cups coarsely
     chopped Swiss
     chard leaves
1   roma tomato, chopped
     Parmesan Cheese
     Crisps (optional)

1 In a large Dutch oven cook sausage, onion, and garlic until meat is brown, stirring to break up meat as it cooks. Drain fat.

2 Stir broth and Italian seasoning into meat mixture. Bring to boiling; reduce heat. Stir in Swiss chard; cook just until wilted. Stir in tomato; cook for 1 minute more. If desired, top each serving with Parmesan Cheese Crisps.

nutrition facts per serving: 227 cal., 16 g total fat (6 g sat. fat), 48 mg chol., 1258 mg sodium, 6 g carb., 1 g dietary fiber, 11 g protein.

parmesan cheese crisps: Preheat oven to 400°F. Coarsely shred 6 ounces Parmesan cheese. Line a baking sheet with parchment paper or nonstick foil. Place about 1 tablespoon of the shredded cheese on prepared sheet; pat into a 2-inch circle. Repeat with remaining cheese, allowing 2 inches between circles. Bake for 7 to 8 minutes or until bubbly and lightly golden. Let stand on baking sheet for 1 to 2 minutes or until cooled but still pliable. Carefully peel off paper or foil. Place cheese crisps on a wire rack; cool completely.

Pork strips get a quick sizzle in a skillet to join beans and seasonings for a hearty soup that's ready to enjoy in just minutes. Crusty rolls and creamy coleslaw make good accompaniments.

quick pork-bean soup

prep: 15 minutes cook: 15 minutes
makes: 4 servings

12 ounces lean boneless
      pork
1   cup chopped onion
      (1 large)
2   tablespoons
      vegetable oil
2   cups water
1   11.5-ounce can
      condensed bean
      with bacon soup
1½ cups sliced carrot
      (3 medium)
1   teaspoon
      Worcestershire
      sauce
¼   teaspoon dry mustard

1 Cut pork into thin bite-size strips. In a large skillet cook the meat and onion in hot oil for 3 to 4 minutes or until meat is brown. Stir in the water, soup, carrot, Worcestershire sauce, and dry mustard.

2 Bring to boiling; reduce heat. Simmer, covered, for 15 minutes.

nutrition facts per serving: 312 cal., 13 g total fat (3 g sat. fat), 52 mg chol., 678 mg sodium, 23 g carb., 6 g dietary fiber, 24 g protein.

Even short simmers, like a brothy smoky ham soup loaded with fresh summer veggies, yield a colorful soup with big flavor.

ham, sweet pepper, and zucchini soup

start to finish: 25 minutes
makes: 6 servings

1 tablespoon butter
1¼ cups coarsely chopped zucchini (1 medium)
¾ cup coarsely chopped yellow sweet pepper (1 medium)
2 cloves garlic, minced
3 14-ounce cans chicken broth
3 cups chopped cooked ham (1 pound)
2 tablespoons snipped fresh basil

In a large saucepan melt butter over medium heat. Add zucchini, sweet pepper, and garlic; cook until tender. Add broth. Bring to boiling; reduce heat. Simmer, covered, for 5 minutes. Stir in ham; heat through. Stir in basil.

nutrition facts per serving: 167 cal., 9 g total fat (3 g sat. fat), 51 mg chol., 1814 mg sodium, 7 g carb., 2 g dietary fiber, 15 g protein.

Apple juice and sautéed leeks give this hearty soup long-simmered flavor in just 25 minutes. Serve with toasted baguette slices brushed with olive oil and a light sprinkling of coarse salt.

lickety-split pea soup with ham

start to finish: 25 minutes
makes: 4 servings

⅔ cup sliced leeks
     (2 medium)*
2 teaspoons olive oil
2 19-ounce cans ready-
     to-serve green split
     pea with bacon
     soup
1½ cups apple juice
     or apple cider
1 cup chopped carrot
     (2 medium)
½ cup diced cooked
     ham
½ teaspoon ground
     black pepper
     Fresh mint leaves
     (optional)

1 In a large saucepan cook leeks in hot oil over medium heat about 3 minutes or just until tender. Using a slotted spoon, remove a few leek slices; set aside.

2 Stir split pea soup, apple juice, carrot, ham, and pepper into leeks in saucepan. Bring to boiling; reduce heat. Simmer, covered, about 15 minutes or until carrot is tender.

3 Top each serving with reserved leek slices and, if desired, mint.

nutrition facts per serving: 291 cal., 4 g total fat (1 g sat. fat), 3 mg chol., 1038 mg sodium, 51 g carb., 7 g dietary fiber, 11 g protein.

＊note: See tip on cleaning leeks, page 464.

Salsa adds a lively beat to the turkey and zucchini in this aromatic meal in a bowl. For a heartier soup, use a salsa with black beans and corn.

turkey-tortilla soup

start to finish: 20 minutes
makes: 6 servings

2 tablespoons
vegetable oil
3 6-inch corn tortillas,
cut into strips
2 14.5-ounce cans
reduced-sodium
chicken broth
1 cup chunky red salsa
2 cups cubed cooked
turkey, chicken,
pork, or beef
1½ cups coarsely
chopped zucchini
Sour cream (optional)
Snipped fresh cilantro
(optional)
Lime wedges
(optional)

1 In a large skillet heat oil over medium heat. Add tortilla strips; cook and stir until crisp. Using a slotted spoon, remove tortilla strips from skillet; drain on paper towels.

2 In a large saucepan combine broth and salsa. Bring to boiling over medium-high heat. Stir in turkey and zucchini; heat through.

3 If desired, top each serving with sour cream and cilantro. Serve with tortilla strips and, if desired, lime wedges.

nutrition facts per serving: 262 cal., 11 g total fat (2 g sat. fat), 53 mg chol., 920 mg sodium, 16 g carb., 3 g dietary fiber, 26 g protein.

Fresh leeks add a natural sweetness to this soup while starchy potatoes give it a wonderful body without the addition of a thickener. Serve the soup hot or cold.

country chicken and potato soup

start to finish: 25 minutes
makes: 4 servings

2   14-ounce cans
     reduced-sodium
     chicken broth
1   20-ounce package
     refrigerated red-
     skinned potato
     wedges
½   cup chopped leek,
     white part only*
2   or 3 cloves garlic,
     minced
2   cups chopped cooked
     chicken (10 ounces)
1   tablespoon snipped
     fresh chives
⅛   teaspoon ground
     black pepper
1   cup half-and-half,
     light cream, or milk
     Whole fresh chives
     Garlic-flavor olive
     oil**(optional)

1 In a large saucepan combine 1 can of the broth, potatoes, leek, and garlic. Bring to boiling; reduce heat. Simmer, covered, for 5 minutes. Remove from heat.

2 Using a potato masher, slightly mash potatoes, leaving some potato pieces. Add chicken, snipped chives, and pepper. Stir in remaining broth and half-and-half; heat through.

3 Top each serving with whole chives and, if desired, a few drops of garlic-flavor oil.

nutrition facts per serving: 319 cal., 12 g total fat (6 g sat. fat), 85 mg chol., 707 mg sodium, 23 g carb., 4 g dietary fiber, 28 g protein.

*note: See tip on cleaning leeks, page 464.

**note: To make your own garlic-flavor olive oil, in a small skillet heat 2 tablespoons olive oil over medium heat. Add 1 clove minced garlic; cook and stir until garlic begins to brown. Remove from heat. Strain to remove garlic. Discard any unused oil (do not store).

Brimming with chicken, broccoli, and ramen noodles, this is one of the quickest soups you can get to the table. Offer it with other Chinese take-out foods, such as egg rolls.

simply ramen chicken soup

start to finish: 15 minutes
makes: 4 servings

2 14-ounce cans
    reduced-sodium
    chicken broth
2 3-ounce packages
    chicken-flavor
    ramen noodles
½ teaspoon dried
    oregano or basil,
    crushed
1 10-ounce package
    frozen cut broccoli
2 cups shredded
    cooked chicken
    or turkey (about
    10 ounces)
¼ cup sliced almonds,
    toasted

1 In a large saucepan combine broth, seasoning packets from ramen noodles, and oregano. Bring to boiling.

2 Break up noodles. Add noodles and broccoli to broth mixture. Return to boiling; reduce heat. Simmer, uncovered, for 3 minutes. Stir in chicken; heat through. Sprinkle each serving with almonds.

nutrition facts per serving: 416 cal., 18 g total fat (2 g sat. fat), 62 mg chol., 1300 mg sodium, 32 g carb., 3 g dietary fiber, 30 g protein.

Jump-start your soup making in one of two ways: buying ready-to-go chopped chicken or chopping meat pulled from a deli-roasted chicken.

mexi-chicken soup

start to finish: 30 minutes
makes: 6 servings

1   32-ounce carton reduced-sodium chicken broth
1   15-ounce can black beans, rinsed and drained
1   15-ounce can golden hominy, rinsed and drained
1   cup bottled salsa
1   cup bottled nopalitos (cactus leaves), drained, or bite-size green sweet pepper strips
1   4-ounce can diced green chiles
1   tablespoon chili powder
1   teaspoon ground cumin
2½ cups chopped cooked chicken
    Snipped fresh herbs of your choice (optional)

In a 4-quart Dutch oven combine broth, black beans, hominy, salsa, nopalitos, undrained chiles, chili powder, and cumin. Bring to boiling; reduce heat. Simmer, covered, for 20 minutes. Add chicken; heat through. If desired, sprinkle each serving with fresh herbs.

nutrition facts per serving: 240 cal., 6 g total fat (1 g sat. fat), 52 mg chol., 1060 mg sodium, 25 g carb., 7 g dietary fiber, 25 g protein.

Ramen noodles are a convenient and inexpensive staple to keep on hand. Frozen mixed vegetables with water chestnuts boost flavor and add nutritional value to this perfect weeknight soup.

easy oriental chicken soup

start to finish: 20 minutes
makes: 3 servings

1   tablespoon cooking
     oil
8   ounces packaged
     chicken breast
     stir-fry strips
3   cups water
½   of a 16-ounce
     package frozen
     broccoli, carrots,
     and water
     chestnuts (2 cups)
1   3-ounce package
     chicken-flavor
     ramen noodles
2   tablespoons reduced-
     sodium soy sauce

1 In a large saucepan heat oil over medium-high heat. Add chicken; cook and stir for 2 to 3 minutes or until no longer pink. Remove from heat; drain off fat.

2 Carefully add the water, vegetables, and seasoning packet from ramen noodles to chicken in saucepan. Bring to boiling. Break up noodles; stir into soup. Reduce heat. Simmer, covered, for 3 minutes. Stir in soy sauce.

nutrition facts per serving: 254 cal., 8 g total fat (1 g sat. fat), 63 mg chol., 829 mg sodium, 22 g carb., 5 g dietary fiber, 22 g protein.

superfast **simmers**

The addition of bok choy, baby carrots, and lemon makes this savory stew light and elegant. The recipe calls for jarred gravy as a convenient way to add richness.

spring chicken stew

start to finish: 30 minutes
makes: 4 servings

1	lemon
1¼	pounds skinless, boneless chicken thighs
	Salt
	Ground black pepper
1	tablespoon olive oil
8	ounces baby carrots with tops, scrubbed, trimmed, and halved lengthwise
1	12-ounce jar chicken gravy
1½	cups water
1	tablespoon Dijon-style mustard
2	heads baby bok choy, quartered
	Fresh lemon thyme (optional)

1 Finely shred zest from lemon; set zest aside. Juice lemon; set juice aside. Season chicken lightly with salt and pepper.

2 In a Dutch oven heat oil over medium-high heat. Add chicken; cook for 2 to 3 minutes or until chicken is brown, turning occasionally.

3 Add carrots, gravy, and the water. Stir in mustard. Bring to boiling. Place bok choy on top. Reduce heat. Simmer, covered, for 10 minutes or until chicken is done and vegetables are tender. Add lemon juice to taste.

4 Top each serving with lemon zest and, if desired, garnish with lemon thyme.

nutrition facts per serving: 273 cal., 12 g total fat (2 g sat. fat), 117 mg chol., 909 mg sodium, 13 g carb., 3 g dietary fiber, 31 g protein.

Enriched with coconut milk and flavored with Thai curry paste, this aromatic soup provides a welcome change from traditional chicken noodle soup.

curried chicken noodle soup

start to finish: 30 minutes
makes: 6 servings

3   14-ounce cans
     reduced-sodium
     chicken broth
1   to 2 tablespoons
     green or red Thai
     curry paste
2   skinless, boneless
     chicken breast
     halves (about
     10 ounces total)
     Salt
1   5-ounce package
     dried Japanese
     curly wheat-flour
     noodles or angel
     hair pasta
1½ cups chopped peeled
     sweet potato
     (1 medium)
½   cup chopped tomato
     (1 medium)
1   cup canned
     unsweetened
     coconut milk
½   cup lightly packed
     fresh cilantro leaves

1 In a 4-quart Dutch oven combine broth and curry paste. Cover and bring to boiling.

2 Meanwhile, slice chicken breasts crosswise into ¼-inch strips; sprinkle lightly with salt and set aside.

3 Add noodles, sweet potato, and tomato to broth mixture. Return to boiling; reduce heat. Simmer, covered, for 2 minutes, stirring once to break up noodles.

4 Add chicken. Return to boiling; reduce heat. Simmer, covered, for 2 to 3 minutes more or until chicken is tender and no longer pink. Stir in coconut milk. Top each serving with cilantro.

nutrition facts per serving: 273 cal., 9 g total fat (7 g sat. fat), 27 mg chol., 690 mg sodium, 30 g carb., 2 g dietary fiber, 18 g protein.

The crushed tortilla chips added to the chili act as a thickener and give it great whole-grain texture.

chunky bean and chicken chili

start to finish: 20 minutes
makes: 4 servings

3   cups tortilla chips
2   teaspoons vegetable oil
1   pound skinless, boneless chicken breasts or thighs, cut into bite-size pieces
2   19-ounce cans cannellini (white kidney) beans, rinsed and drained
1½ cups shredded Monterey Jack cheese with jalapeño peppers (6 ounces)
1   4.5-ounce can diced green chiles, undrained
1   14-ounce can reduced-sodium chicken broth
½   cup water
     Fresh cilantro (optional)

1 Preheat broiler. Coarsely crush 2 cups of the chips.

2 In 4- to 5-quart Dutch oven, heat oil over medium-high heat. Add chicken; cook until brown. Add beans, 1 cup of the cheese, undrained chiles, broth, the water, and crushed chips. Bring to boiling; reduce heat. Simmer, uncovered, for 5 minutes, stirring occasionally.

3 Meanwhile, for tortilla crisps, place remaining 1 cup chips on a baking sheet lined with nonstick foil. Sprinkle with remaining ½ cup cheese. Broil 6 inches from heat for 1 to 2 minutes or until cheese is melted and begins to brown. Serve chili with tortilla crisps. If desired, sprinkle with cilantro.

nutrition facts per serving: 575 cal., 23 g total fat (10 g sat. fat), 111 mg chol., 1172 mg sodium, 52 g carb., 14 g dietary fiber, 55 g protein.

A spoonful of purchased basil pesto gives this quick-to-make soup a fresh and flavorful finish.

chicken and pasta soup with pesto

start to finish: 25 minutes
makes: 4 to 6 servings

2   14-ounce cans reduced-sodium chicken broth
1   pound skinless, boneless chicken breast halves or thighs, cubed
1   14.5-ounce can diced tomatoes with basil, garlic, and oregano, undrained
½   cup dried orzo
1   cup chopped zucchini (1 small)
1   teaspoon finely shredded lemon zest
1   tablespoon lemon juice
    Ground black pepper
4   to 6 tablespoons purchased basil pesto

1 In a large saucepan combine broth, chicken, undrained tomatoes, and orzo. Bring to boiling; reduce heat. Simmer, covered, for 6 minutes.

2 Add zucchini, lemon zest, and lemon juice. Return to boiling; reduce heat. Simmer, uncovered, for 3 to 4 minutes or until orzo and zucchini are tender and chicken is no longer pink. Season to taste with pepper. Top each serving with pesto.

nutrition facts per serving: 371 cal., 12 g total fat (0 g sat. fat), 68 mg chol., 1180 mg sodium, 30 g carb., 1 g dietary fiber, 35 g protein.

Refrigerated pasta lets you put a soup together lickety split. If you can't find vegetable ravioli or herb-chicken tortellini, use a cheese version.

chicken and vegetable ravioli soup

start to finish: 25 minutes
makes: 4 servings

Nonstick cooking
spray
12 ounces skinless,
boneless chicken
breast halves, cut
into ½-inch cubes
6 cups reduced-sodium
chicken broth
½ cup sliced leek or
chopped onion*
1 tablespoon grated
fresh ginger
¼ teaspoon saffron
threads, slightly
crushed (optional)
1 9-ounce package
vegetable ravioli
or refrigerated herb-
chicken tortellini
½ cup fresh baby spinach
leaves or shredded
fresh spinach

1 Lightly coat an unheated large saucepan
with nonstick cooking spray. Preheat over
medium-high heat. Add chicken; cook and stir
for 3 minutes. Carefully add broth, leek, ginger,
and, if desired, saffron.

2 Bring to boiling. Add ravioli. Return to
boiling; reduce heat. Simmer, uncovered,
for 5 to 9 minutes or until ravioli are tender,
stirring occasionally. Remove from heat. Top
each serving with spinach.

nutrition facts per serving: 222 cal., 3 g total fat
(0 g sat. fat), 59 mg chol., 1221 mg sodium, 21 g carb.,
3 g dietary fiber, 29 g protein.

✳note: See tip on cleaning leeks, page 464.

A hearty bowl of soup like this one, chock-full of vegetables, makes a satisfying meal on any cold day. It's also a terrific way to use up leftover chicken or turkey.

creamy chicken-vegetable soup

start to finish: 30 minutes
makes: 4 servings

½ cup chopped celery
(1 stalk)
½ cup sliced leek or
chopped onion*
½ cup thinly sliced
carrot (1 medium)
1 tablespoon butter
or margarine
1 14-ounce can
reduced-sodium
chicken broth
¼ cup all-purpose flour
2 cups milk
1 tablespoon snipped
fresh thyme
or basil or
1 teaspoon dried
thyme or basil,
crushed
¼ teaspoon salt
1½ cups chopped cooked
chicken or turkey
(about 8 ounces)
¼ cup dry white wine
or reduced-sodium
chicken broth
Cracked black pepper

1 In a large saucepan cook celery, leek, and carrot in hot butter until tender. In a medium bowl gradually stir broth into flour; stir flour mixture into vegetables in saucepan. Add milk, dried herb (if using), and salt; cook and stir until slightly thickened and bubbly. Cook and stir for 1 minute more.

2 Stir in chicken, wine, and fresh herb (if using); cook for about 2 minutes more or until heated through.

3 Season each serving with pepper.

nutrition facts per serving: 254 cal., 10 g total fat (5 g sat. fat), 68 mg chol., 560 mg sodium, 16 g carb., 1 g dietary fiber, 23 g protein.

*note: See tip on cleaning leeks, page 464.

Thyme and Dijon-style mustard, along with a sprinkling of fresh parsley, punctuate this creamy soup with wonderfully bright flavors.

chicken soup dijonaise

start to finish: 30 minutes
makes: 4 servings

1   tablespoon butter
1   tablespoon olive oil
1   cup chopped onion
     (2 medium)
2   leeks, trimmed and
     sliced*
1   tablespoon Dijon-
     style mustard
2   14-ounce cans
     reduced-sodium
     chicken broth
1   medium Yukon Gold
     potato, cut into
     ½-inch pieces
     (about 1 cup)
¾   cup half-and-half or
     light cream
2   tablespoons all-
     purpose flour
2   cups chopped cooked
     chicken
1   teaspoon snipped
     fresh thyme
⅛   teaspoon ground
     white pepper
2   tablespoons snipped
     fresh parsley

1 In a large saucepan heat butter and olive oil over medium heat. Add onion and leeks; cook for 4 to 6 minutes or until tender, stirring occasionally. Stir in mustard. Stir in broth and potato. Bring to boiling; reduce heat. Simmer, covered, for 8 to 10 minutes or until potato is tender.

2 In a small bowl whisk together half-and-half and flour until smooth; stir into broth mixture. Add chicken, thyme, and white pepper; cook and stir until thickened and bubbly. Cook and stir for 2 minutes more. Sprinkle with parsley.

nutrition facts per serving: 344 cal., 17 g total fat (7 g sat. fat), 86 mg chol., 674 mg sodium, 21 g carb., 2 g dietary fiber, 26 g protein.

*note: See tip on cleaning leeks, page 464.

Whether you choose the light and brothy version or the cream-based soup, pesto delivers vibrant flavor. When you don't have turkey, use deli-roasted chicken.

turkey and rice soup

start to finish: 20 minutes
makes: 6 servings

4   cups chicken broth
¼   teaspoon dried Italian seasoning, crushed
¼   teaspoon ground black pepper
1   10-ounce package frozen mixed vegetables
1   cup instant white or brown rice
2   cups chopped cooked turkey or chicken (10 ounces)
1   14.5-ounce can diced tomatoes, drained
2   tablespoons basil pesto

1 In a large saucepan combine broth, Italian seasoning, and pepper. Bring to boiling. Stir in frozen vegetables and rice.

2 Return to boiling; reduce heat. Simmer, covered, for 8 to 10 minutes or until vegetables are tender. Stir in turkey, tomatoes, and pesto; heat through.

nutrition facts per serving: 233 cal., 6 g total fat (1 g sat. fat), 38 mg chol., 847 mg sodium, 25 g carb., 2 g dietary fiber, 18 g protein.

creamy turkey and rice soup: Prepare as directed. In a small bowl combine one 8-ounce carton sour cream and 2 tablespoons all-purpose flour. Stir sour cream mixture into hot soup; cook and stir until thickened and bubbly. Cook and stir for 1 minute more.

Whipping cream and tomatoes seasoned with herbs and garlic make a rich base for this simple soup. Serve with sliced country bread that's been lightly toasted and rubbed with a cut garlic clove.

creamy tomato and shrimp chowder

start to finish: 20 minutes
makes: 4 servings

8   ounces fresh or frozen
    peeled, cooked
    medium shrimp
    with tails
1   tablespoon olive oil
1   cup chopped celery
    (2 stalks)
½   cup chopped onion
    (1 medium)
2   14.5-ounce cans diced
    tomatoes with basil,
    garlic, and oregano,
    undrained
½   cup whipping cream
½   cup water
    Ground black pepper
    Slivered fresh basil
    (optional)
    Sliced bread (optional)

1 Thaw shrimp, if frozen. In a large saucepan heat oil over medium heat. Add celery and onion; cook and stir just until tender.

2 Stir in undrained tomatoes; heat through. Stir in shrimp, cream, and the water; cook over medium heat just until heated through. Season to taste with pepper.

3 If desired, garnish each serving with basil and serve with sliced bread.

nutrition facts per serving: 245 cal., 15 g total fat (8 g sat. fat), 152 mg chol., 1056 mg sodium, 14 g carb., 2 g dietary fiber, 15 g protein.

Although great any time of year, this fresh-tasting soup is perfectly light for summer. The savory combination of shrimp, shredded bok choy, and leek is embellished with an accent of lemon pepper.

shrimp and greens soup

start to finish: 20 minutes
makes: 4 servings

12 ounces peeled and deveined fresh or frozen shrimp

1 leek, thinly sliced*

2 cloves garlic, minced

1 tablespoon olive oil

3 14-ounce cans reduced-sodium chicken broth or vegetable broth

1 tablespoon snipped fresh parsley

1 teaspoon snipped fresh marjoram or thyme or ¼ teaspoon dried marjoram or thyme, crushed

¼ teaspoon lemon pepper

3 cups shredded bok choy or spinach leaves

1 Thaw shrimp, if frozen. Rinse shrimp; pat dry with paper towels. Set aside.

2 In a large saucepan cook leek and garlic in hot oil over medium-high heat about 2 minutes or until leek is tender. Carefully add chicken broth, parsley, marjoram, and lemon pepper. Bring to boiling; add shrimp. Return to boiling; reduce heat.

3 Simmer, uncovered, for 2 minutes. Stir in bok choy; cook about 1 minute more or until bok choy is wilted.

nutrition facts per serving: 147 cal., 6 g total fat (1 g sat. fat), 131 mg chol., 1093 mg sodium, 5 g carb., 2 g dietary fiber, 18 g protein.

*note: See tip on cleaning leeks, page 464.

Cod, haddock, and pike are all good varieties of fish to use in this herbed, tomato-based soup.

fabulous fish soup

prep: 10 minutes cook: 15 minutes
makes: 4 servings

2   cups water
1   14.5-ounce can
       tomatoes, undrained
       and cut up
2   cups frozen mixed
       vegetables
1   cup thinly sliced
       celery (2 stalks)
¾   cup chopped onion
1½ teaspoons instant
       chicken bouillon
       granules
1   teaspoon dried
       oregano, crushed
1   clove garlic, minced
       Several dashes
       bottled hot pepper
       sauce
8   ounces fresh or
       frozen fish fillets,
       cut into 1-inch
       pieces

1 In a large saucepan combine the water, undrained tomatoes, mixed vegetables, celery, onion, bouillon granules, oregano, garlic, and hot pepper sauce. Bring to boiling; reduce heat. Simmer, covered, for 10 minutes or until vegetables are tender.

2 Stir in fish. Return just to boiling; reduce heat. simmer gently, covered, for about 5 minutes or until fish flakes easily with a fork.

nutrition facts per serving: 159 cal., 2 g total fat, 27 mg chol., 441 mg sodium, 21 g carb., 16 g protein.

Frozen vegetables are the secret to this quick chowder. A little smoked Gouda cheese produces the robust flavor.

vegetable-cheese chowder

start to finish: 25 minutes
makes: 4 servings

1   16-ounce package frozen broccoli, cauliflower, and carrots
½   cup water
2   cups milk
⅓   cup all-purpose flour
1   14-ounce can chicken broth
1   cup shredded smoked Gouda cheese (4 ounces)

1 In a large saucepan combine frozen vegetables and the water. Bring to boiling; reduce heat. Simmer, covered, about 4 minutes or just until vegetables are tender. Do not drain.

2 Meanwhile, in a screw-top jar combine ⅔ cup of the milk and flour; cover and shake well. Stir milk mixture into vegetable mixture in saucepan. Add remaining 1⅓ cups milk and broth; cook and stir until thickened and bubbly. Cook and stir for 1 minute more. Add cheese; cook and stir over low heat until cheese is nearly melted.

nutrition facts per serving: 370 cal., 20 g total fat (13 g sat. fat), 81 mg chol., 942 mg sodium, 22 g carb., 3 g dietary fiber, 25 g protein.

tortellini florentine soup

start to finish: 30 minutes
makes: 6 servings

1   9-ounce package refrigerated three-cheese tortellini
2   14.5-ounce cans low-sodium chicken broth
1   10-ounce container refrigerated light Alfredo pasta sauce
2   cups shredded purchased roasted chicken
½   cup oil-packed dried tomato strips, drained
½   of a 5-ounce package fresh baby spinach
    Shaved or shredded Parmesan cheese (optional)

1 In a 4-quart Dutch oven cook tortellini according to package directions; drain.

2 In the same Dutch oven combine broth and pasta sauce. Stir in chicken and dried tomatoes. Bring just to boiling; reduce heat. Simmer, uncovered, for 5 minutes.

3 Stir in cooked tortellini and spinach; cook for 1 to 2 minutes or just until tortellini is heated through and spinach is wilted. If desired, top each serving with cheese.

nutrition facts per serving: 286 cal., 15 g total fat (6 g sat. fat), 77 mg chol., 1094 mg sodium, 21 g carb., 1 g dietary fiber, 20 g protein.

superfast **simmers**

Tomato soup and tortellini harmonize in this rich cream cheese–based soup. Bake some quick and easy refrigerated breadsticks to serve alongside.

tomato-tortellini soup

start to finish: 15 minutes
makes: 4 servings

2   14-ounce cans
     reduced-sodium
     chicken broth or
     vegetable broth
1   9-ounce package
     refrigerated
     tortellini
½   of an 8-ounce tub
     cream cheese
     spread with chive
     and onion
1   10.75- or 11-ounce
     can condensed
     tomato or tomato
     bisque soup
     Snipped fresh chives
     (optional)

1 In a medium saucepan bring broth to boiling. Add tortellini; reduce heat. Simmer, uncovered, for 5 minutes.

2 In a small bowl whisk ⅓ cup of the hot broth into cream cheese spread until smooth. Add cream cheese mixture and tomato soup to saucepan; heat through. If desired, sprinkle each serving with chives.

nutrition facts per serving: 363 cal., 14 g total fat (8 g sat. fat), 57 mg chol., 1264 mg sodium, 44 g carb., 1 g dietary fiber, 14 g protein.

Hot Jamaican spices zip up this creamy pasta soup. With a dash of jerk seasoning—a unique island blend of spices, herbs, and fiery chiles—this pasta soup recipe is Jamaica's own.

creamy carrot and pasta soup

start to finish: 30 minutes
makes: 4 servings

2 14-ounce cans
   chicken broth
   (3½ cups)
2 cups sliced carrot
   (4 medium)
1 large potato, peeled
   and diced
1 cup chopped onion
   (1 large)
1 tablespoon grated
   fresh ginger
½ to 1 teaspoon
   Jamaican jerk
   seasoning
8 ounces dried tricolor
   radiatore or rotini
1½ cups milk or one
   12-ounce can
   evaporated skim
   milk
   Fresh chives
   (optional)

1 In a large saucepan combine broth, carrot, potato, onion, ginger, and Jamaican jerk seasoning. Bring to boiling; reduce heat. Simmer, covered, for 15 to 20 minutes or until vegetables are very tender. Cool slightly.

2 Meanwhile, cook pasta according to package directions; drain.

3 Transfer vegetable mixture, one-fourth at a time, to a food processor. Cover and process until smooth. Return pureed mixture to saucepan. Stir in pasta and milk; heat through. If desired, garnish each serving with chives.

nutrition facts per serving: 363 cal., 4 g total fat (2 g sat. fat), 8 mg chol., 750 mg sodium, 65 g carb., 3 g dietary fiber, 16 g protein.

Warm up to big, hearty meals in a bowl, featuring moist, tender chunks of meat. Whether it's familiar combos, such as meatballs and veggies or something entirely new, such as lamb cassoulet or polenta-topped stew, you'll find plenty of savory recipes to satisfy the meat-lovers in your family.

hearty & me

4

aty

A richly flavored wine sauce coats seasoned beef chuck steak and vegetables in this hearty one-dish meal.

polenta meat stew

prep: 30 minutes   slow cook: 8 to 10 hours (low) or 4 to 5 hours (high)
makes: 8 servings

2½ pounds boneless beef chuck roast, pork shoulder roast, or lamb stew meat
¼ cup all-purpose flour
1 teaspoon dried thyme, crushed
1 teaspoon dried basil, crushed
½ teaspoon salt
½ teaspoon ground black pepper
4 medium carrots, cut into 1-inch pieces
8 ounces boiling onions, peeled, or frozen small whole onions
6 cloves garlic, minced
1 teaspoon snipped fresh rosemary or ¼ teaspoon dried rosemary, crushed
1 14.5-ounce can reduced-sodium beef broth
1 cup water
½ cup dry red wine
1 recipe Polenta
½ cup snipped fresh parsley
¼ cup tomato paste
Snipped fresh Italian parsley (optional)

1 Trim fat from meat. Cut meat into 1-inch pieces. In a resealable plastic bag combine flour, thyme, basil, salt, and pepper. Add meat pieces, several at a time, shaking to coat. Place meat in a 3½- or 4-quart slow cooker. Add carrots, onions, garlic, and dried rosemary (if using). Stir in broth, the water, and wine.

2 Cover and cook on low-heat setting for 8 to 10 hours or on high-heat setting for 4 to 5 hours.

3 Shortly before serving, prepare Polenta.

4 To serve, stir fresh rosemary (if using), ½ cup parsley, and tomato paste into meat mixture. Serve stew in shallow bowls with polenta. If desired, garnish with additional parsley.

nutrition facts per serving: 357 cal., 8 g total fat (3 g sat. fat), 92 mg chol., 560 mg sodium, 30 g carb., 3 g dietary fiber, 37 g protein.

polenta: In a large saucepan bring 3 cups milk just to a simmer over medium heat. In a medium bowl combine 1 cup cornmeal, 1 cup water, and 1 teaspoon salt. Slowly stir cornmeal mixture into hot milk; cook and stir until mixture comes to a boil. Reduce heat to low. Cook for 10 to 15 minutes or until mixture is very thick, stirring occasionally. (If mixture is too thick, stir in additional milk.) Stir in 2 tablespoons butter or margarine until melted.

Basic meat and potatoes get bold flavor after simmering in this heady combination of dark beer, onions, thyme, and parsley. It will fill you up on a chilly winter evening.

mustard-herb beef stew

prep: 30 minutes cook: 1 to 1¼ hours
makes: 6 servings

⅓ cup all-purpose flour
1 tablespoon snipped fresh parsley
1 teaspoon snipped fresh thyme or ½ teaspoon dried thyme, crushed
1 teaspoon ground black pepper
½ teaspoon salt
1½ pounds boneless beef chuck, cut in 1- to 1½-inch pieces
2 tablespoons olive oil
8 to 10 ounces cippollini onions, peeled, or 1 medium onion, peeled and cut in wedges
4 carrots, peeled and cut into 1-inch pieces
1 8-ounce package fresh cremini mushrooms, halved if large
8 tiny Yukon Gold potatoes, halved
3 tablespoons tomato paste
2 tablespoons spicy brown mustard
1 14-ounce can beef broth
1 12-ounce bottle dark porter beer or nonalcoholic beer
1 bay leaf

1 In large bowl combine flour, parsley, thyme, pepper, and salt. Add beef, a few pieces at a time; stir to coat. Reserve leftover flour mixture.

2 In 6-quart Dutch oven heat oil over medium-high heat. Add beef; cook until brown. Stir in onions, carrots, mushrooms, and potatoes; cook and stir 3 minutes. Stir in tomato paste, mustard, and remaining flour mixture. Add broth, beer, and bay leaf. Bring to boiling; reduce heat. Simmer, covered, for 1 to 1¼ hours or until beef is tender. Discard bay leaf.

nutrition facts per serving: 426 cal., 11 g total fat (3 g sat. fat), 50 mg chol., 880 mg sodium, 43 g carb., 5 g dietary fiber, 33 g protein.

Beef and barley are a classic combination in soup and one that yields a hearty, meaty richness and pleasantly chewy texture. Add a bit of freshness with a sprinkling of chopped parsley over each serving.

barley-beef soup

prep: 25 minutes cook: 1¾ hours
makes: 8 servings

12   ounces beef or lamb
     stew meat, cut into
     1-inch cubes
1   tablespoon vegetable
     oil
4   14-ounce cans beef
     broth
1   cup chopped onion
     (1 large)
½   cup chopped celery
     (1 stalk)
1   teaspoon dried
     oregano or basil,
     crushed
¼   teaspoon ground
     black pepper
2   cloves garlic, minced
1   bay leaf
1   cup frozen mixed
     vegetables
1   14.5-ounce can diced
     tomatoes, undrained
1   cup ½-inch slices
     peeled parsnip or
     ½-inch cubes peeled
     potato
⅔   cup quick-cooking
     barley

1 In a Dutch oven brown meat in hot oil. Stir in broth, onion, celery, oregano, pepper, garlic, and bay leaf. Bring to boiling; reduce heat. Simmer, covered, for 1½ hours for beef (45 minutes for lamb).

2 Stir in frozen vegetables, undrained tomatoes, parsnip, and barley. Return to boiling; reduce heat. Simmer, covered, about 15 minutes more or until meat and vegetables are tender. Discard bay leaf.

nutrition facts per serving: 171 cal., 4 g total fat (1 g sat. fat), 25 mg chol., 865 mg sodium, 20 g carb., 4 g dietary fiber, 13 g protein.

slow cooker directions: Substitute regular barley for quick-cooking barley. In a large skillet brown cubed beef in hot oil. Drain fat. In a 5- or 6-quart slow cooker combine beef and remaining ingredients. Cover and cook on low-heat setting for 8 to 10 hours or on high-heat setting for 4 to 5 hours.

Dried apricots lend sweetness to this hearty stew punctuated with Dijon mustard and red wine and served over pasta. Finish with a sprinkle of parsley.

zesty apricot-beef stew

prep: 30 minutes cook: 1½ hours
makes: 4 to 6 servings

1 tablespoon olive oil
1 pound beef stew meat, cut into 1-inch cubes
1 medium onion, cut into thin wedges
1 large clove garlic, minced
1 14-ounce can beef broth
1 cup dry red wine or cranberry juice
1½ cups water
½ cup dried apricot halves
2 tablespoons Dijon-style mustard
1½ teaspoons dried thyme, crushed
¼ teaspoon ground black pepper
2 cups sliced carrot (3 large)
⅓ cup water
3 tablespoons all-purpose flour
1 tablespoon snipped fresh Italian parsley
3 cups dried medium noodles, cooked and drained

1 In a 4-quart Dutch oven heat oil over medium heat. Add meat; cook until brown. Add onion; cook about 4 minutes more or until just tender. Add garlic; cook and stir 1 minute more. Add broth, wine, the 1½ cups water, apricot halves, mustard, thyme, and pepper. Bring to boiling; reduce heat. Simmer, covered, for 1 hour, stirring occasionally.

2 Stir in carrots. Return to boiling; reduce heat. Simmer, covered, for 30 to 40 minutes more or until meat and carrots are tender, stirring occasionally.

3 In a small bowl whisk together the ⅓ cup water and flour until smooth. Stir into stew; cook and stir until thickened and bubbly. Cook and stir 1 minute more.

4 Sprinkle with parsley and serve with noodles.

nutrition facts per serving: 448 cal., 10 g total fat (3 g sat. fat), 74 mg chol., 693 mg sodium, 45 g carb., 4 g dietary fiber, 32 g protein.

Italian wedding soup gets its name from the marriage of meat and greens. Use lean ground beef, pork, or lamb.

italian wedding soup

prep: 35 minutes slow cook: 8 to 10 hours (low) or 4 to 5 hours (high) + 20 minutes (high)
makes: 6 servings

1   large onion
1   egg, lightly beaten
3   oil-packed dried
     tomatoes, drained
     and finely snipped
¼   cup fine dry bread
     crumbs
2   teaspoons dried
     Italian seasoning,
     crushed
1   pound lean ground
     beef
2   teaspoons olive oil
1   large fennel bulb
2   14.5-ounce cans
     reduced-sodium
     chicken broth
3½   cups water
6   cloves garlic, thinly
     sliced
½   teaspoon ground
     black pepper
¾   cup dried orzo
5   cups shredded fresh
     spinach

1 Finely chop one-third of the onion; thinly slice remaining onion. In a large bowl combine chopped onion, egg, dried tomatoes, bread crumbs, and 1 teaspoon of the Italian seasoning. Add ground beef; mix well. Shape mixture into 12 meatballs. In a large skillet cook meatballs in hot oil over medium-high heat until brown on all sides. Remove from skillet; drain on paper towels. Transfer meatballs to a 4½- or 5-quart slow cooker.

2 Meanwhile, cut off and discard upper stalks of fennel. If desired, reserve some of the feathery leaves for garnish. Remove any wilted outer layers; cut off and discard a thin slice from fennel base. Cut fennel into thin wedges; add to cooker. Add sliced onion, remaining 1 teaspoon Italian seasoning, broth, the water, garlic, and pepper.

3 Cover and cook on low-heat setting for 8 to 10 hours or on high-heat setting for 4 to 5 hours.

4 If using low-heat setting, turn to high-heat setting. Gently stir in pasta. Cover and cook for 20 to 30 minutes more or until pasta is tender. Stir in spinach.

5 If desired, garnish each serving with the reserved fennel leaves.

nutrition facts per serving: 283 cal., 10 g total fat (3 g sat. fat), 83 mg chol., 515 mg sodium, 26 g carb., 3 g dietary fiber, 21 g protein.

A variety of vegetables, such as mushrooms, escarole, green beans, and yellow sweet pepper, ensures this colorful soup will be a crowd-pleaser.

beefy italian vegetable soup

prep: 25 minutes   cook: 15 minutes
makes: 4 servings

1   teaspoon vegetable oil
12 ounces boneless beef sirloin steak, trimmed of fat and cut into bite-size pieces
8   ounces fresh mushrooms, quartered
½   cup chopped onion (1 medium)
3   cloves garlic, minced
1   tablespoon balsamic vinegar
2   14-ounce cans reduced-sodium beef broth
1   14.5-ounce can no-salt-added diced tomatoes, undrained
¼   cup dry red wine (optional)
½   teaspoon dried Italian seasoning, crushed
¼   teaspoon fennel seed, crushed
¼   teaspoon ground black pepper
3   cups escarole or kale, chopped
1   cup fresh green beans, bias-sliced into bite-size pieces
1   medium yellow sweet pepper, chopped

1 In a 4-quart Dutch oven heat oil over medium-high heat. Add beef; cook until brown, stirring occasionally. Using a slotted spoon, remove beef from Dutch oven.

2 Add mushrooms, onion, and garlic to Dutch oven; cook and stir 6 minutes or until tender and mushrooms are brown. Add vinegar; stir to remove browned bits on the bottom of the pan.

3 Add broth, undrained tomatoes, wine, if desired, Italian seasoning, fennel seed, and pepper. Bring to boiling. Add beef, escarole, green beans, and sweet pepper. Reduce heat. Simmer, covered, about 15 minutes or until vegetables and beef are tender.

nutrition facts per serving: 209 cal., 5 g total fat (1 g sat. fat), 36 mg chol., 469 mg sodium, 17 g carb., 5 g dietary fiber, 25 g protein.

Looking for a new way to serve easy, always satisfying ground beef? Try this family favorite.

hamburger-vegetable soup

start to finish: 35 minutes

makes: 6 servings

1 pound lean ground beef

½ cup chopped onion (1 medium)

½ cup chopped green sweet pepper (1 small)

2 cloves garlic, minced

4 cups beef broth

1 14.5-ounce can diced tomatoes, undrained

1 14- to 16-ounce package desired frozen mixed vegetables

½ cup peeled and cubed potato

1½ teaspoons dried Italian seasoning, crushed

1 teaspoon Worcestershire sauce

½ teaspoon salt

⅛ teaspoon ground black pepper

1 In a large saucepan cook ground beef, onion, sweet pepper, and garlic over medium-high heat until meat is brown, using a wooden spoon to break up meat as it cooks. Drain fat. Stir in broth, undrained tomatoes, frozen vegetables, potato, Italian seasoning, Worcestershire sauce, salt, and black pepper.

2 Bring to boiling; reduce heat. Simmer, covered, about 15 minutes or until vegetables are tender.

nutrition facts per serving: 249 cal., 12 g total fat (5 g sat. fat), 51 mg chol., 1017 mg sodium, 17 g carb., 4 g dietary fiber, 19 g protein.

Ground beef, vegetables, and broken spaghetti noodles are simmered in a rich tomato sauce to make this fun dinner dish.

souper spaghetti

prep: 20 minutes   cook: 25 minutes
makes: 6 servings

1   pound lean ground
    beef
½   cup chopped onion
    (1 medium)
1   small green sweet
    pepper, chopped
½   cup chopped celery
    (1 stalk)
1   medium carrot,
    chopped
2   cloves garlic, minced
2   14.5-ounce cans
    diced tomatoes,
    undrained
2½ cups water
1   13- to 15-ounce jar
    spaghetti sauce
1   tablespoon sugar
½   teaspoon dried Italian
    seasoning, crushed
½   teaspoon salt
¼   teaspoon ground
    black pepper
    Pinch crushed red
    pepper flakes
2   ounces spaghetti,
    broken into 2-inch
    pieces
    Fresh herb sprigs
    of your choice
    (optional)

1 In a large saucepan or Dutch oven cook meat, onion, sweet pepper, celery, carrot, and garlic over medium heat until vegetables are tender and meat is no longer pink, stirring frequently. Drain fat.

2 Add undrained tomatoes, the water, spaghetti sauce, sugar, Italian seasoning, salt, black pepper, and red pepper flakes. Bring to boiling. Add broken spaghetti. Return to boiling; reduce heat. Gently boil, uncovered, for 12 to 15 minutes or until spaghetti is tender. Serve immediately. If desired, top each serving with a fresh herb sprig.

nutrition facts per serving: 263 cal., 9 g total fat (3 g sat. fat), 48 mg chol., 960 mg sodium, 28 g carb., 5 g dietary fiber, 17 g protein.

Black-eyed peas and a trio of beans make this dynamic soup distinctive. A spoonful of sour cream on each serving adds a cooling touch.

taco soup

98

prep: 20 minutes slow cook: 6 to 8 hours (low) or 3 to 4 hours (high)
makes: 8 servings

1   pound ground beef
1   15.5-ounce can black-eyed peas, undrained
1   15-ounce can black beans, undrained
1   15-ounce can chili beans with chili gravy, undrained
1   15-ounce can garbanzo beans (chickpeas), undrained
1   14.5-ounce can Mexican-style stewed tomatoes, undrained
1   11-ounce can whole-kernel corn with sweet peppers, undrained
1   1.25-ounce package taco seasoning mix
Sour cream
Salsa
Tortilla chips

1 In a 4-quart Dutch oven cook ground beef until brown. Drain fat. Stir in undrained black-eyed peas, undrained black beans, undrained chili beans, undrained garbanzo beans, undrained tomatoes, and undrained corn. Stir in taco seasoning; mix until well combined.

2 Bring to boiling; reduce heat. Simmer, covered, for 1 to 2 hours, stirring occasionally. Serve with sour cream, salsa, and tortilla chips.

nutrition facts per serving: 409 cal., 13 g total fat, 41 mg chol., 1423 mg sodium, 52 g carb., 12 g dietary fiber, 26 g protein.

slow cooker directions: Brown ground beef as directed and place in a 3½- or 4-quart slow cooker. Stir in undrained vegetables and taco seasoning mix, as directed. Cover and cook on low-heat setting for 6 to 8 hours or on high-heat setting for 3 to 4 hours. Serve as directed.

Fast, delicious, and sure to please, this chunky soup has everything your family wants for a weeknight dinner. Baking the meatballs is a fuss-free way to cook them without adding any fat.

mediterranean meatball soup

prep: 25 minutes bake: 15 minutes oven: 350°F cook: 20 minutes
makes: 6 servings

¾ cup soft whole wheat
    bread crumbs
¼ cup refrigerated or
    frozen egg product,
    thawed, or 1 egg,
    lightly beaten
4 cloves garlic, minced
2 teaspoons snipped
    fresh rosemary or
    ½ teaspoon dried
    rosemary, crushed
¼ teaspoon ground
    black pepper
1 pound 90% or higher
    lean ground beef
1 tablespoon olive oil
1½ cups coarsely
    chopped carrot
    (3 medium)
2 medium yellow
    and/or red sweet
    peppers, seeded
    and cut into bite-
    size strips
½ cup chopped onion
    (1 medium)
2 cups reduced-sodium
    beef broth
2 cups water
1 15-ounce can Great
    Northern beans,
    rinsed and drained
½ cup quick-cooking
    barley
4 cups fresh baby
    spinach leaves

1 Preheat oven to 350°F. In a large bowl combine bread crumbs, egg, half of the garlic, half of the rosemary, and black pepper. Add ground beef; mix well. Shape meat mixture into 1½-inch meatballs. Place meatballs in a foil-lined 15×10×1-inch baking pan. Bake about 15 minutes or until done in centers (160°F). Set aside.

2 In a 5- to 6-quart Dutch oven heat oil over medium heat. Add carrot, sweet pepper, onion, and remaining garlic; cook for 5 minutes, stirring occasionally. Add stock, the water, beans, barley, and remaining rosemary. Bring to boiling; reduce heat. Simmer, covered about 15 minutes or until barley is tender.

3 Add meatballs to barley mixture; heat through. Stir in spinach just before serving.

nutrition facts per serving: 301 cal., 10 g total fat (3 g sat. fat), 49 mg chol., 400 mg sodium, 31 g carb., 7 g dietary fiber, 25 g protein.

Just five ingredients—frozen meatballs, stewed tomatoes, white beans, basil pesto, and Parmesan cheese—make up this wholesome, filling stew your family's sure to love.

pesto meatball stew

prep: 10 minutes   slow cook: 5 to 7 hours (low) or 2½ to 3½ hours (high)
makes: 6 servings

2 14.5-ounce cans
    Italian-style
    stewed tomatoes,
    undrained
1 16-ounce package
    (32) frozen cooked
    Italian-style
    meatballs, thawed
1 15- to 19-ounce can
    cannellini (white
    kidney) beans,
    rinsed and drained
½ cup water
¼ cup purchased basil
    pesto
½ cup finely shredded
    Parmesan cheese
    (2 ounces)

1 In a 3½- or 4-quart slow cooker, combine undrained tomatoes, meatballs, beans, the water, and pesto.

2 Cover and cook on low-heat setting for 5 to 7 hours or on high-heat setting for 2½ to 3½ hours. Sprinkle each serving with cheese.

nutrition facts per serving: 408 cal., 27 g total fat (10 g sat. fat), 34 mg chol., 1201 mg sodium, 24 g carb., 6 g dietary fiber, 17 g protein.

A trio of winter vegetables—squash, carrots, and parsnips star in this warming soup. Choose regular or Italian-seasoned meatballs, whichever suits your palate.

barley soup with meatballs

prep: 35 minutes   cook: 15 minutes
makes: 6 to 8 servings

4   slices bacon or
     peppered bacon
½   cup chopped onion
     (1 medium)
2   cloves garlic, minced
1   1- to 1½-pound
     butternut or acorn
     squash, peeled
     and cut into ¾-inch
     pieces (about 4 cups)
2   medium carrots,
     peeled and cut into
     ¾-inch pieces
2   medium parsnips,
     peeled and cut into
     ¾-inch pieces
4   14-ounce cans
     reduced-sodium
     chicken broth or
     reduced-sodium
     beef broth (about
     7 cups)
1   cup apple juice
     or water
1   teaspoon dried Italian
     seasoning, dried
     thyme, or dried
     oregano, crushed
1   cup quick-cooking
     barley
24 frozen cooked
     meatballs, thawed
     (about ⅔ of a
     16-ounce package)
     Salt
     Ground black pepper

1 In a 4-quart Dutch oven cook bacon until crisp. Remove bacon from Dutch oven, reserving 1 tablespoon of the drippings in pan. Drain bacon on paper towels; set aside.

2 Cook onion and garlic in reserved drippings over medium heat until tender. Add squash, carrots, and parsnips; cook for 5 minutes more, stirring occasionally. Add broth, apple juice, and Italian seasoning. Bring to boiling; stir in barley. Reduce heat. Simmer, covered, for 10 to 15 minutes or until barley and vegetables are tender. Add meatballs; heat through. Season to taste with salt and pepper.

3 Crumble cooked bacon and sprinkle over each serving.

nutrition facts per serving: 439 cal., 20 g total fat (8 g sat. fat), 51 mg chol., 1296 mg sodium, 50 g carb., 9 g dietary fiber, 18 g protein.

Meatballs hail from Italy, but the spicy sauce is definitely Mexican. Together the pair make a hearty and comforting supper.

mexican meatball stew

prep: 10 minutes slow cook: 6 to 7 hours (low) or 3 to 3½ hours (high)
makes: 8 to 10 servings

2 14.5-ounce cans Mexican-style stewed tomatoes, undrained
2 12-ounce packages frozen cooked Italian-style turkey meatballs, thawed (24 total)
1 15-ounce can black beans, rinsed and drained
1 14-ounce can seasoned chicken broth with roasted garlic
1 10-ounce package frozen whole-kernel corn, thawed
Fresh oregano (optional)

1 In a 4- to 5-quart slow cooker, combine undrained tomatoes, meatballs, beans, broth, and corn.

2 Cover and cook on low-heat setting for 6 to 7 hours or on high-heat setting for 3 to 3½ hours. If desired, garnish each serving with oregano.

nutrition facts per serving: 287 cal., 13 g total fat (6 g sat. fat), 37 mg chol., 1134 mg sodium, 30 g carb., 6 g dietary fiber, 16 g protein.

Nutrient-packed butternut squash is a natural in this flavorful Moroccan-spiced stew. Serve with couscous to scoop up the rich tomatoey sauce.

aromatic beef stew with butternut squash

prep: 40 minutes cook: 30 to 35 minutes
makes: 6 servings

2   teaspoons olive oil
1   pound stew beef
    (round or chuck),
    cut into chunks
1   cup chopped onion
    (1 large)
1   tablespoon grated
    fresh ginger
2   cloves garlic, minced
1   pound peeled cubed
    butternut squash,
    cut into 1½-inch
    cubes (about
    2½ cups)
1   14.5-ounce can
    no-salt-added diced
    tomatoes
1   8-ounce can no-salt-
    added tomato sauce
1½ cups reduced-sodium
    beef broth
1½ teaspoons ground
    cumin
1   teaspoon ground
    cinnamon
½   teaspoon crushed red
    pepper flakes
3   cups cooked whole
    wheat couscous
¼   cup sliced almonds,
    toasted*
1   to 2 tablespoons
    chopped fresh
    parsley

1 Heat oil in a 4-quart saucepan over medium-high heat. Add beef; cook until browned on all sides, about 5 minutes. Transfer meat to plate, leaving juices in saucepan. Add onion to pan; cook 6 minutes, stirring often, or until softened and translucent. Add ginger and garlic; cook, stirring, for 1 minute more.

2 Return beef to pan. Stir in squash, diced tomatoes, tomato sauce, broth, cumin, cinnamon, and red pepper flakes. Bring to boiling; reduce heat. Simmer, covered, for 30 to 35 minutes or until beef is tender.

3 Serve with couscous. Sprinkle with almonds and parsley.

nutrition facts per serving: 421 cal., 11 g total fat (3 g sat. fat), 29 mg chol., 206 mg sodium, 57 g carb., 10 g dietary fiber, 25 g protein.

*note: Toast almonds in a dry skillet over medium-high heat, stirring frequently, for about 2 minutes or until golden brown.

Tender beef and vegetables top garlic mashed potatoes to create a comforting supper that's ready in less than 30 minutes. Packaged roast beef and frozen vegetables are the clever shortcuts.

beef stew and garlic mash

start to finish: 25 minutes
makes: 4 servings

1   1-pound bag frozen
    assorted vegetable
    blend (carrots, peas,
    and onions)
½   cup water
1   17-ounce package
    refrigerated cooked
    beef tips in gravy
2   teaspoons
    Worcestershire
    sauce
6   cloves garlic
1   pound Yukon Gold or
    red potatoes, halved
2   tablespoons olive oil
¼   teaspoon salt
¼   teaspoon ground
    black pepper
2   tablespoons fresh
    oregano leaves

1 In a 4-quart Dutch oven combine vegetables and the water. Bring to boiling over medium heat. Meanwhile, microwave beef tips according to package directions. Add beef and Worcestershire to vegetables; reduce heat to low. Cook, covered, for 5 minutes or until vegetables are tender.

2 In small microwave-safe bowl cover garlic and 2 tablespoons water with vented plastic wrap. Microwave on 100 percent power (high) for 1 minute; set aside. In large microwave-safe bowl microwave potatoes on 100 percent power (high) for 8 to 10 minutes; stirring once halfway through cooking.

3 Peel and mash garlic. Add garlic, oil, salt, and black pepper to potatoes; mash. Divide among four dishes; top with stew. Sprinkle each serving with oregano.

nutrition facts per serving: 368 cal., 14 g total fat (3 g sat. fat), 47 mg chol., 888 mg sodium, 42 g carb., 8 g dietary fiber, 24 g protein.

By using lentils instead of the white beans in a traditional French cassoulet, you can skip the step of soaking and precooking the beans. Unlike dried beans, lentils can be added to the slow cooker straight from the package.

pork and lentil cassoulet

prep: 20 minutes   slow cook: 10 to 12 hours (low) or 4½ to 5½ hours (high)
makes: 4 servings

12   ounces boneless pork
      shoulder
1   large onion, cut into
      wedges
2   cloves garlic, minced
2   teaspoons vegetable
      oil
2½   cups water
1   14.5-ounce can
      tomatoes, undrained
      and cut up
4   medium carrots and/
      or parsnips, sliced
      ½ inch thick (2 cups)
2   stalks celery, thinly
      sliced
¾   cup lentils
1½   teaspoons dried
      rosemary, crushed
1   teaspoon instant beef
      bouillon granules
¼   teaspoon salt
¼   teaspoon ground
      black pepper

1 Trim fat from pork; cut meat into ¾-inch cubes. In a large nonstick skillet brown pork, onion, and garlic in hot oil. Transfer mixture to a 3½- to 4-quart slow cooker. Add the water, undrained tomatoes, carrots, celery, lentils, rosemary, bouillon granules, salt, and pepper to cooker.

2 Cover and cook on low-heat setting for 10 to 12 hours or on high-heat setting for 4½ to 5½ hours.

nutrition facts per serving: 354 cal., 12 g total fat (3 g sat. fat), 37 mg chol., 641 mg sodium, 37 g carb., 5 g dietary fiber, 26 g protein.

Everyday cream of potato soup gets a flavor boost from savory ham and an array of toppers. Set out the toppers—herb, cheese, and broccoli—so your hungry clan can customize their own bowls.

creamy ham and potato chowder

prep: 20 minutes slow cook: 3 hours (high) + 30 minutes (high)
makes: 6 servings

12   ounces tiny yellow
      potatoes, cut into
      ¾-inch pieces
1   cup chopped onion
      (1 large)
2   14.5-ounce cans
      reduced-sodium
      chicken broth
¼   cup cornstarch
½   teaspoon dried
      thyme, crushed
¼   teaspoon ground
      black pepper
1   12-ounce can
      evaporated fat-free
      milk
½   cup diced cooked
      lean ham
1   cup coarsely
      shredded carrot
      (2 medium)
1   cup broccoli florets,
      steamed
¼   cup shredded
      cheddar cheese
      (1 ounce)
2   teaspoons snipped
      fresh thyme

1 In a 4-quart slow cooker combine potatoes and onion. Pour broth over all. Cover and cook on high-heat setting for 3 hours.

2 In a medium bowl combine cornstarch, dried thyme, and pepper. Whisk in evaporated milk. Slowly stir the cornstarch mixture, ham, and carrot into the hot soup. Cover and cook on high-heat setting for 30 minutes more, stirring the soup occasionally.

3 Top each serving with broccoli, cheese, and fresh thyme.

nutrition facts per serving: 171 cal., 2 g total fat (1 g sat. fat), 12 mg chol., 566 mg sodium, 27 g carb., 3 g dietary fiber, 11 g protein.

Hearty comfort food at its most robust, this meat-lover's stew featuring pork loin and spicy chorizo marries well with cooked pasta. Serve with warm garlic bread.

pork and chorizo stew

start to finish: 40 minutes
makes: 4 servings

1 1-pound pork
   tenderloin, cut into
   1-inch cubes
8 ounces cooked
   smoked chorizo
   sausage, cut into
   ¼-inch slices
1 tablespoon cooking
   oil
1 cup coarsely chopped
   onion (1 large)
2 cloves garlic, minced
2 tablespoons all-
   purpose flour
½ teaspoon dried
   thyme, crushed
2½ cups reduced-sodium
   beef broth
1 cup frozen peas and
   carrots
   Salt
   Ground black pepper
2 cups dried egg
   noodles

1 In a 4-quart Dutch oven cook pork cubes and chorizo in hot oil over medium-high heat for 10 minutes or until brown. Using a slotted spoon, transfer meat to a plate; set aside.

2 Add onion and garlic to pan; cook and stir for 4 to 5 minutes or until tender. Return meat and any accumulated juices to pan. Add flour and thyme; cook and stir for 1 minute.

3 Gradually add broth, stirring to loosen any browned bits from bottom of pan. Add frozen peas and carrots. Bring to boiling; reduce heat. Simmer, uncovered, for 15 to 20 minutes. Season to taste with salt and pepper.

4 Meanwhile, in a large pan cook egg noodles according to package directions. Drain well. Serve stew with noodles.

nutrition facts per serving: 555 cal., 30 g total fat (10 g sat. fat), 140 mg chol., 1211 mg sodium, 26 g carb., 3 g dietary fiber, 43 g protein.

This aromatic stew is even better the next day, when the herbs and spices and fruity flavors have had time to really infuse the meat. Serve it with rustic bread.

pork and sweet potato stew

prep: 20 minutes   cook: 25 to 32 minutes
makes: 6 to 8 servings

1   2½- to 3-pound pork loin, cut into 1¼- to 1½-inch cubes
½   teaspoon salt
¼   teaspoon ground black pepper
3   to 4 tablespoons all-purpose flour
3   tablespoons olive oil
1   cup chopped onion (1 large)
2   or 3 stalks celery, chopped
2   or 3 cloves garlic, minced
1   14-ounce can chicken broth
1   10-ounce bottle apple-cranberry juice
1   cup water
2   large sweet potatoes, peeled and cut into 1¼-inch cubes
1   to 2 tablespoons snipped fresh sage
    Grated fresh nutmeg
    Fresh sage leaves

1 Lightly sprinkle pork with salt and pepper. Place flour in a large bowl; add pork and toss to coat. Reserve any remaining flour.

2 In a 5- to 6-quart Dutch oven heat 1 tablespoon of the oil over medium-high heat. Add half the pork; brown on all sides. Transfer pork to a plate; set aside. Repeat with 1 tablespoon oil and remaining pork. Transfer pork to the plate.

3 Add remaining 1 tablespoon oil to pan along with onion and celery; cook 5 to 7 minutes or until tender. Stir in garlic. Sprinkle with any remaining flour; stir to coat. Slowly stir in broth, juice, and the water. Return pork to pan; add sweet potatoes and snipped sage. Bring to a simmer. Reduce heat and cook 20 to 25 minutes more or until potatoes and pork are tender. Season to taste with salt and pepper.

4 Top each serving with nutmeg and fresh sage leaves.

nutrition facts per serving: 481 cal., 24 g total fat (7 g sat. fat), 131 mg chol., 600 mg sodium, 23 g carb., 2 g dietary fiber, 41 g protein.

A slow cooker makes the pork and vegetables extra tender in this main-dish stew recipe. Apples and apple cider tenderize and add sweetness.

cider-pork stew

prep: 20 minutes slow cook: 10 to 12 hours (low) or 5 to 6 hours (high)
makes: 8 servings

2 pounds boneless pork shoulder roast
2½ cups cubed potatoes (3 medium)
1½ cups coarsely chopped carrot (3 medium)
2 medium onions, sliced
1 cup coarsely chopped apple (1 medium)
½ cup coarsely chopped celery (1 stalk)
3 tablespoons quick-cooking tapioca
2 cups apple juice or apple cider
1 teaspoon salt
1 teaspoon caraway seeds
¼ teaspoon ground black pepper
Celery leaves (optional)

1 Cut meat into 1-inch cubes. In a 3½- to 5½-quart slow cooker, combine meat, potatoes, carrots, onions, apple, celery, and tapioca. Stir in apple juice, salt, caraway seeds, and pepper.

2 Cover and cook on low-heat setting for 10 to 12 hours or high-heat setting for 5 to 6 hours. If desired, garnish each serving with celery leaves.

nutrition facts per serving: 272 cal., 7 g total fat (2 g sat. fat), 73 mg chol., 405 mg sodium, 27 g carb., 3 g dietary fiber, 24 g protein.

109

A jar of pasta sauce and diced tomatoes provide the base for this hearty pork and vegetable stew.

pork roast and vegetable stew

prep: 45 minutes cook: 1½ hours
makes: 8 servings

2   pounds boneless pork
      shoulder roast
1   tablespoon olive oil
1   tablespoon butter
1   cup chopped celery
      (2 stalks)
1   cup chopped onion
      (1 large)
1   tablespoon dried
      chives
1   teaspoon dried
      parsley, crushed
1   teaspoon dried basil,
      crushed
½   teaspoon dried dill
½   teaspoon ground
      black pepper
1   26-ounce jar pasta
      sauce
1   14.5-ounce can
      diced tomatoes,
      undrained
2   cups frozen whole-
      kernel corn
1   cup packaged peeled
      fresh baby carrots,
      halved lengthwise
3   Yukon Gold potatoes,
      peeled, if desired,
      and cut into 1-inch
      pieces
      Salt

1 Trim fat from pork; discard fat. Cut pork in 1- to 2-inch pieces.

2 In a 4- to 5-quart Dutch oven cook pork, half at a time, in hot oil over medium-high heat until brown, stirring occasionally. Remove from pan. Add butter to pan. Add celery, onion, chives, parsley, basil, dill, and pepper; cook for 8 to 10 minutes or until vegetables are tender, stirring occasionally.

3 Add pasta sauce, undrained tomatoes, corn, carrots, potatoes, and browned pork to onion mixture. Bring to boiling; reduce heat. Simmer, covered, about 1½ hours or until meat and vegetables are tender, stirring occasionally. Season to taste with salt.

nutrition facts per serving: 363 cal., 12 g total fat (4 g sat. fat), 72 mg chol., 532 mg sodium, 40 g carb., 6 g dietary fiber, 26 g protein.

Gremolata is a traditional garnish of parsley, lemon zest, and garlic that adds a fresh, sprightly flavor to savory and meaty stews.

pork stew with gremolata

prep: 25 minutes   slow cook: 7 to 8 hours (low) or 3½ to 4 hours (high)
makes: 4 servings

1½ pounds boneless pork
     shoulder roast
1   tablespoon olive oil
1   14.5-ounce can
     diced tomatoes,
     undrained
1   14-ounce can beef
     broth
1   large onion, cut into
     thin wedges
1   cup sliced carrot
     (2 medium)
½   cup sliced celery
     (1 stalk)
½   cup dry white wine
1   tablespoon quick-
     cooking tapioca,
     crushed
2   cloves garlic, minced
½   teaspoon dried
     thyme, crushed
¼   teaspoon salt
⅛   teaspoon ground
     black pepper
2   cups hot cooked orzo
     or rice
1   recipe Gremolata

1 Trim fat from meat. Cut meat into 1-inch pieces. In a large skillet cook meat, half at a time, in hot oil over medium heat until brown. Drain fat. Transfer meat to a 3½- or 4-quart slow cooker. Stir in undrained tomatoes, broth, onion, carrot, celery, wine, tapioca, garlic, thyme, salt, and pepper.

2 Cover and cook on low-heat setting for 7 to 8 hours or on high-heat setting for 3½ to 4 hours.

3 Serve over hot cooked orzo. Sprinkle each serving with Gremolata.

nutrition facts per serving: 530 cal., 14 g total fat (4 g sat. fat), 107 mg chol., 805 mg sodium, 49 g carb., 4 g dietary fiber, 44 g protein.

gremolata: In a small bowl stir together ¼ cup snipped fresh Italian parsley, 2 teaspoons finely shredded lemon zest, and 4 cloves minced garlic.

Posole is a traditional soup in Mexico, often served on Christmas Eve. The broth-rich soup is made with pork shoulder, red chile powder, and lots of add-ins, including cabbage and hominy.

red posole

prep: 20 minutes   slow cook: 8 to 9 hours (low) or 4 to 4½ hours (high)
+ 30 minutes (high)
makes: 8 servings

1½ pounds boneless pork shoulder, cut into 1-inch cubes
2 15-ounce cans hominy, rinsed and drained
1 cup chopped onion (1 large)
1 4-ounce can diced green chiles, undrained
1 tablespoon ancho chile powder
1½ teaspoons dried oregano, crushed
2 cloves garlic, minced
½ teaspoon ground cumin
2 14.5-ounce cans reduced-sodium chicken broth
2 cups coarsely chopped cabbage
1 10-ounce can enchilada sauce
   Lime wedges
   Fresh pineapple wedges (optional)

1 In a 4- to 5-quart slow cooker combine pork, hominy, onion, chiles, chile powder, oregano, garlic, and cumin. Pour broth over all.

2 Cover and cook on low-heat setting for 8 to 9 hours or on high-heat setting for 4 to 4½ hours.

3 If using low-heat setting, turn cooker to high-heat setting. Stir in cabbage and enchilada sauce. Cover and cook for 30 minutes more.

4 Garnish each serving with lime wedges and, if desired, pineapple wedges.

nutrition facts per serving: 279 cal., 12 g total fat (4 g sat. fat), 53 mg chol., 659 mg sodium, 23 g carb., 4 g dietary fiber, 19 g protein.

This wonderfully textured soup marries a handful of classic Mexican flavors. For a milder flavor, choose ground pasilla or ancho chile pepper; for a spicy-smoky flavor, choose ground chipotle chile pepper.

pork and hominy soup

prep: 35 minutes cook: 20 minutes
makes: 4 servings

2 teaspoons vegetable oil
12 ounces pork tenderloin, trimmed of fat and cut into bite-size pieces
1 medium poblano or Anaheim pepper, seeded and chopped*
1 large onion, cut into thin wedges
3 cloves garlic, minced
1 15.5-ounce can golden or white hominy, rinsed and drained
1 14.5-ounce can no-salt-added diced tomatoes, undrained
1 14-ounce can reduced-sodium chicken broth
1¾ cups water
1 tablespoon lime juice
2 teaspoons snipped fresh oregano or 1 teaspoon dried oregano, crushed
1 teaspoon ground cumin
1 teaspoon ground pasilla, ancho, or chipotle pepper
¼ teaspoon ground black pepper
¼ cup sliced radishes, shredded cabbage, and/or sliced green onions

1 In a 4-quart Dutch oven heat oil. Add pork, poblano pepper, onion, and garlic; cook over medium heat for 5 minutes or until tender, stirring occasionally. Stir in hominy, undrained tomatoes, broth, the water, lime juice, oregano, cumin, ground pasilla pepper, and black pepper. Bring to boiling; reduce heat. Simmer, covered, for 15 minutes.

2 Top each serving with radishes, cabbage, and/or green onions.

nutrition facts per serving: 258 cal., 6 g total fat (1 g sat. fat), 55 mg chol., 569 mg sodium, 29 g carb., 6 g dietary fiber, 23 g protein.

*note: See tip on handling chile peppers, page 31.

Giant lima beans make this bean soup stand out from the rest. Their mellow, buttery flavor adds a lovely layer of richness.

ham and lima soup

prep: 40 minutes stand: 1 hour slow cook: 11 to 13 hours (low) or 5½ to 6½ hours (high)
makes: 6 servings

1½ cups dried giant lima beans, cannellini (white kidney) beans, or navy beans
6 cups water
2 cooked smoked pork hocks or 1 to 1½ pounds meaty ham bones
2¼ cups water
1 14.5-ounce can reduced-sodium chicken broth
1½ cups sliced celery (3 stalks)
1½ cups sliced carrot (3 medium)
1½ cups sliced leek (4 medium)*
2 tablespoons snipped fresh rosemary or 2½ teaspoons dried rosemary, crushed
¼ teaspoon ground black pepper
1 bay leaf
3 cups torn fresh kale or spinach leaves
Salt

1 Rinse beans. In a 4-quart Dutch oven combine beans and the 6 cups water. Bring to boiling; reduce heat. Simmer, uncovered, for 2 minutes. Remove from heat. Cover and let stand for 1 hour. (Or place beans and the 6 cups water in a 4-quart Dutch oven. Cover and let soak in a cool place overnight.) Drain and rinse beans. Transfer to a 5- to 6-quart slow cooker.

2 Add pork hocks, the 2¼ cups water, broth, celery, carrot, leek, rosemary, ¼ teaspoon pepper, and bay leaf to slow cooker. Cover and cook on low-heat setting for 11 to 13 hours or on high-heat setting for 5½ to 6½ hours.

3 To serve, remove pork hocks and cool slightly. Meanwhile, if desired, mash beans slightly. When hocks are cool enough to handle, cut meat off bones; discard bones. Chop meat. Discard bay leaf. Stir meat and kale into soup. Season to taste with salt and pepper.

nutrition facts per serving: 265 cal., 4 g total fat (1 g sat. fat), 22 mg chol., 826 mg sodium, 40 g carb., 11 g dietary fiber, 19 g protein.

*note: See tip on cleaning leeks, page 464.

This long-simmering soup gets a dose of freshness when you add kale or spinach just before serving

tuscan ham and bean soup

prep: 25 minutes slow cook: 6 to 8 hours (low) or 3 to 4 hours (high)
makes: 8 servings

3   15-ounce cans small white beans, rinsed and drained
2½ cups cubed cooked ham
1½ cups chopped carrot (3 medium)
1   cup thinly sliced celery (2 stalks)
1   cup chopped onion (1 large)
¼   teaspoon ground black pepper
2   14.5-ounce cans diced tomatoes with basil, garlic, and oregano, undrained
2   14.5-ounce cans reduced-sodium chicken broth
8   cups torn fresh kale or spinach leaves
    Finely shredded Parmesan cheese (optional)

1 In a 5- to 6-quart slow cooker combine beans, ham, carrots, celery, onion, and pepper. Stir in undrained tomatoes and broth.

2 Cover and cook on low-heat setting for 6 to 8 hours or on high-heat setting for 3 to 4 hours.

3 Before serving, stir in kale. If desired, sprinkle each serving with cheese.

nutrition facts per serving: 323 cal., 3 g total fat (1 g sat. fat), 21 mg chol., 2099 mg sodium, 53 g carb., 12 g dietary fiber, 25 g protein.

best for last

Add delicate leafy green veggies, such as spinach or kale, to long-simmering soups and stews just before serving. The greens will cook quickly in the hot soup, yet keep their fresh flavor and pleasing texture.

Green peas, parsley, and lime juice make this a brighter, fresher version of pea soup. Dried split peas and pork keep it thick and hearty.

two-pea soup with pork

prep: 30 minutes roast: 15 minutes oven: at 425°F cook: 45 minutes
makes: 6 servings

2　medium carrots, cut into 1-inch pieces
2　stalks celery, cut into 1-inch pieces
1　large onion, cut into wedges
3　cloves garlic, peeled
1　tablespoon olive oil
6　cups water
2　pounds meaty smoked pork hocks
1　cup dried split peas, rinsed and drained
½　teaspoon dried summer savory or marjoram, crushed
¼　teaspoon ground black pepper
1　16-ounce package frozen green peas
⅓　cup packed fresh parsley leaves
2　tablespoons lemon juice
　Salt

1 Preheat oven to 425°F. In a shallow baking pan combine carrots, celery, onion, and garlic. Drizzle with oil; toss gently to coat. Spread vegetables in a single layer. Roast, uncovered, for 15 to 20 minutes or until vegetables are light brown on the edges, stirring once.

2 In a large Dutch oven combine roasted vegetables, the water, pork hocks, split peas, savory, and pepper. Bring to boiling; reduce heat. Simmer, covered, for 45 minutes, stirring occasionally. Remove pork hocks from Dutch oven; set aside.

3 Stir frozen peas and parsley into Dutch oven; cool slightly. Transfer vegetable mixture, half at a time, to a food processor or blender. Cover and process or blend until nearly smooth. Return pureed mixture to Dutch oven. Stir in lemon juice.

4 When pork hocks are cool enough to handle, cut meat from bones; chop meat. Discard bones. Set aside ½ cup of the chopped meat for garnish. Add remaining chopped meat to pureed vegetable mixture; heat through. Season to taste with salt and pepper. Garnish each serving with reserved chopped meat.

nutrition facts per serving: 267 cal., 5 g total fat (1 g sat. fat), 25 mg chol., 663 mg sodium, 35 g carb., 13 g dietary fiber, 21 g protein.

Fresh ginger and Chinese cabbage lend Asian flavors to this hearty soup.

gingered pork
and cabbage soup

start to finish: 40 minutes
makes: 8 servings

6   cups reduced-sodium
    chicken broth
8   ounces boneless pork
    sirloin, cut ½ inch
    thick
1   cup chopped onion
    (1 large)
4   cloves garlic, minced
2   teaspoons grated
    fresh ginger
1   tablespoon vegetable
    oil
3   small tomatoes,
    chopped
1   cup finely chopped
    carrot (2 medium)
½   cup dried anelli pasta
    or other small pasta
4   cups thinly sliced
    Chinese cabbage
¼   cup snipped fresh
    mint

1   In a medium saucepan bring broth to
    boiling. Meanwhile, trim fat from pork.
Cut pork into ½-inch cubes.

2   In a large saucepan cook pork, onion,
    garlic, and ginger in hot oil until pork
is brown.

3   Carefully add hot broth. Bring to boiling.
    Stir in tomato and carrot. Return to boiling;
reduce heat. Simmer, covered, for 15 minutes.

4   Stir in pasta; cook for 6 to 8 minutes more
    or until pasta is tender but still firm. Stir in
sliced Chinese cabbage and mint.

nutrition facts per serving: 118 cal., 3 g total fat
(1 g sat. fat), 18 mg chol., 493 mg sodium, 13 g carb.,
3 g dietary fiber, 10 g protein.

Wild rice lends a chewy texture and nutty, earthy flavor to this aromatic soup. Serve it with a tossed green salad dressed with a raspberry or citrus vinaigrette.

wild rice–ham soup

prep: 20 minutes slow cook: 6½ to 7½ hours (low) or 3½ to 4 hours (high)
makes: 6 servings

5   cups water
1   14.5-ounce can
      reduced-sodium
      chicken broth
1   cup chopped celery
      (2 stalks)
1   cup diced cooked ham
      (about 5 ounces)
¾   cup wild rice, rinsed
      and drained
1   medium onion, cut
      into thin wedges
1½   teaspoons dried
      thyme, crushed
1½   cups chopped red
      sweet peppers
      (2 medium)
4   cups shredded fresh
      spinach

1 In a 4- to 5-quart slow cooker combine the water, broth, celery, ham, wild rice, onion, and thyme.

2 Cover and cook on low-heat setting for 6 to 7 hours or on high-heat setting for 3 to 3½ hours.

3 If using low-heat setting, turn to high-heat setting. Stir in sweet peppers. Cook, covered, for 30 minutes more. Stir in spinach.

nutrition facts per serving: 124 cal., 1 g total fat (0 g sat. fat), 11 mg chol., 584 mg sodium, 20 g carb., 3 g dietary fiber, 10 g protein.

This hearty one-pot meal combines some of fall's best seasonal ingredients—pork, apples, carrots, and butternut squash—into a satisfying soup recipe.

curried pork and apple stew

prep: 25 minutes cook: 1 hour
makes: 8 servings

4   pounds boneless pork
     shoulder
4   medium tart green
     cooking apples
2   tablespoons
     vegetable oil
2   medium onions, cut
     into thin wedges
1   teaspoon curry
     powder
1   teaspoon ground
     coriander
½   teaspoon ground
     cumin
2   14-ounce cans
     chicken broth
½   teaspoon salt
¼   teaspoon ground
     black pepper
2   cups packaged
     peeled baby carrots,
     halved lengthwise
1   2-pound butternut
     squash, peeled,
     seeded, and cubed
     (3 cups)
     Sour cream

1 Trim fat from pork; cut into 1-inch cubes. Peel, core, and chop two of the apples; set aside. In a large pot brown pork, half at a time, in hot oil. Return all pork to pot. Add chopped apples, onions, curry powder, coriander, and cumin; cook and stir for 2 minutes. Add broth, salt, and pepper. Bring to boiling; reduce heat. Simmer, covered, for 30 minutes, stirring occasionally.

2 Add carrots to pork mixture. Return to boiling; reduce heat. Simmer, covered, for 20 minutes, stirring occasionally. Meanwhile, cut remaining apples into ¼-inch-thick wedges. Add apple wedges and squash to pot; cook, covered, for 10 to 12 minutes more or until pork and vegetables are tender.

3 Top each serving with sour cream.

nutrition facts per serving: 510 cal., 23 g total fat (7 g sat. fat), 159 mg chol., 752 mg sodium, 30 g carb., 6 g dietary fiber, 47 g protein.

Early Virginia settlers made this hearty stew recipe with squirrel meat. Our updated version simmers all day in your slow cooker and features chicken and ham.

brunswick-style stew

prep: 20 minutes slow cook: 8 to 10 hours (low) or 4 to 5 hours (high)
+ 30 minutes (high)
makes: 6 to 8 servings

1½ to 2 pounds meaty
      smoked pork hocks
1 14.5-ounce can
      diced tomatoes,
      undrained
1 14.5-ounce can
      chicken broth
3 medium onions, cut
      into thin wedges
½ cup ketchup
¼ cup cider vinegar
2 tablespoons packed
      brown sugar
2 tablespoons
      Worcestershire
      sauce
4 cloves garlic, minced
¼ teaspoon ground
      black pepper
¼ teaspoon bottled hot
      pepper sauce
1½ cups frozen baby lima
      beans
1 cup frozen whole-
      kernel corn

1 In a 5- to 6-quart slow cooker combine pork hocks, undrained tomatoes, broth, onions, ketchup, vinegar, brown sugar, Worcestershire sauce, garlic, black pepper, and hot pepper sauce.

2 Cover and cook on low-heat setting for 8 to 10 hours or on high-heat setting for 4 to 5 hours.

3 Remove pork hocks. When cool enough to handle, cut meat from bones; coarsely chop meat. Discard bones. Return meat to cooker.

4 If using low-heat setting, turn to high-heat setting. Stir in frozen lima beans and frozen corn. Cover and cook for 30 minutes more.

nutrition facts per serving: 224 cal., 4 g total fat (1 g sat. fat), 20 mg chol., 1138 mg sodium, 37 g carb., 4 g dietary fiber, 11 g protein.

This soup is very hearty and is great served with cold beer. You can substitute kielbasa or even a flavored chicken sausage. Serve with hunks of freshly baked rye or pumpernickel bread.

loaded bratwurst stew

prep: 20 minutes   slow cook: 6 to 7 hours (low) or 3 to 3½ hours (high)
makes: 6 servings

1 pound cooked smoked bratwurst, cut into ½-inch slices
4 cups chopped cabbage or packaged shredded cabbage with carrot (coleslaw mix)
1½ cups coarsely chopped red-skinned potatoes
¾ cup chopped red sweet pepper (1 medium)
1 medium onion, cut into thin wedges
2 14.5-ounce cans chicken broth
1 tablespoon spicy brown mustard
1 tablespoon cider vinegar
¼ teaspoon salt
¼ teaspoon ground black pepper
⅛ teaspoon celery seeds
Shredded Swiss cheese (optional)

1 In a 5- to 6-quart slow cooker combine bratwurst, cabbage, potatoes, sweet pepper, and onion. In a medium bowl combine broth, mustard, vinegar, salt, black pepper, and celery seeds. Pour broth mixture over bratwurst mixture in cooker.

2 Cover and cook on low-heat setting for 6 to 7 hours or on high-heat setting for 3 to 3½ hours. If desired, top each serving with cheese.

nutrition facts per serving: 315 cal., 23 g total fat (8 g sat. fat), 49 mg chol., 1348 mg sodium, 15 g carb., 3 g dietary fiber, 12 g protein.

122

Chorizo, a pork sausage popular in Latin dishes, heightens the flavor of the fennel- and carrot-flavored broth. You can substitute your favorite smoked sausage for the chorizo.

lentil and sausage soup

prep: 20 minutes   cook: 30 minutes
makes: 6 servings

1	medium fennel bulb, trimmed, cored, and thinly sliced
1	cup thinly sliced carrot (2 medium)
½	cup chopped onion (1 medium)
2	cloves garlic, minced
1	tablespoon olive oil
2	sweet or hot Italian sausage links, sliced
2	14-ounce cans reduced-sodium chicken broth
1	14.5-ounce can diced tomatoes with basil, garlic, and oregano, undrained
1	cup lentils, rinsed and drained
⅛	teaspoon crushed red pepper flakes

1 In a large saucepan cook fennel, carrot, onion, and garlic in hot oil over medium-high heat for 5 minutes or until tender. Add sausage; cook for 2 to 3 minutes more or until sausage is brown.

2 Stir broth, undrained tomatoes, lentils, and red pepper flakes into saucepan. Bring to boiling; reduce heat. Simmer, covered, for 30 to 35 minutes or until vegetables and lentils are tender.

nutrition facts per serving: 238 cal., 5 g total fat (1 g sat. fat), 9 mg chol., 866 mg sodium, 33 g carb., 12 g dietary fiber, 16 g protein.

Lamb, carrots, and celery lend their flavors to the lentils for this low-fat soup recipe.

lentil and lamb soup

prep: 20 minutes cook: 1 hour
makes: 6 servings

1   pound lean boneless
      lamb
      Nonstick cooking
      spray
½   cup chopped onion
      (1 medium)
4   cups water
1   14.5-ounce can
      tomatoes, undrained
      and cut up
1   cup coarsely chopped
      carrot
1   cup sliced celery
      (2 stalks)
1   teaspoon salt
½   teaspoon dried
      thyme, crushed
¼   teaspoon ground
      black pepper
1   clove garlic, minced
1   bay leaf
¾   cup lentils, rinsed
      and drained

1 Trim fat from lamb; cut lamb into 1-inch pieces.

2 Spray a Dutch oven with nonstick spray. Preheat Dutch oven over medium heat. Add half of the lamb; cook until brown. Remove lamb from Dutch oven. Repeat with remaining lamb and onion. Return all lamb to Dutch oven.

3 Add the water, undrained tomatoes, carrot, celery, salt, thyme, pepper, garlic, and bay leaf. Bring to boiling; reduce heat. Simmer, covered, for 30 minutes.

4 Add lentils. Bring to boiling; reduce heat. Simmer, covered, for 30 minutes more or until lamb and lentils are tender. Remove bay leaf.

nutrition facts per serving: 197 cal., 4 g total fat, 44 mg chol., 527 mg sodium, 21 g carb., 21 g protein.

Classic French cassoulet is a garlic-flavored bean stew that features one or more meats, such as the lamb and chicken combo in this version. Browning the lamb seals in juices and helps develop a rich color.

lamb cassoulet

prep: 30 minutes cook: 1½ hours stand: 1 hour
makes: 6 servings

2 cups dried navy beans
8 cups water
1 pound lean boneless
   lamb, cut into
   1-inch cubes
1 tablespoon vegetable
   oil
1 cup chopped carrot
   (2 medium)
½ cup chopped green
   sweet pepper
   (1 medium)
½ cup chopped onion
   (1 medium)
1 tablespoon instant
   beef bouillon
   granules
1 tablespoon
   Worcestershire
   sauce
2 teaspoons snipped
   fresh thyme or
   1 teaspoon dried
   thyme, crushed
3 cloves garlic, minced
2 bay leaves
4 cups water
8 ounces skinless,
   boneless chicken
   thighs, cut into
   1-inch pieces
1 14.5-ounce can
   diced tomatoes,
   undrained
½ teaspoon salt
   Ground black pepper

1 Rinse beans. In a large pot combine beans and the 8 cups water. Bring to boiling; reduce heat. Simmer, uncovered, for 2 minutes. Remove from heat. Cover and let stand for 1 hour. (Or, place beans in water in pot. Cover and let soak in a cool place for 6 to 8 hours or overnight.) Drain and rinse beans. Wipe pot dry.

2 In the same pot, cook lamb, half at a time, in hot oil until brown. Drain fat. Return all lamb to the pot. Add beans, carrot, sweet pepper, onion, bouillon granules, Worcestershire sauce, dried thyme (if using), garlic, and bay leaves to the pot. Add the 4 cups water. Bring to boiling; reduce heat. Simmer, covered, for 1 to 1½ hours or until beans are tender.

3 Stir in chicken, undrained tomatoes, salt, and fresh thyme (if using). Return to boiling; reduce heat. Simmer, uncovered, for 30 minutes more. Discard bay leaves. Skim fat if necessary. Season to taste with salt and black pepper.

nutrition facts per serving: 417 cal., 8 g total fat (2 g sat. fat), 79 mg chol., 899 mg sodium, 49 g carb., 18 g dietary fiber, 39 g protein.

Overflowing with mushrooms, green beans, carrots, and zucchini, this Mediterranean-style stew makes a great dinner for a blustery night.

lamb stew with pasta

prep: 25 minutes cook: 1 hour
makes: 4 servings

1   pound lamb or beef
    stew meat
1   medium onion, sliced
    and separated into
    rings
2   tablespoons
    vegetable oil
3½ cups water
¼   cup snipped dried
    tomatoes (not oil-
    packed)
1   teaspoon dried Italian
    seasoning, crushed
¼   teaspoon salt
¼   teaspoon ground
    black pepper
2   cups sliced fresh
    mushrooms
1   9-ounce package
    frozen cut green
    beans
1   cup thinly sliced
    carrot (2 medium)
¾   cup dried medium
    bow tie pasta
1   15-ounce can tomato
    sauce

1 In a large saucepan cook lamb and onion in hot oil until the meat is brown.

2 Stir in the water, dried tomatoes, Italian seasoning, salt, and pepper. Bring to boiling; reduce heat. Simmer, covered, about 45 minutes (about 1¼ hours for beef, if using) or until the meat is nearly tender.

3 Stir mushrooms, frozen green beans, carrots, and pasta into meat mixture. Return to boiling; reduce heat. Simmer, covered, for 15 minutes more or until meat, vegetables, and pasta are tender. Stir in tomato sauce; heat through.

nutrition facts per serving: 315 cal., 12 g total fat (2 g sat. fat), 71 mg chol., 806 mg sodium, 24 g carb., 5 g dietary fiber, 29 g protein.

Braising the lamb shanks, relatively tough cuts of meat, transforms them into fork-tender morsels that add flavor and richness to the soup.

lamb and orzo soup with spinach

start to finish: 2 hours
makes: 6 servings

2½ pounds lamb shanks
4 cups water
4 cups chicken or
   vegetable broth
2 bay leaves
1 tablespoon snipped
   fresh oregano or
   1 teaspoon dried
   oregano, crushed
1½ teaspoons snipped
   fresh marjoram or
   ½ teaspoon dried
   marjoram, crushed
½ teaspoon salt
¼ teaspoon ground
   black pepper
2 carrots, cut into
   julienne strips
   (1 cup)
1 cup sliced celery
   (2 stalks)
¾ cup dried orzo
3 cups torn spinach
   or ½ of a 10-ounce
   package frozen
   chopped spinach,
   thawed and well
   drained
   Finely shredded
   Parmesan cheese
   (optional)

1 In a large Dutch oven combine lamb shanks, the water, broth, bay leaves, oregano, marjoram, salt, and pepper. Bring to boiling; reduce heat. Simmer, covered, for 1¼ to 1½ hours or until meat is tender.

2 Remove meat from soup; set aside to cool. Strain broth through a large sieve or colander lined with two layers of 100-percent-cotton cheesecloth; discard herbs. Skim fat from broth; return broth to Dutch oven. When cool enough to handle, cut meat off bones; discard bones. Coarsely chop meat.

3 Stir chopped meat, carrots, celery, and orzo into soup. Return to boiling; reduce heat. Simmer, covered, about 15 minutes or until vegetables and orzo are tender. Stir in spinach. Cook for 1 to 2 minutes more or just until spinach wilts. If desired, serve with Parmesan cheese.

nutrition facts per serving: 226 cal., 5 g total fat (2 g sat. fat), 59 mg chol., 797 mg sodium, 20 g carb., 2 g dietary fiber, 25 g protein.

What do you do with that venison the hunter in your family brought home? Cook it up in this meaty and satisfying stew.

spicy venison stew

prep: 30 minutes   cook: 1½ hours
makes: 4 servings

1   pound boneless
    venison leg or
    shoulder or boneless
    beef chuck roast,
    trimmed and cut
    into 1-inch pieces
1   tablespoon vegetable
    oil
½   cup chopped onion
    (1 medium)
2   cloves garlic, minced
1   14.5-ounce can
    diced tomatoes,
    undrained
1   14-ounce can beef
    broth
1½ teaspoons dried
    oregano, crushed
¼   to ½ teaspoon
    crushed red pepper
    flakes
4   ounces Anaheim
    peppers, poblano
    peppers, banana
    peppers, and/or
    red sweet peppers,
    seeded and cut into
    1-inch pieces (about
    1 cup)*
2   cups cooked long-
    grain rice
    Salt
    Ground black pepper
2   tablespoons snipped
    fresh cilantro

1 In a 4-quart Dutch oven cook half of the meat in hot oil until brown. Remove meat from Dutch oven with a slotted spoon. Add remaining meat, onion, and garlic; cook until meat is brown and onion is tender, stirring occasionally. Drain off fat if necessary. Return all meat to Dutch oven.

2 Stir in undrained tomatoes, broth, oregano, and red pepper flakes. Bring to boiling; reduce heat. Simmer, covered, for 1 hour. Add chile peppers. Return to boiling; reduce heat. Simmer, covered, for 25 to 30 minutes more or until meat is tender.

3 Just before serving, stir in rice and heat through. Season to taste with salt and black pepper. Sprinkle each serving with some cilantro.

nutrition facts per serving: 342 cal., 6 g total fat (1 g sat. fat), 96 mg chol., 779 mg sodium, 38 g carb., 3 g dietary fiber, 31 g protein.

*note: See tip on handling chile peppers, page 31.

pleasing pou

5

ltry

Chicken is one of the easiest go-to ingredients for soups and stews. Its mild taste harmonizes beautifully with greens, grains, and veggies, and even some of the spiciest global seasonings. Here, you'll find everything from a feel-good chicken and pasta soup to a cassoulet with complex, robust flavor.

Using a deli-roasted chicken eases the preparation time for this rich and creamy Thai-seasoned soup. Find canned coconut milk at Asian markets and well-stocked supermarkets.

coconut-lime chicken soup

start to finish: 25 minutes
makes: 4 servings

1   2 to 2½-pound deli-
    roasted chicken
1   15-ounce can
    unsweetened
    coconut milk
2   cups water
¼   cup lime juice
    (2 medium limes)
1½ cups thinly sliced
    carrot (3 medium)
1   tablespoon soy sauce
2   teaspoons Thai
    seasoning blend
¼   teaspoon salt
    Thai seasoning blend
    (optional)
    Fresh cilantro
    (optional)
    Lime wedges
    (optional)

1 Remove and discard skin and bones from chicken. Shred chicken. In large saucepan combine shredded chicken, coconut milk, the water, lime juice, carrot, soy sauce, 2 teaspoons Thai seasoning, and salt. Bring to boiling; reduce heat. Simmer, covered, for 8 minutes or until carrot is crisp-tender.

2 If desired, sprinkle each with Thai seasoning and cilantro and pass lime wedges.

nutrition facts per serving: 487 cal., 38 g total fat (24 g sat. fat), 125 mg chol., 1437 mg sodium, 11 g carb., 1 g dietary fiber, 29 g protein.

Israeli couscous is the perfect pairing for this succulent stew. Compared to regular couscous, it has a slightly more toothy texture. Find it in most grocery stores and specialty food stores.

chicken and duck hunter stew

prep: 1 hour cook: 45 minutes
makes: 12 servings

12 chicken drumsticks, skinless, if desired (about 3 pounds)
3 skinless, boneless duck breast halves, quartered*
¼ cup olive oil
3 cups assorted sliced fresh mushrooms
2 medium onions, sliced
3 cloves garlic, minced
6 medium tomatoes, seeded and chopped (about 3 cups)
3 medium green sweet peppers, cut into 1-inch pieces
1½ cups dry Marsala or beef broth
1 6-ounce can tomato paste
¾ cup pitted kalamata olives and/or green olives
2 tablespoons balsamic vinegar
1 teaspoon salt
¼ teaspoon ground black pepper
¼ cup snipped fresh oregano or marjoram
2 tablespoons snipped fresh rosemary
6 cups hot cooked Israeli couscous or couscous

1 In a 6-quart Dutch oven cook chicken and duck, half at a time, in hot oil about 15 minutes or until lightly browned, turning to brown evenly. Remove chicken and duck, reserving drippings in the Dutch oven; set chicken aside. Cover and chill duck portions in the refrigerator.

2 Add mushrooms, onions, and garlic to drippings in pot; cook and stir about 5 minutes or until vegetables are just tender. Return chicken to Dutch oven.

3 Meanwhile, in a large bowl, combine tomatoes, sweet peppers, Marsala, tomato paste, olives, vinegar, salt, and black pepper. Pour over drumsticks in pot. Bring to boiling; reduce heat. Simmer, covered, for 20 minutes. Add duck; return to boiling. Reduce heat and simmer 25 to 30 minutes more or until poultry is tender. Just before serving, stir in oregano and rosemary. Serve stew with couscous.

nutrition facts per serving: 393 cal., 14 g total fat (3 g sat. fat), 129 mg chol., 407 mg sodium, 28 g carb., 3 g dietary fiber, 33 g protein.

✳note: To make this stew with all chicken: Substitute 12 chicken thighs for the duck; add the thighs and drumsticks back into the pot all at once.

Make this soup at the height of sweet corn season—July and August—for the best and freshest flavor. If you don't want to add crushed red pepper, try a garnish of snipped fresh cilantro.

fresh corn and chicken chowder

start to finish: 30 minutes
makes: 4 servings

12   ounces skinless,
      boneless chicken
      breast halves or
      chicken thighs
4   ears fresh sweet corn
1   32-ounce container
      reduced-sodium
      chicken broth
½   cup chopped green
      sweet pepper,
      chopped (1 small)
1   cup milk
1¼   cups instant mashed
      potato flakes
      Salt
      Ground black pepper
      Crushed red pepper
      flakes (optional)

1 In a 4-quart Dutch oven combine chicken, corn, and broth. Cover and bring to boiling over high heat; reduce heat. Simmer, covered, for 12 minutes or until chicken is no longer pink. Transfer chicken and corn to a cutting board.

2 Add half of the sweet pepper to broth in Dutch oven. Stir in milk and potato flakes. Shred chicken. Return chicken to Dutch oven. Using a kitchen towel to hold hot corn, cut kernels from cobs. Add corn kernels to Dutch oven; heat through. Season to taste with salt and black pepper. Sprinkle each serving with remaining sweet pepper and red pepper flakes.

nutrition facts per serving: 269 cal., 3 g total fat (1 g sat. fat), 54 mg chol., 721 mg sodium, 33 g carb., 3 g dietary fiber, 29 g protein.

This incredibly creamy soup is packed with vegetables, poultry, and just the right amount of seasoning

creamy broccoli-chicken soup

start to finish: 25 minutes
makes: 4 servings

1½ cups small broccoli
    florets
1 cup sliced fresh
    mushrooms
½ cup shredded carrot
    (1 medium)
¼ cup chopped onion
¼ cup butter
¼ cup all-purpose flour
1½ teaspoons snipped
    fresh basil or
    ½ teaspoon dried
    basil, crushed
¼ teaspoon ground
    black pepper
3 cups milk
1 cup half-and-half
    or light cream
1 tablespoon
    white wine
    Worcestershire
    sauce
2 teaspoons instant
    chicken bouillon
    granules
1½ cups chopped cooked
    chicken or turkey
    Coarsely ground
    black pepper

1 In a large saucepan cook and stir broccoli, mushrooms, carrot, and onion in hot butter over medium heat for 6 to 8 minutes or until vegetables are tender.

2 Stir in flour, basil, and pepper. Add milk, half-and-half, Worcestershire sauce, and bouillon granules; cook and stir until thickened and bubbly. Stir in chicken; heat through. Sprinkle each serving with coarsely ground pepper.

nutrition facts per serving: 435 cal., 27 g total fat (15 g sat. fat), 116 mg chol., 764 mg sodium, 23 g carb., 2 g dietary fiber, 26 g protein.

The assertive flavor of the smoky chipotle chile in this hearty stew is tamed by the addition of earthy lentils. You can find chipotles in adobo sauce in the Mexican section of your grocery store.

spicy chipotle chicken-lentil stew

prep: 20 minutes slow cook: 10 hours (low) or 5 hours (high)
makes: 8 to 10 servings

2 cups sliced carrot (4 medium)
8 ounces skinless, boneless chicken breast halves, cut in 1-inch pieces
8 ounces skinless, boneless chicken thighs, cut in 1-inch pieces
1 cup brown lentils, rinsed
1 cup chopped onion (1 large)
1 tablespoon finely chopped canned chipotle peppers in adobo sauce*
1 tablespoon chili powder
2 teaspoons ground cumin
1½ teaspoons dried oregano, crushed
2 cloves garlic, minced
3 14.5-ounce cans reduced-sodium chicken broth
1 14.5-ounce can Italian-style stewed tomatoes, undrained and cut up
1 10-ounce can diced tomatoes and green chiles, undrained
½ cup shredded Monterey Jack cheese (2 ounces)
Avocado slices (optional)
Plain fat-free yogurt (optional)

1 In a 5- to 6-quart slow cooker layer carrot, chicken, lentils, onion, chipotle peppers, chili powder, cumin, oregano, and garlic. Add broth, stewed tomatoes, and tomatoes and green chiles.

2 Cover and cook on low-heat setting for 10 hours or on high-heat setting for 5 hours.

3 Top each serving with cheese and, if desired, avocado slices and yogurt.

nutrition facts per serving: 236 cal., 4 g total fat (2 g sat. fat), 46 mg chol., 737 mg sodium, 26 g carb., 10 g dietary fiber, 24 g protein.

*note: See tip on handling chile peppers, page 31.

Leafy green kale, red lentils, and tomato add nutrients as well as great taste to this home-style soup.

kale, lentil, and chicken soup

prep: 25 minutes cook: 25 minutes
makes: 6 servings

1   tablespoon olive oil
1   cup chopped onion
      (1 large)
1   cup coarsely chopped
      carrot (2 medium)
2   cloves garlic, minced
6   cups reduced-sodium
      chicken broth
1   tablespoon snipped
      fresh basil or
      1 teaspoon dried
      basil, crushed
4   cups coarsely chopped
      kale (about 8 ounces)
½   teaspoon salt
⅛   teaspoon ground
      black pepper
1½ cups cubed cooked
      chicken
1   medium tomato,
      seeded and
      chopped
½   cup dried red lentils

1 In a large saucepan heat oil over medium-low heat. Add onion, carrot, and garlic; cook, covered, for 5 to 7 minutes or until vegetables are nearly tender, stirring occasionally.

2 Add broth and dried basil (if using). Bring to boiling; reduce heat. Simmer, covered, for 10 minutes. Stir in kale, salt, and pepper. Return to boiling; reduce heat. Simmer, covered, for 10 minutes.

3 Stir in chicken, tomato, lentils, and fresh basil (if using). Simmer, covered, for 5 to 10 minutes more or until kale and lentils are tender.

nutrition facts per serving: 199 cal., 5 g total fat (1 g sat. fat), 31 mg chol., 871 mg sodium, 20 g carb., 7 g dietary fiber, 20 g protein.

Regular barley replaces noodles in this whole-grain variation of traditional chicken noodle soup. Sage or rosemary enhances the flavor of the broth.

barley-vegetable chicken soup

prep: 20 minutes cook: 35 minutes
makes: 8 servings

8 cups reduced-sodium
    chicken broth
½ cup regular barley
4 skinless, boneless
    chicken breast
    halves (1 to 1¼
    pounds total), cut
    into ¾-inch cubes
1½ cups sliced celery
    (3 stalks)
1½ cups sliced carrot
    (3 medium)
½ cup chopped onion
    (1 medium)
¼ cup snipped
    fresh parsley or
    2 tablespoons dried
    parsley flakes
1 tablespoon snipped
    fresh sage or
    rosemary or
    1 teaspoon dried
    sage or rosemary,
    crushed
¼ teaspoon ground
    black pepper
1 cup chopped green,
    yellow, and/or red
    sweet pepper
    (1 medium)

1 In a 4-quart Dutch oven bring broth to boiling. Add barley. Return to boiling; reduce heat. Simmer, covered, for 30 minutes.

2 Add chicken, celery, carrot, onion, dried parsley (if using), sage, and black pepper. Return to boiling; reduce heat. Simmer, covered, for 10 minutes. Add sweet pepper. Simmer, covered, about 5 minutes more or until chicken is no longer pink and vegetables are tender. Stir in fresh parsley (if using).

nutrition facts per serving: 137 cal., 1 g total fat (0 g sat. fat), 33 mg chol., 631 mg sodium, 14 g carb., 3 g dietary fiber, 18 g protein.

make-ahead directions: Prepare as directed. Let cool for 30 minutes. Transfer to airtight freezer containers. Seal, label, and freeze for up to 3 months. Thaw in the refrigerator overnight (soup may still be a little icy). Place soup in a saucepan; heat through over medium-low heat, stirring occasionally.

Although this recipe includes a can of condensed soup, tender chicken and sharp American cheese give it a delightful homemade flavor.

cream-of-chicken and cheese soup

start to finish: 40 minutes
makes: 4 servings

2   cups water
1   small whole
      chicken breast
      (about 12 ounces)
⅓   cup chopped onion
      (1 small)
⅓   cup chopped carrot
      (1 small)
⅓   cup chopped celery
      (1 small stalk)
1   10.75-ounce can
      condensed cream of
      chicken soup
½   cup milk
2   ounces American
      cheese, cubed
      (about ½ cup)
      Shredded American
      cheese (optional)

1 In a large saucepan bring the water to boiling. Add chicken breast. Return to boiling; reduce heat. Simmer, covered, for 20 to 25 minutes or until chicken is tender and no longer pink. Remove chicken; reserve cooking liquid.

2 Add onion, carrot, and celery to cooking liquid. Return to boiling; reduce heat. Simmer, uncovered, for 10 minutes.

3 When cool enough to handle, remove chicken from bones; discard bones. Chop chicken. Stir soup and milk into vegetable mixture until smooth. Add chicken and cubed cheese; cook and stir until cheese is melted. If desired, garnish each serving with shredded cheese.

nutrition facts per serving: 209 cal., 11 g total fat (5 g sat. fat), 47 mg chol., 820 mg sodium, 11 g carb., 1 g dietary fiber, 16 g protein.

Blue cheese is the surprise flavor in this rich, cheesy chicken soup.

buffalo chicken soup

prep: 30 minutes   cook: 15 minutes
makes: 6 servings

2	tablespoons butter
½	cup coarsely chopped celery (1 stalk)
½	cup chopped onion (1 medium)
2	14-ounce cans reduced-sodium chicken broth
1½	cups milk
1	teaspoon bottled hot pepper sauce
1½	cups shredded mozzarella cheese (6 ounces)
1¼	cups crumbled blue cheese (5 ounces)
½	cup shredded Parmesan cheese (2 ounces)
⅓	cup all-purpose flour
1	2¼- to 2½-pound deli-roasted chicken, skinned, boned, and coarsely shredded
	Bottled hot pepper sauce (optional)

1 In a 4-quart Dutch oven melt butter over medium heat. Add celery and onion; cook and stir until onion is tender. Stir in broth, milk, and 1 teaspoon hot pepper sauce.

2 In a bowl toss together mozzarella, 1 cup of the blue cheese, Parmesan, and flour. Add gradually to soup, stirring after each addition just until melted. Stir in three-fourths of the shredded chicken; heat through. Top with remaining chicken, blue cheese, and, if desired, hot pepper sauce.

nutrition facts per serving: 490 cal., 28 g total fat (15 g sat. fat), 145 mg chol., 1134 mg sodium, 12 g carb., 1 g dietary fiber, 45 g protein.

Chunky bottled salsa provides the heat in this Mexican-inspired soup. It also makes the soup easy enough to whip together for a quick lunch.

chicken and salsa soup

makes: 4 servings

139

1¾ cups water
1   14.5-ounce can
    reduced-sodium
    chicken broth
8   ounces skinless,
    boneless chicken,
    cut into bite-size
    pieces
1   to 2 teaspoons chili
    powder
1   11-ounce can whole-
    kernel corn with
    sweet peppers,
    drained
1   cup chunky garden-
    style salsa
3   cups broken baked
    tortilla chips
½   cup shredded
    Monterey Jack
    cheese with
    jalapeño peppers
    (2 ounces)

1 In a 3-quart saucepan combine the water, broth, chicken, and chili powder. Bring to boiling; reduce heat. Simmer, covered, for 8 minutes. Add corn. Simmer, uncovered, about 5 minutes more. Stir in salsa; heat through.

2 Top each serving with tortilla chips and sprinkle with cheese.

nutrition facts per serving: 319 cal., 9 g total fat (3 g sat. fat), 42 mg chol., 989 mg sodium, 32 g carb., 3 g dietary fiber, 20 g protein.

Oftentimes, the most delicious soups result from seasoning with a new herb, such as herbes de Provence. This traditional French herb blend contains marjoram, thyme, savory, basil, rosemary, sage, and fennel.

french chicken stew

prep: 30 minutes **slow cook:** 6 to 7 hours (low) or 3 to 4 hours (high)
makes: 8 servings

4 cups sliced fresh button and/or shiitake mushrooms
1 14.5-ounce can diced tomatoes, undrained
1 cup sliced carrot (2 medium)
½ chopped onion (1 medium)
1 medium red potato, cut into 1-inch pieces
½ cup fresh green beans, cut into 1-inch pieces
½ cup pitted ripe olives, halved
1 cup reduced-sodium chicken broth
½ cup dry white wine or chicken broth
2 tablespoons quick-cooking tapioca
1 teaspoon herbes de Provence or dried Italian seasoning, crushed
¾ teaspoon dried thyme, crushed
¼ teaspoon ground black pepper
8 skinless, boneless chicken thighs (1¾ to 2 pounds total)
½ teaspoon seasoned salt
1 14-ounce jar tomato pasta sauce or one 16-ounce jar Alfredo pasta sauce
French bread (optional)

1 In a 5- to 6-quart slow cooker combine mushrooms, undrained tomatoes, carrot, onion, potato, green beans, olives, broth, wine, tapioca, herbes de Provence, thyme, and pepper. Place chicken on top; sprinkle with seasoned salt. Cover and cook on low-heat setting for 6 to 7 hours or on high-heat setting for 3 to 4 hours.

2 Stir in pasta sauce. If desired, serve with French bread.

nutrition facts per serving: 219 cal., 5 g total fat (1 g sat. fat), 83 mg chol., 629 mg sodium, 17 g carb., 3 g dietary fiber, 23 g protein.

Make chicken soup a weeknight favorite with this Asian-inspired twist. Serve it with veggie spring rolls.

chicken-edamame chowder

prep: 30 minutes slow cook: 7 to 8 hours (low) or 3½ to 4 hours (high)
+ 20 minutes (high)
makes: 6 to 8 servings

1 pound skinless, boneless chicken breast halves, cut into 1-inch pieces
1 tablespoon vegetable oil
1 12-ounce package frozen sweet soybeans (edamame)
1 cup coarsely chopped green sweet pepper (1 large)
1 cup chopped onion (1 large)
2 jalapeño peppers, seeded and finely chopped*
2 teaspoons ground cumin
2 teaspoons ground coriander
½ teaspoon salt
¼ teaspoon ground black pepper
2 14.5-ounce cans chicken broth
1 8-ounce carton sour cream
3 tablespoons all-purpose flour
2 medium zucchini, halved lengthwise and thinly sliced
   Shredded Monterey Jack cheese (optional)
   Snipped fresh cilantro (optional)

1 In a large skillet cook chicken in hot oil over medium-high heat until lightly browned. In a 3½- or 4-quart slow cooker combine chicken, soybeans, sweet pepper, onion, chiles, cumin, coriander, salt, and black pepper. Pour broth over all. Stir to combine.

2 Cover and cook on low-heat setting for 7 to 8 hours or on high-heat setting for 3½ to 4 hours.

3 If using low-heat setting, turn to high-heat setting. Combine sour cream and flour. Using a wire whisk, stir sour cream mixture and zucchini into chicken mixture. Cover and cook for 20 to 30 minutes more or until mixture is thickened and zucchini is crisp-tender. If desired, top each serving with cheese and cilantro.

nutrition facts per serving: 314 cal., 14 g total fat (5 g sat. fat), 61 mg chol., 806 mg sodium, 17 g carb., 8 g dietary fiber, 27 g protein.

*note: See tip on handling chile peppers, page 31.

Tender chunks of chicken combine with wild rice, carrots, celery, and mushrooms in this creamy chowder. To save time, buy a roast chicken at your local deli to make it.

chicken and wild rice chowder

prep: 20 minutes cook: 25 minutes
makes: 4 servings

1 cup sliced carrot
   (2 medium)
1 cup sliced celery
   (2 stalks)
1 cup quartered fresh
   mushrooms
3 tablespoons butter
3 tablespoons all-
   purpose flour
2 14-ounce cans
   chicken broth
3 cups chopped cooked
   chicken breast
¾ cup cooked wild rice
¼ teaspoon ground
   black pepper
1½ cups half-and-half

In a saucepan cook carrot, celery, and mushrooms in melted butter over medium heat until tender. Stir in flour. Add broth, chicken, wild rice, and pepper; cook and stir until mixture is bubbly and slightly thickened. Stir in half-and-half and heat through.

nutrition facts per serving: 445 cal., 22 g total fat (13 g sat. fat), 140 mg chol., 1019 mg sodium, 21 g carb., 2 g dietary fiber, 40 g protein.

Let the kids choose which vegetables to add; the more variety, the more colorful the brothy mix will be. It's the perfect weeknight soup.

choose-a-vegetable chicken and pasta soup

start to finish: 40 minutes
makes: 6 servings

2 14-ounce cans reduced-sodium chicken broth
2 cups water
¼ teaspoon ground black pepper
1 cup dried whole wheat rotini or twisted spaghetti or broken fusilli
3 cups vegetable pieces (such as thinly sliced carrots, small broccoli florets, chopped green or red sweet pepper, and/or fresh or frozen whole-kernel corn)
1½ cups cubed cooked chicken (about 8 ounces)
1 tablespoon snipped fresh basil or 1 teaspoon dried basil, crushed
¼ cup finely shredded Parmesan cheese (1 ounce)

In a Dutch oven combine broth, the water, and black pepper; bring to boiling. Stir in pasta. Return to boiling; reduce heat. Simmer, covered, for 5 minutes. Stir in vegetables. Return to boiling; reduce heat. Simmer, covered, for 5 to 8 minutes more or until vegetables and pasta are tender. Stir in chicken and basil; heat through. Top each serving with cheese.

nutrition facts per serving: 170 cal., 4 g total fat (2 g sat. fat), 35 mg chol., 437 mg sodium, 17 g carb., 2 g dietary fiber, 16 g protein.

sodium sense

Consider using reduced-sodium products whenever possible. Look for reduced-sodium or no-salt-added canned tomatoes, beans, or broth. Or you can substitute fresh or frozen vegetables or cooked dried beans. Stir in extra-fresh snipped herbs at the end of cooking time to boost flavor in low-sodium recipes.

Ceramic mugs make great serving bowls for this colorful all-time favorite take on chicken and noodle soup.

chicken-squash noodle soup

start to finish: 40 minutes
makes: 6 servings

1 pound skinless, boneless chicken breast halves, cut into 1-inch pieces
½ teaspoon poultry seasoning
1 tablespoon canola oil
½ cup chopped onion (1 medium)
½ cup chopped celery (1 stalk)
½ cup chopped carrot (1 medium)
2 cloves garlic, minced
3 14-ounce cans reduced-sodium chicken broth
1½ cups dried medium noodles
1 medium zucchini or yellow summer squash, quartered lengthwise and cut into 1-inch-thick pieces
1¾ cups fat-free milk
¼ cup all-purpose flour
¼ cup snipped fresh parsley

1 In a large bowl combine chicken pieces and poultry seasoning; toss to coat. In a 4-quart Dutch oven heat oil over medium heat. Add chicken pieces; cook for 3 to 5 minutes or until chicken pieces are brown. Using a slotted spoon, transfer chicken to a bowl; set aside.

2 In the same Dutch oven cook onion, celery, carrot, and garlic over medium heat about 5 minutes or just until tender, stirring occasionally. Add broth; bring to boiling. Add chicken, noodles, and zucchini. Return to boiling; reduce heat. Simmer, covered, for 5 minutes.

3 In a medium bowl whisk milk and flour together until combined. Stir flour mixture into Dutch oven; cook and stir until bubbly. Cook and stir for 1 minute more. Sprinkle with parsley just before serving.

nutrition facts per serving: 215 cal., 4 g total fat (1 g sat. fat), 53 mg chol., 560 mg sodium, 20 g carb., 2 g dietary fiber, 25 g protein.

With a light, licorice flavor and celery-like texture, fennel melds with the marjoram and thyme in this hearty soup. Look for firm, smooth bulbs without cracks and brown spots. Stalks should be crisp and leaves a fresh bright green.

chicken and garbanzo bean soup

prep: 30 minutes **slow cook:** 6 to 7 hours (low) or 3 to 3½ hours (high)
makes: 6 servings

2½ cups sliced carrot
1 15-ounce can garbanzo beans (chickpeas), rinsed and drained
1 medium fennel bulb, trimmed and cut into ¼-inch slices, or 1½ cups sliced celery
1 cup chopped onion (1 large)
1 pound skinless, boneless chicken breast halves or thighs
1 tablespoon snipped fresh marjoram or 1 teaspoon dried marjoram, crushed
1 tablespoon snipped fresh thyme or 1 teaspoon dried thyme, crushed
¼ teaspoon ground black pepper
1 14-ounce can reduced-sodium chicken broth
2 cups water
1 cup shredded fresh spinach or escarole

1 In a 5- to 6-quart slow cooker combine carrot, beans, fennel, and onion. Top with chicken pieces. Sprinkle with dried marjoram (if using), dried thyme (if using), and pepper. Pour broth and the water over all.

2 Cover and cook on low-heat setting for 6 to 7 hours or on high-heat setting for 3 to 3½ hours. Remove the chicken with a slotted spoon; cool slightly. Shred chicken into bite-size pieces. Return chicken to cooker. Stir in the spinach, fresh marjoram (if using), and fresh thyme (if using). Let stand for 5 minutes before serving.

nutrition facts per serving: 216 cal., 2 g total fat (0 g sat. fat), 44 mg chol., 481 mg sodium, 27 g carb., 6 g dietary fiber, 23 g protein.

Never mind traditional pairings. Beefy onion soup mix and red wine combine with chicken for a succulent stew that's luscious on a cold night. Crusty bread makes an excellent accompaniment.

coq au vin stew

prep: 20 minutes slow cook: 5 to 6 hours (low) or 2½ to 3 hours (high)
makes: 4 servings

Nonstick cooking
   spray
3 pounds skinless
   chicken thighs
1 envelope beefy onion
   soup mix (½ of a
   2.2-ounce package)
1½ cups loose-pack
   frozen small whole
   onions
2 cups fresh button
   or wild mushrooms,
   quartered
½ cup dry red wine
   Hot cooked mashed
   potatoes (optional)
   Snipped fresh basil
   or parsley (optional)

1 Lightly coat a large skillet with nonstick cooking spray; preheat over medium heat. Cook chicken thighs, several at a time, in the hot skillet until brown; drain fat. Place chicken thighs in a 3½- or 4-quart slow cooker.

2 Sprinkle chicken with dry soup mix. Add onions and mushrooms. Pour wine over all.

3 Cover and cook on low-heat setting for 5 to 6 hours or on high-heat setting for 2½ to 3 hours. Using a slotted spoon, remove chicken from slow cooker. Use a fork to remove chicken from bones; discard bones. Shred chicken into bite-size pieces. Return chicken to cooker. If desired, serve with hot mashed potatoes and sprinkle with basil.

nutrition facts per serving: 305 cal., 8 g total fat (2 g sat. fat), 161 mg chol., 759 mg sodium, 12 g carb., 2 g dietary fiber, 41 g protein.

The creamy texture and delightful tang in this soup come from buttermilk. Cultured buttermilk is made by adding a bacterial culture to low-fat milk and can be found in the dairy section of supermarkets.

fennel-chicken-potato soup

prep: 25 minutes cook: 25 minutes
makes: 8 servings

2 medium fennel bulbs (about 2 pounds)
6 medium potatoes, peeled and cubed (about 2 pounds)
4 cups reduced-sodium chicken broth
⅓ cup butter or margarine
½ cup all-purpose flour
½ teaspoon caraway seeds
½ teaspoon ground black pepper
2 cups cultured buttermilk or milk
2½ cups chopped cooked chicken
 Rye croutons (optional)

1 Wash fennel; snip ¼ cup of the leafy tops. Set aside. If desired for garnish, set aside additional leafy tops. Cut off and discard upper stalks of fennel. Remove any wilted outer layers; cut off and discard a thin slice from fennel base. Halve, core, and chop fennel. (You should have about 4 cups.)

2 Combine fennel, potatoes, and broth in a 4-quart Dutch oven. Bring to boiling; reduce heat. Simmer, covered, for 15 to 20 minutes or until potatoes are tender. Drain, reserving broth. Set aside in a medium bowl; mash with a potato masher.

3 Meanwhile, in the same pot, melt butter over medium heat. Stir in flour, caraway seeds, and pepper. Add buttermilk; cook and stir until slightly thickened and bubbly. Cook 1 minute more. Stir in mashed potato and fennel mixture, chicken, snipped fennel tops, and broth; cook and stir until heated through. If necessary, stir in additional broth to achieve desired consistency. If desired, top each serving with rye croutons and additional leafy fennel tops.

nutrition facts per serving: 331 cal., 12 g total fat (6 g sat. fat), 63 mg chol., 556 mg sodium, 35 g carb., 32 g dietary fiber, 21 g protein.

This slow-cooked stew recipe is similar to a Southwestern white chili. The refrigerated Alfredo sauce gives it a creamy texture.

chicken and white bean stew

prep: 35 minutes slow cook: 4 to 5 hours (low) or 2 to 2½ hours (high)
makes: 8 servings

2 pounds skinless, boneless chicken thighs

2 teaspoons ground cumin

⅛ teaspoon ground black pepper

1 tablespoon olive oil

2 10-ounce packages refrigerated light Alfredo sauce

1 15-ounce can Great Northern or cannellini (white kidney) beans, rinsed and drained

1 cup reduced-sodium chicken broth

½ cup chopped red onion (1 medium)

1 4-ounce can diced green chile peppers

4 cloves garlic, minced

¼ cup shredded sharp cheddar cheese or Monterey Jack cheese (1 ounce) (optional)

Fresh parsley leaves (optional)

1 Cut chicken into 1-inch pieces. Sprinkle chicken with cumin and pepper. In a large skillet, cook chicken, half at a time, in hot oil over medium heat until brown. Place chicken in a 3½- or 4-quart slow cooker. Stir in Alfredo sauce, beans, broth, onion, chile peppers, and garlic.

2 Cover and cook on low-heat setting for 4 to 5 hours or on high-heat setting for 2 to 2½ hours. If desired, sprinkle each serving with cheese and parsley.

nutrition facts per serving: 360 cal., 16 g total fat (8 g sat. fat), 122 mg chol., 918 mg sodium, 20 g carb., 3 g dietary fiber, 31 g protein.

Round out the meal with hot-from-the-oven biscuits and a crisp green salad topped with citrus slices and your favorite vinaigrette.

spinach, chicken, and wild rice soup

prep: 20 minutes   slow cook: 7 to 8 hours (low) or 3½ to 4 hours (high)
makes: 6 servings

3   cups water
1   14-ounce can
    reduced-sodium
    chicken broth
1   10.75-ounce can
    reduced-fat and low-
    sodium condensed
    cream of chicken
    soup
⅔   cup wild rice, rinsed
    and drained
½   teaspoon dried
    thyme, crushed
¼   teaspoon ground
    black pepper
3   cups chopped cooked
    chicken or turkey
    (about 1 pound)
2   cups shredded fresh
    spinach

1 In a 3½- or 4-quart slow cooker combine the water, broth, cream of chicken soup, wild rice, thyme, and pepper.

2 Cover and cook on low-heat setting for 7 to 8 hours or on high-heat setting for 3½ to 4 hours.

3 Stir in chicken and spinach and heat through.

nutrition facts per serving: 216 cal., 4 g total fat "(1 g sat. fat), 64 mg chol., 397 mg sodium, 19 g carb., 2 g dietary fiber, 26 g protein.

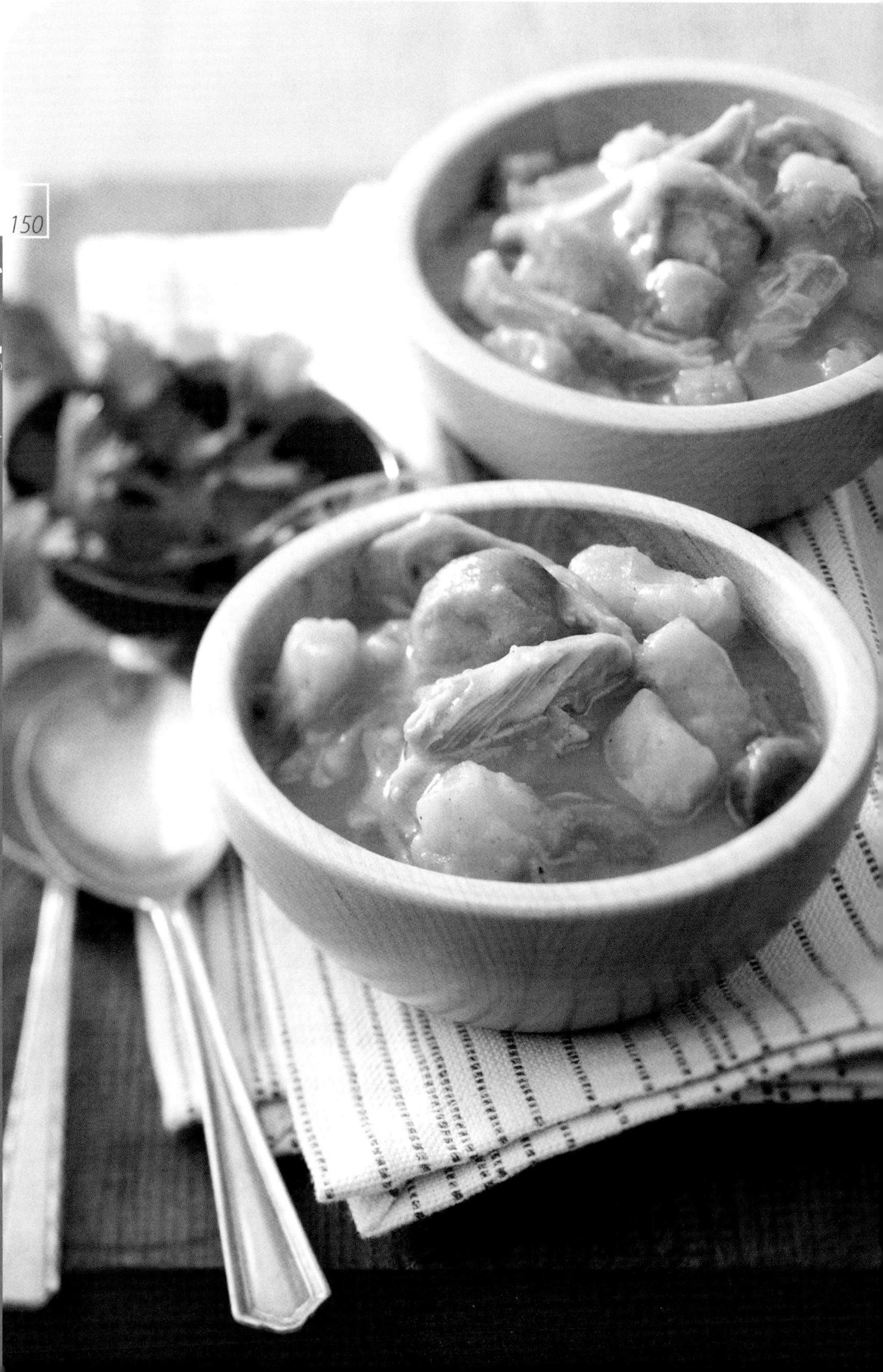

Frozen stew vegetables eliminate peeling and cutting, leaving just 15 minutes prep time before the slow cooker takes over. Top each serving with a sprinkle of toasted slivered almonds and chopped fresh cilantro.

in-a-hurry chicken curry

prep: 15 minutes slow cook: 6 to 7 hours (low) or 3 to 3½ hours (high)
makes: 6 servings

1 16-ounce package
    frozen stew
    vegetables
4 large skinless
    chicken thighs
    (1½ to 1¾ pounds)
    Salt
    Ground black pepper
1 10.75-ounce can
    condensed cream of
    potato soup
2 teaspoons curry
    powder
1 tablespoon snipped
    fresh cilantro

1 Place frozen stew vegetables in a 3½- or 4-quart slow cooker. Top with chicken. Sprinkle with salt and pepper. In a small bowl stir together soup and curry powder. Pour soup mixture over chicken and vegetables in cooker.

2 Cover and cook on low-heat settting for 6 to 7 hours or on high-heat setting for 3 to 3½ hours. Remove chicken from bones and, if desired, break into large pieces. Sprinkle with cilantro.

nutrition facts per serving: 200 cal., 5 g total fat (2 g sat. fat), 97 mg chol., 734 mg sodium, 13 g carb., 1 g dietary fiber, 24 g protein.

Toss the ingredients into the slow cooker for a no-fuss meal that looks as vibrant as it tastes. If you're watching sodium, try using low-sodium chicken broth and soy sauce.

soy-ginger soup with chicken

prep: 20 minutes slow cook: 2 to 3 hours (high) + 3 minutes (high)
makes: 6 servings

1 pound skinless, boneless chicken thighs, cut into 1-inch pieces
1 cup coarsely shredded carrot (2 medium)
2 tablespoons dry sherry (optional)
1 tablespoon soy sauce
1 tablespoon rice vinegar
1 teaspoon grated fresh ginger or ½ teaspoon ground ginger
¼ teaspoon ground black pepper
3 14-ounce cans reduced-sodium chicken broth
1 cup water
2 ounces dried somen noodles
1 6-ounce package frozen snow peapods, thawed
Soy sauce

1 In a 3½- or 4-quart slow cooker combine chicken, carrot, sherry, if desired, 1 tablespoon soy sauce, vinegar, ginger, and pepper. Stir in chicken broth and the water.

2 Cover and cook on high-heat setting for 2 to 3 hours. Stir in noodles and peapods. Cover and cook for 3 minutes more.

3 Serve with additional soy sauce.

nutrition facts per serving: 174 cal., 3 g total fat (1 g sat. fat), 44 mg chol., 1050 mg sodium, 13 g carb., 1 g dietary fiber, 21 g protein.

"Nourishing" and "delicious" are the best words to describe this hearty chicken soup. To reap all the rewards of this Indian-inspired dish, sop up the rich, curried broth with chunks of warm bread.

chicken chili monterey

prep: 25 minutes cook: 35 minutes
makes: 6 servings

1 tablespoon vegetable oil
1 cup chopped onion (1 large)
1 cup coarsely chopped carrot (2 medium)
1 cup sliced celery (2 stalks)
1⅓ cups chopped tart apples
2 to 3 teaspoons curry powder
¼ teaspoon salt
3 cups reduced-sodium chicken broth
3 cups water
1 14.5-ounce can low-sodium stewed tomatoes, undrained
2 cups chopped cooked chicken or turkey

In a Dutch oven heat oil over medium heat. Add onion, carrot, and celery; cook and stir about 10 minutes or until crisp-tender. Reduce heat to medium-low; add apples, curry powder, and salt. Cook, covered, for 5 minutes. Stir in broth, the water, and undrained tomatoes. Bring to boiling; reduce heat. Simmer, covered, for 10 minutes. Stir in chicken. Simmer, covered, for 10 minutes more.

nutrition facts per serving: 197 cal., 7 g total fat (1 g sat. fat), 45 mg chol., 517 mg sodium, 17 g carb., 4 g dietary fiber, 17 g protein.

This cassoulet features white beans and meats slow-cooked so all the flavors meld together. Pasta sauce made with red wine and herbs adds a hearty depth to this one.

chicken cassoulet-style soup

prep: 25 minutes **slow cook:** 5 to 7 hours (low) or 2½ to 3½ hours (high)
makes: 6 servings

1   pound skinless, boneless chicken thighs, cut into ½-inch pieces

8   ounces smoked turkey sausage, cut into ½-inch slices

1   26-ounce jar pasta sauce with red wine and herbs

1   15- to 19-ounce can cannellini (white kidney) beans, rinsed and drained

1⅓   cups water

1   teaspoon dried oregano, crushed

1 In a 3½- or 4-quart slow cooker combine chicken, sausage, pasta sauce, beans, the water, and oregano.

2 Cover and cook on low-heat setting for 5 to 7 hours or on high-heat setting for 2½ to 3½ hours.

nutrition facts per serving: 286 cal., 7 g total fat (2 g sat. fat), 88 mg chol., 1178 mg sodium, 33 g carb., 9 g dietary fiber, 30 g protein.

This thick chowder is a good way to lure picky eaters away from mac and cheese, especially if you have breadsticks to dip into it.

nacho cheese chicken chowder

prep: 10 minutes slow cook: 4 to 5 hours (low) or 2 to 2½ hours (high)
makes: 6 servings

1   pound skinless, boneless chicken breast halves, cut into ½-inch pieces
2   14.5-ounce cans Mexican-style stewed tomatoes, undrained
1   10.75-ounce can condensed nacho cheese soup
1   10-ounce package frozen whole-kernel corn (2 cups)
    Shredded Mexican-style or cheddar cheese

1 In a 3½- or 4-quart slow cooker stir together chicken, undrained tomatoes, soup, and corn.

2 Cover and cook on low-heat setting for 4 to 5 hours or on high-heat setting for 2 to 2½ hours. Sprinkle each serving with cheese.

nutrition facts per serving: 244 cal., 6 g total fat (3 g sat. fat), 55 mg chol., 647 mg sodium, 24 g carb., 2 g dietary fiber, 23 g protein.

This aromatic soup features a medley of Asian flavors, including five-spice powder, which is available at larger supermarkets and in Asian markets.

five-spice chicken noodle soup

start to finish: 20 minutes
makes: 4 servings

2	cups water
1	14-ounce can reduced-sodium chicken broth
2	green onions, thinly bias-sliced
2	teaspoons reduced-sodium soy sauce
2	cloves garlic, minced
¼	teaspoon five-spice powder
⅛	teaspoon ground ginger
2	cups chopped bok choy
1	medium red sweet pepper, thinly sliced into strips
2	ounces dried somen noodles, broken into 2-inch lengths, or 2 ounces dried fine noodles
1½	cups chopped cooked chicken

In a large saucepan combine the water, broth, green onions, soy sauce, garlic, five-spice powder, and ginger. Bring to boiling. Stir in bok choy, sweet pepper, and noodles. Return to boiling; reduce heat. Boil gently, uncovered, for 3 to 5 minutes or until noodles are just tender. Stir in the cooked chicken; heat through.

nutrition facts per serving: 181 cal., 4 g total fat (1 g sat. fat), 51 mg chol., 556 mg sodium, 14 g carb., 1 g dietary fiber, 20 g protein.

This rich, lemony chicken and rice soup features a colorful array of vegetables, making it extra flavorful. Serve with crusty rolls.

cream of chicken and rice florentine

prep: 25 minutes   cook: 40 minutes
makes: 6 servings

2   tablespoons olive oil
1   pound skinless, boneless chicken breast halves
1½ cups finely chopped onion (3 medium)
1   8-ounce package fresh mushrooms, sliced
½   cup shredded carrot (1 medium)
1   tablespoon bottled minced garlic
⅓   cup long-grain rice
1   14-ounce can reduced-sodium chicken broth
1   cup water
¼   teaspoon ground nutmeg
½   teaspoon ground black pepper
2   12-ounce cans evaporated fat-free milk
2   tablespoons all-purpose flour
4   cups packed fresh spinach
2   teaspoons finely shredded lemon zest
2   tablespoons lemon juice

1 In a Dutch oven heat oil over medium-high heat; reduce heat to medium. Add chicken; cook for 12 to 15 minutes or until no longer pink (170°F), turning once halfway through cooking. Transfer chicken to a plate to cool. When cool enough to handle, coarsely shred chicken.

2 Meanwhile, add onion, mushrooms, carrot, and garlic to the Dutch oven; cook for 5 minutes, stirring occasionally. Stir in rice; cook for 1 minute more. Add broth, the water, nutmeg, and ½ teaspoon pepper. Bring to boiling; reduce heat. Simmer, covered, for 15 minutes.

3 In a small bowl stir together 1 can of the evaporated milk and flour; stir into mixture in Dutch oven. Stir in the remaining can of evaporated milk; cook and stir until bubbly.

4 Stir in spinach and the shredded chicken. Simmer, uncovered, for 5 minutes. Stir in lemon zest and lemon juice. If desired, sprinkle with black pepper.

nutrition facts per serving: 300 cal., 6 g total fat (1 g sat. fat), 48 mg chol., 365 mg sodium, 31 g carb., 2 g dietary fiber, 30 g protein.

The classic version of this curry-flavored chicken and rice soup hails from India.

chicken mulligatawny soup

prep: 45 minutes slow cook: 4 hours (low) + 1 hour (low)
makes: 8 servings

1	cup finely chopped celery (2 stalks)
1	cup finely chopped carrot (2 medium)
⅔	cup peeled and finely chopped Granny Smith apple (1 medium)
½	cup chopped onion (1 medium)
2	cloves garlic, minced
1½	teaspoons curry powder
1	teaspoon ground cardamom
1	teaspoon ground coriander
1	teaspoon ground cumin
1	teaspoon ground ginger
1	teaspoon ground turmeric
⅛	to ¼ teaspoon cayenne pepper
6	cups reduced-sodium chicken broth
2	cups water
1	pound skinless, boneless chicken breast halves, cut into bite-size pieces
2	tablespoons all-purpose flour
1½	teaspoons curry powder
1	tablespoon olive oil
½	cup basmati rice
1	cup unsweetened light coconut milk

1 In a 4- to 5-quart slow cooker place celery, carrots, apple, onion, and garlic. Stir in 1½ teaspoons curry powder, cardamom, coriander, cumin, ginger, turmeric, and cayenne pepper. Pour broth and the water over all.

2 Cover and cook on low-heat setting for 4 hours.

3 In a resealable plastic bag place chicken, flour, and 1½ teaspoons curry powder; shake to coat chicken. Chill in refrigerator until needed.

4 In a large skillet brown coated chicken in hot oil over medium heat, stirring often. Add three or four ladles of the cooking liquid from slow cooker to skillet; stir until thickened and gravylike, scraping bottom of skillet to incorporate flour and spices. Stir chicken mixture and rice into the slow cooker. Cover and cook 1 hour more on low-heat setting. Stir in coconut milk before serving.

nutrition facts per serving: 166 cal., 4 g total fat (1 g sat. fat), 21 mg chol., 473 mg sodium, 20 g carb., 2 g dietary fiber, 13 g protein.

Turkey sausage is well seasoned but low in fat, so there's no fat to skim from the soup before serving it. Slightly mashing the beans helps thicken the consistency.

turkey sausage and bean soup

prep: 20 minutes   slow cook: 10 hours (low) or 5 hours (high)
makes: 10 to 12 servings

1   pound dried beans
    (cranberry, kidney,
    Great Northern,
    and/or pinto beans)
8   cups water
4   cups water
2   14-ounce cans
    reduced-sodium
    chicken broth
3   medium red-skinned
    potatoes, cubed
4   cloves garlic, minced
1   tablespoon chili
    powder
1   1-pound link smoked
    turkey sausage,
    halved and sliced
    ½ inch thick
2   cups frozen cut green
    beans

1 Rinse beans; drain. In a large pot combine beans and the 8 cups water. Bring to boiling; reduce heat. Simmer, uncovered, for 10 minutes. Cover and let stand for 1 hour. Or cool; transfer to an extra-large bowl. Cover and chill for up to 24 hours. Drain and rinse beans.

2 In a 6- to 7-quart slow cooker combine beans, the 4 cups water, broth, potatoes, garlic, and chili powder. Cover and cook on low-heat setting for 10 hours or on high-heat setting for 5 hours. Mash beans slightly with a potato masher or the back of a wooden spoon.

3 If using low-heat setting, turn slow cooker to high-heat setting. Add sausage and green beans. Cover and cook for 1 hour more.

nutrition facts per serving: 268 cal., 5 g total fat (1 g sat. fat), 30 mg chol., 604 mg sodium, 38 g carb., 13 g dietary fiber, 20 g protein.

Caraway seed, a sometimes overlooked spice, adds fresh new flavor to this chicken stew.

caraway chicken and vegetable stew

prep: 45 minutes   cook: 40 to 50 minutes
makes: 6 servings

3   pounds skinless
     chicken thighs and/
     or skinless breasts
3¾   cups water
2   teaspoons instant
     chicken bouillon
     granules
1   teaspoon salt
1   teaspoon caraway
     seeds, crushed
¼   teaspoon ground
     black pepper
8   ounces fresh green
     beans, trimmed
     and cut into 2-inch
     pieces
2   medium carrots, cut
     into ¾-inch chunks
2   stalks celery, bias-cut
     into ½-inch-thick
     slices
2   cups sliced fresh
     shiitake, crimini,
     oyster, and/or
     button mushrooms
1   cup pearl onions,
     peeled
¼   cup cold water
¼   cup all-purpose flour

1 In a 4-quart Dutch oven combine chicken, the 3¾ cups water, bouillon granules, salt, caraway seeds, and pepper. Bring to boiling; reduce heat. Simmer, covered, for 40 minutes. Stir in green beans, carrots, celery, mushrooms, and pearl onions. Return to boiling; reduce heat. Simmer, covered, for about 10 minutes or until chicken is tender.

2 Remove chicken pieces from the stew; set aside to cool slightly. When cool enough to handle, remove meat from bones; discard bones. Cut up the meat; add to vegetable mixture in Dutch oven.

3 In a small bowl combine the ¼ cup cold water and flour; whisk until smooth. Add to stew; cook and stir until thickened and bubbly. Cook and stir for 1 minute more.

nutrition facts per serving: 229 cal., 5 g total fat (1 g sat. fat), 107 mg chol., 783 mg sodium, 18 g carb., 4 g dietary fiber, 28 g protein.

A play on traditional chicken soup, this soup is a comforting and creamy low-fat soup. Topping with toasted nuts and dried cranberries makes for a flavorful finish.

creamy turkey soup

prep: 30 minutes slow cook: 9 to 10 hours (low) or 4 ½ to 5 hours (high) + 45 minutes (high)
makes: 8 servings

8 ounces red-skinned potatoes, cut in 1-inch pieces
8 ounces fresh cremini mushrooms, sliced
1 cup coarsely chopped onion (1 large)
1 cup sliced celery (2 stalks)
2 turkey breast tenderloins (about 1½ pounds total)
3 14.5-ounce cans reduced-sodium chicken broth
1½ teaspoons dried thyme, crushed
½ teaspoon ground black pepper
1 12-ounce can evaporated fat-free milk
3 tablespoons cornstarch
½ cup sliced green onions (4)
2 tablespoons lemon juice
   Toasted sliced almonds or chopped pecans* and/or dried cranberries (optional)

1 In a 6-quart slow cooker combine potatoes, mushrooms, onion, and celery. Top with turkey. Add broth, thyme, and pepper.

2 Cover and cook on low-heat setting for 9 to 10 hours or on high-heat setting for 4½ to 5 hours.

3 Transfer turkey to a cutting board; shred turkey. Return to cooker. In a small bowl stir together evaporated milk and cornstarch; stir into mixture in cooker. If using low-heat setting, turn cooker to high-heat setting.

4 Cover and cook for 45 to 60 minutes more or until bubbly at edges. Stir in green onions and lemon juice.

5 If desired, top each serving with nuts and/ or cranberries.

nutrition facts per serving: 188 cal., 1 g total fat (0 g sat. fat), 39 mg chol., 487 mg sodium, 18 g carb., 2 g dietary fiber, 26 g protein.

*note: To toast nuts, preheat oven to 350°F. Spread nuts in a single layer in a shallow baking pan. Bake for 5 to 10 minutes or until light brown, watching carefully and stirring once or twice.

What do you do with leftover turkey? This recipe for turkey soup makes a cozy meal. Toss in the odds and ends of fresh vegetables that you didn't use for your holiday dinner.

turkey frame soup

prep: 30 minutes   cook: 1¾ hours
makes: 6 servings

1   meaty turkey frame
4   cups water
4   cups reduced-sodium
      chicken broth
1   large onion,
      quartered
1   clove garlic, crushed
½   teaspoon salt
¼   cup dried tomatoes
      (not oil-packed),
      cut into thin strips
1½   teaspoons dried
      Italian seasoning,
      crushed
¼   teaspoon ground
      black pepper
3   cups sliced or cubed
      vegetables (such as
      carrot, parsnip, and/
      or turnip)
1½   cups dried high-fiber
      or whole wheat
      rotini or penne
      pasta
1   15-ounce can
      Great Northern or
      cannellini (white
      kidney) beans,
      rinsed and drained

1 Break turkey frame or cut in half with kitchen shears. Place in a large pot. Add the water, broth, onion, garlic, and salt. Bring to boiling; reduce heat. Simmer, covered, for 1½ hours.

2 Remove turkey frame from pot. When cool enough to handle, remove meat from bones; discard bones. Coarsely chop meat. Measure enough turkey to equal 2 cups; set aside. Strain broth; skim off fat.

3 Return broth to pot. Stir in tomatoes, Italian seasoning, and pepper. Stir in vegetables. Return to boiling; reduce heat. Simmer, covered, for 5 minutes. Add pasta. Simmer, uncovered, for 8 to 10 minutes or until pasta is tender and still firm and vegetables are tender. Stir in turkey and beans; heat through.

nutrition facts per serving: 192 cal., 2 g total fat
(1 g sat. fat), 27 mg chol., 610 mg sodium, 27 g carb.,
5 g dietary fiber, 19 g protein.

This recipe starts with sweet peppers, onion, and celery, a trio known as the "holy trinity" of Cajun and Creole cooking. That means you can expect a lively dish!

chicken and turkey sausage soup

prep: 30 minutes slow cook: 8 to 9 hours (low) or 4 to 4½ hours (high)
makes: 6 to 8 servings

1½ cups chopped red and/or green sweet pepper (2 medium)
1 cup chopped onion (1 large)
1 cup chopped celery (2 stalks)
8 skinless, boneless chicken thighs, cut into bite-size pieces
1 tablespoon vegetable oil (optional)
1 pound smoked turkey sausage, cut lengthwise and sliced into ½-inch pieces
4 cloves garlic, minced
1 teaspoon dried thyme, crushed
1 teaspoon dried oregano, crushed
½ teaspoon salt
¼ to ½ teaspoon cayenne pepper
4 cups chicken broth

1 Place sweet pepper, onion, and celery in a 4- to 5-quart slow cooker. If desired, in a large skillet brown chicken, half at a time, in hot oil over medium heat. Place chicken and sausage on top of vegetables in cooker. Add garlic, thyme, oregano, salt, and cayenne pepper. Pour broth over all.

2 Cover and cook on low-heat setting for 8 to 9 hours or high-heat setting for 4 to 4½ hours.

3 Skim fat from soup before serving.

nutrition facts per serving: 273 cal., 12 g total fat (3 g sat. fat), 127 mg chol., 1629 mg sodium, 9 g carb., 1 g dietary fiber, 32 g protein.

While the plump cheesy tortellini cooks gently in the well-seasoned broth you'll have plenty of time to toss a green salad, which pairs nicely with this soup.

turkey tortellini soup

prep: 25 minutes   slow cook: 6 to 8 hours (low) or 3 to 4 hours (high)
+ 30 minutes (high)
makes: 6 servings

4   cups reduced-sodium
     chicken broth
4   cups water
4   cups coarsely chopped
     roasted turkey
     breast (1 pound)
1   14.5-ounce can
     no-salt-added
     diced tomatoes,
     undrained
1   tablespoon dried
     Italian seasoning,
     crushed
1   9-ounce package
     refrigerated cheese
     tortellini
2   cups fresh baby
     spinach
6   tablespoons shredded
     Parmesan cheese
     (optional)

1 In a 5- to 6-quart slow cooker combine broth, the water, turkey, undrained tomatoes, and Italian seasoning.

2 Cover and cook on low-heat setting for 6 to 8 hours or on high-heat setting for 3 to 4 hours. If using low-heat setting, turn to high-heat setting. Stir in tortellini. Cover and cook for 30 minutes more or until tortellini is tender. Stir in spinach. If desired, sprinkle each serving with 1 tablespoon cheese.

nutrition facts per serving: 240 cal., 3 g total fat (2 g sat. fat), 63 mg chol., 656 mg sodium, 25 g carb., 3 g dietary fiber, 28 g protein.

Although this recipe calls for white hominy, you could certainly use yellow or golden hominy as well. The color of the hominy simply reflects the color of the corn from which it was made.

smoked turkey chuckwagon soup

start to finish: 20 minutes
makes: 4 servings

2 14-ounce cans
   reduced-sodium
   chicken broth
1 15-ounce can white
   hominy, drained
1 11-ounce can
   condensed tomato
   rice soup
2 cups chopped
   smoked turkey
   (about 10 ounces)
½ cup chopped yellow
   sweet pepper
   (1 small)
⅓ cup bottled salsa
1 teaspoon ground
   cumin
1½ cups crushed tortilla
   chips (2½ ounces)
   Sour cream (optional)

1 In a large saucepan combine broth, hominy, tomato rice soup, turkey, sweet pepper, salsa, and cumin. Bring to boiling; reduce heat. Simmer, uncovered, for about 5 minutes or until sweet pepper is tender.

2 Top each serving with tortilla chips and, if desired, sour cream.

nutrition facts per serving: 318 cal., 10 g total fat (2 g sat. fat), 38 mg chol., 2013 mg sodium, 39 g carb., 5 g dietary fiber, 20 g protein.

The secret to this nicely thick corn and potato chowder is to mash some of the potatoes after cooking. Chopped cooked chicken can stand in for the turkey if you want variety.

turkey and sweet potato chowder

start to finish: 40 minutes
makes: 5 servings

1 large potato, peeled, if desired, and chopped (about 1½ cups)
1 14-ounce can reduced-sodium chicken broth
2 small ears frozen corn, thawed, or 1 cup loose-pack frozen whole-kernel corn
12 ounces cooked turkey breast, cut into ½-inch cubes (about 2¼ cups)
1½ cups fat-free milk
1 large sweet potato, peeled and cut into ¾-inch cubes (about 1½ cups)
⅛ to ¼ teaspoon ground black pepper
¼ cup coarsely snipped fresh parsley

1 In a 3-quart saucepan combine chopped potato and broth. Bring to boiling; reduce heat. Simmer, uncovered, about 12 minutes or until potato is tender, stirring occasionally. Remove from heat. Do not drain. Using a potato masher, mash potato until mixture is thickened and nearly smooth.

2 If using corn on the cob, cut the kernels from one of the ears of corn. Carefully cut the second ear of corn crosswise into ½-inch-thick slices.

3 Stir corn, turkey, milk, sweet potato, and pepper into potato mixture in saucepan. Bring to boiling; reduce heat. Cover and cook for 12 to 15 minutes or until the sweet potato is tender. Sprinkle each serving with parsley.

nutrition facts per serving: 216 cal., 1 g total fat (0 g sat. fat), 44 mg chol., 271 mg sodium, 29 g carb., 4 g dietary fiber, 23 g protein.

Slices of mushrooms, slivers of bok choy, and chunks of turkey mingle in a soy- and ginger-scented broth, giving stir-fry flavors to this savory soup.

asian turkey and rice soup

prep: 25 minutes   slow cook: 7 to 8 hours (low) or 3½ to 4 hours (high) + 10 minutes (high)
makes: 6 servings

2   14-ounce cans
      reduced-sodium
      chicken broth
1   pound turkey breast
      tenderloin or
      skinless, boneless
      chicken breast
      halves, cut into
      1-inch pieces
2   cups sliced fresh
      mushrooms, such as
      shiitake or button
1½ cups water
2   medium carrots, cut
      into bite-size strips
      (1 cup)
½   cup chopped onion
      (1 medium)
2   tablespoons low-
      sodium soy sauce
2   teaspoons grated
      fresh ginger
4   cloves garlic, minced
1½ cups sliced bok choy
1   cup instant brown
      rice
      Lo mein noodles
      (optional)

1 In a 3½- or 4-quart slow cooker stir together broth, turkey, mushrooms, the water, carrots, onion, soy sauce, ginger, and garlic.

2 Cover and cook on low-heat setting for 7 to 8 hours or on high-heat setting for 3½ to 4 hours.

3 If using low-heat setting, turn slow cooker to high-heat setting. Stir in bok choy and rice. Cover and cook for 10 to 15 minutes more or until rice is tender. If desired, top each serving with lo mein noodles.

nutrition facts per serving: 166 cal., 2 g total fat (0 g sat. fat), 45 mg chol., 572 mg sodium, 15 g carb., 2 g dietary fiber, 22 g protein.

*Double the recipe for the meatballs and freeze half for another meal.
They are especially delicious served over buttered noodles with
shaved Parmesan.*

alphabet soup with turkey meatballs

start to finish: 45 minutes   oven: at 350°F
makes: 6 servings

1   medium onion, sliced
3   cloves garlic, minced
2   teaspoons olive oil
1   cup dry white wine
     or reduced-sodium
     chicken broth
1   32-ounce carton
     reduced-sodium
     chicken broth
1½   cups water
1   recipe Turkey
     Meatballs
1   pound fresh
     asparagus spears,
     trimmed and cut
     into bite-size pieces
     (about 2 cups)
1   medium yellow
     and/or red sweet
     pepper, seeded and
     cut into bite-size
     pieces
1   cup dried alphabet-
     shape pasta
2   tablespoons snipped
     fresh basil or
     1 teaspoon dried
     Italian seasoning,
     crushed
     Salt
     Cracked black pepper
     Finely shredded
     Parmesan cheese
     (optional)

1 In a 4-quart Dutch oven cook onion and garlic in hot oil over medium-high heat about 5 minutes or until tender. Remove from heat. Add wine; return to heat. Bring to boiling; reduce heat. Simmer, uncovered, about 5 minutes or until wine is reduced by half. Add broth and the water. Return to boiling. Stir in Turkey Meatballs, asparagus, sweet pepper, pasta, and Italian seasoning (if using).

2 Simmer, covered, about 8 minutes or until pasta is tender but still firm. Stir in basil (if using). Season to taste with salt and black pepper.

3 If desired, sprinkle each serving with cheese.

nutrition facts per serving: 268 cal., 5 g total fat (1 g sat. fat), 27 mg chol., 565 mg sodium, 33 g carb., 3 g dietary fiber, 16 g protein.

turkey meatballs: Preheat oven to 350°F. Line a 15×10×1-inch baking pan with foil. Coat foil with nonstick cooking spray; set pan aside. In a medium bowl combine 8 ounces lean ground turkey, ⅓ cup seasoned fine dry bread crumbs, and pinch of cayenne pepper. If desired, stir in 1 teaspoon grated Parmesan cheese or 1 teaspoon low-sodium Worcestershire sauce. Shape turkey mixture into twenty-four 1-inch meatballs. Place meatballs in the prepared baking pan. Bake for 12 to 15 minutes, until no longer pink (165°F).

6

A simmering pot of chili will warm up any occasion; it's the quintessential food for both family meals and stress-free entertaining. However you like your chili—mild or spicy, meaty or strictly beans—these richly spiced recipes offer inspiring new ways to whip up the ultimate winter comfort food.

hot bowls of

ch

Calling all chili aficionados! Here's our favorite take on the traditional bowl of red with all the convenience of slow cooker cooking. Let everyone create their own version with the innovative topper ideas on pages 204–205.

all-american chili

prep: 10 minutes   **slow cook:** 6 hours (low) or 4 hours (high)
makes: 6 servings

1½ pounds lean ground
     beef
 2 15.5-ounce cans
     kidney beans,
     rinsed and drained
 1 14.5-ounce can diced
     tomatoes, drained
 1 cup chopped onion
     (1 large)
 1 8-ounce can no-salt-
     added tomato sauce
 1 cup reduced-sodium
     chicken broth
 ¾ cup chopped yellow
     sweet pepper
     (1 medium)
 3 tablespoons chili
     powder
 2 cloves garlic, minced
 1 teaspoon ground
     cumin
 1 teaspoon dried
     oregano, crushed
 ½ teaspoon salt
 1 8.5-ounce box corn
     bread mix, prepared
     according to
     package directions
     (optional)

1 In a 3½- or 4-quart slow cooker combine beef, beans, drained tomatoes, onion, tomato sauce, broth, sweet pepper, 2 tablespoons of the chili powder, garlic, ½ teaspoon of the cumin, and ½ teaspoon of the oregano.

2 Cover and cook on low-heat setting for 6 hours or on high-heat setting for 4 hours.

3 To serve, stir in remaining 1 tablespoon chili powder, remaining ½ teaspoon cumin, remaining ½ teaspoon oregano, and salt. Serve with corn bread.

nutrition facts per serving: 353 cal., 7 g total fat (3 g sat. fat), 71 mg chol., 710 mg sodium, 37 g carb., 13 g dietary fiber, 35 g protein.

The Chili Seasoning Puree in this chili boosts peppery flavor without being too hot and spicy. Dried plums sweeten and thicken the mix while balancing the spiciness.

game day chili

prep: 40 minutes **slow cook:** 6 to 7 hours (low) or 3 to 3½ hours (high)
makes: 8 servings

1½ pounds ground beef chuck

1 cup chopped onion (1 large)

½ cup sliced celery (1 stalk)

1 recipe Chili Seasoning Puree

1 28-ounce can diced tomatoes, undrained

1 14-ounce can beef broth

1½ cups pitted dried plums (prunes), chopped

1½ cups water

1 6-ounce can tomato paste

2 tablespoons smoked paprika

2 teaspoons ground coriander

1 teaspoon crushed red pepper flakes

¼ teaspoon ground cloves

1 ounce bittersweet chocolate, chopped

1 In a 6-quart Dutch oven cook ground beef, onion, and celery over medium-high heat until meat is brown and onion is tender, using a wooden spoon to break up meat as it cooks. Drain fat.

2 Transfer meat mixture to a 5- or 6-quart slow cooker. Stir in Chili Seasoning Puree, undrained tomatoes, broth, dried plums, the water, tomato paste, paprika, coriander, red pepper flakes, and cloves.

3 Cover and cook on low-heat setting for 6 to 7 hours or on high-heat setting for 3 to 3½ hours. Stir in chocolate.

nutrition facts per serving: 343 cal., 14 g total fat (5 g sat. fat), 58 mg chol., 702 mg sodium, 38 g carb., 7 g dietary fiber, 20 g protein.

*note: See tip on handling chile peppers, page 31.

chili seasoning puree: In a small bowl combine 2 dried ancho, mulato, or pasilla peppers and enough boiling water to cover. Let stand for 30 minutes; drain well. Remove stems and seeds from peppers.* In a food processor or blender combine the drained chile peppers, ¾ cup beef broth, 5 pitted dried plums (prunes), and 1 fresh jalapeño chile pepper, seeded and chopped.* Cover and process or blend until smooth.

If you have leftovers, create another meal by spooning this spunky chili over baked potatoes.

mexican chili

prep: 25 minutes slow cook: 8 to 10 hours (low) or 4 to 5 hours (high)
makes: 8 to 10 servings

1 pound lean ground beef
3 14.5-ounce cans Mexican-style stewed tomatoes, undrained and cut up
2 15.5-ounce cans red kidney beans, rinsed and drained
1 cup chopped celery (2 stalks)
1 cup finely chopped onion (2 medium)
1 cup water
1 6-ounce can tomato paste
1 4-ounce can diced green chile peppers, undrained
2 cloves garlic, minced
4 teaspoons chili powder
1 teaspoon ground cumin
1 cup shredded cheddar cheese (4 ounces)
½ cup sour cream
Fresh cilantro sprigs (optional)

1 In a large skillet cook ground beef until brown, using a wooden spoon to break up meat as it cooks. Drain fat.

2 Meanwhile, in a 4- to 6-quart slow cooker combine undrained tomatoes, beans, celery, onion, the water, tomato paste, undrained chile peppers, garlic, chili powder, and cumin. Stir in cooked ground beef.

3 Cover and cook on low-heat setting for 8 to 10 hours or on high-heat setting for 4 to 5 hours. Serve with shredded cheddar cheese and sour cream. If desired, garnish with cilantro.

nutrition facts per serving: 340 cal., 13 g total fat (7 g sat. fat), 56 mg chol., 695 mg sodium, 34 g carb., 9 g dietary fiber, 25 g protein.

Rich, chunky, and filled with fabulous flavor, this chipotle-flavored chili easily satisfies a large crowd. Add an extra sprinkle of cheese and a dollop of sour cream for a smooth finish.

chili for a crowd

prep: 30 minutes **slow cook:** 10 to 12 hours (low) or 5 to 6 hours (high)
makes: 10 to 12 servings

2   pounds boneless beef round steak or boneless pork shoulder, trimmed and cut into ½-inch cubes
2   large onions, chopped
2   large yellow, red, and/or green sweet peppers, chopped
2   15-ounce cans chili beans in chili gravy
2   14.5-ounce cans Mexican-style stewed tomatoes, undrained and cut up
1   15-ounce can kidney or pinto beans, rinsed and drained
1   cup beer or beef broth
1   to 2 tablespoons chopped canned chipotle peppers in adobo sauce*
2   teaspoons garlic salt
2   teaspoons ground cumin
1   teaspoon dried oregano, crushed

1 In a 5½- to 6-quart slow cooker combine meat, onions, sweet pepper, chili beans in chili gravy, undrained tomatoes, beans, beer, chile peppers, garlic salt, cumin, and oregano.

2 Cover and cook on low-heat setting for 10 to 12 hours or on high-heat setting for 5 to 6 hours. Spoon off fat.

nutrition facts per serving: 294 cal., 5 g total fat (1 g sat. fat), 52 mg chol., 823 mg sodium, 32 g carb., 8 g dietary fiber, 29 g protein.

*note: See tip on handling chile peppers, page 31.

tame the heat

If a spicy chili is too hot to take, counter its heat with a dairy product, such as a sour cream topping or a glass of milk.

Serve up your chili like they do in Cincinnati—heaped over swirls of spaghetti and topped with oodles of onions and cheese.

cincinnati chili

prep: 25 minutes **cook:** 20 minutes
makes: 6 servings

1   pound ground beef chuck
1   pound ground lamb or beef
½   cup chopped onion (1 medium)
2   cloves garlic, minced
2   tablespoons chili powder
1   teaspoon salt
½   teaspoon ground cumin
¼   teaspoon ground allspice
¼   teaspoon ground cinnamon
¼   teaspoon ground cloves
⅛   teaspoon cayenne pepper
1   28-ounce can crushed tomatoes
1   cup beef broth
1   ounce unsweetened chocolate, chopped
2   tablespoons honey
2   tablespoons cider vinegar
⅓   cup seeded and chopped roma tomato (1 medium)
¼   cup chopped green onion (2)
    Hot cooked spaghetti
    Grated cheddar cheese

1 In a Dutch oven cook ground beef, ground lamb, onion, and garlic over medium-high heat until meat is brown, using a wooden spoon to break up meat as it cooks. Drain fat. Stir in chili powder, salt, cumin, allspice, cinnamon, cloves, and cayenne pepper; cook and stir for 2 to 3 minutes or until fragrant.

2 Stir in crushed tomatoes, broth, chocolate, honey, and vinegar. Bring to boiling; reduce heat. Simmer, uncovered, for 20 to 30 minutes.

3 In a small bowl combine roma tomato and green onion. Serve chili over spaghetti and top each serving with roma tomato mixture and cheese.

nutrition facts per serving: 486 cal., 33 g total fat (14 g sat. fat), 107 mg chol., 836 mg sodium, 21 g carb., 5 g dietary fiber, 30 g protein.

If you love barbecue and you love chili, you'll love how they taste great together in one bowl!

barbecue chili

prep: 15 minutes cook: 1 hour
makes: 12 servings

1   tablespoon vegetable oil
1   pound lean ground beef
1   cup chopped onion (1 large)
¼   cup chili powder
1   tablespoon ground cumin
2   cloves garlic, minced
1   14.5-ounce can stewed tomatoes, undrained
1   cup ketchup
⅓   cup packed brown sugar*
¼   cup molasses
¼   cup Worcestershire sauce
1   tablespoon dry mustard
2   15.5-ounce cans dark red kidney beans, rinsed and drained
2   15.5-ounce cans pinto beans, rinsed and drained
1   15-ounce can cannellini (white kidney) beans, rinsed and drained
12   cooked bacon strips (optional)
     Jalapeño pepper strips (optional) **

1 In a large Dutch oven heat oil over medium-high heat. Add ground beef, onion, chili powder, cumin, and garlic; cook about 10 minutes or until meat is brown and onion is tender, using a wooden spoon to break up meat as it cooks.

2 Stir in undrained tomatoes, ketchup, brown sugar, molasses, Worcestershire sauce, and mustard. Bring to boiling; reduce heat. Simmer, covered, for 20 minutes, stirring occasionally. Stir in kidney beans, pinto beans, and cannellini beans. Return to boiling; reduce heat. Simmer, covered, for 30 minutes more.

3 If desired, garnish each serving with bacon and chile strips.

nutrition facts per serving: 343 cal., 6 g total fat (2 g sat. fat), 14 mg chol., 675 mg sodium, 53 g carb., 14 g dietary fiber, 20 g protein.

*note: You can substitute ⅓ cup granulated sugar plus 2 teaspoons molasses for the brown sugar.

**note: See tip on handling chile peppers, page 31.

178

This colorful chili's wow factor comes from a combo of butternut squash, fresh spinach, and dried cranberries, which add a hint of sweetness. Sprinkle servings with roasted pepitas (pumpkin seeds) for added crunch.

new world chili

prep: 25 minutes   **slow cook:** 10 to 12 hours (low) or 5 to 6 hours (high)
makes: 6 servings

1   pound turkey breast
    tenderloins, cut into
    1-inch pieces
1   28-ounce can
    diced tomatoes,
    undrained
1   15-ounce can black
    beans, rinsed and
    drained
1   8-ounce can tomato
    sauce
1   cup seeded, peeled,
    and cubed butternut
    squash
½   cup dried cranberries
½   cup chopped onion
    (1 medium)
½   cup frozen whole-
    kernel corn
½   cup chicken broth
1   jalapeño pepper,
    seeded and finely
    chopped*
1   tablespoon chili
    powder
1   clove garlic, minced
    Chicken broth
    (optional)
2   cups shredded fresh
    spinach leaves
1   cup shredded
    Monterey Jack
    cheese with jalapeño
    peppers (4 ounces)
    (optional)

1 In a 5-quart slow cooker combine turkey, undrained tomatoes, beans, tomato sauce, squash, dried cranberries, onion, frozen corn, ½ cup broth, chile pepper, chili powder, and garlic.

2 Cover and cook on low-heat setting for 10 to 12 hours or on high-heat setting for 5 to 6 hours. If desired, stir in additional broth to reach desired consistency.

3 Before serving, stir in spinach. If desired, sprinkle each serving with cheese.

nutrition facts per serving: 234 cal., 1 g total fat (0 g sat. fat), 47 mg chol., 776 mg sodium, 35 g carb., 8 g dietary fiber, 26 g protein.

*note: See tip on handling chile peppers, page 31.

Salsa, a time-saving ingredient, provides both the tomatoes and sauce for this meaty chili. Choose the type of salsa according to how spicy you like your chili.

easy texas-style chili

start to finish: 20 minutes
makes: 6 servings

12   ounces lean ground beef
1   15-ounce can pinto beans, undrained
1   cup bottled salsa
½   cup beef broth
1   teaspoon chili powder
½   teaspoon ground cumin

1 In a large skillet cook meat over medium heat until brown, using a wooden spoon to break up meat as it cooks. Drain fat.

2 Stir undrained beans, salsa, broth, chili powder, and cumin into meat. Bring to boiling; reduce heat. Simmer, covered, for 10 minutes.

nutrition facts per serving: 178 cal., 8 g total fat (3 g sat. fat), 36 mg chol., 442 mg sodium, 12 g carb., 4 g dietary fiber, 15 g protein.

three-bean chili

prep: 15 minutes   slow cook: 6 to 8 hours (low) or 3 to 4 hours (high)
makes: 4 servings

1   15-ounce can no-salt-added red kidney beans, rinsed and drained
1   15-ounce can small white beans, rinsed and drained
1   15-ounce can low-sodium black beans, rinsed and drained
1   14.5-ounce can diced tomatoes and green chiles, undrained
1   cup beer or chicken broth
3   tablespoons chocolate-flavor syrup
1   tablespoon chili powder
2   teaspoons Cajun seasoning

1 In a 3½- or 4-quart slow cooker combine kidney beans, white beans, black beans, undrained tomatoes, beer, chocolate syrup, chili powder, and Cajun seasoning.

2 Cover and cook on low-heat setting for 6 to 8 hours or on high-heat setting for 3 to 4 hours.

nutrition facts per serving: 308 cal., 1 g total fat (0 g sat. fat), 0 mg chol., 569 mg sodium, 60 g carb., 21 g dietary fiber, 21 g protein.

Longer cooking at a low temperature makes the blade steak wonderfully tender in this zesty beef and two-bean chili.

chipotle steak chili

prep: 30 minutes cook: 1 hour
makes: 8 servings

1½ pounds boneless beef shoulder top blade steak (flat iron)
1 tablespoon vegetable oil
2 cups chopped onion (2 large)
1 cup chopped green sweet pepper (2 small)
4 cloves garlic, minced
2 15- to 16-ounce cans kidney beans, pinto beans, and/or black beans, rinsed and drained
2 14.5-ounce cans diced tomatoes, undrained
1 15-ounce can tomato sauce
½ cup water
2 tablespoons chili powder
1 to 2 teaspoons chopped canned chipotle peppers in adobo sauce
1 teaspoon dried basil, crushed
½ teaspoon ground black pepper
    Shredded cheddar cheese (optional)

1 Trim fat from meat. Cut meat into ¾-inch pieces. In a 4-quart Dutch oven heat oil over medium heat. Add meat, half at a time; cook until brown. Remove meat, reserving drippings in Dutch oven. Add onion, sweet pepper, and garlic to drippings; cook until tender.

2 Return meat to Dutch oven. Stir beans, undrained tomatoes, tomato sauce, the water, chili powder, chile peppers, basil, and black pepper into meat mixture. Bring to boiling; reduce heat. Simmer, covered, about 1 hour or until meat is tender, stirring occasionally. If desired, top each serving with cheese.

nutrition facts per serving: 288 cal., 8 g total fat (3 g sat. fat), 54 mg chol., 639 mg sodium, 32 g carb., 8 g dietary fiber, 24 g protein.

This ground beef chili comes together in just 20 minutes. Letting it simmer for a couple hours yields intriguing spicy flavor. Hot cooked macaroni is a serve-along that makes this unique.

firehouse chili

prep: 20 minutes cook: 2 hours
makes: 10 servings

2   pounds lean ground
    beef
1   cup chopped onion
    (1 large)
1½ cups chopped celery
    (3 stalks)
3   cloves garlic, minced
1   30-ounce can chili
    beans, undrained
1   29-ounce can tomato
    sauce
1   28-ounce can stewed
    tomatoes, undrained
    and cut up
2   tablespoons chili
    powder
1   tablespoon bottled
    hot pepper sauce
    Hot cooked macaroni
    Sour cream (optional)
    Shredded cheddar
    cheese (optional)
    Sliced green onions
    (optional)
    Bottled hot pepper
    sauce (optional)

1 In a 6- to 8-quart Dutch oven cook meat, onion, celery and garlic until meat is brown and onion is tender, using a wooden spoon to break up meat as it cooks. Drain fat. Stir in undrained chili beans, tomato sauce, undrained tomatoes, chili powder, and 1 tablespoon hot pepper sauce. Bring to boiling; reduce heat. Simmer, covered, for 2 hours.

2 Serve chili over hot cooked macaroni. If you like, top each serving with sour cream, cheddar cheese, and green onions, and pass hot pepper sauce.

nutrition facts per serving: 433 cal., 15 g total fat (6 g sat. fat), 68 mg chol., 1251 mg sodium, 48 g carb., 7 g dietary fiber, 28 g protein.

Ancho chiles are actually dried poblano chile peppers that lend a sweet, earthy flavor and medium heat level to Mexican stews. Add a portion of the liquid from the tomatoes to the chiles to make blending easier.

spicy ancho chili with tomatillos

prep: 45 minutes cook: 1 hour
makes: 6 to 8 servings

2   11-ounce cans tomatillos, rinsed and drained
¾   cup lightly packed fresh cilantro leaves
3   dried ancho peppers, stemmed and seeded*
1   jalapeño pepper, seeded*
2   14.5-ounce cans whole or diced fire-roasted tomatoes, undrained
1½ pounds boneless beef chuck roast
    Salt
    Ground black pepper
2   tablespoons olive oil
2   cups chopped onion (2 large)
1   cup chopped green sweet pepper (2 small)
4   cloves garlic, minced
2   15-ounce cans kidney beans and/or black beans, rinsed and drained
1   cup frozen whole-kernel corn, thawed
2   tablespoons chili powder
1   teaspoon dried oregano, crushed
    Desired toppings, such as sliced avocado, sour cream, and/or shredded cheddar cheese

1 In a blender or food processor combine tomatillos, cilantro, ancho peppers, and jalapeño pepper. Cover and blend or process until smooth. Remove mixture from blender and set aside. Add undrained tomatoes to blender or food processor. Cover and blend or process until smooth; set aside.

2 Trim fat from meat. Cut meat into ½-inch pieces. Lightly sprinkle meat with salt and black pepper. In a Dutch oven cook half of the meat in 1 tablespoon of the hot oil over medium-high heat until brown. Remove from Dutch oven; drain fat. Cook remaining meat in remaining 1 tablespoon hot oil until nearly brown. Stir in onions, sweet peppers, and garlic; cook and stir until meat is brown and vegetables are tender. Drain fat. Return all meat to Dutch oven.

3 Stir in tomatillo mixture, pureed tomatoes, beans, corn, chili powder, and oregano. Bring to boiling; reduce heat. Simmer, covered, about 1 hour or until meat is tender and mixture is desired consistency.

4 Serve with desired toppings.

nutrition facts per serving: 651 cal., 30 g total fat (10 g sat. fat), 93 mg chol., 919 mg sodium, 54 g carb., 15 g dietary fiber, 49 g protein.

*note: See tip on handling chile peppers, page 31.

slow cooker directions: Prepare as directed through Step 2, except place meat mixture in a 5- to 6-quart slow cooker. Stir in the remaining ingredients. Cover and cook on low-heat setting for 8 to 10 hours or on high-heat setting for 4 to 5 hours. Serve with desired toppings.

Lean pork tenderloin cooks up tender in just 5 minutes. As for the simmered-all-day flavor, give credit to smoky chipotle chile peppers.

chunky beer-pork chili

start to finish: 30 minutes
makes: 4 servings

12   ounces pork
        tenderloin
2   teaspoons chili
        powder
2   teaspoons ground
        cumin
1   tablespoon canola oil
½   cup chopped onion
        (1 medium)
4   cloves garlic, minced
1   yellow or red sweet
        pepper, seeded
        and cut into ½-inch
        pieces
1   cup beer or reduced-
        sodium beef broth
¼   cup bottled picante
        sauce or salsa
2   to 3 teaspoons finely
        chopped canned
        chipotle pepper in
        adobo sauce*
1   15- to 16-ounce can
        small red beans or
        pinto beans, rinsed
        and drained
½   cup light sour cream
2   tablespoons snipped
        fresh cilantro

1 Trim fat from meat. Cut meat into ¾-inch pieces. Place meat in a medium bowl. Add chili powder and cumin; toss gently to coat. Set aside.

2 In large saucepan heat oil over medium heat. Add onion and garlic; cook and stir for 3 minutes. Add meat; cook and stir until meat is brown.

3 Stir in sweet pepper, beer, picante sauce, and chipotle chile pepper. Bring to boiling; reduce heat. Simmer, covered, about 5 minutes or until pork is tender. Stir in beans; heat through.

4 Top each serving with sour cream. Garnish with cilantro.

nutrition facts per serving: 313 cal., 9 g total fat (2 g sat. fat), 64 mg chol., 510 mg sodium, 29 g carb., 7 g dietary fiber, 27 g protein.

*note: See tip on handling chile peppers, page 31.

Venison—an extra-lean meat with a woody, almost fruity flavor— mingles with veggies and seven aromatic spices to deliver a knockout chili.

venison chili

prep: 45 minutes cook: 1 hour
makes: 6 servings

1½ pounds boneless
    venison leg or
    shoulder or boneless
    beef round steak
2   tablespoons canola oil
½   cup chopped onion
    (1 medium)
½   cup chopped celery
    (1 stalk)
3   cloves garlic, minced
1   jalapeño pepper,
    seeded and finely
    chopped*
1   tablespoon dried
    oregano, crushed,
    or 3 tablespoons
    snipped fresh
    oregano
4   teaspoons chili powder
4   teaspoons paprika
4   teaspoons ground
    cumin
½   teaspoon salt
½   teaspoon ground black
    pepper
1   cup dark beer or
    reduced-sodium beef
    broth
1   28-ounce can diced
    tomatoes, undrained
1½ cups chopped red
    sweet pepper
    (2 medium)
1   15-ounce can black
    beans, rinsed and
    drained, or 1½ cups
    cooked black beans
¼   cup lime juice
¼   cup snipped fresh
    cilantro
¼   cup snipped fresh
    parsley

1 Trim fat from meat. Cut meat into ½-inch pieces. In a 4- to 6-quart Dutch oven heat 1 tablespoon of the oil over medium-high heat. Add meat, half at a time; cook until brown. Using a slotted spoon, remove meat from Dutch oven; set aside. Drain fat.

2 In the same Dutch oven heat remaining 1 tablespoon oil over medium heat. Add onion, celery, garlic, jalapeño chile pepper, dried oregano (if using), chili powder, paprika, cumin, salt, and black pepper; cook and stir about 5 minutes or until vegetables are tender (mixture will be dry). Add beer; bring to boiling. Boil gently about 5 minutes or until liquid is reduced by about half, stirring occasionally. Add meat and undrained tomatoes. Return to boiling; reduce heat. Simmer, covered, for 45 to 60 minutes or until meat is tender.

3 Stir in red sweet pepper and black beans. Return to simmering. Cover and cook for 15 minutes more.

4 Stir in lime juice, cilantro, parsley, and fresh oregano (if using).

nutrition facts per serving: 302 cal., 8 g total fat (2 g sat. fat), 96 mg chol., 814 mg sodium, 26 g carb., 9 g dietary fiber, 32 g protein.

*note: See tip on handling chile peppers, page 31.

This beef chili packs a two-tomato wallop with both dried and canned tomatoes. Crushed red pepper adds bite, balanced by mild and sweet red and green peppers. Golden raisins are another element of surprise.

two-tomato stew chili

prep: 30 minutes cook: 1 hour
makes: 8 to 10 servings

1	8- to 8.5-ounce jar oil-packed dried tomatoes
2	pounds beef chuck, cut in 1-inch cubes
3	cups chopped onion (3 large)
6	cloves garlic, minced
1	cup chopped red sweet pepper (2 medium)
1	cup chopped green sweet pepper (2 medium)
1	cup coarsely chopped carrot (2 medium)
½	cup golden raisins
4	teaspoons ground cumin
½	to 1 teaspoon crushed red pepper flakes
1	4.5-ounce can diced green chiles, undrained
1	28-ounce can crushed tomatoes
2	cups water
¼	teaspoon salt
¼	teaspoon ground black pepper
8	ounces smoked mozzarella cheese, shredded

1 Drain dried tomatoes, reserving 2 tablespoons of the oil. Chop tomatoes; set aside. In a Dutch oven heat reserved oil over medium-high heat. Add beef, half at a time; cook until brown.

2 Return all beef to Dutch oven. Add onion, garlic, red sweet pepper, green sweet pepper, and carrot; cook for 2 minutes. Stir in chopped dried tomatoes, raisins, cumin, and red pepper flakes; cook for 2 minutes. Stir in undrained green chiles; cook for 1 minute. Add crushed tomatoes and the water; bring to boiling. Reduce heat to medium. Simmer, covered, for 1 to 1¼ hours, stirring occasionally, until meat is tender. Remove from heat. Add salt and pepper. Top with cheese.

nutrition facts per serving: 429 cal., 18 g total fat (7 g sat. fat), 82 mg chol., 676 mg sodium, 36 g carb., 7 g dietary fiber, 34 g protein.

Chili powder, curry powder, and ground cinnamon spice up the mix of apples, almonds, and cocoa powder in this tomato-laden meat and bean chili.

fruit and nut chili

prep: 40 minutes cook: 1 hour
makes: 8 servings

1½ pounds lean ground beef
2 cups chopped onion (2 large)
3 cloves garlic, minced
2 14.5-ounce cans tomatoes, undrained and cut up
1 15-ounce can tomato sauce
1 15-ounce can red kidney beans, rinsed and drained
1 14-ounce can chicken broth
2¼ cups chopped green, red, and/or yellow sweet pepper (3 medium)
2 cooking apples (such as Granny Smith or Jonathan), cored and chopped
2 4-ounce cans diced green chiles, drained
3 tablespoons chili powder
2 tablespoons unsweetened cocoa powder
1 tablespoon curry powder
1 teaspoon ground cinnamon
⅔ cup slivered almonds

1 In a 6-quart Dutch oven cook meat, onion, and garlic until meat is brown and onion is tender, using a wooden spoon to break up meat as it cooks. Drain fat.

2 Stir undrained tomatoes, tomato sauce, beans, and broth into meat mixture. Add sweet pepper, apples, drained chile peppers, chili powder, cocoa powder, curry powder, and cinnamon. Bring to boiling; reduce heat. Simmer, covered, for 1 hour.

3 Top each serving with almonds.

nutrition facts per serving: 357 cal., 16 g total fat (4 g sat. fat), 54 mg chol., 782 mg sodium, 34 g carb., 10 g dietary fiber, 26 g protein.

It's likely that there are as many versions of mole—a flavorful Mexican Indian sauce—as there are cooks in Mexico. Combining chili powder, cinnamon, and chocolate, we patterned the flavors in this intriguing chili after the brown version of mole.

mole-style pork and squash chili

prep: 30 minutes   cook: 30 minutes
makes: 6 servings

12   ounces boneless pork sirloin chops, cut ½ inch thick
½   cup chopped onion (1 medium)
2   cloves garlic, minced
2   tablespoons olive oil or vegetable oil
2   14.5-ounce cans stewed tomatoes, undrained
8   ounces butternut squash, peeled and cut into ½-inch cubes (about 1½ cups)
1   15-ounce can red kidney beans, rinsed and drained
1   15-ounce can black beans, rinsed and drained
1   cup frozen whole-kernel corn
1   cup water
1   tablespoon chili powder
1   tablespoon grated unsweetened chocolate
½   teaspoon ground cumin
¼   teaspoon ground cinnamon
¼   teaspoon dried oregano, crushed

1 Trim fat from meat. Cut meat into ½-inch pieces. In a Dutch oven cook and stir meat, onion, and garlic in hot oil over medium-high heat until meat is brown. Stir in undrained tomatoes, squash, beans, frozen corn, the water, chili powder, chocolate, cumin, cinnamon, and oregano.

2 Bring to boiling; reduce heat. Simmer, covered, about 30 minutes or until meat and squash are tender, stirring occasionally.

nutrition facts per serving: 289 cal., 9 g total fat (2 g sat. fat), 23 mg chol., 678 mg sodium, 41 g carb., 11 g dietary fiber, 20 g protein.

Mango adds a tropical note to this chili. Save a step by using a jar of refrigerated ready-to-eat mangoes from your grocer's produce section rather than a fresh mango. Drain and chop the mangoes and use about 1 cup in the chili; combine the remainder with chopped red onion for a sprightly topper.

caribbean pork chili

prep: 20 minutes slow cook: 4 to 5 hours (low) or 2 to 2½ hours (high)
makes: 6 servings

1½ pounds boneless pork loin roast
1 tablespoon chili powder
2 cloves garlic, minced
½ teaspoon ground chipotle chile pepper (optional)
½ teaspoon ground cumin
¼ teaspoon salt
1 tablespoon canola oil
2 14.5-ounce cans no-salt-added diced tomatoes, undrained
1 15-ounce can no-salt-added black beans, rinsed and drained
1 8-ounce can no-salt-added tomato sauce
1 cup frozen whole-kernel corn
1 medium mango, seeded, peeled, and chopped
¼ cup snipped fresh cilantro
¼ cup red onion shards (optional)

1 Trim fat from meat. Cut meat into 1-inch pieces. In a medium bowl combine meat, chili powder, garlic, ground chipotle pepper, if desired, cumin, and salt; toss to coat. In a large nonstick skillet heat oil over medium-high heat. Add meat, half at a time; cook until brown. Drain fat.

2 Transfer meat to a 3½- or 4-quart slow cooker. Add undrained tomatoes, beans, tomato sauce, and frozen corn.

3 Cover and cook on low-heat setting for 4 to 5 hours or on high-heat setting for 2 to 2½ hours.

4 In a small bowl combine mango, cilantro, and, if desired, onion shards. Top each serving with mango mixture.

nutrition facts per serving: 315 cal., 7 g total fat (2 g sat. fat), 78 mg chol., 246 mg sodium, 32 g carb., 8 g dietary fiber, 32 g protein.

Chorizo, a sausage spiked with chili powder and garlic, punctuates this Southwestern-style chili. Carrots, peppers, and grape tomatoes bring a lighter touch. Corn hominy is a tasty stand-in for beans.

hominy and chorizo chili

prep: 45 minutes   cook: 20 minutes
makes: 8 servings

1½   pounds fresh or
       1 pound hard
       (cured) chorizo
       sausage links*
¼   cup water
1   tablespoon olive oil
3   cups chopped onion
       (3 large)
6   cloves garlic, minced
1½   cups chopped carrot
       (3 medium)
¾   cup chopped green
       sweet pepper
       (1 large)
1   teaspoon fresh thyme
1   tablespoon chili
       powder
½   teaspoon smoked
       paprika
3   15-ounce cans hominy,
       rinsed and drained
1   14.5-ounce can
       reduced-sodium
       chicken broth
2   tablespoons tomato
       paste
2   cups grape tomatoes,
       halved
       Snipped fresh oregano

1 In a 12-inch skillet over medium-high heat, bring sausage and the water to boiling. Cook, covered, for 15 minutes, turning occasionally. Cook, uncovered, for 8 to 10 minutes more, turning to brown. Cool for 5 minutes on cutting board. Diagonally cut into ½-inch slices.

2 In a large Dutch oven heat oil over medium-high heat. Add onion, garlic, carrot, sweet pepper, and thyme; cook for 7 to 8 minutes, stirring occasionally, until almost tender. Stir in chili powder and paprika; cook for 30 seconds. Add cooked sausage; cook for 1 minute. Add hominy, broth, and tomato paste; bring to boiling. Reduce heat to medium. Simmer, covered, for 10 minutes, stirring occasionally. Stir in tomatoes; cook for 2 minutes, until tomatoes just begin to wilt. Top each serving with oregano.

nutrition facts per serving: 576 cal., 36 g total fat (13 g sat. fat), 75 mg chol., 1456 mg sodium, 37 g carb., 7 g dietary fiber, 25 g protein.

✳note: If you can only find the hard or "cured" kind of chorizo, cut it into ½-inch pieces. Skip the first step and sauté the chorizo in the oil in the Dutch oven, then add the vegetables and follow the recipe as directed except for the adding the sausage, which has already been done.

*Seeds and membranes give chile peppers
their kick. If you like your chili spicy hot,
use the seeds and membranes; leave
them out if mild chili fits your style.*

pork and poblano chili

prep: 25 minutes **slow cook:** 7 to 8 hours
(low) or 3½ to 4 hours (high)
makes: 6 to 8 servings

2   poblano peppers,
      halved and seeded*
1   green sweet pepper,
      halved and seeded
3   cloves garlic
1½ pounds lean ground
      pork
1   cup chopped onion
      (1 large)
2   15-ounce cans Great
      Northern beans,
      rinsed and drained
1   16-ounce jar mild or
      medium green salsa
      (salsa verde)
1   14.5-ounce can
      chicken broth
1½ teaspoons ground
      cumin
¼   cup snipped fresh
      cilantro
      Fresh cilantro leaves,
      sour cream, and/or
      red salsa (optional)
1   recipe Tortilla Strips
      (optional)

*note: See tip on handling
chile peppers, page 31.

1 In a food processor combine poblano chile
peppers, sweet pepper, and garlic. Cover
and process until finely chopped; set aside.
In a large skillet cook ground pork and onion
over medium-high heat until meat is brown
and onion is tender, using a wooden spoon to
break up meat as it cooks. Drain fat. Add pepper
mixture; cook and stir for 2 to 3 minutes or until
peppers are tender.

2 Transfer meat mixture to a 3½- or 4-quart
slow cooker. Stir in beans, green salsa,
broth, and cumin.

3 Cover and cook on low-heat setting for
7 to 8 hours or on high-heat setting for
3½ to 4 hours; cool slightly. If desired, mash
beans slightly with a potato masher.

4 Before serving, stir in snipped cilantro.
If desired, top each serving with cilantro
leaves, sour cream, and/or red salsa. If desired,
serve with Tortilla Strips.

nutrition facts per serving: 430 cal., 19 g total fat
(7 g sat. fat), 74 mg chol., 1152 mg sodium, 37 g carb.,
9 g dietary fiber, 27 g protein.

tortilla strips: Preheat oven to 350°F. Brush flour tortillas with
vegetable oil and sprinkle with chili powder. Cut tortillas into
½-inch strips. Place in a single layer on a baking sheet. Bake for
5 to 10 minutes or until golden and crisp; cool.

Satisfy your family with this hearty chili that includes bacon and beef. Top with cheese and cilantro for a delicious flavor twist.

winter woods chili

prep: 30 minutes cook: 2 hours
makes: 6 servings

4   slices bacon
3   pounds beef stew
      meat
1   large onion, sliced
      ½ inch thick
4   cloves garlic, minced
2   28-ounce cans
      whole tomatoes,
      undrained
1   15.5-ounce can navy
      beans, rinsed and
      drained
1   15.5-ounce can red
      beans, rinsed and
      drained
2   to 3 tablespoons chili
      powder
2   tablespoons red wine
      vinegar
    Salt
    Ground black pepper
    Shredded cheddar
      cheese
    Snipped fresh oregano
    Cooked bacon,
      crumbled

1 In 4- to 6-quart Dutch oven cook bacon and beef, half at a time, over medium heat until beef is brown. Drain fat. Reduce heat. Add onions and half of the garlic; cook and stir until onion is tender.

2 Add undrained tomatoes, beans, and 1 tablespoon of the chili powder. Bring to boiling; reduce heat. Simmer, covered, for 1 hour, stirring occasionally. Stir in remaining garlic, remaining chili powder, and vinegar. Cook, covered, for 1 hour. Add enough water for desired consistency. Season to taste with salt and pepper. Top each serving with cheese, oregano, and crumbled bacon.

nutrition facts per serving: 546 cal., 23 g total fat (9 g sat. fat), 107 mg chol., 1222 mg sodium, 31 g carb., 8 g dietary fiber, 54 g protein.

Rich, creamy, and packed with spicy flavors of Southeast Asia, this coconut milk–based chili is brimming with vegetables. Offer crusty bread for a complete meal.

coconut-chicken chili

prep: 30 minutes cook: 20 minutes
makes: 4 servings

12 ounces skinless, boneless chicken breast halves, chopped into bite-size pieces
1 cup chopped onion (1 large)
1½ teaspoons chili powder
1½ teaspoons ground ginger
½ teaspoon salt
½ teaspoon ground black pepper
¼ teaspoon cayenne pepper
1 tablespoon olive oil
1 tablespoon all-purpose flour
1 14-ounce can unsweetened coconut milk
1 tablespoon peanut butter
1 cup water
1 15- to 19-ounce can cannellini (white kidney) beans, rinsed and drained
1½ cups shredded carrot (3 medium)
½ cup sliced celery (1 stalk)
2 tablespoons sliced green onion
5 cloves garlic, minced
2 tablespoons chopped fresh basil
   Hot cooked jasmine rice
   Fresh basil leaves
   Sliced jalapeño peppers* (optional)

1 In a large saucepan cook chicken, onion, chili powder, ginger, salt, black pepper, and cayenne pepper in hot oil over medium heat for 6 to 8 minutes or until chicken is no longer pink. Stir in flour and cook for 1 minute more. Stir in coconut milk, peanut butter, and the water. Bring to boiling, stirring occasionally.

2 Stir in beans, carrot, celery, green onion, garlic, and chopped basil. Return to boiling; reduce heat. Simmer, covered, for 10 minutes. Serve with rice. If desired, top each serving with basil leaves and chile pepper.

nutrition facts per serving: 556 cal., 31 g total fat (22 g sat. fat), 49 mg chol., 890 mg sodium, 47 g carb., 11 g dietary fiber, 32 g protein.

*note: See tip on handling chile peppers, page 31.

Get ready for a fiesta with this richly satisfying Mexican-style meal, featuring fajita-spiced chicken, frozen sweet peppers and onions, and cannellini beans.

chicken fajita chili

prep: 25 minutes   **slow cook:** 4 to 5 hours (low) or 2 to 2½ hours (high)
makes: 6 servings

2   pounds skinless, boneless chicken breast halves, cut into 1-inch pieces
1   tablespoon chili powder
1   teaspoon fajita seasoning
2   cloves garlic, minced
½   teaspoon ground cumin
   Nonstick cooking spray
2   14.5-ounce cans no-salt-added diced tomatoes, undrained
1   16-ounce package frozen sweet pepper and onion stir-fry vegetables
1   19-ounce can cannellini (white kidney) beans, rinsed and drained
3   tablespoons shredded reduced-fat cheddar cheese (optional)
3   tablespoons light sour cream (optional)
3   tablespoons guacamole (optional)

1 In a medium bowl combine chicken, chili powder, fajita seasoning, garlic, and cumin; toss gently to coat.

2 Coat a large skillet with cooking spray; heat skillet over medium-high heat. Add chicken, half at a time; cook until brown, stirring occasionally. Transfer chicken mixture to a 3½- or 4-quart slow cooker. Stir in undrained tomatoes, frozen vegetables, and beans.

3 Cover and cook on low-heat setting for 4 to 5 hours or on high-heat setting for 2 to 2½ hours. If desired, top each serving with cheese, sour cream, and guacamole.

nutrition facts per serving: 261 cal., 2 g total fat (1 g sat. fat), 88 mg chol., 294 mg sodium, 22 g carb., 7 g dietary fiber, 41 g protein.

This off-the-shelf chili relies on jars of salsa, cans of beans, and frozen chicken for its super-quick prep.

chicken-salsa chili

prep: 15 minutes cook: 20 minutes
makes: 6 servings

1 16-ounce jar thick and chunky salsa
1 15-ounce can yellow hominy or garbanzo beans (chickpeas), rinsed and drained
1 15-ounce can dark red kidney beans or black beans, rinsed and drained
1 14-ounce can chicken broth
1 9-ounce package (2 cups) frozen diced cooked chicken
1 4-ounce can diced green chiles
1 tablespoon chili powder
2 teaspoons bottled minced garlic or ½ teaspoon garlic powder
¼ to ½ teaspoon crushed red pepper flakes
¼ cup snipped fresh cilantro
2 tablespoons lime juice
Sour cream or plain low-fat yogurt (optional)
Chopped red onion and/or sliced green onion (optional)
Shredded sharp cheddar cheese (optional)
Chopped avocado (optional)

1 In a 4-quart Dutch oven combine salsa, hominy, beans, broth, chicken, chile peppers, chili powder, garlic, and red pepper flakes. Bring to boiling; reduce heat. Simmer, covered, for 20 minutes.

2 Just before serving, stir in cilantro and lime juice. If desired, top each serving with sour cream, red onion, cheese, and/or avocado.

nutrition facts per serving: 190 cal., 2 g total fat (0 g sat. fat), 23 mg chol., 1200 mg sodium, 27 g carb., 7 g dietary fiber, 17 g protein.

more chili, please!

Next time you're lucky enough to have leftover chili, try one of these quick and simple ideas for another busy weeknight supper.

- chili mac: *Combine equal parts chili and prepared macaroni and cheese. Bake until heated through. Top with chopped fresh tomatoes.*

- chili pie: *Prepare a package of corn bread mix. Pour the batter over the top of chili in a baking dish and sprinkle with cheese. Bake according to corn bread package directions.*

- chili scramble: *Use chili as a topping for scrambled eggs. Sprinkle with snipped fresh cilantro.*

- chili tators: *Top baked potatoes with chili, shredded Monterey Jack cheese, and a mixture of sour cream and chopped fresh cilantro.*

Brimming with tender chicken and white kidney beans, this fiery slow cooker favorite owes its bold flavor to a zesty mix of cumin, oregano, garlic, and chile peppers.

white chicken chili

prep: 25 minutes slow cook: 8 to 10 hours (low) or 4 to 5 hours (high)
makes: 6 servings

3   15-ounce cans Great
    Northern, pinto, or
    cannellini (white
    kidney) beans,
    rinsed and drained
2½ cups chopped cooked
    chicken
1½ cups chopped red,
    green, and/or yellow
    sweet pepper
    (2 medium)
1   cup chopped onion
    (1 large)
2   jalapeño peppers,
    seeded and
    chopped*
2   teaspoons ground
    cumin
2   cloves garlic, minced
½   teaspoon salt
½   teaspoon dried
    oregano, crushed
3½ cups chicken broth
    Shredded Monterey
    Jack cheese
    (optional)
    Broken tortilla chips
    (optional)

1 In a 3½- or 4-quart slow cooker combine beans, chicken, sweet pepper, onion, chile peppers, cumin, garlic, salt, and oregano. Pour broth over all.

2 Cover and cook on low-heat setting for 8 to 10 hours or on high-heat setting for 4 to 5 hours.

3 If desired, top each serving with cheese and/or tortilla chips.

nutrition facts per serving: 422 cal., 6 g total fat (2 g sat. fat), 52 mg chol., 709 mg sodium, 54 g carb., 13 g dietary fiber, 38 g protein.

*note: See tip on handling chile peppers, page 31.

This hearty vegetarian chili is packed with nutrient-rich veggies and grains. It's also delicious topped with nonfat plain yogurt and baked corn chips.

sweet potato and barley chili

prep: 20 minutes slow cook: 6 to 7 hours (low) or 3 to 3½ hours (high)
makes: 6 servings

1 28-ounce can crushed tomatoes
1 15-ounce can red beans, rinsed and drained
1 14.5-ounce can chicken broth
1 medium sweet potato, peeled and cut into 1-inch pieces
¾ cup chopped red sweet pepper (1 medium)
½ cup chopped onion (1 medium)
½ cup regular barley
½ cup water
1 tablespoon chili powder
1 tablespoon lime juice
3 cloves garlic, minced
1 teaspoon ground cumin
½ teaspoon salt
½ teaspoon dried oregano, crushed
¼ teaspoon ground black pepper
   Snipped fresh cilantro (optional)
   Lime wedges (optional)

1 In a 3½- or 4-quart slow cooker combine tomatoes, beans, broth, sweet potato, sweet pepper, onion, barley, the water, chili powder, lime juice, garlic, cumin, salt, oregano, and black pepper.

2 Cover and cook on low-heat setting for 6 to 7 hours or on high-heat setting for 3 to 3½ hours.

3 If desired, top each serving with cilantro and serve with lime wedges.

nutrition facts per serving: 198 cal., 1 g total fat (0 g sat. fat), 1 mg chol., 930 mg sodium, 41 g carb., 11 g dietary fiber, 9 g protein.

Rustic and rich in deep flavors, this hearty chili satisfies big appetites with complete vegetarian protein from the combination of rice and beans.

sassy bean and brown rice chili

prep: 25 minutes slow cook: 7 to 8 hours (low) or 3½ to 4 hours (high)
makes: 6 servings

2 cups reduced-sodium vegetable broth
2 cups water
1 16-ounce jar picante sauce
1 15-ounce can no-salt-added pinto or red kidney beans, rinsed and drained
1 15-ounce can no-salt-added black beans, rinsed and drained
1 15-ounce can no-salt-added garbanzo beans (chickpeas), rinsed and drained
¾ cup brown rice
1 4-ounce can diced green chiles, undrained
½ cup chopped onion (1 medium)
2 tablespoons chili powder
1 tablespoon unsweetened cocoa powder
2 cloves garlic, minced
⅓ cup plain fat-free yogurt
⅓ cup crumbled cotija cheese or shredded reduced-fat Monterey Jack cheese (optional)
¼ cup roasted pumpkin seeds (pepitas)

1 In a 3½- or 4-quart slow cooker combine broth, the water, picante sauce, pinto beans, black beans, garbanzo beans, brown rice, chile peppers, onion, chili powder, cocoa powder, and garlic.

2 Cover and cook on low-heat setting for 7 to 8 hours or on high-heat setting for 3½ to 4 hours.

3 Top each serving with yogurt and sprinkle with cheese and pumpkin seeds.

nutrition facts per serving: 415 cal., 11 g total fat (1 g sat. fat), 11 mg chol., 937 mg sodium, 61 g carb., 12 g dietary fiber, 22 g protein.

Frozen hash brown potatoes and zucchini are the surprise ingredients in this meatless chili. Polenta makes a pleasant alternative to traditional corn bread

vegetarian chili with polenta

prep: 20 minutes   cook: 20 minutes
makes: 4 servings

1 tablespoon olive oil
½ cup chopped onion (1 medium)
1 cup loose-pack frozen hash brown potatoes
1 cup chopped zucchini
1 10-ounce can diced tomatoes and green chiles, undrained
1 8-ounce can tomato sauce
2 teaspoons chili powder
2 cloves garlic, minced
1 15- to 16-ounce can kidney beans, rinsed and drained
1 16-ounce tube refrigerated cooked polenta, cut into 8 slices
½ cup shredded Monterey Jack cheese (2 ounces)
 Sour cream (optional)

1 In a large skillet heat oil over medium heat. Add onion; cook and stir until tender. Stir in potatoes, zucchini, undrained tomatoes and chiles, tomato sauce, chili powder, and garlic. Bring to boiling; reduce heat. Simmer, covered, for 15 minutes. Stir in beans. Simmer, uncovered, for 5 minutes more or to reach desired consistency.

2 Meanwhile, prepare polenta according to package directions. Serve with chili. Sprinkle with cheese. If desired, top each serving with sour cream.

nutrition facts per serving: 350 cal., 9 g total fat (3 g sat. fat), 15 mg chol., 1251 mg sodium, 58 g carb., 12 g dietary fiber, 17 g protein.

Once you cut up the vegetables for this meatless chili, your slow cooker will do the rest of the work. Select mild, medium, or hot salsa to adjust the level of heat.

garden chili

prep: 20 minutes slow cook: 8 to 10 hours (low) or 4 to 5 hours (high)
makes: 6 servings

1   zucchini, halved
    lengthwise and cut
    into ½-inch pieces
¾   cup coarsely chopped
    green sweet pepper
    (1 medium)
½   cup chopped onion
    (1 medium)
½   cup thinly sliced
    celery (1 stalk)
2   to 3 teaspoons chili
    powder
1   teaspoon dried
    oregano, crushed
½   teaspoon ground
    cumin
2   14.5-ounce cans
    diced tomatoes,
    undrained
1   15-ounce can black
    beans, rinsed and
    drained
1   10-ounce package
    frozen whole-kernel
    corn
1   cup salsa
¾   cup shredded
    cheddar cheese
    (3 ounces)
⅓   cup sour cream

1 In a 3½- to 5-quart slow cooker combine zucchini, sweet pepper, onion, celery, chili powder, oregano, and cumin. Stir in undrained tomatoes, beans, frozen corn, and salsa.

2 Cover and cook on low-heat setting for 8 to 10 hours or on high-heat setting for 4 to 5 hours.

3 Top each serving with cheese and sour cream.

nutrition facts per serving: 203 cal., 6 g total fat (3 g sat. fat), 15 mg chol., 598 mg sodium, 32 g carb., 7 g dietary fiber, 11 g protein.

Red lentils blend right in with classic chili ingredients—diced tomatoes, kidney beans, and chopped veggies—in this hearty meatless dish. It easily feeds a large crowd, and it freezes beautifully.

big-batch red lentil chili

prep: 15 minutes cook: 35 minutes
makes: 12 servings

4 14.5-ounce cans diced tomatoes, undrained
2 15-ounce cans red kidney beans, rinsed and drained
3 cups water
1 12-ounce package frozen chopped green sweet pepper
1 12-ounce package frozen chopped onion
2 cups dried red lentils, rinsed and drained
¼ cup chili powder
2 tablespoons garlic powder
1 8-ounce can tomato sauce
1 6-ounce can tomato paste
⅛ teaspoon ground black pepper
2 cups shredded cheddar cheese (8 ounces)
   Tortilla chips (optional)

1 In an 8-quart Dutch oven combine undrained tomatoes, beans, the water, frozen sweet pepper, frozen onion, lentils, chili powder, and garlic powder. Bring to boiling; reduce heat. Simmer, covered, for 30 minutes, stirring occasionally.

2 Stir in tomato sauce, tomato paste, and black pepper; heat through. Serve with shredded cheese and, if desired, tortilla chips.

nutrition facts per serving: 314 cal., 7 g total fat (4 g sat. fat), 20 mg chol., 752 mg sodium, 47 g carb., 19 g dietary fiber, 21 g protein.

Two kinds of beans plus five vegetables yield a warming and surprisingly substantial meatless dinner.

spicy vegetable chili

prep: 30 minutes **slow cook:** 9 to 10 hours (low) or 4½ to 5 hours (high)
makes: 10 to 12 servings

2   28-ounce cans diced tomatoes, undrained
2   15-ounce cans dark red kidney beans, rinsed and drained
2   15-ounce cans pinto beans, rinsed and drained
2   cups chopped onion (2 large)
1   15.25-ounce can whole-kernel corn, drained
1½ cups chopped green sweet pepper (2 medium)
1   cup chopped celery (2 stalks)
1   cup water
1   6-ounce can tomato paste
2   tablespoons chili powder
8   cloves garlic, minced
1   tablespoon Worcestershire sauce
1   teaspoon ground cumin
1   teaspoon dried oregano, crushed
1   teaspoon bottled hot pepper sauce
¼   teaspoon cayenne pepper (optional)
    Sour cream (optional)

1 In a 6- to 7-quart slow cooker combine undrained tomatoes, beans, onion, frozen corn, sweet pepper, celery, the water, tomato paste, chili powder, garlic, Worcestershire sauce, cumin, oregano, hot pepper sauce, and, if desired, cayenne pepper.

2 Cover and cook on low-heat setting for 9 to 10 hours or on high-heat setting for 4½ to 5 hours.

3 If desired, top each serving with sour cream.

nutrition facts per serving: 244 cal., 2 g total fat (0 g sat. fat), 0 mg chol., 916 mg sodium, 49 g carb., 12 g dietary fiber, 13 g protein.

Toasting the cumin seeds intensifies their flavor, which gives the chili a rich, nutty taste.

white bean and toasted cumin chili

prep: 20 minutes slow cook: 9 to 10 hours (high) or 4½ to 5 hours (low)
makes: 4 servings

2   14.5-ounce cans tomatoes, undrained and cut up
1   12-ounce can beer or nonalcoholic beer
1   cup chopped onion (1 large)
3   cloves garlic, minced
1   canned chipotle pepper in adobo sauce, chopped*
1   tablespoon cumin seeds, toasted and crushed**
1   teaspoon sugar
½   teaspoon salt
2   19-ounce cans cannellini (white kidney) beans, rinsed and drained
1½ cups peeled, seeded, and coarsely chopped Golden Nugget or acorn squash (about 12 ounces)
½   cup sour cream
2   tablespoons lime juice
1   tablespoon snipped fresh chives
    Whole fresh chives (optional)
    Lime wedges (optional)

1 In a 3½- or 4-quart slow cooker stir together undrained tomatoes, beer, onion, garlic, chile pepper, cumin seeds, sugar, and salt. Stir in beans and squash.

2 Cover and cook on low-heat setting for 9 to 10 hours or on high-heat setting for 4½ to 5 hours.

3 In a small bowl stir together sour cream, lime juice, and snipped chives. Top each serving with sour cream mixture. If desired, garnish with whole chives and lime wedges.

nutrition facts per serving: 327 cal., 7 g total fat (3 g sat. fat), 11 mg chol., 1070 mg sodium, 60 g carb., 16 g dietary fiber, 20 g protein.

*note: See tip on handling chile peppers, page 31.

**note: To toast cumin seeds, place seeds in a dry skillet over low heat. Cook about 8 minutes or until fragrant, stirring often. Remove from heat; let cool. To crush the toasted seeds, use a spice grinder or a mortar and pestle.

1

2

10

10 chili toppers **to try**

For a crowd-pleasing chili buffet, serve up All-American Chili (recipe, page 172) and set out a variety of toppers so everyone can create his or her own one-of-a-kind bowl.

1 Cheese and Nuts: Sprinkle chili with shredded Monterey Jack cheese, chopped lime-and-chili-flavor almonds or chopped toasted almonds, and snipped fresh herb.

2 Bacon and Onion: Top chili with crisp-cooked bacon and onion slices.

3 Jicama and Radish: Top chili with slivered jicama, slivered radishes, and finely shredded lime zest. Drizzle with fresh lime juice and sprinkle with cayenne pepper.

4 Popcorn: Top chili with popped popcorn seasoned with taco seasoning mix.

5 Avocado-Tomato Salsa: Top chili with peeled, seeded, and chopped avocado tossed with lime juice; quartered cherry tomatoes; and seeded and chopped jalapeño chile pepper.*

9

8

6 Fried Tortilla Crisps: Cut flour or corn tortillas into ½-inch strips. Fry strips in vegetable oil until crisp and golden; sprinkle strips with ground cumin. Top chili with strips.

7 Mango and Green Onions: Top chili with fresh mango and sliced green onions.

8 Cilantro Sour Cream: Combine one 8-ounce carton sour cream and ¼ cup snipped fresh cilantro. Top chili with sour cream mixture.

9 Jalapeño and Cheese: Top chili with shredded Chihuahua or cheddar cheese and sliced pickled jalapeño peppers.

10 Corn Bread Croutons: Cut an 8-inch square pan of baked corn bread into ¾-inch cubes. Spread cubes in an even layer in a 15×10×1-inch baking pan. Bake at 350°F for 8 minutes. Toss the cubes with ¼ cup melted butter. Bake for 2 minutes more; cool. Top chili with croutons and shredded cheddar cheese.

*note: See tip on handling chile peppers, page 31.

dumpling

deli

7

If you think dumplings are something only your grandmother had the time and talent to make, think again! These light and fluffy toppers stir together quickly and puff up magically in soups and stews your family will love.

ghts

Corn muffin mix is the secret for these quick-to-fix dumplings. If you have a round rather than an oval slow cooker, bake the extra dumpling batter in the oven to make two or three muffins.

chili with cheesy corn bread dumplings

prep: 25 minutes slow cook: 8 to 10 hours (low) or 4 to 5 hours (high)
+ 25 minutes (high)
makes: 6 to 8 servings

1 pound boneless beef round steak or boneless pork shoulder, trimmed and cut into ½-inch cubes
½ cup chopped onion (1 medium)
¾ cup chopped green, red, or yellow sweet pepper (1 medium)
1 15-ounce can chili beans with chili gravy
1 15-ounce can kidney or pinto beans, rinsed and drained
1 14.5-ounce can Mexican-style stewed tomatoes, undrained and cut up
1 cup beef broth
1 to 2 teaspoons chopped canned chipotle peppers in adobo sauce*
1 teaspoon ground cumin
¾ teaspoon garlic salt
½ teaspoon dried oregano, crushed
1 recipe Corn Bread Dumplings
  Shredded cheddar cheese
  Green onion strips (optional)

1 In a 3½- or 4-quart slow cooker stir together meat, onion, sweet pepper, chili beans with chili gravy, beans, undrained tomatoes, broth, chipotle chile pepper, cumin, garlic salt, and oregano.

2 Cover and cook on low-heat setting for 8 to 10 hours or on high-heat setting for 4 to 5 hours.

3 If using low-heat setting, turn to high-heat setting. If you have an oval slow cooker, drop all of the Corn Bread Dumplings batter onto the bubbling mixture in slow cooker. (If you have a round cooker, preheat oven to 400°F. Drop half of the Corn Bread Dumplings batter onto the bubbling mixture. Spoon remaining batter into two or three greased muffin cups. Bake for 15 to 18 minutes or until a toothpick inserted in the center comes out clean.)

4 Cover cooker and cook for 20 to 25 minutes more or until a toothpick inserted into dumplings comes out clean. Top individual servings with shredded cheddar cheese. If desired, garnish with green onion strips.

nutrition facts per serving: 529 cal., 17 g total fat (6 g sat. fat), 101 mg chol., 1256 mg sodium, 61 g carb., 9 g dietary fiber, 35 g protein.

*note: See tip on handling chile peppers, page 31.

corn bread dumplings: In a large bowl combine one 8.5-ounce package corn muffin mix; ½ cup shredded cheddar cheese, Monterey Jack cheese, or Mexican cheese blend (2 ounces); and ¼ cup sliced green onion. In a small bowl beat 1 egg with a fork. Stir in ¼ cup sour cream. Stir egg mixture into corn muffin mixture.

Greet the first days of autumn with a steaming meal-in-a-bowl topped with cheesy corn bread muffins. For perfect dumplings, resist the urge to lift the lid and peek while they simmer.

beef stew with cornmeal–green onion dumplings

prep: 30 minutes cook: 1 hour 40 minutes
makes: 8 servings

1 tablespoon vegetable oil
2 pounds beef stew meat
1 28-ounce can diced tomatoes, undrained
1 cup beef broth
¼ cup coarse-grain Dijon-style mustard
2 cloves garlic, minced
1 teaspoon dried thyme, crushed
½ teaspoon salt
½ teaspoon dried oregano, crushed
½ teaspoon ground black pepper
1 20-ounce package refrigerated diced potatoes with onion
1 cup peeled baby carrots
1 9-ounce package frozen cut green beans
1 recipe Cornmeal–Green Onion Dumplings

1 In a 4-quart Dutch oven heat oil over medium heat. Add meat, half at a time; cook until brown. Return all meat to pan. Add undrained tomatoes, broth, mustard, garlic, thyme, salt, oregano, and pepper. Bring to boiling; reduce heat. Simmer, covered, for 1 hour.

2 Add potatoes and carrots. Return to boiling; reduce heat. Simmer, covered, for 20 minutes. Stir in frozen green beans. Return to boiling; reduce heat.

3 Using two spoons, drop Cornmeal–Green Onion Dumplings dough in small mounds onto hot stew. Cook, covered, about 20 minutes more or until a toothpick inserted into a dumpling comes out clean. (Do not lift cover during cooking.)

nutrition facts per serving: 446 cal., 13 g total fat (4 g sat. fat), 104 mg chol., 1092 mg sodium, 47 g carb., 4 g dietary fiber, 33 g protein.

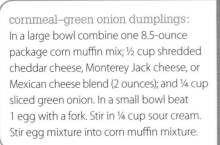

cornmeal–green onion dumplings:
In a large bowl combine one 8.5-ounce package corn muffin mix; ½ cup shredded cheddar cheese, Monterey Jack cheese, or Mexican cheese blend (2 ounces); and ¼ cup sliced green onion. In a small bowl beat 1 egg with a fork. Stir in ¼ cup sour cream. Stir egg mixture into corn muffin mixture.

*Savor extra-light dumplings that cook on top of a carrot-
and corn-filled bubbling chowder.*

chicken chowder
with dilly dumplings

start to finish: 40 minutes
makes: 4 servings

1 tablespoon vegetable
   oil
1 pound skinless,
   boneless chicken
   thighs, cut into
   1-inch pieces
1 cup all-purpose flour
1 teaspoon baking
   powder
½ teaspoon kosher
   salt or ¼ teaspoon
   regular salt
2 tablespoons
   shortening
1 tablespoon snipped
   fresh chives
2 teaspoons snipped
   fresh dill or ¾
   teaspoon dried dill
¼ cup plain yogurt
¼ cup milk
3 cups reduced-sodium
   chicken broth
1 cup sliced leek or
   chopped onion*
1 cup chopped carrot
   (2 medium)
1 cup frozen whole-
   kernel corn
1 teaspoon snipped
   fresh dill or ½
   teaspoon dried dill
2 tablespoons all-
   purpose flour
½ cup half-and-half
   or light cream

1 In a large saucepan heat oil over medium
heat. Add chicken; cook and stir until
chicken is brown and no longer pink. Using a
slotted spoon, remove chicken from saucepan;
set aside. Drain fat.

2 Meanwhile, for dumplings, in a medium
bowl combine 1 cup flour, baking powder,
and half of the salt. Cut in shortening until
mixture resembles coarse crumbs. Stir in
chives and 2 teaspoons dill. Add yogurt and
milk, stirring just until moistened; set aside.

3 In the same saucepan combine broth, leek,
carrot, frozen corn, 1 teaspoon dill, and
remaining salt. Bring to boiling; reduce heat.
Drop dumpling batter into simmering liquid,
making 8 mounds. Return to a gentle boil;
reduce heat. Cover and simmer for 12 to 15
minutes or until a wooden toothpick inserted
into dumplings comes out clean. (Do not lift
lid during cooking.) Using a slotted spoon,
transfer dumplings to a platter.

4 Stir chicken into mixture in saucepan.
Stir 2 tablespoons flour into half-and-half.
Stir flour mixture into the mixture in saucepan;
cook and stir over medium heat until mixture
is thickened and bubbly. Cook and stir for
1 minute more.

5 Top each serving with 2 dumplings.

nutrition facts per serving: 479 cal., 19 g total fat
(6 g sat. fat), 107 mg chol., 914 mg sodium, 46 g carb.,
3 g dietary fiber, 32 g protein.

*note: See tip on cleaning leeks, page 464.

Old-time recipes called for roasting the chicken, stirring together the soup base, and making dumpling batter by hand. Today's up-to-date version relies on convenient deli-roasted chicken, frozen veggies, condensed soup, and refrigerated corn bread twists.

easy chicken and dumplings

prep: 25 minutes cook: 15 minutes
makes: 4 to 6 servings

1 **2- to 2½-pound deli-roasted chicken**

1 **16-ounce package frozen mixed vegetables**

1¼ **cups reduced-sodium chicken broth or water**

1 **10.75-ounce can condensed cream of chicken soup**

⅛ **teaspoon ground black pepper**

1 **11.5-ounce package refrigerated corn bread twists**

1 Remove string from chicken, if present. Remove and discard skin from chicken. Remove meat from bones. Chop or shred chicken (you should have 3½ to 4 cups chopped chicken). In a large saucepan stir together chicken, frozen vegetables, broth, cream of chicken soup, and pepper. Bring to boiling; reduce heat. Simmer, covered, about 15 minutes or until vegetables are tender.

2 Meanwhile, remove corn bread twists from package; cut along perforations. Lay twists on a baking sheet; roll 2 twists together to make a spiral. Repeat with remaining twists. Bake according to package directions.

3 Spoon chicken mixture into bowls. Top each serving with corn bread spirals.

nutrition facts per serving: 683 cal., 32 g total fat (9 g sat. fat), 106 mg chol., 1553 mg sodium, 56 g carb., 5 g dietary fiber, 44 g protein.

A refreshing hint of citrus accents thyme, sage, and marjoram in these tender dumplings.

chicken with lemon-thyme dumplings

prep: 35 minutes cook: 10 minutes
makes: 4 servings

¼ cup butter
¼ cup all-purpose flour
2½ cups chicken stock
    or broth
1 cup cake flour or
    all-purpose flour
1 teaspoon baking
    powder
½ teaspoon snipped
    fresh thyme or
    ⅛ teaspoon dried
    thyme, crushed
½ teaspoon sugar
¼ teaspoon salt
    Pinch white pepper
    Pinch ground sage
    Pinch dried marjoram,
    crushed
½ cup milk
1 teaspoon finely
    shredded lemon zest
1 pound skinless,
    boneless chicken
    breasts, cut into
    1-inch pieces
2 cups chicken stock
    or broth
¼ cup dry white wine,
    chicken stock,
    or broth
1 cup chopped celery
    (2 stalks)
1 cup chopped carrot
    (2 medium)
1 cup chopped, peeled
    celeriac or chopped,
    peeled potato
1 teaspoon snipped
    fresh thyme or
    ¼ teaspoon dried
    thyme, crushed

1 For sauce, in a small saucepan melt butter. Stir in ¼ cup flour. Cook and stir over medium heat for 3 minutes. Stir in 2½ cups stock. Simmer gently, uncovered, for 20 minutes, stirring often. Set aside.

2 Meanwhile, for dumplings, in a medium mixing bowl stir together 1 cup flour, baking powder, ½ teaspoon thyme, sugar, salt, white pepper, sage, and marjoram. Add milk and lemon zest; stir until just moistened. Set aside.

3 In a 3-quart saucepan combine chicken pieces, 2 cups stock, wine, celery, carrot, celeriac, and 1 teaspoon thyme. Bring to boiling. Reduce heat; let simmer.

4 Using a small ice-cream scoop or 2 spoons, drop dumpling batter onto simmering liquid, making 8 mounds. Simmer, covered, for about 10 minutes or until chicken is no longer pink and a wooden toothpick inserted into dumplings comes out clean. (Do not lift lid during cooking.)

5 Using a slotted spoon, remove dumplings from vegetable mixture. Drain and discard chicken liquid from vegetable mixture. Stir in sauce. Return dumplings to saucepan; heat through. Top each serving with 2 dumplings.

nutrition facts per serving: 452 cal., 17 g total fat (9 g sat. fat), 92 mg chol., 1048 mg sodium, 43 g carb., 3 g dietary fiber, 37 g protein.

Watch the dumplings through the transparent cooker lid as they cook in this Italian-inspired stew. Lifting the lid during cooking slows down the process.

vegetable stew with cornmeal dumplings

prep: 25 minutes **slow cook:** 8 to 10 hours (low) or 4 to 5 hours (high) + 50 minutes (high)
makes: 6 servings

3 cups chopped, peeled butternut or acorn squash (1 pound)
2 cups sliced fresh mushrooms
2 14.5-ounce cans diced tomatoes, undrained
1 15-ounce can Great Northern beans, rinsed and drained
1 cup water
4 cloves garlic, minced
1 teaspoon dried Italian seasoning, crushed
¼ teaspoon ground black pepper
½ cup all-purpose flour
⅓ cup cornmeal
2 tablespoons grated Parmesan cheese
1 tablespoon snipped fresh Italian parsley
1 teaspoon baking powder
¼ teaspoon salt
1 egg, lightly beaten
2 tablespoons milk
2 tablespoons vegetable oil
1 9-ounce package frozen Italian green beans or cut green beans
  Paprika

1 In a 3½- or 4-quart slow cooker combine squash and mushrooms. Stir in undrained tomatoes, Great Northern beans, the water, garlic, Italian seasoning, and pepper.

2 Cover and cook on low-heat setting for 8 to 10 hours or on high-heat setting for 4 to 5 hours.

3 Shortly before serving, for dumplings, in a medium bowl stir together flour, cornmeal, cheese, parsley, baking powder, and salt. In a small bowl combine egg, milk, and oil. Stir egg mixture into flour mixture just until combined.

4 If using low-heat setting, turn to high-heat setting. Stir in frozen green beans. Drop dumpling dough by the tablespoon onto the mixture. Sprinkle with paprika; cook, covered, for 50 minutes more. (Do not lift lid during cooking.)

nutrition facts per serving: 288 cal., 7 g total fat (2 g sat. fat), 37 mg chol., 442 mg sodium, 45 g carb., 7 g dietary fiber, 12 g protein.

While canned soup adds extra flavor and richness, frozen broccoli and ready-made cooked chicken make this a quick-to-fix soup. Dress it up with savory dumplings for a family-pleasing meal

chicken-broccoli soup with dumplings

prep: 15 minutes   cook: 10 minutes
makes: 4 servings

2	10.75-ounce cans condensed cream of chicken soup
3	cups milk
1½	cups frozen cut broccoli
1	9-ounce package frozen chopped, cooked chicken breast
½	cup coarsely shredded carrot (1 medium)
1	teaspoon Dijon-style mustard
¼	teaspoon dried thyme, crushed
1	recipe Savory Dumplings
½	cup shredded cheddar cheese (2 ounces)

1 In a 4-quart Dutch oven, combine soup, milk, frozen broccoli, frozen chicken, carrot, mustard, and thyme. Bring to boiling; reduce heat.

2 Using 2 spoons, drop Savory Dumplings dough onto hot soup, making 4 or 5 mounds. Reduce heat. Simmer, covered, for 10 to 12 minutes more or until a toothpick inserted into a dumpling comes out clean. (Do not lift cover during cooking.) Sprinkle dumplings with cheese.

nutrition facts per serving: 535 cal., 26 g total fat (9 g sat. fat), 75 mg chol., 1701 mg sodium, 42 g carb., 3 g dietary fiber, 23 g protein.

savory dumplings: In a small bowl combine ⅔ cup all-purpose flour and 1 teaspoon baking powder. Add ¼ cup milk and 2 tablespoons vegetable oil. Stir just until moistened.

what's the secret?

Here's how to get the best-quality dumplings:

- *Be sure the stew is bubbling before dropping the dough on top.*

- *Cover the Dutch oven and don't peek until the minimum cooking time is up. The hot, steamy environment creates tender dumplings that won't deflate.*

- *Insert a wooden toothpick into one of the dumplings. If it comes out clean, the dumplings are done.*

This traditional German-Russian soup, also known as knoephla, *is commonly served in the upper Midwest.*

potato soup with dumplings

prep: 25 minutes cook: 25 minutes

makes: 10 servings

- 2 14-ounce cans reduced-sodium chicken broth or 3½ cups chicken stock
- 1 1.8-ounce envelope dry white sauce mix
- 4 cups chopped potato (4 large)
- 1 cup chopped onion (1 large)
- 1 cup diced cooked ham or Canadian-style bacon (5 ounces)
- 1 12-ounce can evaporated milk
- ½ teaspoon ground white or black pepper
- 1 recipe Old-Fashioned Dumplings
- ¼ cup snipped fresh parsley

1 In a 4-quart Dutch oven gradually stir broth into white sauce mix until smooth. Stir in potato, onion, ham, evaporated milk, and pepper. Bring to boiling; reduce heat. Simmer, covered, for 15 minutes, stirring occasionally.

2 Using rounded teaspoonfuls, drop Old-Fashioned Dumplings dough onto hot soup. Return to boiling; reduce heat. Simmer, uncovered, for 10 to 15 minutes more or until potatoes are tender and a toothpick inserted into a dumpling comes out clean. Sprinkle with parsley.

nutrition facts per serving: 241 cal., 8 g total fat (3 g sat. fat), 38 mg chol., 671 mg sodium, 33 g carb., 2 g dietary fiber, 9 g protein.

old-fashioned dumplings: In a medium bowl stir together 1½ cups all-purpose flour, 1 teaspoon baking powder, and ¼ teaspoon salt. Make a well in the center of the flour mixture. In a small bowl lightly beat 1 egg with a fork. Stir in ½ cup milk and 2 tablespoons vegetable oil. Add egg mixture to flour mixture. Stir with a fork until flour mixture is moistened.

The key to creating light and fluffy dumplings is to drop the dough into the bubbling stew and cover the slow cooker immediately. The hot, steamy environment creates tender dumplings every time.

turkey stew with biscuit-style dumplings

prep: 20 minutes   slow cook: 6 to 7 hours (low) or 3 to 3½ hours (high) + 45 minutes (high)   stand: 15 minutes
makes: 6 servings

1½ cups thinly sliced carrot (3 medium)
1½ cups thinly sliced celery (3 stalks)
1 medium onion, cut in very thin wedges
1¼ pounds turkey breast tenderloin, cut into ¾-inch cubes
1 14-ounce can reduced-sodium chicken broth
1 10.75-ounce can reduced-fat and low-sodium condensed cream of chicken soup
2 teaspoons dried sage, crushed
¼ teaspoon ground black pepper
1 cup all-purpose flour
1 teaspoon baking powder
⅛ teaspoon salt
2 tablespoons shortening
½ cup fat-free milk
¼ cup all-purpose flour

1 In a 3½- or 4-quart slow cooker combine carrot, celery, and onion; stir in turkey. Set aside ½ cup of the broth. In a medium bowl combine remaining broth, cream of chicken soup, sage, and pepper; stir into mixture in slow cooker.

2 Cover and cook on low-heat setting for 6 to 7 hours or on high-heat setting for 3 to 3½ hours.

3 For dumplings, stir together 1 cup flour, baking powder, and salt. Using a pastry blender, cut in shortening until mixture resembles coarse crumbs. Add milk and stir just until moistened.

4 If using low-heat setting, turn to high-heat setting. In a small bowl, whisk together reserved ½ cup broth and ¼ cup flour; stir into mixture in slow cooker. Drop biscuit dough by teaspoonfuls onto mixture in slow cooker. Cover and cook for 45 minutes more. (Do not lift cover during cooking.)

5 Remove insert from slow cooker, if possible, or turn off slow cooker. Let stand, covered, for 15 minutes before serving.

nutrition facts per serving: 300 cal., 6 g total fat (2 g sat. fat), 63 mg chol., 516 mg sodium, 32 g carb., 3 g dietary fiber, 29 g protein.

Kalamata olives, lemon juice, and sage lend a Mediterranean note to this creamy chicken soup. Serve it with focaccia, a crisp green salad, and gelato for dessert.

sage and chicken soup with dumplings

prep: 30 minutes   cook: 18 minutes
makes: 8 servings

2   cups sliced fresh mushrooms
1   cup chopped onion (2 large)
1   tablespoon olive oil
¼   cup all-purpose flour
6   cups reduced-sodium chicken broth
1   2- to 2½-pound deli-roasted chicken, skinned, boned, and cut into chunks
2   cups frozen peas
½   cup pitted kalamata olives, halved
1   tablespoon lemon juice
1   teaspoon ground sage
1   recipe Buttermilk Dumplings
    Thinly sliced green onion (optional)
    Fried Sage Leaves (optional)

1 In a 4-quart Dutch oven cook mushrooms and onions in hot oil over medium heat for 6 to 8 minutes or until liquid has evaporated. Stir in flour until combined. Add broth all at once; cook and stir until thickened and bubbly. Stir in chicken, frozen peas, olives, lemon juice, and ground sage. Return to boiling.

2 Prepare Buttermilk Dumplings dough; drop dough, ⅓ cup at a time, onto boiling soup. Simmer, covered, for 10 minutes or until toothpick inserted near centers comes out clean. (Do not lift cover during cooking.) If desired, sprinkle servings with green onion and Fried Sage Leaves.

nutrition facts per serving: 367 cal., 12 g total fat (2 g sat. fat), 56 mg chol., 776 mg sodium, 37 g carb., 4 g dietary fiber, 25 g protein.

buttermilk dumplings: Combine 2 cups all-purpose flour, ½ teaspoon baking powder, ¼ teaspoon baking soda, and ¼ teaspoon salt. Stir in ¼ cup sliced green onion and 1 tablespoon snipped Italian parsley. Add 1 cup buttermilk and 2 tablespoons olive oil; stir until moistened.

fried sage leaves: Heat ¼ cup olive oil over medium heat. Add 8 sage sprigs, 2 at a time. Cook for 30 to 60 seconds, until crisp; drain on paper towels.

This hearty and delicious soup, crowned with tender corn bread dumplings, gets an extra burst of flavor from the zesty salsa.

white bean–turkey chili with corn bread dumplings

start to finish: 22 minutes
makes: 4 servings

1   pound cooked turkey
1   16-ounce jar chunky
     salsa
1   15-ounce can
     cannellini (white
     kidney) beans,
     rinsed and drained
1   teaspoon chili
     powder
⅔   cup water
1   8.5-ounce package
     corn bread mix
1   egg
¼   cup water
¼   cup shredded
     cheddar cheese
     (1 ounce) (optional)
     Slivered green onion
     (optional)
     Chili powder
     (optional)

1 Chop turkey. In a Dutch oven combine turkey, salsa, beans, chili powder, and the ⅔ cup water. Bring to boiling.

2 Meanwhile, for dumplings, in a medium bowl mix together corn bread mix, egg, and the ¼ cup water. Drop batter by rounded tablespoonfuls onto boiling turkey chili.

3 Reduce heat. Simmer, covered, for 10 to 15 minutes or until a wooden pick inserted into a dumpling comes out clean. (Do not lift cover during cooking.) Top each serving with cheese, green onion, and chili powder, if desired.

nutrition facts per serving: 555 cal., 15 g total fat (4 g sat. fat), 140 mg chol., 1618 mg sodium, 64 g carb., 11 g dietary fiber, 47 g protein.

This hearty, home-style stew will win your family's approval. You'll love the simplicity of not having to brown the chicken and using biscuit mix for the tender dumplings.

chicken stew with cheesy garlic dumplings

prep: 20 minutes cook: 25 minutes
makes: 6 servings

1½ cups water
½ of a 1.8-ounce package dry onion-mushroom soup mix
1½ pounds skinless, boneless chicken breasts or thighs, cut into bite-size pieces
3 cups cubed, peeled potato (3 medium)
1½ cups sliced carrot (3 medium)
1 teaspoon dried sage, crushed
⅛ teaspoon ground black pepper
1 recipe Cheesy Garlic Dumplings

1 In a 4-quart Dutch oven stir together the water and soup mix. Add chicken, potato, carrot, dried sage, and pepper. Bring to boiling; reduce heat. Simmer, covered, for 10 to 15 minutes or until vegetables are almost tender.

2 Using 2 spoons, drop Cheesy Garlic Dumplings dough into simmering chicken mixture, making 6 mounds. Simmer, covered, for 15 to 20 minutes more or until a toothpick inserted in center of a dumpling comes out clean. (Do not lift cover during cooking.)

nutrition facts per serving: 379 cal., 9 g total fat (3 g sat. fat), 66 mg chol., 651 mg sodium, 42 g carb., 3 g dietary fiber, 30 g protein.

cheesy garlic dumplings: Prepare one 7.75-ounce package cheese-garlic or three-cheese complete biscuit mix according to package directions, except stir ¼ cup cornmeal into dry biscuit mix and increase the water to ¾ cup.

Dainty basil-flavored dumplings set this delicious soup apart from any tomato soup you've sampled before.

chunky tomato soup with basil dumplings

prep: 40 minutes cook: 30 minutes
makes: 6 servings

2 tablespoons olive oil
1 cup coarsely chopped onion (1 large)
2 tablespoons chopped shallot
2 cloves garlic, minced
1 14-ounce can reduced-sodium chicken broth
½ cup coarsely chopped carrot (1 medium)
½ cup coarsely chopped celery (1 stalk)
½ cup coarsely chopped red sweet pepper (1 small)
1 tablespoon lemon juice
½ teaspoon sugar
1 14.5-ounce can diced tomatoes, undrained
Pinch cayenne pepper
1 recipe Basil Dumplings
Salt
Ground black pepper
Fresh basil sprigs (optional)

1 In a large saucepan heat oil over medium heat. Add onion, shallot, and garlic; cook about 5 minutes or until onion is tender, stirring frequently. Add broth, carrot, celery, sweet pepper, lemon juice, and sugar. Bring to boiling; reduce heat. Simmer, covered, for 20 to 25 minutes or until vegetables are very tender. Cool slightly (do not drain).

2 Transfer vegetable mixture, half at a time, to a blender or food processor. Cover and blend or process until smooth. Return pureed mixture to saucepan.

3 Stir in undrained tomatoes and cayenne pepper. Cook, uncovered, over low heat about 10 minutes or until heated through, stirring often.

4 Meanwhile, fill a Dutch oven half-full with water; bring to boiling. Using a slightly rounded ½-teaspoon measuring spoon, drop Basil Dumplings dough into boiling water. Cook for 4 to 5 minutes (start timing after dough rises to the surface) or until a toothpick inserted into a dumpling comes out clean. Using a slotted spoon, remove the dumplings; drain in a colander. Rinse dumplings under cold running water; drain again.

5 Add half of the dumplings to soup in saucepan; heat through. Season to taste with salt and black pepper. Ladle into soup bowls. Top with remaining dumplings. If desired, garnish with basil sprigs.

nutrition facts per serving: 141 cal., 8 g total fat (1 g sat. fat), 35 mg chol., 817 mg sodium, 15 g carb., 2 g dietary fiber, 3 g protein.

basil dumplings: In a small bowl combine ⅓ cup all-purpose flour, 1 tablespoon snipped fresh basil, ½ teaspoon salt, and ¼ teaspoon baking powder. In a small bowl, beat 1 egg with a fork; add 2 teaspoons vegetable oil, stirring until mixed. Add the egg mixture to flour mixture. Using a wooden spoon, beat until a soft, sticky dough forms.

This cheese-topped vegetable stew gets a winning twist from the carrot dumplings on top.

hearty vegetable stew with carrot dumplings

prep: 50 minutes cook: 12 minutes
makes: 8 servings

2   tablespoons
     vegetable oil
4   carrots, cut into
     ¼-inch slices
     (2 cups)
1½   cups chopped onion
     (3 medium)
3   stalks celery, cut into
     ¼-inch slices
3   cups water
4   potatoes, peeled,
     if desired, and cut
     into ¼-inch slices
     (about 4 cups)
2⅔   cups coarsely
     chopped tomato
     (8 small)
3   vegetable bouillon
     cubes
2   cloves garlic, minced
½   teaspoon ground
     black pepper
½   cup cold water
¼   cup all-purpose flour
1   cup coarsely chopped
     cabbage
1   cup frozen peas
1   recipe Carrot
     Dumplings
2   cups shredded
     cheddar cheese
     (8 ounces)

1 In a Dutch oven heat oil over medium heat. Add carrots, onion, and celery; cook, covered, about 5 minutes or until tender, stirring occasionally. Stir in the 3 cups water, potatoes, tomato, bouillon cubes, garlic, and pepper. Bring to boiling; reduce heat. Simmer, covered, for 15 to 20 minutes or until potatoes are almost tender.

2 In a screw-top jar combine the ½ cup cold water and flour; cover and shake until well mixed. Stir flour mixture into vegetable mixture in Dutch oven; cook and stir until thickened and bubbly.

3 Gently stir cabbage and frozen peas into stew. Using 2 spoons, drop Carrot Dumplings dough onto hot stew, making 8 mounds. Simmer, covered, about 12 minutes more or until a toothpick inserted into a dumpling comes out clean. (Do not lift cover during cooking.) Sprinkle each serving with cheese.

nutrition facts per serving: 328 cal., 22 g total fat (2 g sat. fat), 105 mg chol., 921 mg sodium, 55 g carb., 3 g dietary fiber, 12 g protein.

carrot dumplings: In a large bowl stir together 2¼ cups packaged biscuit mix, 1 cup finely shredded carrot, and 1 tablespoon snipped fresh parsley. Add 1 cup water; stir with a fork just until combined.

8

make it

meat

Toothsome grains—barley, bulgur, and rice—and protein-rich legumes, including beans, split peas, and lentils, star in these bright, beautiful bowls, making it easy to incorporate meatless options into everyday cooking. It's hearty vegetarian fare that even meat lovers will rave about.

less

Spunky Cajun seasoning, velvety black beans, and colorful vegetables keep this lively, loaded gumbo interesting. There's plenty of saucy liquid to flavor accompanying rice.

cajun-seasoned vegetarian gumbo

prep: 10 minutes   **slow cook:** 6 to 8 hours (low) or 3 to 4 hours (high)
makes: 6 servings

2   15-ounce cans black beans, rinsed and drained
1   28-ounce can diced tomatoes, undrained
1   16-ounce package frozen sweet pepper and onion stir-fry vegetables
2   cups frozen cut okra
2   to 3 teaspoons Cajun seasoning
3   cups hot cooked white or brown rice
    Chopped green onion (optional)

1 In a 3½- to 4½-quart slow cooker combine beans, undrained tomatoes, frozen stir-fry vegetables, frozen okra, and Cajun seasoning.

2 Cover and cook on low-heat setting for 6 to 8 hours or on high-heat setting for 3 to 4 hours.

3 Serve gumbo in shallow bowls over rice. If desired, sprinkle with green onion.

nutrition facts per serving: 250 cal., 1 g total fat (0 g sat. fat), 0 mg chol., 675 mg sodium, 52 g carb., 10 g dietary fiber, 14 g protein.

Stock your pantry and fridge with the ingredients here so you'll be ready to whip up a soup on a weeknight that offers home-cooked comfort.

spicy tortellini stew

start to finish: 40 minutes
makes: 6 servings

8 ounces fresh mushrooms, sliced (3 cups)
½ cup chopped onion (1 medium)
2 tablespoons olive oil
2 14.5-ounce cans diced tomatoes, undrained
1 14-ounce can vegetable broth
1 8-ounce can tomato sauce
½ cup bottled salsa
2 teaspoons dried Italian seasoning, crushed
1 7-ounce package dried cheese tortellini

1 In a Dutch oven cook mushrooms and onion in hot oil over medium heat for 5 to 8 minutes or until mushrooms are tender, stirring occasionally.

2 Stir in undrained tomatoes, vegetable broth, tomato sauce, salsa, and Italian seasoning. Add tortellini. Bring to boiling; reduce heat. Simmer, covered, about 20 minutes or until tortellini is tender, stirring occasionally.

nutrition facts per serving: 237 cal., 8 g total fat (1 g sat. fat), 0 mg chol., 1153 mg sodium, 33 g carb., 4 g dietary fiber, 10 g protein.

Hearty and rustic French lentils—or lentilles du Puy—are smaller and darker than regular brown lentils and hold their shape better during cooking. Look for them at specialty or natural food stores or online. If French lentils aren't available, brown lentils will work just as well.

french lentil, leek, and mushroom soup

prep: 30 minutes   **cook:** 35 minutes
makes: 8 servings

1   32-ounce carton
     reduced-sodium
     vegetable broth
2½ cups water
1½ cups French lentils
     or brown lentils,
     rinsed and drained
3   cups sliced fresh
     cremini and/or
     button mushrooms
     (8 ounces)
3   medium carrots
     or 2 yellow beets,
     peeled and coarsely
     chopped (1½ cups)
⅔   cup thinly sliced leek
     (2 medium)*
1   tablespoon olive oil
4   cups chopped kale
     or chopped fresh
     spinach
1   teaspoon dried
     thyme or marjoram,
     crushed
½   teaspoon salt
¼   teaspoon cracked
     black pepper
2   14.5-ounce cans
     no-salt-added diced
     tomatoes, drained
⅓   cup purchased basil
     pesto

1 In a Dutch oven bring broth and the water to boiling. Add lentils. Return to boiling; reduce heat. Simmer, covered, for 15 minutes.

2 Meanwhile, in a large skillet cook mushrooms, carrots, and leek in hot oil over medium heat about 5 minutes or until leek is tender. Stir mushroom mixture, kale, thyme, salt, and pepper into the lentil mixture. Bring to boiling; reduce heat. Simmer, covered, about 15 minutes or until lentils are tender. Stir in drained tomatoes; heat through.

3 Top each serving with a spoonful of pesto.

nutrition facts per serving: 267 cal., 7 g total fat (1 g sat. fat), 3 mg chol., 383 mg sodium, 39 g carb., 15 g dietary fiber, 14 g protein.

*note: See tip on cleaning leeks, page 464.

This dish is inspired by the much-loved cuisine of Tuscany, Italy, where native diners enjoy white beans so much in their hearty and satisfying cuisine, they've earned the nickname mangiafagioli— *"bean eaters."*

rustic italian stew

prep: 20 minutes slow cook: 7 to 8 hours (low) or 3½ to 4 hours (high)
makes: 8 servings

Nonstick cooking
 spray
2 yellow summer
 squash, halved
 lengthwise and
 sliced (2½ cups)
8 ounces fresh button
 mushrooms,
 quartered (3 cups)
1 15-ounce can navy
 beans, rinsed and
 drained
2 green sweet peppers,
 cut into 1-inch
 pieces (1 cup)
1 zucchini, halved
 lengthwise and
 sliced (1¼ cups)
1 onion, cut into thin
 wedges (1 cup)
1 tablespoon olive oil
1 teaspoon salt
1 teaspoon dried Italian
 seasoning, crushed
⅛ to ¼ teaspoon
 crushed red pepper
 flakes (optional)
2 14.5-ounce cans
 stewed tomatoes,
 undrained and
 cut up
2 cups shredded
 mozzarella cheese
 (8 ounces)

1 Lightly coat the inside of a 5- to 6-quart slow cooker with cooking spray. In prepared cooker combine yellow squash, mushrooms, navy beans, sweet pepper, zucchini, onion, oil, salt, Italian seasoning, and, if desired, red pepper flakes. Pour undrained tomatoes over all.

2 Cover and cook on low-heat setting for 7 to 8 hours or on high-heat setting for 3½ to 4 hours.

3 Sprinkle each serving with mozzarella cheese.

nutrition facts per serving: 433 cal., 9 g total fat (4 g sat. fat), 22 mg chol., 959 mg sodium, 25 g carb., 6 g dietary fiber, 14 g protein.

This hearty vegetarian soup features three kinds of beans, split peas, and lentils. It pairs well with a slice of crunchy toasted ciabatta.

fava bean and chard soup

prep: 50 minutes **soak:** overnight **cook:** 2 hours
makes: 8 servings

8   ounces dried fava
     beans
4   ounces dried red
     kidney beans
4   ounces dried
     garbanzo beans
     (chickpeas)
4   ounces dried split
     peas, rinsed and
     drained
4   ounces lentils, rinsed
     and drained
2   teaspoons salt
9   cups water
8   ounces Swiss chard,
     chopped
1   cup chopped celery
     (2 stalks)
½   cup chopped onion
     (1 medium)
2   tablespoons snipped
     dried tomatoes
     (not oil-packed)
3   cloves garlic, minced
1   teaspoon fennel
     seeds, crushed
     Ground black pepper
     Fennel leaves
     (optional)
     Olive oil

1 Rinse fava, kidney, and garbanzo beans. Place beans in a 4- to 5-quart Dutch oven; add enough water to cover. Cover and let soak overnight.*

2 Drain and rinse beans. Remove fava beans and squeeze off skins. Return kidney and garbanzo beans to Dutch oven; add fava beans. Stir in split peas, lentils, and 2 teaspoons salt. Add the 9 cups water. Bring to boiling; reduce heat. Simmer, covered, for 1 hour.

3 Stir in chard, celery, onion, dried tomatoes, garlic, and fennel seeds. Return to boiling; reduce heat. Simmer, covered, about 1 hour more or until beans are very tender and mixture is thick, adding additional water during cooking if necessary. Season to taste with salt and pepper.

4 If desired, garnish each serving with fennel leaves and drizzle with oil.

nutrition facts per serving: 341 cal., 5 g total fat (1 g sat. fat), 0 mg chol., 755 mg sodium, 55 g carb., 22 g dietary fiber, 22 g protein.

*note: If you don't want to soak the beans overnight, use this method: Rinse fava beans. In a large saucepan combine fava beans and 4 cups water. Bring to boiling; reduce heat. Simmer, covered, for 15 to 20 minutes or until skins are softened. Remove from heat. Cover and let stand for 1 hour. Drain and rinse fava beans; squeeze off skins. Meanwhile, rinse kidney and garbanzo beans. Place beans in a 4- to 5-quart Dutch oven; add 8 cups water. Bring to boiling; reduce heat. Simmer, uncovered, for 2 minutes. Remove from heat. Cover and let stand for 1 hour. Drain and rinse beans. Return kidney and garbanzo beans to Dutch oven; add fava beans. Continue as directed in Step 2.

Lentils come in several colors—green, brown, red, and yellow. Any would work well in this hearty, healthy soup, which comes with a tasty hint of citrus.

lemony lentil soup
with greens

prep: 25 minutes cook: 30 to 35 minutes
makes: 8 servings

2 teaspoons canola oil
⅓ cup chopped onion
   (1 small)
½ cup chopped carrot
   (1 medium)
1 cup chopped celery
   (2 stalks)
2 cloves garlic, minced
12 cups reduced-sodium
   chicken broth, plus
   more as needed
1 1-pound package
   green lentils
1 teaspoon dried basil
1 teaspoon dried thyme
1 teaspoon salt
8 cups chopped kale
   leaves (about
   6 ounces)
3 tablespoons lemon
   juice
1 teaspoon finely
   grated lemon zest

1 In a 6-quart pot heat oil over medium-high heat. Add onion; cook for 3 to 5 minutes or until tender. Add carrot, celery, and garlic; cook covered, stirring occasionally, for 5 minutes or until the carrot is tender.

2 Add 12 cups broth, lentils, basil, thyme, and salt. Bring to boiling; reduce heat. Add kale. Simmer, covered, for 30 to 35 minutes, or until lentils are tender, adding additional broth if necessary. Stir in lemon juice and top with lemon zest before serving.

nutrition facts per serving: 313 cal., 4 g total fat (1 g sat. fat), 0 mg chol., 445 mg sodium, 48 g carb., 19 g dietary fiber, 24 g protein.

This soup recipe is a vegetarian delight. It's full of vegetables, mushrooms, barley, and red beans—all slow cooked to perfection for those busy weeknights. Using regular barley instead of instant will give you a pleasantly chewy texture.

barley-vegetable soup

prep: 25 minutes   **slow cook:** 8 to 10 hours (low) or 4 to 5 hours (high)
makes: 6 servings

1   cup chopped onion
      (1 large)
½   cup bias-sliced carrot
      (1 medium)
½   cup sliced celery
      (1 stalk)
2   cups sliced fresh
      mushrooms
1   15-ounce can red
      beans, rinsed and
      drained
1   14.5-ounce can
      stewed tomatoes,
      undrained
1   10-ounce package
      frozen whole-kernel
      corn
½   cup regular barley
      (not quick-cooking)
2   teaspoons dried
      Italian seasoning,
      crushed
¼   teaspoon ground
      black pepper
3   cloves garlic, minced
5   cups vegetable
      or chicken broth

1 In a 3½- to 5-quart slow cooker toss together onion, carrot, and celery. Add mushrooms, beans, undrained tomatoes, frozen corn, barley, Italian seasoning, pepper, and garlic. Pour broth over all.

2 Cover and cook on low-heat setting for 8 to 10 hours or on high-heat setting for 4 to 5 hours.

nutrition facts per serving: 228 cal., 2 g total fat (0 g sat. fat), 0 mg chol., 1212 mg sodium, 47 g carb., 8 g dietary fiber, 9 g protein.

A medley of spices—cumin, mustard, and curry—adds beautiful depth to this stew. Sautéing the cumin and mustard seeds in the beginning toasts the spices, further enhancing their flavors.

indian-style vegetable and lentil stew

prep: 30 minutes   cook: 45 minutes
makes: 5 servings

1   tablespoon mustard
    seeds
1   tablespoon cumin
    seeds
1   tablespoon olive oil
1½ cups chopped carrot
    (3 medium)
¾   cup chopped green
    sweet pepper
    (1 medium)
½   cup chopped onion
    (1 medium)
½   teaspoon salt
¼   teaspoon ground
    black pepper
4   cups water
1   6-ounce can tomato
    paste
1   15- to 16-ounce can
    garbanzo beans
    (chickpeas), rinsed
    and drained
1   14.5-ounce can diced
    tomatoes, drained
1   tablespoon lemon
    juice
3   cloves garlic, minced
1   teaspoon curry
    powder
1   teaspoon ground
    cumin
½   teaspoon crushed
    red pepper flakes
1   sweet potato, peeled
    and cut into ½-inch
    pieces
1   cup red lentils
½   cup coarsely chopped
    fresh cilantro

1 In a Dutch oven toast mustard and cumin seeds in hot oil over medium heat until fragrant and beginning to pop.

2 Add carrot, sweet pepper, onion, salt, and black pepper; cook, stirring occasionally, for 8 minutes or until vegetables begin to soften.

3 Stir in the water, tomato paste, beans, drained tomatoes, lemon juice, garlic, curry powder, ground cumin, and red pepper flakes. Bring to boiling. Add sweet potato and lentils. Reduce heat. Simmer, covered, for 30 minutes or until lentils and sweet potato are tender, stirring occasionally. Stir in cilantro before serving.

nutrition facts per serving: 378 cal., 5 g total fat (.7 g sat. fat), 0 mg chol., 975 mg sodium, 68 g carb., 22 g dietary fiber, 19 g protein.

Serve this fiber-rich soup with a salad of fresh romaine, marinated artichoke hearts, and thinly sliced red onions, tossed with Caesar dressing.

curry-ginger lentil soup

prep: 20 minutes   **cook:** 30 minutes
makes: 4 to 6 servings

1	tablespoon olive oil
½	cup chopped onion (1 medium)
1	jalapeño pepper, seeded and finely chopped*
1	teaspoon grated fresh ginger
3	cloves garlic, minced
2	14-ounce cans vegetable broth or 3½ cups homemade vegetable stock
2	cups cubed, peeled sweet potato
2	cups chopped tomato
1	cup water
1	cup brown lentils
1	tablespoon curry powder
	Salt
	Plain yogurt or sour cream (optional)

In a 4-quart Dutch oven heat oil. Add onion, chile pepper, ginger, and garlic; cook and stir over medium heat until tender. Add broth, sweet potato, tomato, the water, lentils, curry powder, and salt. Bring to boiling; reduce heat. Simmer, covered, for 25 to 30 minutes or until lentils are tender. If desired, top each serving with yogurt.

nutrition facts per serving: 328 cal., 5 g total fat (1 g sat. fat), 0 mg chol., 886 mg sodium, 57 g carb., 19 g dietary fiber, 18 g protein.

✱note: See tip on handling chile peppers, page 31.

Nothing says comfort like a hot bowl of cheese soup. This version uses reduced-fat milk and cheese to keep it healthful.

cheddar soup

prep: 40 minutes **cook:** 25 minutes
makes: 6 servings

½   cup sliced celery
      (1 stalk)
1   cup chopped onion
      (1 large)
4   cloves garlic, sliced
1   tablespoon olive oil
3   14-ounce cans
      reduced-sodium
      chicken broth
2   12-ounce cans
      evaporated fat-free
      milk
½   cup all-purpose flour
2   cups reduced-fat
      shredded cheddar
      cheese (8 ounces)
¼   teaspoon ground
      white pepper
      (optional)
½   cup reduced-fat
      shredded cheddar
      cheese (2 ounces)
      (optional)

1 In a Dutch oven cook celery, onion, and garlic in hot oil until tender. Add broth. Bring to boiling; reduce heat. Simmer, covered, for 25 minutes.

2 Strain vegetables, reserving broth. Return broth to Dutch oven; discard vegetables. In a medium bowl stir together evaporated milk and flour. Stir into broth; cook and stir until thickened and bubbly. Reduce heat to low.

3 Add 2 cups cheese; cook and stir until cheese is melted. If desired, stir in white pepper. If desired, sprinkle each serving with some of the ½ cup cheese.

nutrition facts per serving: 294 cal., 10 g total fat (6 g sat. fat), 32 mg chol., 928 mg sodium, 26 g carb., 0 g dietary fiber, 22 g protein.

Cilantro, spinach, edamame, and green onions send a healthy message while sparking fresh flavor. A jar of salsa verde (green chile sauce) is a time-saving addition that makes this chili unique.

vegetarian green chili

prep: 25 minutes **cook:** 28 minutes
makes: 8 servings

2   cups long-grain rice
½   cup chopped green
     onion (4)
6   cloves garlic, minced
2   tablespoons
     vegetable oil
2   cups chopped green
     sweet pepper
     (2 large)
1½ cups chopped celery
     (3 stalks)
2   12-ounce bags
     shelled frozen
     sweet soybeans
     (edamame)
1   4.5-ounce can
     chopped green
     chiles
3   cups vegetable broth
     or reduced-sodium
     chicken broth
1   16-ounce jar green
     salsa (salsa verde)
6   cups fresh spinach
¼   cup chopped fresh
     cilantro
3   avocados, pitted,
     peeled, and
     chopped
     Plain lowfat yogurt
     or sour cream
     (optional)

1 Cook rice according to package directions.

2 Meanwhile, in a Dutch oven cook and stir onion and garlic in hot oil over medium-high heat for 2 minutes. Add sweet pepper and celery; cook for 5 minutes or until crisp-tender. Add edamame and green chiles; cook for 5 minutes. Add broth and salsa verde. Bring to boiling; reduce heat. Simmer, covered, for 15 minutes. Stir in spinach; cook about 1 minute or until wilted.

3 Remove from heat; stir in cilantro and two of the chopped avocados. Top with the remaining avocado and yogurt. Serve with rice.

nutrition facts per serving: 413 cal., 16 g total fat (1 g sat. fat), 0 mg chol., 753 mg sodium, 56 g carb., 11 g dietary fiber, 14 g protein.

Rich, creamy avocado and snipped fresh cilantro provide a refreshing contrast to the lively flavors in this easy chili.

two-bean chili with avocado

prep: 15 minutes cook: 28 minutes
makes: 4 or 5 servings

1 cup chopped onion (1 large)
2 teaspoons dried oregano, crushed
2 teaspoons canola or olive oil
2 14.5-ounce cans diced tomatoes, undrained
1 15-ounce can black beans or kidney beans, rinsed and drained
1 15-ounce can pinto beans, rinsed and drained
½ cup salsa (preferably guajillo chile salsa)
1 medium ripe avocado, pitted, peeled, and diced
¼ cup snipped fresh cilantro

In a large saucepan cook onion and oregano in hot oil over medium-high heat for 3 minutes or until tender. Stir in undrained tomatoes, beans, and salsa. Bring to boiling; reduce heat. Simmer, uncovered, about 25 minutes. Top each serving with avocado and snipped cilantro.

nutrition facts per serving: 325 cal., 10 g total fat (1 g sat. fat), 0 mg chol., 985 mg sodium, 50 g carb., 15 g dietary fiber, 14 g protein.

the call of protein

When you choose to go meatless for a meal but still want the protein, pick one of these ingredients to add to your soup.

• beans: *An easy way to add protein to any meatless meal, especially soup, is to stir in a can of beans. Try varieties such as black, navy, kidney, Great Northern, pinto, garbanzo (chickpeas), or cannellini (white kidney) beans. Just rinse and drain them before using.*

• other legumes: *Lentils, split peas, and peanuts are all good sources of protein. Lentils and split peas require a longer cooking time before you add them to your soup, so plan ahead. Peanuts can be chopped and sprinkled over thicker soups.*

• dairy products: *While they are not always low in fat, adding dairy products, such as cheese or milk, boosts the protein in soup. Add a swirl of milk to thicker soups or try some cheese as a garnish.*

• whole grains: *Add cooked brown rice or whole-grain pasta, or serve whole-grain bread on the side.*

238

Beans and rice add creamy texture to this hearty stew, while kale offers an excellent source of vitamins and minerals.

savory bean and kale soup

prep: 20 minutes   **slow cook:** 5 to 7 hours (low) or 2½ to 3½ hours (high)
makes: 6 servings

3   14.5-ounce cans vegetable broth
1   15-ounce can tomato puree
1   15-ounce can small white beans or Great Northern beans, rinsed and drained
½   cup converted rice
½   cup finely chopped onion (1 medium)
2   cloves garlic, minced
1   teaspoon dried basil, crushed
¼   teaspoon salt
¼   teaspoon ground black pepper
8   cups coarsely chopped fresh kale leaves
    Finely shredded Parmesan cheese (optional)

1 In a 3½- or 4-quart slow cooker combine broth, tomato puree, beans, rice, onion, garlic, basil, salt, and pepper.

2 Cover and cook on low-heat setting for 5 to 7 hours or on high-heat setting for 2½ to 3½ hours.

3 Before serving, stir in kale. If desired, sprinkle each serving with cheese.

nutrition facts per serving: 188 cal., 1 g total fat (0 g sat. fat), 0 mg chol., 1306 mg sodium, 42 g carb., 7 g dietary fiber, 10 g protein.

savory bean and spinach soup: Prepare as directed, except substitute fresh baby spinach leaves for the kale. (Pictured on page 256.)

As members of the protein-rich legume family, split peas are high in fiber and carbohydrates and relatively low in fat. Unlike dried beans, the peas do not require presoaking, making them as convenient as they are nutritious.

split pea soup with herbed crostini

prep: 20 minutes cook: 50 minutes
makes: 6 servings

lowfat

239

1 pound dry split peas
4 cups water
1 14-ounce can
    vegetable broth
1 cup chopped carrot
    (2 medium)
½ cup chopped onion
    (1 medium)
2 tablespoons snipped
    fresh basil
2 tablespoons snipped
    fresh oregano
1 tablespoon snipped
    fresh sage
    Salt
    Ground black pepper
1 recipe Herbed
    Crostini

1 Rinse and drain split peas. In 4- to 5-quart Dutch oven combine split peas, the water, and broth. Bring to boiling; reduce heat. Simmer, covered, for 30 minutes. Add carrot and onion; cook, covered, for 20 to 30 minutes more or until peas and vegetables are tender.

2 Stir in basil, oregano, and sage; cook and stir for 1 minute. Season to taste with salt and pepper.

3 Top each serving with Herbed Crostini.

nutrition facts per serving: 442 cal., 9 g total fat (2 g sat. fat), 1 mg chol., 623 mg sodium, 69 g carb., 21 g dietary fiber, 23 g protein.

herbed crostini: Preheat oven to 425°F. Brush six ½-inch-thick slices French bread with mixture of 3 tablespoons olive oil and 1 tablespoon each finely snipped basil and oregano. Place on greased baking sheet. Bake for 6 to 8 minutes or until lightly toasted, turning once. Sprinkle hot crostini with 2 tablespoons finely shredded Parmesan cheese.

If you like the traditional Middle Eastern dip made with chickpeas, tahini, and lemon juice, you'll love the lively flavors in this soup. Serve with toasted pita bread.

thick hummus-style soup

prep: 35 minutes **stand:** 1 hour **slow cook:** 10 to 12 hours (low) or 5 to 6 hours (high) **bake:** 12 minutes **oven:** at 300°F
makes: 8 servings

1 pound dried garbanzo beans (chickpeas)
8 cups vegetable broth or reduced-sodium chicken broth
6 cloves garlic, minced
1 tablespoon ground cumin
1 teaspoon ground coriander
1 teaspoon ground turmeric
½ teaspoon salt
1 6-ounce carton plain fat-free Greek yogurt
⅓ cup tahini (sesame seed paste)
⅓ cup lemon juice
⅓ cup snipped fresh Italian parsley
1 to 2 whole-grain pita bread rounds
1 tablespoon olive oil
1¼ cups chopped red sweet pepper (1 large)
Toasted sesame seeds* (optional)

*note: To toast sesame seeds, preheat oven to 350°F. Spread sesame seeds in a shallow baking pan. Bake for 5 to 10 minutes or until light brown, watching carefully and stirring once or twice.

1 Rinse beans; drain. In a large saucepan or Dutch oven combine beans and enough water to cover beans by 2 inches. Bring to boiling; reduce heat. Simmer, uncovered, for 10 minutes. Remove from heat. Cover and let stand for 1 hour. Drain and rinse beans.

2 Place drained beans in a 4- to 5-quart slow cooker. Add broth, garlic, cumin, coriander, turmeric, and salt. Cover and cook on low-heat setting for 10 to 12 hours or on high-heat setting for 5 to 6 hours.

3 Stir in yogurt, tahini, and lemon juice. Cool slightly. Transfer mixture in batches to a blender or food processor. Cover and blend or process until smooth. Stir in parsley.

4 Meanwhile, preheat oven to 300°F. Chop enough of the pita bread into ½- to ¾-inch pieces to measure 2 cups; toss with oil. Spread in a shallow baking pan. Bake for 12 to 13 minutes or until crisp, stirring once.

5 Serve soup topped with pita bread pieces, sweet pepper, and, if desired, sesame seeds.

nutrition facts per serving: 351 cal., 11 g total fat (1 g sat. fat), 0 mg chol., 768 mg sodium, 47 g carb., 12 g dietary fiber, 18 g protein.

A quartet of seasonings—garlic, cilantro, oregano, and adobo seasoning—adds a zesty kick to this savory bean and rice stew. You'll find adobo seasoning at Hispanic markets.

red bean and brown rice stew

start to finish: 20 minutes
makes: 4 servings

1 teaspoon vegetable oil
⅔ cup chopped red onion
3 cloves garlic, minced
1 cup water
2 tablespoons tomato paste
1 tablespoon snipped fresh cilantro
1 teaspoon snipped fresh oregano or ¼ teaspoon dried oregano, crushed
½ teaspoon adobo seasoning*
1 15-ounce can red kidney beans, rinsed and drained
2 cups hot cooked brown rice
Fresh cilantro sprigs (optional)

1 In a large skillet heat oil over medium heat. Add onion and garlic; cook about 5 minutes or until onion is tender. Carefully add the water, tomato paste, snipped cilantro, oregano, and adobo seasoning. Stir in beans. Bring to boiling; reduce heat. Cook and stir over medium heat for 5 to 10 minutes or until soup is slightly thickened, mashing beans slightly while stirring.

2 Serve stew over rice. If desired, garnish with cilantro sprigs.

nutrition facts per serving: 220 cal., 2 g total fat (0 g sat. fat), 0 mg chol., 427 mg sodium, 44 g carb., 8 g dietary fiber, 11 g protein.

*note: Look for this seasoning blend at a market that specializes in Hispanic foods.

Carrots and garden-fresh asparagus make corn-and-bean chowder a delightful one-bowl meal that's full of healthy veggies.

creamy succotash soup

start to finish: 35 minutes
makes: 4 servings

2 teaspoons canola oil
1 cup thinly sliced carrot (2 medium)
½ cup chopped sweet onion, such as Vidalia or Maui (1 medium)
2 cloves garlic, minced
1 14-ounce can vegetable broth
1½ cups frozen lima beans
2 teaspoons snipped fresh dill or ½ teaspoon dried dill weed
1 cup 1-inch pieces fresh asparagus
½ cup frozen whole-kernel corn
2 cups evaporated fat-free milk
2 tablespoons all-purpose flour
Fresh dill sprigs (optional)

1 In a large nonstick saucepan, heat oil over medium heat. Add carrot, onion, and garlic; cook for 5 minutes, stirring occasionally. Add broth, frozen lima beans, and dried dill weed (if using). Bring to boiling; reduce heat. Simmer, covered, for 5 minutes.

2 Add asparagus and frozen corn. Return to boiling. Cook, covered, for 1 minute. In a large screw-top jar, combine 1 cup of the evaporated milk and flour; cover and shake until smooth. Add flour mixture, remaining 1 cup evaporated milk, and snipped fresh dill (if using) to soup; cook and stir until slightly thickened and bubbly. Cook and stir for 1 minute more. If desired, garnish each serving with fresh dill sprigs.

nutrition facts per serving: 269 cal., 3 g total fat (0 g sat. fat), 5 mg chol., 591 mg sodium, 45 g carb., 6 g dietary fiber, 17 g protein.

Dried shiitake mushrooms have a wonderful smoky flavor and meaty texture that add character to this soup. The water used to reconstitute the dried mushrooms becomes a flavorful broth.

savory barley, bean, and mushroom soup

prep: 20 minutes   cook: 45 minutes
makes: 4 or 5 servings

½   cup dried shiitake
     mushrooms
     (¼ ounce)
2   cups boiling water
2   tablespoons olive oil
1   cup chopped onion
     (2 medium)
½   cup chopped celery
     (1 stalk)
½   cup chopped carrot
     (1 medium)
2   cloves garlic, minced
½   teaspoon dried
     thyme, crushed
½   teaspoon dried
     oregano, crushed
1   bay leaf
2   14-ounce cans
     vegetable broth
1   15-ounce can navy
     beans or cannellini
     (white kidney)
     beans, rinsed and
     drained
½   cup regular (not
     quick-cooking)
     barley
½   teaspoon salt
¼   teaspoon ground
     black pepper
1   tablespoon olive oil
1   cup sliced fresh
     mushrooms
½   cup sliced zucchini
1   cup shredded fresh
     spinach
¼   cup chopped fresh
     parsley (optional)
1   tablespoon cider
     vinegar (optional)

1 In a medium bowl cover shiitake mushrooms with boiling water. Let stand for 15 to 20 minutes or until tender. Drain, reserving liquid. Strain liquid; set aside. Chop mushrooms; set aside.

2 In a large saucepan heat 1 tablespoon of the oil over medium heat. Add onion, celery, and carrot; cook about 8 minutes or until tender. Stir in garlic, thyme, oregano, and bay leaf; cook and stir 2 minutes more. Stir in reserved mushroom liquid, soaked mushrooms, broth, beans, barley, salt, and pepper. Bring to boiling; reduce heat. Simmer, covered, for 35 minutes or until barley is tender.

3 In a large skillet heat remaining 1 tablespoon oil over medium heat. Add mushrooms and zucchini; cook until tender. Add mushrooms, zucchini, spinach, parsley, and vinegar to soup. Heat through. Discard bay leaf.

nutrition facts per serving: 304 cal., 9 g total fat (1 g sat. fat), 0 mg chol., 1616 mg sodium, 51 g carb., 18 g dietary fiber, 13 g protein.

This hearty soup full of beans, mushrooms, tomatoes, and orzo—a Greek pasta shaped like grains of rice—can be on the table in just 30 minutes.

minestrone with mushrooms and feta

prep: 15 minutes   cook: 15 minutes
makes: 4 servings

2   cloves garlic, minced
1   tablespoon extra-virgin olive oil
2   cups stemmed fresh shiitake mushrooms, sliced
3   14-ounce cans vegetable broth
1   15-ounce can cannellini (white kidney) beans, rinsed and drained
½   cup dried orzo
1½   cups quartered cherry tomatoes
¼   cup small fresh oregano leaves
½   cup feta cheese, crumbled
Ground black pepper
1   tablespoon extra-virgin olive oil

In a 4-quart Dutch oven cook garlic in hot oil for 15 seconds. Add mushrooms; cook, stirring frequently, until mushrooms are tender. Stir in broth and beans. Bring to boiling. Add orzo. Return to boiling; reduce heat. Simmer, covered, for 15 minutes or until orzo is tender. Stir in cherry tomatoes and 3 tablespoons of the oregano; heat through. Sprinkle with remaining oregano, feta, and pepper. Drizzle with olive oil.

nutrition facts per serving: 312 cal., 11 g total fat (3 g sat. fat), 13 mg chol., 1497 mg sodium, 48 g carb., 8 g dietary fiber, 14 g protein.

Loaded with fiber and iron, lentils are especially delicious in this meatless soup because they absorb the snappy flavors of the garlic, Italian seasoning, and tomatoes.

italian-style lentil soup

prep: 25 minutes   cook: 40 minutes
makes: 6 servings

1   tablespoon olive oil
    or canola oil
½   cup chopped onion
    (1 medium)
6   cloves garlic, minced
1   32-ounce box
    reduced-sodium
    chicken broth
    (4 cups)
2   cups water
1   cup lentils
1½ teaspoons dried
    Italian seasoning,
    crushed
½   teaspoon ground
    black pepper
1   14.5-ounce can
    no-salt-added
    diced tomatoes,
    undrained
1   6-ounce can no-salt-
    added tomato paste
2   cups frozen peas and
    carrots
2   ounces dried
    multigrain penne
    pasta or multigrain
    elbow macaroni
¼   cup finely shredded
    Parmesan cheese
    (optional)

1 In a large saucepan or 4-quart Dutch oven heat oil over medium heat. Add onion and garlic; cook about 5 minutes or until onion is tender, stirring occasionally.

2 Add broth, the water, lentils, Italian seasoning, and pepper to onion mixture. Bring to boiling; reduce heat. Simmer, covered, for 30 minutes.

3 Stir in tomatoes and tomato paste. Stir in frozen peas and carrots and pasta. Return to boiling; reduce heat. Simmer, uncovered, about 10 minutes or until pasta is tender.

4 If desired, sprinkle each serving with cheese.

nutrition facts per serving: 251 cal., 3 g total fat (0 g sat. fat), 0 mg chol., 467 mg sodium, 42 g carb., 15 g dietary fiber, 15 g protein.

A combination French onion and bean soup, this mix tastes great ladled over melted cheese–topped toasts.

hearty onion-lentil soup

prep: 20 minutes **slow cook:** 6 to 8 hours (low) or 3 to 4 hours (high)
broil: 2 minutes
makes: 6 servings

4   cups water
2   10.5-ounce cans
      condensed French
      onion soup
2   cups sliced celery
      (4 stalks) or carrot
      (4 medium)
1   cup lentils
6   ¾-inch slices crusty
      country French
      bread, toasted
1   cup shredded Swiss
      or Gruyère cheese
      (4 ounces)

1 In a 3½- or 4-quart slow cooker combine the water, condensed French onion soup, celery, and lentils.

2 Cover and cook on low-heat setting for 6 to 8 hours or on high-heat setting for 3 to 4 hours.

3 Before serving, preheat broiler. Arrange toasted bread slices on a baking sheet; sprinkle with cheese. Broil 3 to 4 inches from the heat for 2 to 3 minutes or until cheese is light brown and bubbly.

4 Divide cheese-topped bread among 6 soup bowls; ladle soup over bread.

nutrition facts per serving: 345 cal., 9 g total fat (4 g sat. fat), 19 mg chol., 1130 mg sodium, 48 g carb., 12 g dietary fiber, 20 g protein.

Enjoy hearty winter vegetables in this light and satisfying soup. A fresh cabbage topper adds delightful crunch.

chunky vegetable-lentil soup

prep: 25 minutes **cook:** 30 minutes
makes: 6 servings

1   tablespoon olive oil
1   medium onion, cut
      into thin rings
1   clove garlic, minced
1   cup green (French)
      lentils
1   pound whole small
      fresh mushrooms
      (halve or quarter
      any larger
      mushrooms)
2   cups thinly sliced
      carrot (4 medium)
1   cup chopped celery
      (2 stalks)
4   cups water
1   14-ounce can
      vegetable broth
¼   teaspoon salt
¼   teaspoon ground
      black pepper
¼   of a head napa or red
      cabbage, sliced into
      strips (2 cups)

1 In a 4-quart saucepan or Dutch oven heat oil over medium heat. Add onion and garlic; cook for 4 to 5 minutes or until onion is tender, stirring occasionally. Stir in lentils; cook and stir 1 minute.

2 Add mushrooms, carrot, celery, the water, broth, salt and pepper. Bring to boiling; reduce heat. Simmer, covered, about 25 minutes or until lentils are tender.

3 Divide among soup bowls; top with cabbage.

nutrition facts per serving: 185 cal., 3 g total fat (0 g sat. fat), 0 mg chol., 408 mg sodium, 30 g carb., 13 g dietary fiber, 12 g protein.

Potatoes blend with cheddar cheese, cream, and roasted garlic in this chunky, good-to-the-last-spoonful soup.

smashed potato soup

prep: 25 minutes   slow cook: 8 to 10 hours (low) or 4 to 5 hours (high)
makes: 8 servings

3½ pounds potatoes, peeled and cut into ¾-inch cubes
½ cup chopped yellow and/or red sweet pepper
1½ teaspoons bottled roasted garlic
½ teaspoon ground black pepper
4½ cups chicken broth
½ cup whipping cream, half-and-half, or light cream
1 cup shredded cheddar cheese (4 ounces)
½ cup thinly sliced green onion
Sliced green onion (optional)

1 In a 4- to 6-quart slow cooker combine potatoes, sweet pepper, garlic, and black pepper. Pour broth over all.

2 Cover and cook on low-heat setting for 8 to 10 hours or on high-heat setting for 4 to 5 hours.

3 Mash potatoes slightly with a potato masher. Stir in whipping cream, cheese, and ½ cup green onion. If desired, top each servings with sliced green onion.

nutrition facts per serving: 243 cal., 11 g total fat (6 g sat. fat), 37 mg chol., 644 mg sodium, 30 g carb., 3 g dietary fiber, 8 g protein.

Cumin, paprika, and cayenne pepper add a nice level of spice and heat to this brothy bean and potato stew. Accompany with whole-grain bread.

garbanzo bean stew

prep: 20 minutes   **slow cook:** 9 to 10 hours (low) or 4½ to 5 hours (high)
makes: 6 servings

3   15-ounce cans no-salt-added garbanzo beans (chickpeas), rinsed and drained
1   pound red-skinned potatoes, cut into ¾-inch pieces
1   14.5-ounce can no-salt-added diced tomatoes, undrained
¾   cup chopped red sweet pepper (1 medium)
½   cup chopped onion (1 medium)
3   cloves garlic, minced
1   teaspoon ground cumin
½   teaspoon paprika
¼   teaspoon cayenne pepper
2   14.5-ounce cans vegetable broth or chicken broth

1 In a 5- to 6-quart slow cooker combine beans, potatoes, undrained tomatoes, sweet pepper, onion, garlic, cumin, paprika, and cayenne pepper. Pour broth over mixture in cooker.

2 Cover and cook on low-heat setting for 9 to 10 hours or on high-heat setting for 4½ to 5 hours.

nutrition facts per serving: 293 cal., 3 g total fat (0 g sat. fat), 0 mg chol., 590 mg sodium, 53 g carb., 12 g dietary fiber, 14 g protein.

The lentils, brown rice, vegetables, and herbs contribute plenty of fiber in this winter chill chaser.

tomato-lentil soup

prep: 20 minutes cook: 45 minutes
makes: 5 or 6 servings

7   cups water
1   14.5-ounce can diced
    tomatoes, undrained
1   cup chopped carrot
    (2 medium)
1   cup lentils
1   cup chopped onion
    (2 medium)
½   cup chopped celery
    (1 stalk)
1   tablespoon instant
    chicken bouillon
    granules
2   cloves garlic, minced
1   bay leaf
½   teaspoon dried basil,
    crushed
½   teaspoon dried
    oregano, crushed
½   teaspoon dried
    thyme, crushed
¾   cup brown rice
¼   cup snipped fresh
    parsley
½   teaspoon salt
½   teaspoon cider
    vinegar
¼   teaspoon ground
    black pepper
    Chopped green onion
    (optional)

1 In a Dutch oven or large pot combine the water, undrained tomatoes, carrot, lentils, onion, celery, bouillon granules, garlic, bay leaf, basil, oregano, and thyme. Bring to boiling; reduce heat. Simmer, covered, for 45 minutes.

2 Meanwhile, cook rice according to package directions. Discard the bay leaf from lentil mixture. Stir in parsley, salt, vinegar, and pepper. Stir in rice. If desired, garnish each serving with green onion.

nutrition facts per serving: 283 cal., 0 g total fat (0 g sat. fat), 0 mg chol., 988 mg sodium, 53 g carb., 15 g dietary fiber, 14 g protein.

A takeoff on the French classic, cassoulet, this stew features a trio of beans simmered with leeks, carrots, celery, and turnips.

vegetable stew with parmesan toast

prep: 35 minutes   **slow cook:** 10 to 11 hours (low) or 5 to 5½ hours (high)
bake: 7 minutes   **oven:** at 400°F
makes: 8 servings

2   14.5-ounce cans vegetable broth
1   15- to 16-ounce can navy beans, rinsed and drained
1   15- to 16-ounce can cannellini (white kidney) beans, rinsed and drained
1   15- to 16-ounce can butter beans, rinsed and drained
4   medium leeks, sliced*
4   carrots, cut into ½-inch-thick slices
2   medium turnips, peeled and diced
2   cups sliced celery (4 stalks)
4   cloves garlic, minced
2   teaspoons dried Italian seasoning, crushed
2   bay leaves
½   to 1 teaspoon cracked black pepper
¼   teaspoon salt
16   slices baguette-style French bread
1   tablespoon olive oil
½   cup finely shredded Parmesan cheese (2 ounces)
1   14.5-ounce can fire-roasted diced tomatoes or diced tomatoes, drained

1 In a 5- to 6-quart slow cooker stir together broth, navy beans, cannellini beans, butter beans, leeks, carrots, turnips, celery, garlic, Italian seasoning, bay leaves, pepper, and salt.

2 Cover and cook on low-heat setting for 10 to 11 hours or on high-heat setting for 5 to 5½ hours.

3 For Parmesan toast, preheat oven to 400°F. Brush baguette slices with oil; sprinkle with cheese. Place on a baking sheet. Bake about 7 minutes or until lightly toasted and cheese is melted.

4 Discard bay leaves. Stir drained tomatoes into bean mixture in cooker. Serve stew with Parmesan toast.

nutrition facts per serving: 288 cal., 4 g total fat (1 g sat. fat), 4 mg chol., 1409 mg sodium, 50 g carb., 10 g dietary fiber, 15 g protein.

*note: See tip on cleaning leeks, page 464.

Curry blends with grated fresh ginger and colorful sweet potatoes to give this lentil soup a different flavor.

curried lentil soup

prep: 20 minutes cook: 25 minutes
makes: 4 to 6 servings

1 medium onion,
    chopped (½ cup)
1 medium jalapeño
    pepper*, seeded
    and finely chopped
3 cloves garlic, minced
1 teaspoon grated fresh
    ginger
1 tablespoon olive oil
1 cup lentils
2 medium sweet
    potatoes, peeled
    and cut into ½-inch
    pieces
2 medium tomatoes,
    chopped
2 14-ounce cans
    vegetable broth
1 cup water
1 tablespoon curry
    powder
    Pinch salt
    Plain yogurt or sour
    cream (optional)
    Small fresh chile
    peppers* and/or
    crushed red pepper
    flakes (optional)

1 In a 4-quart Dutch oven, cook onion, chile pepper, garlic, and ginger in hot oil over medium heat until tender. Add lentils, sweet potatoes, tomatoes, broth, the water, curry powder, and salt. Bring mixture to boiling; reduce heat.

2 Simmer, covered, 25 to 30 minutes or until lentils are tender. If desired, top each serving with yogurt and garnish with chile peppers.

nutrition facts per serving: 328 cal., 5 g total fat (0 g sat. fat), 0 mg chol., 886 mg sodium, 57 g carb., 19 g dietary fiber, 18 g protein.

*note: See tip on handling chile peppers, page 31.

254

An aromatic base of tomatoes, garlic, and onions blends deliciously with the earthy flavor of navy beans and buttery texture and nutty flavor of fava beans.

italian bean and pasta soup

start to finish: 30 minutes
makes: 6 servings

1   cup chopped onion
      (1 large)
2   cloves garlic, minced
1   tablespoon olive oil
2   14-ounce cans
      vegetable broth
½   cup chopped green
      sweet pepper
      (1 medium)
½   cup dried orzo
2   14.5-ounce cans diced
      tomatoes with basil,
      garlic, and oregano,
      undrained
1   19-ounce can fava
      beans, rinsed and
      drained
1   15-ounce can navy
      beans, rinsed and
      drained
¼   cup snipped fresh
      parsley

1 In a 4- to 5-quart Dutch oven cook onion and garlic in hot oil over medium heat for 5 minutes or until tender, stirring occasionally. Add broth; bring to boiling.

2 Add sweet pepper and orzo. Return to boiling; reduce heat. Simmer, uncovered, for 8 to 10 minutes or until orzo is tender. Stir in undrained tomatoes, fava beans, and navy beans. Cover and simmer for 5 minutes. Stir in parsley.

nutrition facts per serving: 295 cal., 3 g total fat (0 g sat. fat), 0 mg chol., 1953 mg sodium, 54 g carb., 9 g dietary fiber, 15 g protein.

The greens in this soup stay flavorful and brightly colored, as they're not cooked but just slightly wilted when added to the hot soup after it's ladled into the bowls. Sharp and nutty-flavored Gouda melts marvelously and perfectly complements the assortive greens.

broccoli-potato soup with greens

start to finish: 20 minutes
makes: 4 servings

2 red-skinned potatoes, chopped
1 14-ounce can reduced-sodium chicken broth
3 cups small broccoli florets
2 cups milk
3 tablespoons all-purpose flour
2 cups smoked Gouda cheese, shredded (8 ounces)
   Ground black pepper
2 cups winter greens (such as curly endive, chicory, romaine, escarole, or spinach)
   Smoked Gouda cheese, shredded (optional)

1 In a large saucepan combine potatoes and broth. Bring to boiling; reduce heat. Simmer, covered, for 8 minutes. Mash potatoes slightly. Add broccoli and milk; bring just to simmering.

2 In a medium bowl toss flour with 2 cups cheese; gradually add to soup, stirring cheese until melted. Season to taste with pepper. Top each serving with greens and cheese.

nutrition facts per serving: 365 cal., 18 g total fat (11 g sat. fat), 74 mg chol., 782 mg sodium, 28 g carb., 4 g dietary fiber, 23 g protein.

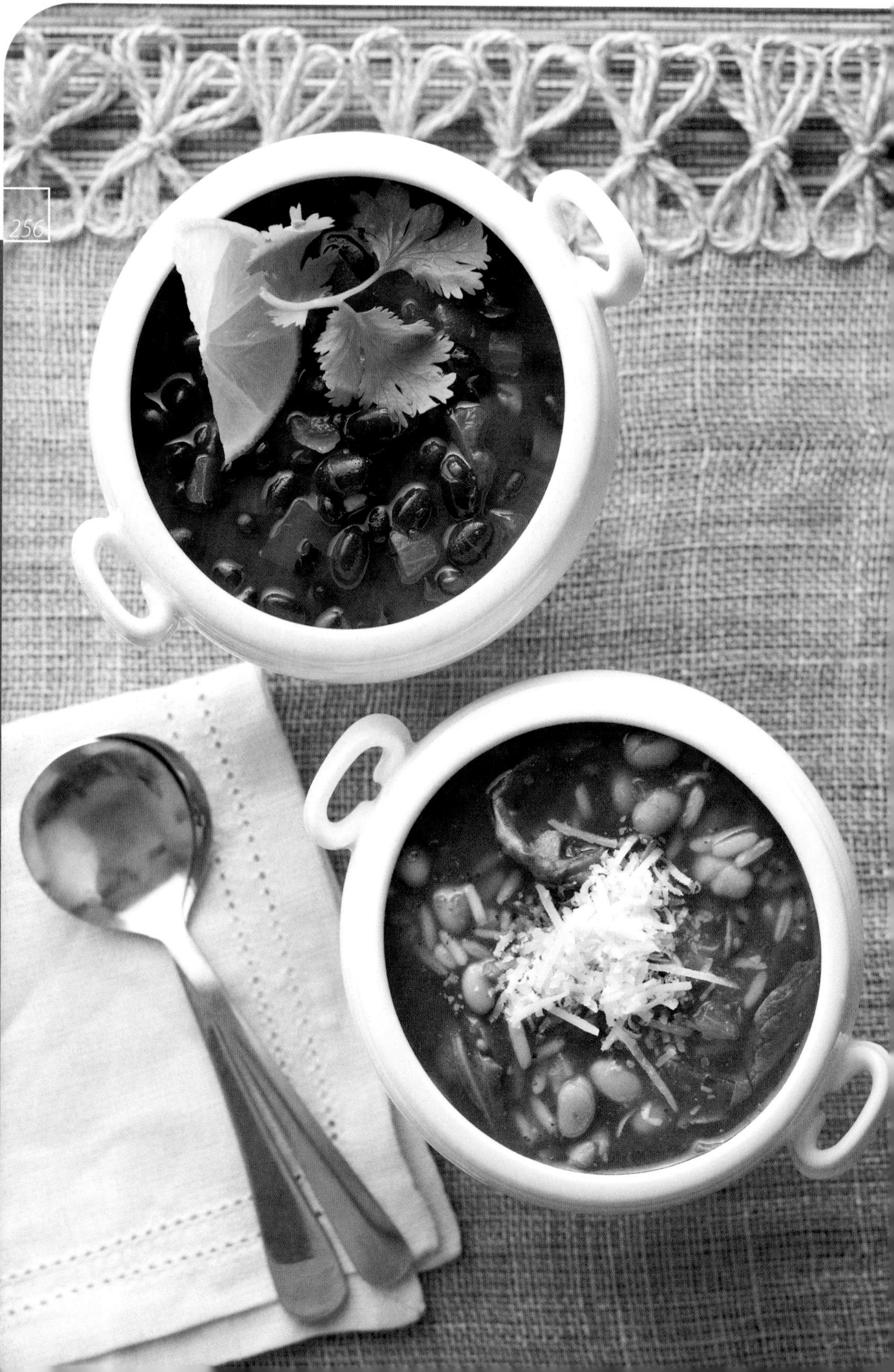

Thick, rich, hearty, and healthy — you can't go wrong with a meatless soup like this one that gets a spicy punch from ground cumin and chili powder.

vegetarian black bean soup

prep: 10 minutes **stand:** 1 hour **slow cook:** 9 to 10 hours (low) or 4½ to 5 hours (high)
makes: 6 servings

1½ cups dried black beans, rinsed and drained
8 cups water
½ cup chopped onion (1 medium)
1 jalapeño pepper, seeded and chopped*
3 cloves garlic, minced
6 cups no-salt-added vegetable broth
2 tablespoons ground cumin
1 tablespoon chili powder
½ teaspoon salt
½ cup chopped fresh cilantro
 Lime wedges
 Light sour cream (optional)

1 In a large pot combine beans and the water. Bring to boiling; reduce heat. Simmer, uncovered, for 10 minutes. Remove from heat. Cover and let stand for 1 hour. Drain and rinse beans.

2 In a 4-quart slow cooker combine beans, onion, chile pepper, garlic, broth, cumin, chili powder, and salt.

3 Cover and cook on low-heat setting for 9 to 10 hours or on high-heat setting for 4½ to 5 hours. Using a potato masher, coarsely mash the beans. Top each serving with cilantro and serve with lime wedges for squeezing. If desired, top each serving with sour cream.

nutrition facts per serving: 204 cal., 1 g total fat (0 g sat. fat), 0 mg chol., 367 mg sodium, 37 g carb., 10 g dietary fiber, 11 g protein.

＊note: See tip on handling chile peppers, page 31.

Tofu is amazingly versatile in meatless soups like this one. It absorbs the flavors of the ingredients while supplying adequate amounts of protein. Be sure to drain the tofu well before adding to the soup so you don't dilute the flavor of the broth.

tofu-carrot soup

prep: 30 minutes **cook:** 25 minutes
makes: 6 servings

3 cups sliced fresh
    button mushrooms
    (8 ounces)
1 cup sliced celery
    (2 stalks)
1 medium onion, sliced
2 cloves garlic, minced
2 tablespoons
    vegetable oil
3 14.5-ounce cans
    vegetable broth
    or chicken broth
4 cups sliced carrot
    (8 medium)
1 12-ounce package
    firm, silken-style
    tofu (fresh bean
    curd)
1 5-ounce can
    evaporated milk
1 teaspoon snipped
    fresh thyme
    Salt
    Ground black pepper
½ cup sour cream
2 to 3 teaspoons water
    Fresh thyme
    (optional)
    Cayenne pepper
    (optional)

1 In a 4- to 6-quart Dutch oven cook mushrooms, celery, onion, and garlic in hot oil over medium heat about 5 minutes or until softened. Add broth and carrot. Bring to boiling; reduce heat. Simmer, covered, about 20 minutes or until vegetables are tender; cool slightly.

2 Cut up tofu. Place tofu and half of the broth mixture in a large food processor or blender. (If you don't have a large food processor or blender, process mixture in smaller batches.) Cover and process or blend until smooth. Repeat with the remaining broth mixture and evaporated milk.

3 Return all of the pureed mixture to Dutch oven; heat through. Stir in 1 teaspoon thyme. Season to taste with salt and black pepper. In a small bowl combine sour cream and enough of the water to reach drizzling consistency. Top each serving of soup with sour cream mixture and, if desired, thyme and cayenne pepper.

nutrition facts per serving: 205 cal., 11 g total fat (4 g sat. fat), 15 mg chol., 1003 mg sodium, 18 g carb., 3 g dietary fiber, 8 g protein.

Brimming with pumpkin and carrots, this tomato-based stew makes a delicious cold-weather supper. Lentils and beans pack filling protein, while nonfat yogurt adds creaminess without the fat.

pumpkin, chickpea, and red lentil stew

prep: 25 minutes   slow cook: 8 to 10 hours (low) or 4 to 5 hours (high)
makes: 6 servings

1   pound pie pumpkin or winter squash, peeled, seeded, and cut into 1-inch cubes
1   15-ounce can garbanzo beans (chickpeas), rinsed and drained
3   carrots, sliced ½ inch thick
1   cup chopped onion (1 large)
1   cup red lentils
2   tablespoons tomato paste
1   tablespoon grated fresh ginger
1   tablespoon lime juice
1   teaspoon ground cumin
¼   teaspoon salt
¼   teaspoon ground turmeric
¼   teaspoon gound black pepper
4   cups chicken or vegetable broth
¼   cup chopped peanuts
2   tablespoons chopped fresh cilantro
    Plain nonfat yogurt (optional)

1 In a 3½- or 4-quart slow cooker combine pumpkin, beans, carrots, onion, lentils, tomato paste, ginger, lime juice, cumin, salt, turmeric, and pepper. Pour broth over all.

2 Cover and cook on low-heat setting for 8 to 10 hours or on high-heat setting for 4 to 5 hours. Top each serving with peanuts, cilantro, and, if desired, yogurt.

nutrition facts per serving: 275 cal., 4 g total fat (1 g sat. fat), 2 mg chol., 1027 mg sodium, 46 g carb., 10 g dietary fiber, 14 g protein.

make it **meatless**

Green onions bring a mild onion flavor to this delicious cheese and potato soup recipe that's perfect for a cold winter night. The sweet and roasty flavors of a lager blend in nicely with the natural richness of the cheese.

cheesy potato soup

start to finish: 25 minutes
makes: 4 servings

1   bunch green onions
3   tablespoons olive oil
2   cups refrigerated
      shredded hash
      brown potatoes
¾   cup roasted red
      sweet peppers
¾   cup pale lager or
      nonalcoholic beer
2   cups milk
2   cups shredded
      American cheese
      (8 ounces)
¼   teaspoon paprika
      Paprika

1 Slice green onions, separating white portions from green portions. In a Dutch oven heat 1 tablespoon of the oil over medium heat. Add white portions of the green onions; cook until tender.

2 In a blender combine cooked onions, 1 cup of the potatoes, roasted sweet peppers, and lager. Cover and blend until smooth. Transfer pureed mixture to Dutch oven. Bring to boiling; reduce heat. Simmer, uncovered, for 5 minutes. Add milk and cheese; cook and stir over medium heat until cheese is melted and mixture is heated through (do not boil).

3 In a medium skillet heat remaining 2 tablespoons oil over medium-high heat. Add the remaining 1 cup potatoes; cook about 8 minutes or until golden, stirring occasionally. Using a slotted spoon, remove potatoes from skillet; drain on paper towels. Sprinkle potatoes with the ¼ teaspoon paprika.

4 Top each serving with cooked potatoes, sliced green onion tops, and additional paprika.

nutrition facts per serving: 467 cal., 30 g total fat (14 g sat. fat), 63 mg chol., 1096 mg sodium, 28 g carb., 2 g dietary fiber, 19 g protein.

Adding beans to a classic potato chowder boosts the protein, turning the creamy soup into a tasty main dish. Chopped carrot and fresh herbs add texture and boost flavor.

potato and white bean chowder

start to finish: 30 minutes
makes: 4 servings

Nonstick cooking
   spray
½   cup sliced green
   onion (4)
2   tablespoons snipped
   fresh herbs (such
   as oregano, basil,
   and/or parsley) or
   ¾ teaspoon dried
   Italian seasoning,
   crushed
4   cloves garlic, minced
2   cups water
2   medium potato,
   peeled and chopped
   (2 cups)
1   cup chopped carrot
   (2 medium)
½   teaspoon salt
¼   teaspoon coarsely
   ground black
   pepper
2   cups fat-free milk
2   tablespoons all-
   purpose flour
1   15-ounce can
   cannellini (white
   kidney) beans,
   rinsed and drained
   Ground nutmeg

1 Coat an unheated nonstick large saucepan with nonstick cooking spray. Heat over medium heat. Add green onion, dried Italian seasoning (if using), and garlic to hot saucepan. Cook until green onion is tender. Add the water, potato, carrot, salt, and pepper. Bring to boiling; reduce heat. Simmer, covered, about 12 minutes or until potato and carrot are tender. Do not drain. Slightly mash potato and carrot with a fork or potato masher.

2 In a screw-top jar combine milk and flour; cover and shake well. Stir milk mixture into potato mixture; cook and stir until thickened and bubbly. Stir in fresh herbs (if using) and beans; cook and stir for 1 minute more. Sprinkle individual servings with nutmeg.

nutrition facts per serving: 236 cal., 1 g total fat (0 g sat. fat), 2 mg chol., 380 mg sodium, 46 g carb., 7 g dietary fiber, 14 g protein.

Serve a pot of rich tomato-laced seafood stew, a fresh fish chowder, or any of the other delectable seafood specialties featured here, and you'll get rave reviews.

deep-sea

trea

9

sures

If you have a great seafood market nearby, try this with other firm white fish such as snapper, cod, flounder, or sea bass. You can also toast the cumin seeds in a skillet to bring out the flavor and aroma.

hot 'n' spicy fish soup

start to finish: 35 minutes
makes: 2 servings

2 6-ounce fresh or frozen halibut steaks, cut 1 inch thick
2 teaspoons vegetable oil
¼ teaspoon cumin seeds
1 small onion, chopped
2 to 3 teaspoons grated fresh ginger
1 serrano pepper, seeded and finely chopped*
½ cup chopped tomato (1 medium)
¾ cup water
½ teaspoon ground coriander
¼ teaspoon ground turmeric
¼ teaspoon salt
   Fresh cilantro leaves (optional)

1 Thaw fish, if frozen. Rinse fish; pat dry with paper towels. Remove skin and bones. Cut into 1-inch pieces; set aside.

2 In a medium saucepan heat oil over medium heat. Add cumin seeds; cook and stir about 1 minute or until toasted. Add onion; cook and stir for 4 to 5 minutes or until tender. Add ginger and chile pepper; cook and stir for 1 minute more. Add tomato; cook and stir for 2 to 3 minutes more or until tomato has softened. Stir in the water, coriander, turmeric, and salt. Bring to boiling; reduce heat. Stir in fish. Cook, covered, about 5 minutes or just until fish pieces flake easily when tested with a fork. Serve immediately. If desired, garnish with cilantro.

nutrition facts per serving: 252 cal., 9 g total fat (1 g sat. fat), 54 mg chol., 392 mg sodium, 5 g carb., 1 g dietary fiber, 36 g protein.

✳note: See tip on handling chile peppers, page 31.

For a more dramatic presentation, use shrimp with tails left on. Start with 8 ounces shrimp; peel and devein the shrimp, leaving the tails intact. Topping with gremolata adds a jolt of color and freshness to the stew.

quick fish stew with basil gremolata

start to finish: 25 minutes

makes: 4 servings

6 ounces fresh or frozen cod fillets

6 ounces fresh or frozen peeled and deveined shrimp

1 cup green sweet pepper strips (1 medium)

1 cup chopped onion (1 large)

2 cloves garlic, minced

1 tablespoon olive oil or vegetable oil

2 14.5-ounce cans Italian-style stewed tomatoes, undrained and cut up

½ cup water

¼ teaspoon salt

¼ teaspoon ground black pepper

3 tablespoons snipped fresh basil

1 tablespoon finely shredded lemon zest

2 cloves garlic, minced

1 Thaw cod and shrimp, if frozen. Rinse cod and shrimp; pat dry with paper towels. Cut cod into 1-inch pieces. Set cod and shrimp aside.

2 In a large saucepan or Dutch oven cook and stir sweet pepper, onion, and 2 cloves garlic in hot oil over medium heat until tender. Stir in undrained tomatoes, the water, salt, and black pepper. Bring to boiling. Stir in cod and shrimp. Return to boiling; reduce heat. Simmer, covered, for 2 to 3 minutes or until cod flakes easily when tested with a fork and shrimp turn opaque.

3 In a small bowl combine basil, lemon zest, and 2 cloves garlic. Sprinkle each serving with basil mixture.

nutrition facts per serving: 197 cal., 5 g total fat (1 g sat. fat), 83 mg chol., 686 mg sodium, 19 g carb., 5 g dietary fiber, 19 g protein.

freshen up a soup with gremolata

Traditionally served over osso buco (braised veal shanks), a gremolata is a fragrant blend of chopped parsley, lemon zest, and garlic. Here are several ways to make this herb condiment to liven up a soup or stew.

· parsley gremolata: *3 tablespoons snipped parsley, 1 tablespoon finely shredded lemon zest, and 2 cloves garlic, minced, is the classic recipe for gremolata. It adds a jolt of freshness to long-simmered meat and poultry stews.*

· basil gremolata: *Using basil as the herb, this fragrant mixture enhances tomato, seafood, and Italian stews with a light citrusy flavor.*

· cilantro-lime gremolata: *Substituting cilantro for the parsley and lime zest for the lemon creates a vibrant topper for Tex-Mex pork or chicken soups.*

· other gremolatas: *Experiment with different combinations. Use chives as the herb, or mix the chives with basil and/or thyme, and replace the lemon or lime zest with orange zest. If desired, add a pinch of sea salt.*

A garlic-flavored tomato broth and fresh parsley inject bright flavor into this fish and vegetable soup. For more robust flavor, try substituting some red wine for some of the vegetable broth.

chunky fish soup

prep: 25 minutes cook: 20 minutes
makes: 6 servings

½ cup chopped onion
   (1 medium)
½ cup chopped celery
   (1 stalk)
½ cup chopped carrot
   (1 medium)
1 clove garlic, minced
2 tablespoons olive oil
5 cups vegetable broth
1 14.5-ounce can diced
   tomatoes, undrained
1½ pounds assorted
   white fish (such
   as halibut, red
   snapper, or cod), cut
   into bite-size pieces
2 tablespoons snipped
   fresh Italian parsley
6 slices country-style
   bread, toasted

1 In a Dutch oven cook onion, celery, carrot, and garlic in hot oil over medium-high heat about 5 minutes or until tender. Add broth and undrained tomatoes. Heat to boiling; reduce heat. Simmer, covered, for 15 minutes. Stir in fish. Simmer, covered, about 5 minutes more or until fish flakes easily when tested with a fork. Stir in parsley.

2 Serve with toasted bread.

nutrition facts per serving: 286 cal., 8 g total fat (1 g sat. fat), 36 mg chol., 1146 mg sodium, 23 g carb., 2 g dietary fiber, 27 g protein.

The firm texture and mild flavor of tilapia make it ideal for this tomato-based soup. Herbs and lemon infuse bright flavor while the fish simmers with fresh vegetables.

tilapia chowder with sage

start to finish: 30 minutes
makes: 6 servings

2   small carrots, peeled
1   medium onion,
     quartered
1   stalk celery
1   medium zucchini,
     halved lengthwise
3   tablespoons butter
3   14-ounce cans
     reduced-sodium
     chicken broth
1   14.5-ounce can diced
     tomatoes with basil,
     garlic, and oregano,
     undrained
¼   teaspoon salt
⅛   teaspoon ground
     black pepper
1½ pounds tilapia fillets,
     cut into 2-inch
     pieces
3   tablespoons chopped
     fresh sage
1   tablespoon lemon
     or lime juice
½   cup sour cream
     Snipped fresh sage
     (optional)

1 Thinly slice the carrots, onion, celery, and zucchini. In a Dutch oven cook carrots, onion, and celery in hot butter over medium heat for 4 minutes or until crisp-tender.

2 Add broth, undrained tomatoes, salt, and pepper. Cover and bring to boiling. Add tilapia, zucchini, and sage. Return to boiling; reduce heat. Simmer, uncovered, for 3 minutes or until fish flakes easily when tested with a fork, stirring occasionally. Stir in lemon juice. Top each serving with dollop of sour cream. If desired, sprinkle with sage.

nutrition facts per serving: 254 cal., 11 g total fat (7 g sat. fat), 78 mg chol., 1054 mg sodium, 12 g carb., 2 g dietary fiber, 28 g protein.

veggie-fish chowder

prep: 20 minutes   cook: 10 minutes
makes: 4 to 6 servings

1   pound cod, salmon,
    or other firm-
    textured fish,
    cut into 4 pieces
    Ground black pepper
1   32-ounce carton
    reduced-sodium
    chicken broth
1   cup water
1   cup thinly sliced
    carrot (2 medium)
1   cup sugar snap peas,
    halved diagonally
1   4-ounce package
    (or ½ a 7.2-ounce
    package) butter-
    and-herb-flavored
    instant mashed
    potatoes
¼   cup finely shredded
    Parmesan cheese

1 Season fish lightly with pepper; set aside. In a 4-quart pot bring broth and water to boiling. Add carrot. Cook, covered for 5 minutes. Add fish and peas. Return to boiling. Reduce heat. Simmer, covered, for 3 minutes or until fish flakes easily when tested with a fork. Stir in mashed potatoes and simmer for 2 minutes.

2 Break fish into bite-size pieces. Top each serving with cheese.

nutrition facts per serving: 269 cal., 5 g total fat (2 g sat. fat), 52 mg chol., 1269 mg sodium, 28 g carb., 3 g dietary fiber, 28 g protein.

Flounder and shrimp cook in a spicy tomato broth with corn and potatoes, two traditional staples of Peruvian cuisine. Cream cheese stirred in at the end adds flavor and richness.

peruvian shrimp chowder

prep: 15 minutes cook: 30 minutes
makes: 6 servings

8 ounces fresh or
   frozen flounder
   fillets (about
   2 medium)
8 ounces fresh or
   frozen peeled and
   deveined medium
   shrimp
1 cup chopped onion
   (2 medium)
2 cloves garlic, minced
1 tablespoon canola oil
1 14.5-ounce can
   diced tomatoes,
   undrained
1 14-ounce can
   vegetable or
   chicken broth
1 cup water
12 ounces potatoes,
   scrubbed and cubed
1½ teaspoons Creole
   seasoning
⅛ to ¼ teaspoon
   crushed red pepper
   flakes
   Dash bottled hot
   pepper sauce
1 3-ounce package
   cream cheese,
   softened
1 cup milk
1½ cups frozen whole-
   kernel corn

1 Thaw flounder and shrimp, if frozen. Rinse fish and shrimp; pat dry with paper towels. Cut flounder into bite-size pieces. Set aside. In a 4- to 5-quart Dutch oven cook onion and garlic in hot oil over medium heat for 12 to 15 minutes or until onion is tender and lightly browned. Turn heat down as needed to prevent onions from overbrowning.

2 Stir in undrained tomatoes, broth, the water, potatoes, Creole seasoning, red pepper flakes, and hot pepper sauce. Bring to boiling; reduce heat. Simmer, covered, 15 to 20 minutes or until potatoes are just tender.

3 Meanwhile, in medium bowl beat cream cheese with an electric mixer on medium to high speed until smooth. Gradually beat in milk on low speed until mixture is very smooth.

4 Add flounder, shrimp, cream cheese mixture, and corn to soup. Return to boiling; reduce heat. Simmer, uncovered, 3 to 5 minutes or until shrimp are opaque.

nutrition facts per serving: 276 cal., 10 g total fat (4 g sat. fat), 94 mg chol., 593 mg sodium, 28 g carb., 4 g dietary fiber, 21 g protein.

Stir-fry veggies and the kick of Cajun seasoning start this delicious seafood meal. Add tilapia and tomatoes and this 20-minute soup is done.

cajun fish soup

start to finish: 20 minutes
makes: 4 servings

12 ounces fresh or frozen
sea bass, cod, or
orange roughy fillets

4 cups assorted stir-fry
vegetables from
a salad bar or
produce department
or one 16-ounce
package frozen
stir-fry vegetables

4 cups reduced-sodium
chicken broth

2 teaspoons Cajun
seasoning

1 14.5-ounce can diced
tomatoes, undrained

1 Thaw fish, if frozen. Rinse fish; pat dry with paper towels. Cut fish into 1-inch pieces. Set aside.

2 In a large saucepan combine vegetables, broth, and Cajun seasoning. Bring to boiling; reduce heat. Simmer, covered, for 3 to 5 minutes or until vegetables are crisp-tender. Stir in fish and undrained tomatoes. Return to boiling; reduce heat. Simmer, covered, for 2 to 3 minutes more or until fish flakes easily when tested with a fork.

nutrition facts per serving: 157 cal., 2 g total fat (0 g sat. fat), 35 mg chol., 968 mg sodium, 12 g carb., 3 g dietary fiber, 21 g protein.

Ginger, jerk seasoning, lime, and garlic turn simple white fish into a tropical delight. This lively combo is easy to throw into the slow cooker anytime.

caribbean fish stew

prep: 30 minutes   slow cook: 6 to 8 hours (low) or 3 to 4 hours (high) + 15 minutes (high)

makes: 6 servings

2   pounds sweet potatoes, peeled and coarsely chopped

1¼ cups chopped red sweet pepper (1 large)

½   cup chopped onion (1 medium)

1   tablespoon grated fresh ginger

½   teaspoon finely shredded lime zest

1   tablespoon lime juice

1   teaspoon Jamaican jerk seasoning

2   cloves garlic, minced

2   14-ounce cans chicken broth

1   14.5-ounce can diced tomatoes, undrained

1   pound fresh or frozen firm white fish

2   tablespoons snipped fresh cilantro

1 In a 4- to 5-quart slow cooker combine sweet potatoes, sweet pepper, onion, ginger, lime zest, lime juice, jerk seasoning, and garlic. Pour broth and undrained tomatoes over all.

2 Cover and cook on low-heat setting for 6 to 8 hours or on high-heat setting for 3 to 4 hours.

3 Thaw fish, if frozen. Cut into 1-inch pieces. If using low-heat setting, turn to high-heat setting. Stir in fish. Cover and cook about 15 minutes more or until fish flakes easily when tested with a fork. Sprinkle each serving with cilantro.

nutrition facts per serving: 232 cal., 5 g total fat (1 g sat. fat), 45 mg chol., 792 mg sodium, 29 g carb., 4 g dietary fiber, 17 g protein.

Lemongrass infuses a refreshing citrusy flavor in this hot-and-sour soup, which also receives a flavor boost from hot chiles and fresh basil. Look for fresh or frozen lemongrass at Asian markets or in some gourmet grocery stores.

thai shrimp soup

prep: 30 minutes cook: 22 minutes
makes: 4 servings

12 ounces fresh or frozen
     peeled and deveined
     shrimp (tails intact,
     if desired)
1   14-ounce can
     reduced-sodium
     chicken broth
2¾ cups water
2   lemongrass stalks
     (white part only),
     cut into ½-inch-
     thick slices
2   jalapeño peppers,
     halved lengthwise
     and seeded*
1   cup stemmed and
     sliced fresh shiitake
     and/or button
     mushrooms or
     ½ of a 15-ounce
     can whole straw
     mushrooms, drained
1   cup chopped red
     sweet pepper
     (1 large)
1   cup sliced carrot
     (2 medium)
2   tablespoons lime
     juice
2   tablespoons rice
     vinegar or white
     wine vinegar
2   teaspoons packed
     brown sugar
2   teaspoons bottled
     fish sauce
¼   cup slivered fresh
     basil

1 Thaw shrimp, if frozen. Rinse shrimp; pat dry with paper towels. Set aside.

2 In a large saucepan combine broth and the water. Bring to boiling. Add lemongrass and chile peppers. Return to boiling; reduce heat. Simmer, covered, for 10 minutes. Using a slotted spoon, remove lemongrass and chile peppers; discard.

3 Stir mushrooms, sweet pepper, carrot, lime juice, rice vinegar, brown sugar, and fish sauce into liquid in saucepan. Bring to boiling; reduce heat. Simmer, covered, for 10 to 15 minutes or until vegetables are crisp-tender. Add shrimp. Cook, covered, for 2 to 4 minutes more or until shrimp are opaque. Sprinkle each serving with basil.

nutrition facts per serving: 146 cal., 2 g total fat (0 g sat. fat), 129 mg chol., 623 mg sodium, 11 g carb., 2 g dietary fiber, 20 g protein.

*note: See tip on handling chile peppers, page 31.

The sweet essence of fresh fennel blends nicely with fish, tomatoes, garlic, and onion in this classic French soup.

fish provençale

start to finish: 30 minutes
makes: 4 servings

8   ounces fresh or
    frozen skinless
    haddock, grouper,
    or halibut fillets
1   fennel bulb
3   cups vegetable broth
    or chicken broth
1   cup finely chopped
    onion (1 large)
1   cup cubed yellow
    summer squash
    (1 small)
1   cup dry white wine
3   cloves garlic, minced
1   teaspoon finely
    shredded orange
    zest or lemon zest
2   cups chopped
    tomatoes or one
    14.5-ounce can
    diced tomatoes,
    undrained
2   tablespoons snipped
    fresh thyme

1 Thaw fish, if frozen. Rinse fish; pat dry with paper towels. Cut fish into 1-inch pieces; set aside.

2 Cut off and discard upper stalks of fennel. Remove any wilted outer layers; cut off and discard a thin slice from fennel base. Wash fennel; cut in half lengthwise and thinly slice.

3 In a large saucepan combine fennel slices, broth, onion, squash, wine, garlic, and orange zest. Bring to boiling; reduce heat. Simmer, covered, for 10 minutes. Stir in fish, undrained tomatoes, and thyme; cook about 3 minutes more or until fish flakes easily when tested with a fork.

nutrition facts per serving: 165 cal., 1 g total fat (0 g sat. fat), 32 mg chol., 798 mg sodium, 17 g carb., 4 g dietary fiber, 13 g protein.

Swiss chard, a member of the beet family, has dark green leaves and reddish celerylike stalks. The vitamin-rich vegetable tastes bitter in the raw form and milder when cooked in soups like this.

shrimp and swiss chard soup with arborio rice

prep: 30 minutes cook: 47 minutes
makes: 6 servings

1 pound fresh or frozen
   medium shrimp in
   shells
3 tablespoons olive oil
4 russet potatoes,
   peeled and cut into
   ¼-inch cubes
1 cup shredded carrot
   (2 medium)
1 tablespoon tomato
   paste
4 14-ounce cans
   reduced-sodium
   chicken broth
12 ounces Swiss chard,
   stems removed
   and cut into ½-inch
   strips (about 6 cups)
¾ cup Arborio rice
1 tablespoon snipped
   fresh oregano
¼ teaspoon salt
⅛ teaspoon ground
   black pepper

1 Thaw shrimp, if frozen. Peel and devein shrimp, leaving tails intact, if desired. Cut shrimp in half lengthwise. Rinse shrimp; pat dry with paper towels. Set aside.

2 In a Dutch oven heat oil over medium-high heat. Add potatoes; cook about 10 minutes or until potatoes start to brown, stirring occasionally.

3 Stir in carrot; cook and stir about 3 minutes or until carrot is wilted. Stir in tomato paste; cook and stir for 1 minute. Add broth. Bring to boiling; reduce heat. Simmer, covered, for 30 minutes.

4 Stir in Swiss chard and rice. Simmer, covered, about 15 minutes or just until rice is tender. Stir in shrimp, oregano, salt, and pepper. Simmer, covered, for about 2 minutes or until shrimp are opaque.

nutrition facts per serving: 304 cal., 8 g total fat (1 g sat. fat), 86 mg chol., 954 mg sodium, 40 g carb., 3 g dietary fiber, 19 g protein.

Add unique flavor to this soup by substituting white wine for some of the steaming liquid for the mussels. Watch the pot carefully because the tender, sweet morsels only need to cook for a short time.

creamy mussel soup

prep: 35 minutes stand: 45 minutes cook: 15 minutes
makes: 8 servings

2 pounds mussels in shells
1 14-ounce can reduced-sodium chicken broth
1½ cups water
1 tablespoon olive oil
1 cup finely chopped leek (3 medium)*
2 cloves garlic, minced
¼ teaspoon saffron threads or
   ⅛ teaspoon ground turmeric
¼ teaspoon ground black pepper
1 cup fat-free half-and-half
1 tablespoon finely shredded fresh basil

1 Scrub live mussels under cold running water. Using your fingers, pull out the beards that are visible between the shells. In a very large bowl combine 4 quarts (16 cups) cold water and ⅓ cup salt. Add mussels; soak for 15 minutes. Drain in a colander. Rinse mussels, discarding water. Repeat soaking, draining, and rinsing two more times. Rinse well.

2 In a Dutch oven combine broth and the 1½ cups water; bring to boiling. Add mussels; reduce heat. Simmer, covered, for 5 to 7 minutes or until shells open and mussels are cooked through. Discard any mussels that do not open. Using a slotted spoon, remove mussels from steaming liquid; set aside until cool enough to handle.

3 Line a sieve with 100-percent-cotton cheesecloth. Strain cooking liquid into a large bowl; discard solids. Set liquid aside. Remove meat from mussel shells; discard shells. Set aside.

4 In a large saucepan heat oil over medium heat. Add leek and garlic; cook for 3 to 5 minutes or until tender. Stir in reserved cooking liquid, saffron, and pepper. Bring to boiling; reduce heat. Boil gently about 15 minutes or until reduced to 3 cups. Stir in half-and-half; heat through.

5 Just before serving, stir mussels into soup. Sprinkle each serving with basil.

nutrition facts per serving: 79 cal., 4 g total fat (1 g sat. fat), 16 mg chol., 456 mg sodium, 7 g carb., 0 g dietary fiber, 3 g protein.

*note:See tip on cleaning leeks, page 464.

Serve a seafood stew loaded with fish, shrimp, beans, and corn. Accompany it with garlic toasts and a bright lemon-dressed salad to accent the fresh flavor of the seafood.

seafood cioppino

prep: 35 minutes stand: 20 minutes chill: Up to 2 hours cook: 25 minutes
makes: 6 servings

1 pound fresh or frozen firm white fish (such as orange roughy or cod), cut into 1-inch pieces
1 pound fresh or frozen monkfish, cut into 1-inch pieces
8 ounces fresh or frozen medium shrimp
2 dried pasilla chile peppers
  Boiling water
1 teaspoon salt
¾ teaspoon chili powder
4 teaspoons olive oil
1 large onion, chopped
1 cup frozen whole-kernel corn
1 tablespoon bottled minced garlic (6 cloves)
1 15-ounce can cannellini (white kidney) beans, rinsed and drained
1 14.5-ounce can diced tomatoes, undrained
1 8-ounce bottle clam juice
1 cup dry white wine
1 cup water
2 tablespoons canned diced green chiles
1 avocado, pitted, peeled, and chopped (optional)
⅓ cup snipped fresh cilantro (optional)

1 Thaw fish and shrimp, if frozen. Peel and devein shrimp. Rinse fish and shrimp; pat dry with paper towels.

2 In a small bowl combine pasilla chile peppers and enough boiling water to cover. Let stand for 20 minutes. Remove chile peppers with a slotted spoon, reserving ¼ cup of the soaking liquid. Remove seeds and stems from chile peppers and discard. In a blender combine chile peppers and reserved liquid. Cover and blend until smooth. Set aside.

3 Meanwhile, in a large, shallow bowl, combine fish and shrimp. In a small bowl combine ½ teaspoon of the salt and chili powder; sprinkle over fish.

4 In a 4-quart nonstick Dutch oven heat 2 teaspoons of the oil over medium-high heat. Add half of the fish and half of the shrimp; cook about 4 minutes or just until done, gently turning mixture with a spatula occasionally. Transfer with a slotted spatula to a clean bowl. Repeat with remaining seafood (add additional oil, if necessary). Chill bowl of seafood until needed (up to 2 hours).

5 In same Dutch oven heat remaining 2 teaspoons oil. Add onion, frozen corn, and garlic; cook for 3 minutes, stirring occasionally. Stir in pureed chile mixture, beans, undrained tomatoes, clam juice, wine, the 1 cup water, green chiles, and remaining ½ teaspoon salt. Bring to boiling; reduce heat. Simmer, covered, for 20 minutes. Add seafood. Simmer, uncovered, for 5 minutes more. If desired, serve with avocado and cilantro.

nutrition facts per serving: 285 cal., 6 g total fat (1 g sat. fat), 74 mg chol., 774 mg sodium, 23 g carb., 5 g dietary fiber, 32 g protein.

Jambalaya is a classic Cajun stew made with shrimp, sausage, and plenty of seasonings. If you've never had it, try this simple recipe.

jambalaya

prep: 25 minutes   cook: 20 minutes
makes: 6 servings

1   pound fresh or frozen peeled and deveined shrimp
2   tablespoons vegetable oil
½   cup chopped onion (1 medium)
⅓   cup chopped celery
¼   cup chopped green sweet pepper
2   cloves garlic, minced
2   cups chicken broth
1   14.5-ounce can diced tomatoes, undrained
8   ounces andouille or kielbasa sausage, halved lengthwise and cut into ½-inch slices
¾   cup long-grain rice
1   teaspoon dried thyme, crushed
½   teaspoon dried basil, crushed
¼   teaspoon ground black pepper
¼   teaspoon cayenne pepper
1   bay leaf
4   ounces cooked boneless ham, cut into bite-size cubes (1 cup)

1 Thaw shrimp, if frozen. Set aside.

2 In a 12-inch skillet heat oil over medium heat. Add onion, celery, sweet pepper, and garlic; cook and stir for 5 minutes. Stir in broth, undrained tomatoes, sausage, rice, thyme, basil, black pepper, cayenne pepper, and bay leaf. Bring to boiling; reduce heat. Simmer, covered, for 15 minutes. Stir in shrimp. Return to boiling; reduce heat. Simmer, covered, about 5 minutes more or until shrimp turn opaque and rice is tender. Stir in ham; heat through. Discard bay leaf.

nutrition facts per serving: 416 cal., 20 g total fat (6 g sat. fat), 154 mg chol., 1199 mg sodium, 27 g carb., 1 g dietary fiber, 30 g protein.

A symbol of Creole cooking, gumbo is ubiquitous in homes and restaurants across Louisiana. Here, rice adds extra body and red and black pepper add the heat. If you prefer a less spicy soup, omit the cayenne pepper.

shrimp gumbo

start to finish: 50 minutes
makes: 6 servings

1 pound fresh or frozen medium shrimp
8 ounces bulk hot Italian sausage
1½ cups chopped green sweet pepper (1 large)
1 cup chopped onion (1 large)
1 cup thinly sliced celery (2 stalks)
2 14.5-ounce cans reduced-sodium stewed tomatoes, undrained
1 14-ounce can reduced-sodium chicken broth
3 cloves garlic, minced
1 teaspoon paprika
¼ teaspoon ground black pepper
⅛ to ¼ teaspoon cayenne pepper
1 cup instant white rice

1 Thaw shrimp, if frozen. Peel and devein shrimp. Rinse shrimp; pat dry with paper towels. Set aside.

2 In a large saucepan cook sausage, sweet pepper, onion, and celery until sausage is brown, stirring to break up sausage as it cooks. Drain fat.

3 Add undrained tomatoes, broth, garlic, paprika, black pepper, and cayenne pepper to sausage mixture. Return to boiling; reduce heat. Simmer, covered, for 10 minutes. Add shrimp; cover and cook about 4 minutes more or until shrimp are opaque. Remove from heat. Stir in rice. Cover and let stand for 5 minutes.

nutrition facts per serving: 338 cal., 14 g total fat (5 g sat. fat), 144 mg chol., 971 mg sodium, 28 g carb., 4 g dietary fiber, 24 g protein.

The tasty juices called the oyster's "liquor" add a tantalizing smell and flavor to this rich and creamy stew. The key here is to cook the oysters gently until they're nice and tender; when the edges begin to curl, they've had enough heat.

classic oyster stew

start to finish: 25 minutes
makes: 10 servings

1   pint (about 3 dozen)
    shucked oysters,
    undrained (about
    1 pound)
4   cups whole milk
2   cups whipping cream
7   tablespoons unsalted
    butter
1   cup finely chopped
    yellow onion
    (1 large)
½   cup finely chopped
    celery (1 stalk)
¾   teaspoon kosher salt
3   tablespoons all-
    purpose flour
    Ground black pepper
    Pinch cayenne pepper
    Snipped fresh parsley

1 Drain oysters, reserving liquor. Remove any shell pieces. Set oysters and liquor aside.

2 In medium saucepan heat milk and cream just to simmering; keep warm.

3 In Dutch oven melt 4 tablespoons of the butter over medium heat until bubbling. Add onion, celery, and ½ teaspoon of the salt, stirring well to coat in butter; cook slowly, stirring often, about 10 minutes or until onion is tender and translucent. Sprinkle flour over vegetable mixture; cook for 2 minutes more, stirring well to blend in the flour. Slowly whisk in hot milk-cream mixture. Bring mixture back to a low simmer, stirring occasionally.

4 Meanwhile, in a 12-inch nonstick skillet melt remaining 3 tablespoons butter over medium heat until bubbling. Add drained oysters in a single layer. Sprinkle with remaining ¼ teaspoon salt and a few grinds of black pepper. Cook just until oysters begin to curl around the edges and gills are slightly exposed. Transfer oysters to the milk mixture in Dutch oven. Turn off heat under Dutch oven.

5 Add oyster liquor to hot skillet; cook 2 to 3 minutes, until boiling. Immediately transfer to Dutch oven; stir. Stir in cayenne pepper. Cover and let stand for 10 minutes. Sprinkle each serving with parsley.

nutrition facts per serving: 342 cal., 30 g total fat (18 g sat. fat), 121 mg chol., 303 mg sodium, 11 g carb., 0 g dietary fiber, 8 g protein.

This Italian-style fish stew is often served over crostini or toast.
Or if you like, sprinkle each serving with garlic-flavored croutons.

italian fish stew

start to finish: 30 minutes
makes: 4 servings

8   ounces fresh or
    frozen skinless cod
    or sea bass fillets
6   ounces fresh or
    frozen peeled and
    deveined shrimp
⅓   cup chopped onion
1   cup sliced celery
    (2 stalks)
1   clove garlic, minced
2   teaspoons olive oil
1   cup reduced-sodium
    chicken broth
¼   cup dry white wine
    or reduced-sodium
    chicken broth
1   14.5-ounce can
    no-salt-added diced
    tomatoes, drained
1   8-ounce can no-salt-
    added tomato sauce
1   teaspoon dried
    oregano, crushed
¼   teaspoon salt
⅛   teaspoon ground
    black pepper
1   tablespoon snipped
    fresh parsley

1 Thaw fish and shrimp, if frozen. Rinse fish and shrimp; pat dry with paper towels. Cut fish into 1½-inch pieces. Cut shrimp in half lengthwise. Cover and chill fish and shrimp until needed.

2 In large saucepan, cook onion, celery, and garlic in hot oil until tender. Carefully stir in broth and wine. Bring to boiling; reduce heat. Simmer, uncovered, for 5 minutes. Stir in drained tomatoes, tomato sauce, oregano, salt, and pepper. Return to boiling; reduce heat. Simmer, covered, for 5 minutes.

3 Gently stir in fish and shrimp. Return just to boiling; reduce heat to low. Simmer, covered, for 3 to 5 minutes or until fish flakes easily with a fork and shrimp are opaque. Sprinkle with parsley.

nutrition facts per serving: 165 cal., 4 g total fat (1 g sat. fat), 87 mg chol., 459 mg sodium, 12 g carb., 2 g dietary fiber, 19 g protein.

pick the best

Visit your local seafood market or shop around to find the best fresh fish selection. Fish should smell like the ocean and not fishy. When buying fillets, choose those that are springy to the touch and have firm, translucent flesh without tears or blemishes.

When only skin-on salmon fillets are available, bake as directed, skin sides down. When done, use a large spatula to lift the fillets from the skins; discard skins.

smoky tomato-salmon chowder

start to finish: 55 minutes oven: at 425°F
makes: 6 servings

3   6-ounce fresh or frozen skinless salmon fillets
2   medium red sweet peppers, halved lengthwise and seeded
1   medium sweet onion, cut in ½-inch slices
1   jalapeño pepper, halved lengthwise and seeded*
1   to 2 teaspoons chili powder
½   teaspoon salt
2   14.5-ounce cans reduced-sodium chicken broth
1   14.5-ounce can no-salt-added diced tomatoes or diced fire-roasted tomatoes, undrained
    Ground black pepper
¾   cup chopped tomato (1 large)
2   tablespoons coarsely chopped fresh Italian parsley
1   medium avocado, pitted, peeled, and sliced
    Chili powder

1 Thaw salmon, if frozen. Preheat oven to 425°F. Place sweet peppers, onion, and chile pepper, cut sides down, on a foil-lined baking sheet. Roast for 20 to 25 minutes or until vegetables are charred and very tender. Bring foil up around vegetables and fold edges together to enclose. Let stand about 15 minutes or until cool enough to handle.

2 Meanwhile, grease a shallow baking pan; set aside. Rinse salmon; pat dry with paper towels. Sprinkle with 1 to 2 teaspoons chili powder and ½ teaspoon salt. Place salmon in prepared baking pan, tucking under any thin edges. Bake for 4 to 6 minutes per ½-inch thickness or until salmon flakes easily when tested with a fork. Remove from oven; cover and keep warm.

3 Using a sharp knife, loosen edges of skins from peppers; gently pull off skins in strips and discard. Coarsely chop peppers and onion; transfer to a large saucepan. Add broth and undrained tomatoes. Bring to boiling, stirring occasionally. Remove from heat. Season to taste with salt and black pepper. Stir in chopped tomato and parsley.

4 Ladle soup into bowls. Break salmon into pieces and divide among bowls. Top with avocado and sprinkle with chili powder.

nutrition facts per serving: 218 cal., 9 g total fat (1 g sat. fat), 47 mg chol., 606 mg sodium, 14 g carb., 3 g dietary fiber, 20 g protein.

∗note: See tip on handling chile peppers, page 31.

Lemon and dill bring fresh and lively flavors to this warming chowder. To speed preparation, substitute a 15-ounce can of canned salmon for the fresh and omit the poaching step.

salmon and asparagus chowder

prep: 20 minutes   cook: 20 minutes
makes: 8 servings

1	pound fresh skinless salmon fillets
1½	cups water
2	14-ounce cans vegetable broth or 3½ cups vegetable stock
2	cups frozen whole small onions or ½ cup frozen chopped onion
2½	cups cubed red-skinned potato (3 medium)
1	tablespoon snipped fresh dill or ½ teaspoon dried dill
1	teaspoon finely shredded lemon zest
½	teaspoon salt
½	teaspoon ground black pepper
2½	cups whole milk, half-and-half, or light cream
2	tablespoons cornstarch
1	10-ounce package frozen cut asparagus, thawed and well-drained, or 2 cups cut-up trimmed fresh asparagus
	Fresh dill sprigs (optional)

1 Rinse salmon; pat dry with paper towels. To poach salmon, in a large skillet bring the water to boiling. Add salmon. Return to boiling; reduce heat. Simmer, covered, for 6 to 8 minutes or until fish flakes easily when tested with a fork. Remove salmon from skillet; discard poaching liquid. Flake salmon into ½-inch pieces; set aside.

2 Meanwhile, in a large pot combine broth, onions, potato, snipped dill, lemon zest, salt, and pepper. Bring to boiling; reduce heat. Simmer, covered, for 15 minutes or until vegetables are tender, stirring occasionally.

3 In a large screw-top jar combine milk and cornstarch. Cover and shake well; stir into soup. Stir in asparagus; cook and stir until soup is slightly thickened and bubbly. Cook and stir for 2 minutes more. Gently stir in salmon; heat through. If desired, garnish with fresh dill sprigs.

nutrition facts per serving: 235 cal., 10 g total fat (3 g sat. fat), 39 mg chol., 609 mg sodium, 19 g carb., 2 g dietary fiber, 16 g protein.

When choosing poblano chiles for this soup, go for the ones with the darkest color—they will be the sweetest.

crab and pepper soup with fresh tomato salsa

start to finish: 30 minutes
makes: 8 servings

¼ cup butter
2 poblano peppers, seeded and chopped*
¾ cup chopped red sweet pepper (1 medium)
½ cup chopped onion (1 medium)
2 cloves garlic, minced
¼ cup all-purpose flour
¼ teaspoon salt
¼ teaspoon ground black pepper
1 14.5-ounce can chicken broth
2 cups milk
1½ cups shredded asadero cheese or Monterey Jack cheese (6 ounces)
1 6.5-ounce can lump crabmeat, drained, or 8 ounces fresh lump crabmeat, picked over and cut into bite-size pieces
1 recipe Fresh Tomato Salsa
Crisp Tortilla Strips (optional)

1 In a large saucepan melt butter over medium heat. Add chile peppers, sweet pepper, onion, and garlic; cook until tender, stirring occasionally. Stir in flour, salt, and black pepper. Gradually stir in broth; cook and stir until mixture is thickened and bubbly. Cook and stir for 1 minute more.

2 Reduce heat to medium-low. Stir in milk and cheese; cook and stir for 3 to 5 minutes or until cheese is melted. Stir in crabmeat; heat through.

3 Top each serving with Fresh Tomato Salsa. If desired, serve with Crisp Tortilla Strips.

nutrition facts per serving: 203 cal., 12 g total fat (8 g sat. fat), 60 mg chol., 664 mg sodium, 11 g carb., 1 g dietary fiber, 14 g protein.

*note: See tip on handling chile peppers, page 31.

fresh tomato salsa: In a small bowl stir together 3 roma tomatoes, seeded and chopped; 1 green onion, thinly sliced; 1 tablespoon snipped fresh cilantro; 2 teaspoons lime juice; and 1 teaspoon finely chopped jalapeño pepper*. Season to taste with salt and ground black pepper.

crisp tortilla strips: Preheat oven to 350°F. Roll up each flour tortilla; slice crosswise, which will result in long, thin strips. Lightly coat tortilla strips with nonstick cooking spray and spread on a baking sheet. Bake about 5 minutes or until golden. Cool.

To tailor the spiciness of this smooth and silky soup, start with 2 tablespoons of the red curry paste, taste, and add more if desired. For an equally good vegetarian soup, omit the shrimp and use vegetable broth.

creamy butternut squash–shrimp curry soup

prep: 35 minutes slow cook: 8 to 10 hours (low) or 4 to 5 hours (high)
+ 20 minutes (high)
makes: 8 servings

8   cups cubed butternut
       squash (about
       3½ pounds)
2   14.5-ounce cans
       reduced-sodium
       chicken broth
1   tablespoon butter
½   teaspoon salt
1   12-ounce can (1½
       cups) evaporated
       fat-free milk
2   to 3 tablespoons Thai
       red curry paste
1   pound peeled and
       deveined medium
       fresh shrimp,
       halved lengthwise
Water (optional)

1 In a 4- to 5-quart slow cooker combine squash, broth, butter, and salt.

2 Cover and cook on low-heat setting for 8 to 10 hours or on high-heat setting for 4 to 5 hours.

3 Stir evaporated milk and curry paste into mixture in cooker. Using an immersion blender, carefully blend soup. Stir in shrimp.

4 If using low-heat setting, turn cooker to high-heat setting. Cover and cook about 20 minutes more or until shrimp are opaque.

5 To serve, if desired, thin soup with a little water.

nutrition facts per serving: 187 cal., 3 g total fat (1 g sat. fat), 90 mg chol., 660 mg sodium, 20 g carb., 3 g dietary fiber, 16 g protein.

This spectacular shrimp and vegetable soup turns into an egg drop soup when a beaten egg is added at the end of cooking. To achieve nice strands of egg, stir the egg slowly into the broth mixture.

hot-and-sour soup with shrimp

start to finish: 35 minutes
makes: 4 servings

12 ounces fresh or frozen shrimp in shells
4 ounces fresh shiitake mushrooms, stems removed and sliced, or button mushrooms, sliced
1 tablespoon vegetable oil
2 14-ounce cans chicken broth
¼ cup rice vinegar or white vinegar
2 tablespoons soy sauce
1 teaspoon sugar
1 teaspoon grated fresh ginger or ¼ teaspoon ground ginger
½ teaspoon ground black pepper
1 tablespoon cornstarch
1 tablespoon cold water
½ cup frozen peas
½ cup shredded carrot (1 medium)
2 tablespoons thinly sliced green onion (1)
1 egg, lightly beaten

1 Thaw shrimp, if frozen. Peel and devein shrimp. Rinse shrimp; pat dry with paper towels. Set aside. In a large saucepan cook and stir mushrooms in hot oil until tender. Add broth, vinegar, soy sauce, sugar, ginger, and pepper. Bring to boiling; reduce heat. Simmer, covered, for 2 minutes. Stir in shrimp. Return to boiling; reduce heat. Simmer, covered, for 1 minute more.

2 Stir together cornstarch and the cold water. Stir into chicken broth mixture; cook and stir until slightly thickened and bubbly. Cook and stir for 2 minutes more. Stir in peas, carrot, and green onion. Pour egg into soup in a steady stream, stirring a few times to create shreds.

nutrition facts per serving: 212 cal., 7 g total fat (1 g sat. fat), 184 mg chol., 1430 mg sodium, 13 g carb., 2 g dietary fiber, 22 g protein.

spin the glo

Take your palate on an amazing expedition with ethnic flavorings straight from some of the best soup kettles around the world. These signature concoctions from Italy, Mexico, India, and other faraway places showcase authentic flavors that tingle taste buds.

"Tagine" is the name of savory Moroccan meat or poultry stews as well as the ceramic vessel in which they are cooked. A slow cooker creates the same kind of moist, gentle cooking environment.

moroccan lamb tagine

prep: 40 minutes slow cook: 8 to 10 hours (low) or 4 to 5 hours (high)
makes: 6 servings

1½   to 2 pounds boneless
       lamb shoulder roast
       or lamb stew meat
½   teaspoon salt
½   teaspoon ground
       cumin
½   teaspoon ground
       ginger
¼   teaspoon ground
       cinnamon
¼   teaspoon ground
       turmeric
1½   cups coarsely chopped,
       peeled sweet potato
       (1 large)
2   medium carrots, cut
       into 1-inch pieces
½   cup chopped onion
       (1 medium)
⅓   cup chopped roma
       tomato (1 medium)
⅓   cup pitted whole
       dates, quartered
¼   cup pitted green
       olives, halved
2   tablespoons quick-
       cooking tapioca
½   teaspoon finely
       shredded lemon zest
1   tablespoon lemon
       juice
1   tablespoon honey
2   cloves garlic, minced
1   14.5-ounce can
       chicken broth
1   teaspoon orange-
       blossom water*
3   cups hot cooked
       couscous
       Sliced almonds,
       toasted

1 Trim fat from meat. Cut meat into 1-inch pieces. Place meat in a large bowl. In a small bowl combine salt, cumin, ginger, cinnamon, and turmeric. Sprinkle mixture over meat; toss to coat.

2 In a 3½- or 4-quart slow cooker combine seasoned meat, sweet potato, carrots, onion, tomato, dates, olives, tapioca, lemon zest, lemon juice, honey, and garlic. Pour broth over all.

3 Cover and cook on low-heat setting for 8 to 10 hours or on high-heat setting for 4 to 5 hours. Stir in orange-blossom water.

4 Serve meat mixture over couscous. Sprinkle with almonds.

nutrition facts per serving: 368 cal., 8 g total fat (2 g sat. fat), 70 mg chol., 674 mg sodium, 45 g carb., 5 g dietary fiber, 28 g protein.

*note: Orange-blossom water, stirred in at the end of cooking, is a distilled water that contains the essential oils of orange blossoms. Just a little is all you need for a nice hint of citrus. If you can't find it, squeeze fresh orange juice over each serving.

Just 20 minutes of prep work, and you'll be ready to plug in your slow cooker for a broth-based soup that's richly seasoned with ginger. Use curly dried Chinese egg noodles, rather than rice sticks or rice noodles, for easier serving.

teriyaki beef-noodle soup

prep: 20 minutes slow cook: 6 to 8 hours (low) or 3 to 4 hours (high)
stand: 5 minutes
makes: 6 servings

1 pound beef stir-fry
    strips
2 14-ounce cans beef
    broth
2 cups water
2 medium red or green
    sweet peppers, cut
    into ½-inch pieces
1 8-ounce can sliced
    water chestnuts,
    drained and
    chopped
6 green onions, cut into
    1-inch pieces
3 tablespoons soy
    sauce
1 teaspoon ground
    ginger
¼ teaspoon ground
    black pepper
5 to 6 ounces dried
    Chinese noodles
    Green onion, cut into
    thin strips (optional)

1 In a 3½- or 4-quart slow cooker combine beef, beef broth, the water, sweet peppers, water chestnuts, green onions, soy sauce, ginger, and black pepper.

2 Cover and cook on low-heat setting for 6 to 8 hours or on high-heat setting for 3 to 4 hours. Turn off cooker. Stir in noodles. Cover and let stand for 5 minutes. If desired, top with green onion strips.

nutrition facts per serving: 230 cal., 4 g total fat (1 g sat. fat), 46 mg chol., 1628 mg sodium, 26 g carb., 3 g dietary fiber, 22 g protein.

Starting with an already cooked rotisserie chicken makes this Mexican-style soup go together in less than an hour. For an extra dimension of flavor in this soup, substitute two 15-ounce cans of fire-roasted diced tomatoes for the 28-ounce can of plum tomatoes.

mexican posole soup with avocado

prep: 30 minutes cook: 30 minutes
makes: 8 servings

1 2- to 2½-pound deli-roasted chicken
¾ cup chopped yellow onion (1 large)
2 teaspoons ground cumin
1 teaspoon chili powder
2 teaspoons vegetable oil
2 14.5-ounce cans reduced-sodium chicken broth
1 28-ounce can peeled plum tomatoes in puree, undrained and cut up*
1 15-ounce can yellow or white hominy, drained
1 10-ounce package frozen whole-kernel corn
2 4-ounce cans diced green chiles, undrained
1 cup shredded Mexican cheese blend (4 ounces)
   Snipped fresh cilantro, halved grape tomatoes, sliced avocado, and/or corn tortilla chips
   Lime wedges (optional)

1 Remove and discard skin from chicken. Pull meat from bones; discard bones. Cube chicken (you should have about 3½ cups); set aside.

2 In a 4-quart Dutch oven cook onion, cumin, and chili powder in hot oil over medium heat for 4 to 6 minutes or until onion is tender. Add chicken, broth, undrained plum tomatoes, hominy, corn, and chile peppers. Bring to boiling; reduce heat. Simmer, uncovered, for 30 minutes, stirring occasionally.

3 Top each serving with cheese, cilantro, grape tomatoes, avocado, and/or tortilla chips. If desired, serve with lime wedges.

nutrition facts per serving: 392 cal., 21 g total fat (7 g sat. fat), 75 mg chol., 1191 mg sodium, 32 g carb., 7 g dietary fiber, 22 g protein.

*note: Use a pair of clean kitchen scissors to cut up the tomatoes in the can.

The flavors of India emerge when you mix lamb, potatoes, and tomatoes with garam masala. You'll find the spice mix at ethnic grocers, but most supermarkets stock it too. Dollops of cool yogurt complement the warm stew.

lamb korma

prep: 15 minutes slow cook: 8 to 10 hours (low) or 4 to 5 hours (high)
makes: 6 servings

2 pounds lean boneless lamb
1 tablespoon garam masala
¼ teaspoon salt
¼ teaspoon ground black pepper
3 cups cubed, peeled potatoes (3 medium)
1 14.5-ounce can diced tomatoes with onion and garlic, undrained
¼ cup water
¾ cup plain yogurt (optional)

1 Trim fat from meat. Cut meat into 1-inch pieces. In a medium bowl combine meat, garam masala, salt, and pepper; toss to coat. Place potatoes in a 3½- or 4-quart slow cooker. Add seasoned meat. Pour undrained tomatoes and the water over all.

2 Cover and cook on low-heat setting for 8 to 10 hours or on high-heat setting for 4 to 5 hours. If desired, top each serving with yogurt.

nutrition facts per serving: 282 cal., 8 g total fat (3 g sat. fat), 97 mg chol., 538 mg sodium, 18 g carb., 1 g dietary fiber, 33 g protein.

a perfect bowl

The secret to a successful soup buffet is keeping the soup at the perfect temperature. Slow cookers with serving burners are two easy options to keep soup warm, with only occasional stirring required. For cold soups, nestle a soup tureen in a bed of ice and serve the soup in chilled bowls.

Nothing is more Irish than this rich and flavorful stew full of carrots, potatoes, and lamb. Some cooks also add turnips or parsnips, when available.

luck of the irish stew

prep: 25 minutes cook: 1¼ hours
makes: 6 servings

1 pound boneless lamb
   or boneless beef
   chuck roast, cut into
   ¾-inch pieces
4 cups beef broth
2 medium onions, cut
   into wedges
¼ teaspoon ground
   black pepper
1 bay leaf
4 medium potatoes
   (1½ pounds), peeled
   and quartered
6 medium carrots,
   sliced ½-inch thick
   (3 cups)
½ teaspoon dried
   thyme, crushed
¼ teaspoon dried basil,
   crushed
½ cup cold water
¼ cup all-purpose flour
   Salt
   Sprigs of fresh thyme
   (optional)

1 In a large saucepan combine lamb, broth, onions, pepper, and bay leaf. Bring to boiling; reduce heat. Simmer, covered, for 45 minutes. Skim off the fat.

2 Add potatoes, carrots, dried thyme, and basil. Bring to boiling; reduce heat. Simmer, covered, for 30 to 35 minutes more or until vegetables are tender. Discard bay leaf.

3 Stir together the cold water and flour. Add flour mixture to stew; cook and stir until thickened and bubbly. Cook and stir for 1 minute more. Season to taste with salt. If desired, garnish with fresh thyme.

nutrition facts per serving: 315 cal., 13 g total fat (3 g sat. fat), 50 mg chol., 615 mg sodium, 30 g carb., 5 g dietary fiber.

Herbes de Provence, an essential herb blend in Provencal cooking, gives this stew complex fragrance and flavor. Find it at specialty stores. Or, to make your own blend, start by combining equal parts of lavender, fennel, thyme, rosemary, dill, and tarragon. Adjust amounts of each herb to achieve the flavor you like best.

french-style beef stew

prep: 35 minutes cook: 1¾ hours
makes: 4 servings

1   tablespoon olive oil
1   pound boneless beef
      top round steak, cut
      into 1-inch cubes
½   cup chopped onion
      (1 medium)
1   cup dry white wine
2   cups water
1   teaspoon dried
      herbes de Provence,
      crushed
¼   teaspoon salt
¼   teaspoon ground
      black pepper
16   baby carrots
8   tiny new potatoes,
      halved or quartered
8   pearl onions, peeled
1   tomato, peeled,
      seeded, and
      chopped
¼   cup pitted niçoise
      or kalamata olives
2   tablespoons capers,
      drained
8   ounces steamed
      haricots verts or
      small green beans
1   tablespoon snipped
      fresh parsley

1 In a 4-quart Dutch oven heat oil. Add beef cubes and onion, half at a time; cook and stir until beef is brown. Drain fat. Return all beef to Dutch oven.

2 Add wine to Dutch oven; cook and stir over medium heat, scraping up browned bits in bottom of Dutch oven. Add the water, herbes de Provence, salt, and pepper. Bring to boiling; reduce heat. Simmer, covered, about 1¼ hours or until meat is nearly tender. Add carrots, potatoes, and onions. Return to boiling; reduce heat. Simmer, covered, about 30 minutes more or until meat and vegetables are tender. Stir in tomato, olives, and capers; heat through.

3 Place haricots verts in shallow soup bowls; top with stew. Sprinkle each serving with parsley.

nutrition facts per serving: 377 cal., 10 g total fat (2 g sat. fat), 72 mg chol., 399 mg sodium, 31 g carb., 5 g dietary fiber, 31 g protein.

A soy-ginger topping, sparked with fresh cilantro, jalapeño, and garlic, makes a lively topper for this Asian soup.

chinese hot pot

prep: 1 hour cook: 15 minutes
makes: 6 to 8 servings

8 ounces fresh or frozen peeled and deveined shrimp
8 ounces fresh or frozen sole fillets
8 ounces boneless beef top loin steak
3 cups shredded napa cabbage
1 cup sliced fresh shiitake mushrooms
1 cup fresh bean sprouts, trimmed
1 cup thinly bias-sliced carrot (2 medium)
1 8-ounce can sliced bamboo shoots, drained
8 cups water
1 teaspoon salt
4 ounces wide rice noodles
2 tablespoons sliced green onion (1)
1 1-inch piece fresh ginger, peeled and thinly sliced
1 recipe Soy-Ginger Topping

soy-ginger topping: In a small bowl stir together ½ cup reduced-sodium soy sauce; ¼ cup snipped fresh cilantro; ¼ cup sliced green onions (2); 1 tablespoon roasted sesame oil; 1 small jalapeño pepper, seeded and finely chopped (optional; see tip on handling chile peppers, page 31); 2 teaspoons grated fresh ginger; and 2 cloves garlic, minced. Cover and let stand for 1 hour before serving. Makes about ¾ cup.

1 Thaw shrimp and fish if frozen.

2 Trim fat from meat. If desired, in a lightly oiled large skillet cook meat over medium-high heat until brown on both sides. Thinly slice meat into bite-size strips. Arrange meat on a serving platter. Rinse shrimp and fish; pat dry with paper towels. Cut fish into 2-inch pieces. Add shrimp and fish to platter; set aside.

3 Arrange cabbage, mushrooms, bean sprouts, carrots, and bamboo shoots on a separate serving platter; set aside.

4 In a large saucepan bring the water and salt to boiling. Pour boiling water into an electric wok or electric skillet. Heat wok or skillet over medium heat at the table.

5 Place meat, shrimp, and fish into simmering water and cook until done. Allow 1 minute for meat or until slightly pink in center, 1 to 2 minutes for shrimp or until opaque, and 1 to 2 minutes for fish or until it flakes easily when tested with a fork. Remove from liquid with a slotted spoon and divide among bowls. Add cabbage, mushrooms, bean sprouts, carrot, and bamboo shoots to pot; cook for 1 to 2 minutes or until crisp-tender. Remove from liquid and divide among bowls. When all meat, shrimp, fish, and vegetables are cooked, add noodles, green onion, and ginger to pot; cook about 3 minutes or until noodles are tender. Discard ginger slices. Spoon hot liquid and noodles over meat, shrimp, fish, and vegetables in each bowl. Add spoonfuls of Soy-Ginger Topping to each bowl to taste.

nutrition facts per serving: 270 cal., 5 g total fat (1 g sat. fat), 93 mg chol., 1293 mg sodium, 29 g carb., 3 g dietary fiber, 26 g protein.

Dried chiles often come in packages that contain many more chiles than are needed for a singular dish. The good news is that chiles, stored tightly sealed in a cool and dark place, keep for at least a year.

mexican pork and chile stew

prep: 40 minutes slow cook: 6 to 8 hours (low) or 3 to 4 hours (high)
makes: 8 servings

3   dried ancho chile peppers, seeded and torn into pieces
3   dried guajillo chile peppers, seeded and torn into pieces
2   dried pasilla chile peppers, seeded and torn into pieces
4   cloves garlic, chopped
½   teaspoon ground cinnamon
½   teaspoon dried oregano
¼   teaspoon ground cloves
¼   teaspoon ground cumin
3   cups reduced-sodium chicken broth
2   tablespoons vegetable oil
2½ pounds boneless pork shoulder, cut into ¾-inch cubes
1   cup chopped onion (1 large)
½   cup raisins
½   cup orange juice
2   bay leaves
1   ounce Mexican chocolate, grated
2   teaspoons packed brown sugar
2   teaspoons cider vinegar
½   teaspoon salt
    Flour tortillas, warmed*

1 In a small bowl combine ancho chile peppers, guajillo chile peppers, and pasillo chile peppers. Pour boiling water over peppers to cover. Let stand for 20 minutes. Drain peppers; discard water.

2 In a food processor combine drained peppers, garlic, cinnamon, oregano, cloves, and cumin. Add ½ cup of the broth. Cover and process until smooth; set aside.

3 In a large skillet heat oil over medium heat. Add pork, half at time; cook and stir until brown. Transfer pork to a 3½- or 4-quart slow cooker. Add onion to skillet; cook and stir for about 6 minutes or until tender. Transfer onion to slow cooker. Add pureed pepper mixture, remaining 2½ cups broth, raisins, orange juice, and bay leaves to cooker.

4 Cover and cook on low-heat setting for 6 to 8 hours or on high-heat setting for 3 to 4 hours. Skim fat from cooking liquid. Discard bay leaves. Add chocolate, brown sugar, vinegar, and salt. Stir until chocolate melts.

5 Serve stew with warm flour tortillas.

nutrition facts per serving: 618 cal., 32 g total fat (10 g sat. fat), 99 mg chol., 707 mg sodium, 48 g carb., 3 g dietary fiber, 32 g protein.

*note: To warm tortillas, preheat oven to 350°F. Stack tortillas and wrap them tightly in foil. Heat for about 10 minutes or until tortillas are heated through.

Satay is an Indonesian specialty of spicy marinated meat that's skewered, then broiled or grilled. Bring its lively flavors home with this easy stew.

pork satay stew

prep: 15 minutes   slow cook: 7 to 8 hours (low) or 3½ to 4 hours (high)
makes: 6 servings

1½   pounds boneless pork
        shoulder roast
2   red and/or green
        sweet peppers, cut
        into 1-inch pieces
1   red onion, cut into
        wedges
1   cup bottled thick and
        chunky salsa
½   cup creamy peanut
        butter
1   tablespoon reduced-
        sodium soy sauce
1   tablespoon lime juice
1½   teaspoons grated
        fresh ginger
½   teaspoon ground
        coriander
¾   cup half-and-half or
        light cream
3   cups hot cooked
        white or brown rice
⅓   cup chopped dry-
        roasted peanuts
¼   cup sliced green
        onion (2)

1 Trim fat from meat. Cut meat into 1-inch pieces. In a 3½-quart slow cooker combine meat, sweet pepper, red onion, salsa, peanut butter, soy sauce, lime juice, ginger, and coriander.

2 Cover and cook on low-heat setting for 7 to 8 hours or on high-heat setting for 3½ to 4 hours. Stir in half-and-half.

3 Serve meat mixture over rice. Sprinkle with peanuts and green onion.

nutrition facts per serving: 502 cal., 25 g total fat (7 g sat. fat), 84 mg chol., 462 mg sodium, 36 g carb., 3 g dietary fiber, 34 g protein.

The tender bits of shredded pork in a rich chipotle-tomato sauce can simply be eaten out of a bowl or used to fill corn or flour tortillas. Transfer leftover chipotles in adobo to a small container. Cover and refrigerate them for up to 1 month.

tinga poblana

prep: 30 minutes **slow cook:** 8 hours (low)
makes: 8 servings

1 2-pound boneless pork shoulder roast
8 ounces uncooked chorizo sausage, casings removed
2 cups cubed red-skin potatoes (2 medium)
1 cup chopped onion (1 large)
1 14.5-ounce can diced fire-roasted tomatoes, undrained
3 canned chipotle peppers in adobo sauce, chopped*
1 tablespoon canned adobo sauce
2 bay leaves
4 cloves garlic, minced
1 teaspoon dried thyme, crushed
1 teaspoon dried Mexican oregano or oregano, crushed
½ teaspoon salt
¼ teaspoon sugar
1 10-ounce package tortilla chips or 16 corn tortillas, warmed
2 avocados, pitted, peeled, and thinly sliced
2 cups crumbled queso fresco (8 ounces)
   Fresh cilantro sprigs (optional)

1 Trim fat from pork roast. Cut roast into 1-inch pieces; set aside. In a large skillet cook sausage over medium-high heat until brown, using a wooden spoon to break up meat as it cooks. Remove sausage; drain on paper towels.

2 In a 3½- or 4-quart slow cooker combine sausage, pork roast, potatoes, and onion. Add undrained tomatoes, chile peppers, adobo sauce, bay leaves, garlic, thyme, oregano, salt, and sugar. Cover and cook on low-heat setting for 8 hours.

3 Using a slotted spoon, remove pork roast from cooker. Using 2 forks, pull roast apart into coarse shreds. Discard bay leaves. Skim fat from tomato mixture. Return shredded meat to cooker.

4 Serve meat mixture in shallow bowls with tortilla chips. Garnish each serving with avocado, queso fresco, and, if desired, cilantro.

nutrition facts per serving: 661 cal., 37 g total fat (12 g sat. fat), 119 mg chol., 1022 mg sodium, 42 g carb., 6 g dietary fiber, 41 g protein.

*note: See tip on handling chile peppers, page 31.

A vibrant blend of fresh parsley, garlic, and lime makes up the gremolata, which brightens this stew and boosts its robust flavor.

caribbean pork stew with lime gremolata

prep: 25 minutes cook: 50 minutes
makes: 6 servings

Nonstick cooking spray
1 pound lean boneless pork, cut into ½-inch cubes
3 onions, cut into wedges
1 14.5-ounce can no-salt-added diced tomatoes, undrained
1 14-ounce can reduced-sodium chicken broth
1 8-ounce can no-salt-added tomato sauce
¼ teaspoon cayenne pepper
2 sweet potatoes, peeled, halved lengthwise, and cut into ½-inch slices
2 green, yellow, and/or red sweet peppers, seeded and cut into bite-size strips
1 cup canned black beans, rinsed and drained
3 tablespoons lime juice
1 recipe Lime Gremolata
Lime wedges (optional)

1 Coat an unheated 4-quart Dutch oven with nonstick cooking spray. Heat Dutch oven over medium heat. Add pork to hot Dutch oven; cook and stir until browned. Add onions, undrained tomatoes, broth, tomato sauce, and cayenne pepper. Bring to boiling; reduce heat. Simmer, covered, for 30 minutes.

2 Add sweet potatoes, sweet peppers, and black beans. Return to boiling; reduce heat. Simmer, covered, for about 20 minutes or until vegetables are tender. Stir in lime juice. Top each serving with Lime Gremolata. If desired, garnish with lime wedges.

nutrition facts per serving: 231 cal., 4 g total fat (1 g sat. fat), 47 mg chol., 433 mg sodium, 29 g carb., 7 g dietary fiber, 22 g protein.

lime gremolata: In a bowl stir together ½ cup snipped fresh parsley, 1 teaspoon finely shredded lime zest, and 1 clove garlic, minced.

This wonderful Asian-style stew tastes like egg roll filling. Miso, a healthful paste of fermented grains and soybeans, adds superlative flavor. If you can't find miso in your supermarket, try a natural foods store.

japanese cabbage stew

prep: 30 minutes **slow cook:** 6 hours (low) or 3 hours (high)
makes: 8 to 10 servings

Nonstick cooking
    spray
6 cups packaged
    shredded cabbage
    with carrot
    (coleslaw mix)
1¼ pounds lean ground
    pork
1 cup chopped bok
    choy leaves or fresh
    spinach leaves
1 cup chopped red
    sweet pepper
    (2 small)
½ cup finely chopped
    onion (1 medium)
½ cup finely chopped
    celery (1 stalk)
¼ cup finely chopped
    green onion (2)
2 tablespoons red miso
    paste
½ teaspoon salt
¼ teaspoon ground
    black pepper
4 cups reduced-sodium
    chicken broth
¼ cup soy sauce
3 tablespoons tomato
    paste
2 tablespoons sake or
    cream sherry
1 tablespoon rice
    vinegar
1 teaspoon dried
    thyme, crushed

1 Lightly coat the inside of a 3½- or 4-quart slow cooker with cooking spray. In a large bowl combine coleslaw mix, ground pork, bok choy, sweet peppers, onion, celery, green onion, red miso paste, salt, and black pepper. Transfer mixture to prepared cooker.

2 In a medium bowl whisk together broth, soy sauce, tomato paste, sake, vinegar, and thyme. Pour broth mixture over pork mixture; stir to combine.

3 Cover and cook on low-heat setting for 6 hours or on high-heat setting for 3 hours.

nutrition facts per serving: 247 cal., 15 g total fat (6 g sat. fat), 51 mg chol., 1215 mg sodium, 10 g carb., 2 g dietary fiber, 16 g protein.

A ginger and garlic infused broth is bulked up with Chinese cabbage, which lends a mild flavor and lovely crunch to this simple soup. A splash of dry sherry adds a nice flavor note.

asian pork soup

start to finish: 20 minutes
makes: 6 servings

Nonstick cooking
    spray
12 ounces lean boneless
    pork, cut into bite-
    size pieces
2   cups sliced fresh
    shiitake mushrooms
2   cloves garlic, minced
3   14-ounce cans
    reduced-sodium
    chicken broth
2   tablespoons dry
    sherry
2   tablespoons reduced-
    sodium soy sauce
2   teaspoons grated
    fresh ginger or
    ½ teaspoon ground
    ginger
¼   teaspoon crushed
    red pepper flakes
2   cups thinly sliced
    Chinese (napa)
    cabbage
1   green onion, thinly
    sliced

1 Coat an unheated large nonstick saucepan with nonstick cooking spray. Heat saucepan over medium heat. Add pork to hot saucepan; cook for 2 to 3 minutes or until slightly pink in center. Remove from saucepan; set aside. Add mushrooms and garlic to saucepan; cook and stir until tender.

2 Stir in broth, sherry, soy sauce, ginger, and red pepper flakes. Bring to boiling. Stir in pork, Chinese cabbage, and green onion; heat through.

nutrition facts per serving: 140 cal., 3 g total fat (1 g sat. fat), 31 mg chol., 691 mg sodium, 10 g carb., 1 g dietary fiber, 16 g protein.

Three German favorites—sausage, caraway, and beer—star in this surprisingly light soup. Using turkey sausage instead of pork sausage cuts fat by more than 50 percent.

german potato-sausage soup

prep: 20 minutes   **cook:** 17 minutes
makes: 6 servings

12   ounces bulk turkey
        sausage
 8   ounces fresh
        mushrooms, sliced
 ½   cup chopped onion
        (1 medium)
 ½   cup chopped celery
        (1 stalk)
 1   teaspoon caraway
        seeds, crushed
 ¼   teaspoon ground
        black pepper
1¾   cups reduced-sodium
        beef broth
 ½   cup light beer,
        nonalcoholic beer,
        or reduced-sodium
        beef broth
 2   potatoes, cubed
 1   cup small broccoli
        florets
 2   cups shredded
        cabbage
1½   cups fat-free milk

1 In a 4-quart Dutch oven cook sausage, mushrooms, onion, and celery over medium heat until sausage is brown, using a wooden spoon to break up sausage as it cooks. Drain fat.

2 Add caraway seeds and pepper to sausage mixture in Dutch oven. Add broth and beer. Bring to boiling. Add potatoes. Simmer, covered, for 10 minutes. Add broccoli. Simmer, covered, about 5 minutes more or until potatoes and broccoli are tender.

3 Stir cabbage and milk into sausage-broccoli mixture; cook for 2 to 3 minutes or just until cabbage is tender and soup is heated through.

nutrition facts per serving: 179 cal., 5 g total fat (1 g sat. fat), 44 mg chol., 522 mg sodium, 16 g carb., 3 g dietary fiber, 17 g protein.

This zesty stick-to-the-ribs soup boasts six seasonings plus Italian sausage. Vary the spiciness by choosing either sweet or hot sausage.

italian sausage soup

prep: 30 minutes slow cook: 8 to 10 hours (low) or 4 to 5 hours (high) + 20 minutes (high)
makes: 8 servings

1 pound Italian sausage (remove casings, if present)
½ cup chopped onion (1 medium)
1 clove garlic, chopped
1 cup chopped carrot (1 medium)
½ cup chopped celery (1 stalk)
1 14.5-ounce can diced tomatoes, undrained
1 8-ounce can tomato sauce
1 teaspoon dried oregano
½ teaspoon dried rosemary
½ teaspoon dried basil
¼ teaspoon dried thyme
¼ teaspoon fennel seeds
1 bay leaf
3 14-ounce cans reduced-sodium chicken broth
½ cup dried orzo or finely broken capellini pasta
Finely shredded Parmesan cheese (optional)

1 In a large skillet combine Italian sausage, onion, and garlic over medium heat; cook until sausage is cooked through, using a wooden spoon to break sausage into bite-size pieces. Drain fat.

2 In 4½- to 6-quart slow cooker combine carrot and celery. Place sausage mixture on top of vegetables. In a medium bowl combine tomatoes, tomato sauce, oregano, rosemary, basil, thyme, fennel seeds, and bay leaf. Pour over sausage mixture. Pour broth over all.

3 Cover and cook on low-heat setting for 8 to 10 hours or on high-heat setting for 4 to 5 hours.

4 If using low-heat setting, turn to high-heat setting. Stir in pasta. Cover and cook for 20 minutes more. Discard bay leaf. If desired, serve with cheese.

nutrition facts per serving: 250 cal., 13 g total fat (5 g sat. fat), 38 mg chol., 923 mg sodium, 17 g carb., 2 g dietary fiber, 12 g protein.

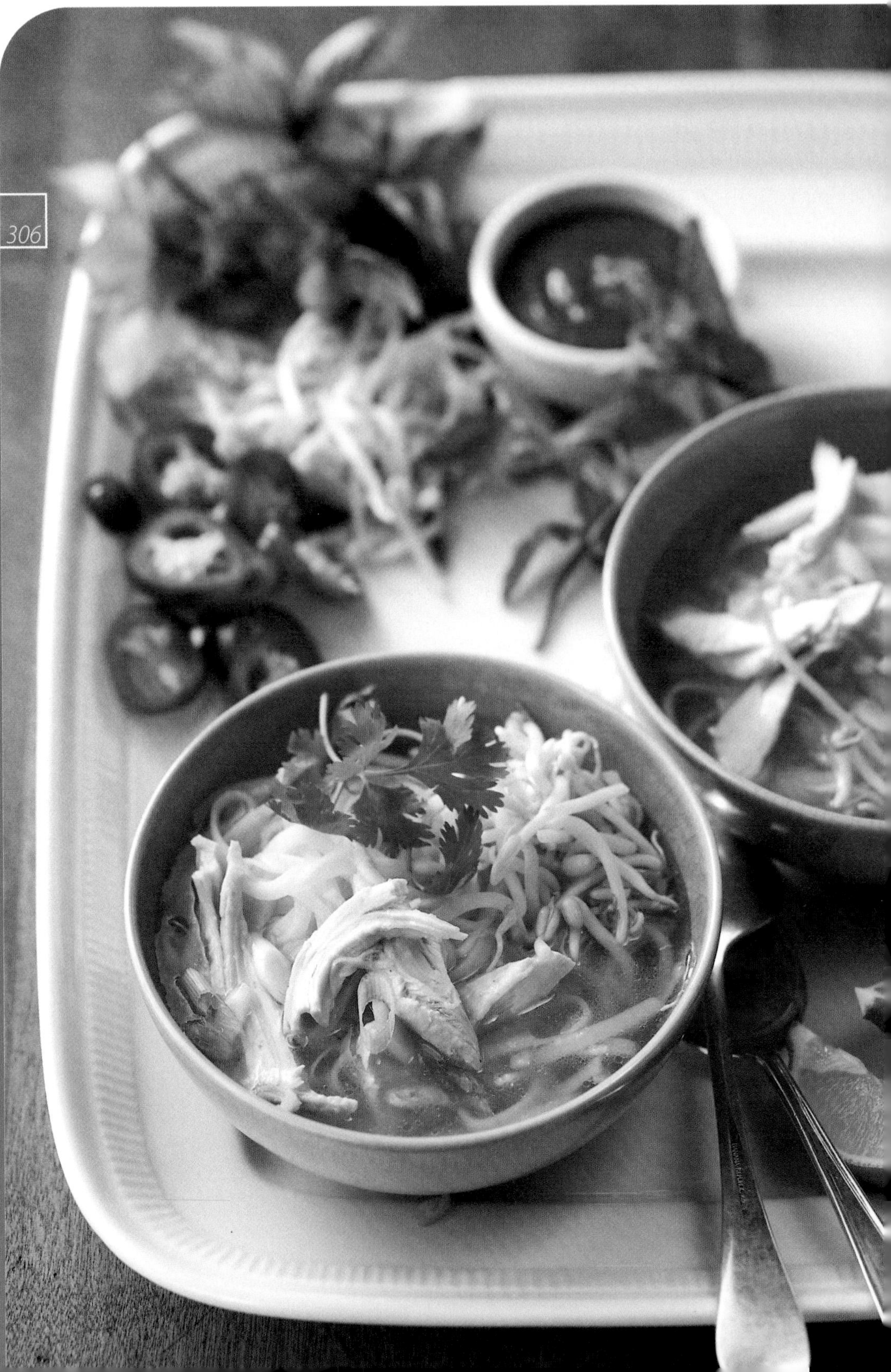

To bring out the fragrance in coriander, toast the seeds. Put them in a dry heavy skillet over medium heat for 1 to 2 minutes or until the seeds are toasted and aromatic, shaking the skillet frequently.

chicken pho ga (vietnamese chicken soup)

prep: 40 minutes cook: 2¼ hours
makes: 10 servings

1   3½- to 4-pound whole broiler chicken
2   pounds chicken necks, backs, and/or wings
2   onions, peeled and quartered
1   2-inch piece unpeeled fresh ginger, cut into ½-inch slices
2   tablespoons coriander seeds, toasted
2   teaspoons sugar
2   teaspoons salt
6   whole cloves
½   small bunch fresh cilantro
    Cold water (about 4 quarts)
3   to 4 tablespoons fish sauce
8   ounces dried thin rice noodles (¼ inch thick)
3   green onions, thinly sliced (include 2 inches of green portions)
2   cups fresh bean sprouts
½   cup fresh Thai or Italian basil leaves, torn or shredded
¼   cup fresh mint leaves, torn or shredded
1   to 2 jalapeño peppers, sliced*
    Limes, cut into wedges
    Asian chili-garlic sauce

1 In a 6- to 8-quart Dutch oven place whole chicken and chicken pieces. Add quartered onions, ginger, coriander seeds, sugar, salt, and cloves. Remove leaves and tender stems from cilantro; set aside. Add remaining stems to pot. Add enough of the cold water to cover. Bring just to simmering over medium heat. Skim off any foam. Simmer, uncovered, for 35 to 40 minutes or until chicken is no longer pink (180°F in thigh).

2 Remove whole chicken and pieces from pot; continue simmering onion mixture. When chicken is cool enough to handle, remove meat from bones. Return skin and bones to pot. Simmer for 1½ hours. Coarsely shred chicken. Cover and chill chicken until needed. Strain broth through two layers of 100-percent-cotton cheesecloth placed in a colander; discard solids. Skim fat from broth. Return broth to pot; stir in fish sauce.

3 Meanwhile, soak noodles in warm water about 20 minutes or until pliable; drain and set aside.

4 To serve, place noodles in a large saucepan of boiling, lightly salted water to heat. Drain and divide noodles among warmed large bowls. Top with green onions. Add shredded chicken to broth; heat through. Ladle broth and chicken over noodles. Serve with the reserved cilantro, bean sprouts, basil, mint, chile peppers, lime wedges, and chili-garlic sauce.

nutrition facts per serving: 535 cal., 34 g total fat (9 g sat. fat), 141 mg chol., 1115 mg sodium, 26 g carb., 2 g dietary fiber, 30 g protein.

*note: See tip on handling chile peppers, page 31.

Broccoli rabe, a leafy green vegetable widely used in Italian dishes, resembles broccoli but has thinner stems, smaller florets, and a sharper flavor. You can substitute regular broccoli or kale.

tuscan ravioli stew

start to finish: 30 minutes
makes: 4 servings

1   tablespoon olive oil
⅓   cup sliced leek
      (1 medium)*
3   cloves garlic, minced
1   14-ounce can
      vegetable broth
      or beef broth
¾   cup water
¼   teaspoon crushed
      red pepper flakes
      (optional)
5   cups coarsely
      chopped broccoli
      rabe or broccoli
      florets
1   14.5-ounce can
      no-salt-added
      stewed tomatoes,
      undrained
1   9-ounce package
      refrigerated cheese-
      filled ravioli
1   tablespoon snipped
      fresh rosemary or
      1 teaspoon dried
      rosemary, crushed
¼   cup grated Asiago or
      Parmesan cheese
      (optional)

1 In a large saucepan heat oil over medium heat. Add leek and garlic; cook for 5 minutes. Add broth, the water, and, if desired, red pepper flakes. Bring to boiling.

2 Add broccoli rabe, undrained tomatoes, ravioli, and rosemary. Return to boiling; reduce heat. Simmer, covered, for 7 to 8 minutes or until broccoli rabe and ravioli are tender. If desired, sprinkle each serving with cheese.

nutrition facts per serving: 363 cal., 16 g total fat (9 g sat. fat), 55 mg chol., 995 mg sodium, 41 g carb., 5 g dietary fiber, 13 g protein.

*note: See tip on cleaning leeks, page 464.

*Loaded with tender, chunky chicken and potatoes, this satisfying
Spanish stew takes a Mediterranean turn with the addition of olives.*

basque chicken stew

start to finish: 30 minutes
makes: 6 servings

1¼ pounds skinless,
   boneless chicken
   thighs, cut into
   2-inch pieces
¼ teaspoon salt
¼ teaspoon ground
   black pepper
1 tablespoon olive oil
1 onion, thinly sliced
1 red sweet pepper, cut
   into ¼-inch-thick
   strips
2 cloves garlic, minced
1 14.5-ounce can diced
   tomatoes, drained
1 cup chicken broth
12 ounces red-skinned
   potatoes, cut into
   ½-inch wedges
½ teaspoon dried
   savory, crushed
1 teaspoon fresh
   snipped thyme or
   ¼ teaspoon dried
   thyme, crushed
¼ teaspoon salt
⅓ cup small pimiento-
   stuffed olives
   (optional)
   Fresh thyme

1 Season chicken with salt and black pepper.
Heat oil in large Dutch oven over medium-
high heat. Add chicken and cook until lightly
browned, about 2 minutes per side.

2 Add onion and sweet pepper; cook
3 minutes or until crisp-tender. Add
garlic; cook 30 seconds more. Add drained
tomatoes, broth, potatoes, savory, 1 teaspoon
fresh thyme, and salt. Bring to boil; reduce
heat. Simmer, covered, for 20 minutes or until
chicken and potatoes are tender. Remove
from heat. Stir in olives, if desired, and garnish
with additional fresh thyme.

nutrition facts per serving: 204 cal., 6 g total fat
(1 g sat. fat), 79 mg chol., 576 mg sodium, 16 g carb.,
3 g dietary fiber, 21 g protein.

slow cooker directions: In a 3½- or
4-quart slow cooker combine chicken,
potatoes, sweet pepper, and onion. Stir in
tomatoes, broth, garlic, thyme, salt, and
black pepper. Cover and cook on low-heat
setting for 10 to 11 hours or on high-heat
setting for 5 to 5½ hours. Stir in olives
and, if desired, garnish with additional
fresh thyme.

An intriguing blend of spices makes this slow-simmer chicken and potato dish sizzle with flavors that are typical of Indian cuisine.

indian curry chicken stew

prep: 25 minutes   slow cook: 8 to 10 hours (low) or 4 to 5 hours (high) + 15 minutes (high)
makes: 4 servings

4   white potatoes (about 1½ pounds), peeled
1   green sweet pepper, seeded and cut into 1-inch pieces
1   onion, sliced
1   pound skinless, boneless chicken breast halves or thighs, cut into 1-inch pieces
1½ cups chopped tomato (3 medium)
1   tablespoon ground coriander
1½ teaspoons paprika
1   teaspoon grated fresh ginger or ¼ teaspoon ground ginger
¾   teaspoon salt
½   teaspoon ground turmeric
¼   to ½ teaspoon crushed red pepper flakes
¼   teaspoon ground cinnamon
⅛   teaspoon ground cloves
1   cup chicken broth
2   tablespoons cold water
4   teaspoons cornstarch

1 In a 3½- to 6-quart slow cooker combine potatoes, sweet pepper, and onion. Add chicken.

2 In a medium bowl combine tomato, coriander, paprika, ginger, salt, turmeric, red pepper flakes, cinnamon, and cloves; stir in broth. Pour over mixture in cooker.

3 Cover and cook on low-heat setting for 8 to 10 hours or on high-heat setting for 4 to 5 hours.

4 If using low-heat setting, turn to high-heat setting. In a small bowl combine the water and cornstarch; stir into mixture in cooker. Cover and cook for 15 to 20 minutes more or until slightly thickened and bubbly.

nutrition facts per serving: 282 cal., 2 g total fat (0 g sat. fat), 66 mg chol., 828 mg sodium, 25 g carb., 6 g dietary fiber, 32 g protein.

Coconut milk, a staple in Caribbean kitchens, gives this stew rich, thick body. For best results, use unsweetened coconut milk, not the sweetened product labeled "cream of coconut."

caribbean chicken stew

prep: 50 minutes   cook: 40 minutes
makes: 8 servings

2   onions, cut into
    1-inch pieces
1   tablespoon vegetable
    oil
1   3- to 3½-pound
    broiler-fryer chicken,
    cut into 8 pieces,
    wing tips removed
2   14-ounce cans
    chicken broth
2½ pounds sweet
    potatoes, peeled
    and cut into 1-inch
    pieces
1   14.5-ounce can
    diced tomatoes,
    undrained
1   10-ounce package
    frozen whole-kernel
    corn
½   to 1 teaspoon crushed
    red pepper flakes
½   teaspoon salt
2   tablespoons grated
    fresh ginger or
    1 teaspoon ground
    ginger
1   cup unsweetened
    coconut milk
4   cups hot cooked rice

1 In a 4- to 5-quart Dutch oven cook onions in hot oil over medium heat for 4 to 6 minutes or until tender, stirring occasionally. Add chicken and broth. Bring to boiling; reduce heat. Simmer, covered, for 30 minutes. Transfer chicken to a bowl; set aside.

2 Add sweet potatoes, undrained tomatoes, corn, red pepper flakes, and salt to Dutch oven. Return to boiling; reduce heat. Simmer, covered, for 10 to 15 minutes or until vegetables are tender. Meanwhile, remove chicken meat from bones; discard bones and skin. Chop or shred meat; set aside.

3 Skim fat from soup. Using a slotted spoon, transfer 1½ cups of the vegetables to a blender or food processor; add 1 cup of the broth. Let cool slightly. Cover and blend until smooth; return to Dutch oven. Add chicken and ginger; heat through. Stir in coconut milk. Serve over rice.

nutrition facts per serving: 587 cal., 26 g total fat (10 g sat. fat), 86 mg chol., 731 mg sodium, 60 g carb., 5 g dietary fiber, 28 g protein.

312

Lemongrass is a popular herb used in Thai cooking. It resembles a very large green onion. Use only the fibrous white bulb to impart a lemon fragrance and flavor.

thai chicken soup

prep: 20 minutes   **slow cook:** 6 to 7 hours (low) or 3 to 3½ hours (high)
stand: 5 minutes
makes: 6 servings

1 In a 3½- to 5-quart slow cooker combine chicken, broth, carrot, onion, ginger, garlic, lemongrass, and red pepper flakes.

2 Cover and cook on low-heat setting for 6 to 7 hours or on high-heat setting for 3 to 3½ hours. If necessary, skim fat. Stir coconut milk, sweet pepper, mushrooms, and cilantro into chicken mixture. Cover; let stand 5 to 10 minutes. Discard lemongrass. Sprinkle each serving with peanuts.

nutrition facts per serving: 328 cal., 20 g total fat (13 g sat. fat), 40 mg chol., 764 mg sodium, 15 g carb., 4 g dietary fiber, 23 g protein.

1 pound skinless, boneless chicken breasts or thighs, cut into ¾-inch pieces
4 cups chicken broth
2 cups bias-sliced carrot (4 medium)
1 cup chopped onion (1 large)
2 tablespoons grated fresh ginger
3 cloves garlic, minced
2 stalks lemongrass, cut into 1-inch pieces, or 1 teaspoon finely shredded lemon zest
½ teaspoon crushed red pepper flakes
1 15-ounce can unsweetened coconut milk
1 medium red, yellow, and/or green sweet pepper, cut into ½-inch pieces
2 4-ounce cans straw or button mushrooms, drained
¼ cup snipped fresh cilantro
⅓ cup chopped roasted peanuts

Borscht is a classic Eastern European and Russian soup that features beets and cabbage. The addition of beef makes it a main dish. Serve it with dark rye or pumpernickel and butter.

beef and borscht stew

prep: 40 minutes   slow cook: 8 to 10 hours (low) or 4 to 4½ hours (high) + 30 minutes (high)
makes: 6 to 8 servings

1   pound beef stew meat, cut into 1-inch cubes
1   tablespoon vegetable oil
4   beets, peeled and cut into ½-inch pieces, or one 16-ounce can diced beets, drained
2   cups chopped, peeled potato (2 medium)
1   cup coarsely chopped tomato (2 medium)
1   cup coarsely shredded carrot (2 medium)
½   cup chopped onion (1 medium)
3   cloves garlic, minced
1   bay leaf
4   cups reduced-sodium beef broth
1   6-ounce can tomato paste
2   tablespoons red wine vinegar
1   tablespoon packed brown sugar
½   teaspoon salt
½   teaspoon dried dill
¼   teaspoon ground black pepper
3   cups shredded cabbage
    Sour cream or plain yogurt (optional)

1 In a large skillet cook meat, half at a time, in hot oil over medium heat until brown. Drain fat. In a 4- to 5-quart slow cooker combine beets, potato, tomato, carrot, onion, garlic, and bay leaf. Add meat to cooker.

2 In a large bowl combine broth, tomato paste, vinegar, brown sugar, salt, dill, and pepper. Pour over all.

3 Cover and cook on low-heat setting for 8 to 10 hours or on high-heat setting for 4 to 4½ hours. If using low-heat setting, turn to high-heat setting. Stir in cabbage. Cover and cook for 30 minutes more.

4 Discard bay leaf. If desired, serve with sour cream.

nutrition facts per serving: 248 cal., 5 g total fat (2 g sat. fat), 45 mg chol., 623 mg sodium, 29 g carb., 5 g dietary fiber, 22 g protein.

Few things smell better than Moroccan food as it cooks. Throw this kaleidoscope of ingredients into the slow cooker in the morning, then return home later to amazing aromas and fabulous flavors.

moroccan chicken stew

prep: 30 minutes slow cook: 6½ to 7 hours (low) or 3½ to 4 hours (high)
makes: 4 servings

2 cups sliced carrot
    (4 medium)
2 large onions, halved
    and thinly sliced
½ teaspoon salt
3 pounds skinless
    meaty chicken
    pieces (breast
    halves, thighs, and
    drumsticks)
½ cup raisins
½ cup dried apricots,
    coarsely chopped
1 14-ounce can chicken
    broth
¼ cup tomato paste
2 tablespoons all-
    purpose flour
2 tablespoons lemon
    juice
2 cloves garlic, minced
1½ teaspoons ground
    cumin
1½ teaspoons ground
    ginger
1 teaspoon ground
    cinnamon
¾ teaspoon ground
    black pepper
    Hot cooked couscous
    Pine nuts, toasted
    Fresh cilantro
    (optional)

1 In a 5- to 6-quart slow cooker place carrot and onions. Sprinkle chicken with salt. Add to cooker; top chicken with raisins and apricots.

2 In bowl whisk broth, tomato paste, flour, lemon juice, garlic, cumin, ginger, cinnamon, and pepper. Pour over all.

3 Cover and cook on low-heat setting for 6 ½ to 7 hours or on high-heat setting for 3½ to 4 hours. Serve in bowls with couscous. Sprinkle each serving with pine nuts. Garnish with cilantro.

nutrition facts per serving: 600 cal., 15 g total fat (3 g sat. fat), 139 mg chol., 997 mg sodium, 65 g carb., 8 g dietary fiber, 52 g protein.

This stew is based on a spicy Italian tomato based sauce that is traditionally served with pasta. Make this as spicy as you like by adding more hot pepper sauce and/or red pepper flakes.

puttanesca turkey stew

prep: 25 minutes   slow cook: 7½ hours (low) + 25 minutes (high)
makes: 4 servings

2 pounds skinless turkey drumsticks (about 1½ pounds)
1 28-ounce can plum tomatoes, undrained
1 8-ounce can tomato sauce
½ cup finely chopped red onion (1 medium)
2 tablespoons tomato paste
¼ cup pitted green olives, halved
3 tablespoons drained capers
½ teaspoon dried Italian seasoning
¼ teaspoon salt
¼ teaspoon ground black pepper
¼ teaspoon crushed red pepper flakes
Dash bottled hot pepper sauce
¼ cup dry red wine
Grated Parmesan cheese (optional)

1 In a 5-quart slow cooker combine drumsticks, undrained tomatoes, tomato sauce, red onion, tomato paste, green olives, capers, Italian seasoning, salt, black pepper, red pepper flakes, and hot pepper sauce.

2 Cover and cook on low-heat setting for 7½ hours. Once turkey reaches the proper temperature (160°F to 170°F on an instant-read thermometer inserted into the thickest part of drumstick without touching bone), transfer turkey drumsticks to platter and let cool.

3 Stir red wine into mixture in slow cooker. Using the back of a large spoon, crush tomatoes in slow cooker. Turn to high-heat setting. Cook, uncovered, for 20 minutes.

4 Once turkey is cool enough to handle, remove meat from bones; discard bones. Chop or shred turkey and return to cooker. Cook, uncovered, for 5 to 10 minutes more or until sauce thickens slightly. If desired, sprinkle each serving with cheese.

nutrition facts per serving: 238 cal., 8 g total fat (2 g sat. fat), 66 mg chol., 1338 mg sodium, 18 g carb., 2 g dietary fiber, 26 g protein.

Popular throughout Mexico, this zesty soup gets much of its deep flavor from roasting the tomatoes and poblanos. Crumbled queso fresco, a fresh Mexican cheese, adds a nice salty bite.

roasted tomato soup with shrimp and queso fresco

prep: 40 minutes broil: 10 minutes roast: 20 minutes oven: at 425°F
stand: 15 minutes cook: 47 minutes
makes: 6 servings

1	pound fresh or frozen medium shrimp in shells
	Nonstick cooking spray
2½	pounds roma tomatoes
6	poblano peppers*
1	tablespoon olive oil
1	onion, halved and thinly sliced
3	cloves garlic, minced
1	teaspoon dried oregano, crushed, or 2 teaspoons snipped fresh oregano
1	teaspoon ground cumin
¼	teaspoon salt
3	14.5-ounce cans chicken broth
2	cups crumbled queso fresco (8 ounces)
	Snipped fresh oregano (optional)

nutrition facts per serving:
283 cal., 7 g total fat (1 g sat. fat),
117 mg chol., 1020 mg sodium,
25 g carb., 4 g dietary fiber,
29 g protein.

*note: See tip on handling chile peppers, page 31.

1 Thaw shrimp if frozen. Peel and devein shrimp. Rinse shrimp; pat dry with paper towels. Cover and chill until needed.

2 Preheat broiler. Line a 15×10×1-inch baking pan with foil; lightly coat foil with cooking spray. Place whole tomatoes in prepared baking pan. Broil about 4 inches from heat for 10 to 12 minutes or until skins are charred, carefully turning once halfway through broiling. When tomatoes are cool enough to handle, peel over a medium bowl to catch the juices. Remove tomato cores; discard cores and skins. Transfer tomatoes and juices to a food processor or blender. Cover and process or blend with several on/off pulses until nearly smooth; set aside.

3 Preheat oven to 425°F. Line a large baking sheet with foil. Cut chile peppers in half lengthwise; remove stems, seeds, and membranes. Place pepper halves, cut sides down, on prepared baking sheet. Roast for 20 to 25 minutes or until peppers are charred and very tender. Bring foil up around peppers and fold edges together to enclose. Let stand about 15 minutes or until cool enough to handle. Using a sharp knife, loosen edges of skins; gently pull off skins in strips; discard skins. Cut peppers into ½-inch-wide strips; set aside.

4 In a Dutch oven heat oil over medium heat. Add onion; cook for 8 to 10 minutes or until golden, stirring frequently. Add pureed tomatoes, roasted peppers, garlic, oregano, cumin, and salt. Bring to boiling over medium-high heat. Boil gently, uncovered, for 7 to 8 minutes or until mixture is quite thick, stirring frequently. Stir in broth. Return to boiling; reduce heat. Simmer, covered, for 30 minutes.

5 Stir in shrimp. Simmer, uncovered, for 2 to 3 minutes more or until shrimp are opaque.

6 Top each serving with cheese and, if desired, oregano.

All of the great flavors of a long-cooking stew come together in less than an hour in this stovetop version, featuring hearty vegetables, crunchy peanuts, and some crushed red pepper flakes.

hot african stew

prep: 25 minutes **cook:** 25 minutes
makes: 6 servings

1   tablespoon canola oil
1¼   cups thinly sliced onion (1 large)
1¼   cups chopped green sweet pepper (1 large)
½   teaspoon crushed red pepper flakes
2   14-ounce cans reduced-sodium beef broth
1   cup chopped unsalted peanuts
6   tiny new potatoes, cut into 1-inch pieces
1   sweet potato, peeled and cut into 1-inch pieces
1   19-ounce can fava beans, rinsed and drained
1   14.5-ounce can diced tomatoes, undrained
   Light sour cream (optional)
   Snipped fresh chives (optional)

1 In a large saucepan or Dutch oven heat oil over medium heat. Add onion and sweet pepper; cook until golden and tender, stirring occasionally. Stir in red pepper flakes; cook for 1 minute. Add broth and peanuts. Bring to boiling.

2 Stir in new potatoes and sweet potato. Return to boiling; reduce heat. Simmer, covered, about 25 minutes or until potatoes are tender, stirring occasionally. Stir in beans and undrained tomatoes; heat through. If desired, top each serving with sour cream and chives.

nutrition facts per serving: 296 cal., 15 g total fat (2 g sat. fat), 0 mg chol., 669 mg sodium, 30 g carb., 11 g dietary fiber, 13 g protein.

Cauliflower, potatoes, and carrots make up the vegetable puree that's warmly spiced with garam masala, a classic Indian spice. You can find it in the spice section at larger supermarkets.

indian cauliflower soup with garam masala

start to finish: 35 minutes
makes: 6 servings

Nonstick cooking
   spray
½ cup coarsely chopped
   onion (1 medium)
3 cloves garlic, minced
1 32-ounce carton
   reduced-sodium
   chicken broth
½ of a head cauliflower
   (14 ounces), cut up
2 cups peeled and
   cubed Yukon Gold
   or red-skinned
   potato (2 medium)
½ cup chopped carrot
   (1 medium)
1 tablespoon grated
   fresh ginger
1½ teaspoons
   garam masala
   (or ¾ teaspoon
   curry powder
   and ¾ teaspoon
   ground cumin)
½ cup yogurt
   Salt
   Cayenne pepper
   Snipped fresh chives
   or parsley (optional)

1 Lightly coat a large saucepan with cooking spray; heat saucepan over medium heat. Add onion and garlic; cook for 3 to 5 minutes or until tender, stirring frequently.

2 Stir in broth, cauliflower, potato, carrot, ginger, and garam masala. Bring to boiling; reduce heat. Simmer, covered, about 12 minutes or until vegetables are tender; cool slightly.

3 Transfer vegetable mixture, half at a time, to a blender or food processor. Cover and blend or process until nearly smooth. Return pureed mixture to saucepan. Stir in yogurt; heat through (do not boil).

4 Season to taste with salt and cayenne pepper. If desired, garnish each serving with chives.

nutrition facts per serving: 85 cal., 2 g total fat
(0 g sat. fat), 0 mg chol., 406 mg sodium, 16 g carb.,
3 g dietary fiber, 6 g protein.

Concocted long ago in Scotland, this hearty, traditional soup features chicken, leeks, and barley, with a surprising garnish of dried plums.

scottish cock-a-leekie soup

prep: 20 minutes cook: 50 minutes
makes: 6 servings

1¼ pounds meaty chicken pieces (breast halves, thighs, and/ or drumsticks)
4 cups chicken broth
4 cups water
4 medium carrots, cut into 1-inch pieces (2 cups)
1 stalk celery, sliced (½ cup)
3 bay leaves
1 teaspoon salt
1 teaspoon ground black pepper
4 medium leeks, sliced ¼ inch thick, white and pale green parts only (1⅓ cups)*
1 tablespoon snipped fresh thyme
¾ cup quick-cooking barley
½ cup snipped dried plums (prunes)
⅓ cup snipped fresh parsley
2 slices bacon, crisp-cooked, drained, and crumbled

1 In a Dutch oven combine chicken, broth, the water, carrots, celery, bay leaves, salt, and pepper. Bring to simmering over medium heat. Simmer, covered, for 30 to 35 minutes or until chicken is tender and no longer pink (180°F on an instant-read thermometer inserted into the thickest part of thigh without touching bone). Remove chicken pieces.

2 When cool enough to handle, remove and discard skin from chicken. Pull meat from bones; discard bones. Coarsely chop chicken; return to pot.

3 Add leeks and thyme to pot. Simmer, covered, for 10 minutes. Stir in barley; simmer, covered, for 10 to 15 minutes more or until leeks and barley are tender.

4 In a small bowl combine dried plums, parsley, and bacon. Ladle soup into bowls and top with bacon mixture.

nutrition facts per serving: 399 cal., 16 g total fat (5 g sat. fat), 75 mg chol., 1205 mg sodium, 41 g carb., 6 g dietary fiber, 24 g protein.

*note: See tip on cleaning leeks, page 464.

This traditional stew, also known as a bouillabaisse, is typically made with tomatoes, onion, olive oil, garlic, herbs, fish, and shellfish. Wine also makes it authentic, but in this case, clam juice is added for the fresh, briny flavors. Soak up the flavorful broth with a crusty French baguette.

provençal seafood stew

start to finish: 30 minutes
makes: 4 servings

4   jumbo shrimp
       (about 4 ounces)
8   ounces cod fillet
       (or other firm-
       fleshed fish),
       cut into 4 pieces
12   mussels in shells
       (about 8 ounces),
       cleaned*
½   cup thinly sliced
       onion
1   clove garlic, minced
⅛   teaspoon ground
       allspice
2   teaspoons olive oil
1   14.5-ounce can whole
       peeled tomatoes in
       puree
1   8-ounce bottle clam
       juice
¼   teaspoon salt
¼   teaspoon ground
       black pepper
⅛   teaspoon crushed
       red pepper flakes
1   teaspoon snipped
       fresh thyme
½   teaspoon finely
       shredded orange
       zest
   Fresh thyme sprigs
       (optional)

1 Peel and devein shrimp. Rinse shrimp, cod, and mussels; pat dry with paper towels. Set aside.

2 In a large saucepan cook onion, garlic, and allspice in hot oil over medium-high heat about 5 minutes or until onions are softened.

3 Meanwhile, press tomatoes and their juices through a fine-mesh sieve. Discard pulp and seeds. Add tomato mixture, clam juice, salt, black pepper, and red pepper flakes to the saucepan. Bring to boiling; reduce heat. Simmer, covered, for 10 minutes.

4 Stir in snipped thyme and orange zest. Add mussels, shrimp, and cod to saucepan. Gently stir to combine. Return to boiling; reduce heat. Simmer, covered, for 3 minutes more or until mussel shells open, shrimp are opaque, and fish flakes easily when tested with a fork. Discard any mussels that do not open.

5 Serve in shallow bowls and, if desired, garnish each serving with fresh thyme sprigs.

nutrition facts per serving: 189 cal., 4 g total fat (1 g sat. fat), 83 mg chol., 997 mg sodium, 11 g carb., 2 g dietary fiber, 29 g protein.

*note: To clean live mussels, scrub mussels under cold running water. Remove beards.

This citrus-scented stew is an adaptation of feijoada, a Portuguese pork, beef, and bean stew considered by many Brazilians to be the country's national dish. Brazilians customarily serve the stew on Wednesdays and Saturdays with rice, cold cuts, and finely shredded kale.

brazilian black bean stew

prep: 1 hour 30 minutes **slow cook:** 8 to 10 hours (low) or 4 to 5 hours (high)
makes: 8 servings

12	ounces dried black beans
8	cups water
2	large smoked ham hocks
4	cups reduced-sodium chicken broth
1½	cups chopped onion (3 medium)
3	jalapeño peppers, seeded and minced*
4	cloves garlic, minced
1	tablespoon finely shredded orange zest
½	cup orange juice
½	cup dry sherry
¼	cup snipped fresh cilantro
	Hot cooked rice (optional)

1 Rinse beans. In a large saucepan combine beans and the water. Bring to boiling; reduce heat. Simmer, uncovered, for 10 minutes. Remove from heat. Cover and let stand for 1 hour. (Or place beans in water in saucepan. Cover and let soak in a cool place overnight.) Drain and rinse beans. Place beans in a 4-quart slow cooker.

2 Add ham hocks, broth, onions, chile peppers, garlic, orange zest, orange juice, and sherry to cooker.

3 Cover and cook on low-heat setting for 8 to 10 hours or on high-heat setting for 4 to 5 hours. Transfer ham hocks to a cutting board. When cool enough to handle, cut meat from bones; discard bones. Shred ham; return shredded ham to slow cooker. Stir in cilantro.

4 If desired, serve stew over rice.

nutrition facts per serving: 253 cal., 5 g total fat (2 g sat. fat), 19 mg chol., 333 mg sodium, 34 g carb., 7 g dietary fiber, 16 g protein.

*note: See tip on handling chile peppers, page 31.

Japanese soba noodles have a nutty taste from the buckwheat flour that is used to make them. Combining them in a spicy broth with sweet potato and shredded cabbage brings out the soba's earthiness. You'll find the noodles in the Asian section of your supermarket.

indonesian chicken and soba noodle soup

start to finish: 45 minutes
makes: 6 servings

1 tablespoon canola oil
   or peanut oil
1 cup sliced onion
2 tablespoons grated
   fresh ginger
2 cups shredded green
   cabbage or napa
   cabbage
1 cup peeled and diced
   sweet potato
   (1 small)
½ cup sliced celery
   (1 stalk)
4 cups reduced-sodium
   chicken broth
1 tablespoon reduced-
   sodium soy sauce
½ teaspoon crushed red
   pepper flakes
8 ounces cooked
   chicken breast,
   coarsely chopped
1 tablespoon lime juice
¼ cup chopped green
   onion (2)
¼ cup snipped fresh
   cilantro
8 ounces whole-grain
   soba or udon
   noodles, cooked
   according to
   package directions
   Chopped unsalted
   dry-roasted peanuts
   (optional)

1 In a large saucepan heat oil over medium-high heat. Add onion and ginger; cook for 3 minutes, stirring occasionally.

2 Add cabbage, sweet potato, and celery; cook for 4 minutes more, stirring occasionally. Stir in broth, soy sauce, and red pepper flakes. Bring to boiling; reduce heat. Simmer, covered, about 15 minutes or until vegetables are tender.

3 Stir in chicken and lime juice. Just before serving, stir in green onion and cilantro. Serve soup over soba noodles and, if desired, garnish with peanuts.

nutrition facts per serving: 266 cal., 5 g total fat (1 g sat. fat), 32 mg chol., 581 mg sodium, 35 g carb., 4 g dietary fiber, 20 g protein.

North to South, East to West, every region of the United States adds its own touch to soups and stews, utilizing ingredients and flavors reflective of the land and the people who live in the region. Now's as good a time as any to bring these wonderfully long simmers to your soup pot.

coast-to-coast

regi

11

onal

Packed with Southwestern flavors, this hearty soup offers a variety of textures, from chewy meatballs to tender corn and beans to crunchy golden tortilla strips. The meatballs can be made ahead and frozen, making this a weeknight-friendly meal.

meatball-tortilla soup

prep: 45 minutes cook: 20 minutes
makes: 6 servings

2 tablespoons
    vegetable oil
3 corn or flour tortillas,
    cut into strips
1 recipe Tex-Mex
    Meatballs
2 14.5-ounce cans
    Mexican-style
    stewed tomatoes,
    undrained and
    cut up
2 14.5-ounce cans
    chicken broth
1 15-ounce can black
    beans, rinsed and
    drained
1 cup frozen whole-
    kernel corn
2 teaspoons chili
    powder
    Snipped fresh cilantro
    leaves

1 In a large skillet heat oil over medium-high heat. Add tortilla strips; cook and stir for 3 to 4 minutes or until crisp. Using a slotted spoon, remove tortilla strips from skillet and drain on paper towels.

2 In a large saucepan combine Tex-Mex Meatballs, undrained tomatoes, broth, beans, frozen corn, and chili powder. Bring to boiling; reduce heat. Simmer, covered, for 20 minutes.

3 Top each serving with tortilla strips. If desired, sprinkle with cilantro.

nutrition facts per serving: 393 cal., 18 g total fat (5 g sat. fat), 88 mg chol., 1485 mg sodium, 36 g carb., 8 g dietary fiber, 24 g protein.

tex-mex meatballs: Preheat oven to 350°F. In a large bowl combine 1 lightly beaten egg, half of a 4-ounce can undrained diced green chile peppers, ¼ cup fine dry bread crumbs, ¼ cup finely chopped onion, and half of a 1.25-ounce envelope taco seasoning mix. Add 1 pound lean ground beef; mix well. On a cutting board pat mixture into a 6×4-inch rectangle. Cut into twenty-four 1-inch squares. Shape each square into a ball. Arrange meatballs in a 15×10×1-inch baking pan. Bake for 15 to 20 minutes or until done (160°F), rotating pan once.

Missouri stockyards once helped deliver some of the finest steaks to the world. This version of the KC steak soup uses lean ground sirloin mixed with veggies and seasoned with a blast of steak sauce and Worcestershire. It cooks in just 25 minutes.

kansas city steak soup

prep: 20 minutes cook: 25 minutes
makes: 6 servings

1½ pounds ground beef
    sirloin
1   cup chopped onion
    (1 large)
1   cup sliced celery
    (2 stalks)
2   14.5-ounce cans
    reduced-sodium
    beef broth
1   28-ounce can
    diced tomatoes,
    undrained
1   10-ounce package
    frozen mixed
    vegetables
2   tablespoons steak
    sauce
2   teaspoons
    Worcestershire
    sauce
¼   teaspoon salt
¼   teaspoon ground
    black pepper
¼   cup all-purpose flour

1 In a Dutch oven cook meat, onion, and celery over medium-high heat until meat is brown, using a wooden spoon to break up meat as it cooks. Drain fat.

2 Stir in 1 can of the broth, undrained tomatoes, frozen vegetables, steak sauce, Worcestershire sauce, salt, and pepper. Bring to boiling; reduce heat. Simmer, covered, for 20 minutes.

3 In a medium bowl whisk together remaining 1 can of broth and flour. Stir into meat mixture; cook and stir until thickened and bubbly. Cook and stir for 1 minute more.

nutrition facts per serving: 306 cal., 12 g total fat (5 g sat. fat), 74 mg chol., 747 mg sodium, 21 g carb., 4 g dietary fiber, 27 g protein.

A brilliant twist on traditional fajitas, this weeknight-friendly soup is sure to become a family favorite. Partially freeze the beef for about 30 minutes for easier slicing into strips.

beef fajita soup

start to finish: 40 minutes
makes: 4 servings

½ teaspoon garlic
  powder
½ teaspoon ground
  cumin
½ teaspoon paprika
⅛ teaspoon cayenne
  pepper
12 ounces boneless
  beef sirloin steak,
  trimmed and cut
  into very thin bite-
  size strips
  Nonstick cooking
  spray
2 teaspoons canola oil
2 medium yellow
  or green sweet
  peppers, cut into
  thin bite-size strips
1 medium onion, halved
  and thinly sliced
2 14-ounce cans
  reduced-sodium
  beef broth
1 14.5-ounce can no-
  salt-added diced
  tomatoes, undrained
¼ cup light sour cream
½ teaspoon finely
  shredded lime zest
1 ounce baked tortilla
  chips, coarsely
  crushed (⅔ cup)
½ of an avocado, pitted,
  peeled, and chopped
  (optional)
¼ cup snipped fresh
  cilantro (optional)

1 In a medium bowl combine garlic powder, cumin, paprika, and cayenne pepper. Add steak strips and toss to coat. Coat an unheated 4-quart nonstick Dutch oven with cooking spray. Heat over medium-high heat. Add steak strips, half at a time; cook for 2 to 4 minutes or until brown, stirring occasionally. Remove meat from the pan.

2 Heat oil in Dutch oven over medium heat. Add sweet peppers and onion; cook for 5 minutes or until lightly browned and just tender, stirring occasionally. Add broth and undrained tomatoes. Bring to boiling. Stir in steak strips and heat through.

3 Add a dollop of sour cream to each serving and sprinkle with lime zest and tortilla chips. If desired, top with avocado and cilantro.

nutrition facts per serving: 244 cal., 8 g total fat (2 g sat. fat), 40 mg chol., 515 mg sodium, 21 g carb., 4 g dietary fiber, 24 g protein.

Texans like chili made with cubed meat and no beans or canned tomatoes. So that's how we made this recipe. Give it a try for dinner some night.

texas bowls o' red chili

prep: 30 minutes cook: 1½ hours
makes: 6 servings

3   pounds boneless beef
    chuck roast, cut into
    ½-inch cubes
1   teaspoon salt
½   teaspoon ground
    black pepper
1   tablespoon vegetable
    oil
4   cups chopped onion
    (4 large)
3   tablespoons chili
    powder
3   tablespoons yellow
    cornmeal
6   cloves garlic, minced
1   tablespoon ground
    cumin
2   teaspoons dried
    oregano, crushed
¼   teaspoon cayenne
    pepper
1   14-ounce can beef
    broth
1¼ cups water
1   tablespoon packed
    brown sugar
    Chopped onion
    (optional)
    Fresh oregano
    (optional)

1 Sprinkle beef with ½ teaspoon of the salt and ¼ teaspoon of the black pepper. In a 4-quart Dutch oven heat oil. Add beef, one-third at a time; cook until brown. Using a slotted spoon, remove beef, reserving drippings in pan, and adding more oil, if necessary.

2 Add 4 cups chopped onion to drippings; cook over medium-high heat for about 5 minutes or until tender. Stir in chili powder, cornmeal, garlic, cumin, oregano, and cayenne pepper; cook for 30 seconds.

3 Stir in beef, broth, water, brown sugar, and remaining ½ teaspoon salt and ¼ teaspoon black pepper. Bring to boiling; reduce heat. Simmer, covered, for 1½ to 2 hours or until meat is tender. If desired, top each serving with additional chopped onion and fresh oregano.

nutrition facts per serving: 448 cal., 17 g total fat (5 g sat. fat), 107 mg chol., 812 mg sodium, 19 g carb., 4 g dietary fiber, 53 g protein.

Purchased salsa is the shortcut ticket to the bold flavors in this slow-cooker soup. Simply choose your favorite brand for your own house specialty version.

southwestern steak and potato soup

prep: 30 minutes   slow cook: 8 to 10 hours (low) or 4 to 5 hours (high)
makes: 12 to 14 servings

2   pounds boneless beef
    sirloin steak, cut
    ¾ inch thick
3   cups cubed potato
    (3 medium)
1   16-ounce package
    frozen cut green
    beans
1   medium onion, sliced
    and separated into
    rings
2   teaspoons dried basil,
    crushed
4   cloves garlic, minced
2   16-ounce jars thick
    and chunky salsa
2   14.5-ounce cans beef
    broth
    Shredded Monterey
    Jack cheese or
    Mexican cheese
    blend (optional)

1 Trim fat from meat. Cut meat into ¾-inch pieces. Set aside.

2 In a 6-quart slow cooker combine potato, frozen green beans, and onion. Add meat. Sprinkle with basil and garlic. Pour salsa and broth over all.

3 Cover and cook on low-heat setting for 8 to 10 hours or on high-heat setting for 4 to 5 hours. Stir before serving. If desired, sprinkle each serving with cheese.

nutrition facts per serving: 224 cal., 9 g total fat (4 g sat. fat), 56 mg chol., 983 mg sodium, 16 g carb., 3 g dietary fiber, 19 g protein.

Here's a hearty meal-in-a-bowl for those who love pork. The recipe makes several servings, but the stew tastes even better served as leftovers the next day.

pork and green chile stew

prep: 30 minutes roast: 20 minutes stand: 20 minutes bake: 1½ hours
oven: at 425°F/ 325°F
makes: 8 servings

4	poblano peppers* or 2 green sweet peppers
1½	pounds lean boneless pork shoulder
3	cups chopped onion (6 medium)
¼	cup finely chopped fresh jalapeño pepper*
6	cloves garlic, minced
1	teaspoon salt
½	teaspoon dried oregano, crushed, or 1½ teaspoons snipped fresh oregano
1½	pounds red potatoes, cut into 1-inch pieces
3	medium zucchini, halved lengthwise and cut into ½-inch-thick slices
1	10-ounce package frozen whole-kernel corn, thawed
½	cup snipped fresh cilantro
	Lime wedges (optional)

1 Preheat oven to 425°F. Line a baking sheet with foil. To roast poblano or sweet peppers, halve peppers and remove stems, seeds, and membranes. Place peppers, cut sides down, on prepared baking sheet. Roast about 20 minutes or until skins are bubbly and browned. Wrap peppers in the foil; let stand for 20 to 25 minutes or until cool enough to handle. Using a paring knife, pull the skins off gently and slowly. Coarsely chop peppers. Reduce oven to 325°F.

2 Trim fat from pork. Cut pork into bite-size pieces. In a Dutch oven combine roasted peppers, pork, onion, jalapeño pepper, garlic, salt, and dried oregano (if using). Cover and bake for 45 minutes.

3 Stir in potatoes. Cover and bake for 30 minutes. Stir in zucchini and corn. Cover and bake about 15 minutes more or until pork and vegetables are tender. Stir in cilantro and fresh oregano (if using). If desired, serve stew with lime wedges.

nutrition facts per serving: 269 cal., 6 g total fat (2 g sat. fat), 55 mg chol., 377 mg sodium, 34 g carb., 5 g dietary fiber, 22 g protein.

*note: See tip on handling chile peppers, page 31.

In the South, ham hocks and black-eyed peas are often on the New Year's Day menu. They are thought to bring good luck. The peas and hominy are what make this a high-fiber soup.

southern ham soup with black-eyed peas and hominy

prep: 25 minutes cook: 40 minutes
makes: 4 servings

2	tablespoons olive oil
1	cup chopped celery (2 stalks)
1	cup chopped onion (1 large)
¾	cup chopped green sweet pepper (1 medium)
2	cloves garlic, minced
1¼	cups diced cooked ham
1	teaspoon paprika
½	teaspoon sugar
½	teaspoon dry mustard
½	teaspoon ground cumin
½	teaspoon dried basil, crushed
½	teaspoon dried oregano, crushed
½	teaspoon dried thyme, crushed
¼	teaspoon ground cloves
¼	teaspoon ground black pepper
⅛	teaspoon cayenne pepper
1	15.5-ounce can black-eyed peas, rinsed and drained
1	15.5-ounce can golden hominy, rinsed and drained
1	14.5-ounce can diced tomatoes, undrained
1	14.5-ounce can chicken broth
1	tablespoon snipped fresh parsley
1	tablespoon mild-flavor molasses

1 In a 4-quart Dutch oven heat oil over medium heat. Add celery, onion, sweet pepper, and garlic; cook and stir for 5 minutes. Stir in ham, paprika, sugar, dry mustard, cumin, basil, oregano, thyme, cloves, black pepper, and cayenne pepper; cook and stir for 5 minutes more.

2 Stir in black-eyed peas, hominy, undrained tomatoes, broth, parsley, and molasses. Bring to boiling; reduce heat. Simmer, covered, for 30 minutes.

nutrition facts per serving: 384 cal., 14 g total fat (3 g sat. fat), 24 mg chol., 1627 mg sodium, 47 g carb., 10 g dietary fiber, 17 g protein.

*Cilantro-flavored salsa perks up the
flavor of the pork and vegetables in
this broth-based soup. The recipe calls
for bottled cilantro-flavored salsa, for
convenience, but you can use regular
salsa and stir in 2 tablespoons snipped
fresh cilantro.*

southwest pork-salsa stew

start to finish: 25 minutes
makes: 4 servings

Nonstick cooking
   spray
12 ounces boneless pork
   loin or sirloin, cut
   into bite-size strips
1 14.5-ounce can
   reduced-sodium
   chicken broth
½ cup bottled cilantro-
   flavored salsa
1 6-ounce can no-salt-
   added tomato paste
½ teaspoon ground
   cumin
1 zucchini, halved
   lengthwise and
   thinly sliced (2 cups)
1 cup frozen sweet
   soybeans (edamame)
   or baby lima beans
½ cup chopped peeled
   mango (1 small)

Lightly coat a large saucepan with cooking
spray. Heat saucepan over medium-high heat.
Add pork; cook and stir about 2 minutes or
until brown. Stir in broth, salsa, tomato paste,
and cumin. Stir in zucchini and edamame. Bring
to boiling; reduce heat. Simmer, covered, about
10 minutes or until vegetables are tender. Top
each serving with chopped mango.

nutrition facts per serving: 243 cal., 7 g total fat
(2 g sat. fat), 47 mg chol., 594 mg sodium, 19 g carb.,
6 g dietary fiber, 26 g protein.

This savory stew plays up two Midwest mainstays—pork and corn. After browning the pork, the stew mixture bakes for 2 hours, which creates a rich, gravylike base and tender meat.

vegetable-pork oven stew

prep: 20 minutes cook: 10 minutes bake: 2 hours oven: at 325°F
makes: 6 servings

1½   pounds boneless pork shoulder or pork stew meat, cut into ¾-inch cubes
1   tablespoon vegetable oil
1½   cups coarsely chopped onions (3 medium)
2   14-ounce cans reduced-sodium chicken broth or vegetable broth or 3½ cups chicken stock
1   teaspoon dried thyme, crushed
1   teaspoon dried oregano, crushed
1   teaspoon lemon pepper
½   teaspoon salt
¼   cup all-purpose flour
1   16-ounce package frozen whole-kernel corn
1   pound tiny new potatoes, halved
2   cups fresh green beans, cut into 2-inch pieces, or frozen cut green beans

1 Preheat oven to 325°F. In a 4-quart Dutch oven brown half of the meat in hot oil. Remove meat from Dutch oven. Add remaining meat and onion. Cook and stir until meat is brown and onion is just tender. Return all meat to Dutch oven. Reserve ½ cup of the broth. Stir in remaining broth, thyme, oregano, lemon pepper, and salt. Bring to boiling; remove from heat. Cover tightly and bake for 1 hour.

2 In a small bowl combine reserved ½ cup chicken broth and flour; stir into stew. Stir in frozen corn, potatoes, and green beans. Bake, covered, for 1 hour more or until meat and vegetables are tender and mixture is thickened.

nutrition facts per serving: 308 cal., 8 g total fat (2 g sat. fat), 46 mg chol., 625 mg sodium, 41 g carb., 6 g dietary fiber, 20 g protein.

This thick stew originated in Louisiana and combines the ingredients or methods of several cultures, including French, African, and Choctaw. This chicken and sausage combo is thickened with roux and flavored with okra, a Southern staple.

louisiana chicken and sausage gumbo

prep: 40 minutes   cook: 40 minutes
makes: 6 servings

⅓   cup all-purpose flour
⅓   cup vegetable oil
½   cup chopped onion
      (1 medium)
½   cup chopped green or
      red sweet pepper
      (1 small)
½   cup sliced celery
      (1 stalk)
3   cloves garlic, minced
1½ to 2 teaspoons Cajun
      seasoning
1   14.5-ounce can beef
      broth
¾   cup water
1   10-ounce package
      frozen cut okra*
      or cut green beans
1½ cups chopped cooked
      chicken
8   ounces cooked
      smoked sausage
      links, sliced
3   cups hot cooked
      long-grain white
      or brown rice
      Bottled hot pepper
      sauce (optional)

1 For roux, in a 3-quart heavy saucepan combine flour and oil until smooth; cook over medium-high heat for 5 minutes, stirring constantly. Reduce heat to medium; cook, stirring constantly, for 8 to 10 minutes more or until roux is dark reddish brown.

2 Stir in onion, sweet pepper, celery, and garlic; cook about 10 minutes or until vegetables are tender, stirring frequently. Stir in Cajun seasoning. Add broth and the water. Stir in okra. Bring to boiling; reduce heat. Simmer, covered, for 15 minutes. Stir in chicken and sausage; heat through.

3 Serve gumbo in bowls over rice. If desired, serve with hot pepper sauce.

nutrition facts per serving: 355 cal., 14 g total fat (2 g sat. fat), 114 mg chol., 487 mg sodium, 34 g carb., 2 g dietary fiber, 22 g protein.

*note: If you can't find cut okra, buy whole; thaw slightly and slice.

Plan ahead, because you'll need to soak the dried beans overnight. Although canned beans are more convenient, dried beans create superior taste and texture in stews like this one and will allow you to control the sodium content.

chicken-chile stew with beans

stand: 8 hours start to finish: 2 hours
makes: 6 servings

1   pound dried navy beans
6   chicken thighs
      (2¼ pounds)
    Kosher salt
    Ground black pepper
2   thick slices salt pork
      (about 4 ounces)
2   dried whole pasilla
      peppers (optional)
8   cups chicken broth
      or water
2   large yellow onions,
      finely chopped
2   large Anaheim or
      poblano peppers,
      seeded, ribs
      removed, and cut
      into ⅓-inch dice*
1   small serrano or
      jalapeño peppers,
      seeded and minced*
      (optional)
1   tablespoon chopped
      garlic
1   tablespoon paprika
1   tablespoon chili
      powder
1   tablespoon
      unsweetened
      cocoa powder
1   tablespoon tomato
      paste
1   tablespoon honey
2   cups peeled, cubed
      pumpkin or winter
      squash (1-inch cubes)
    Hot cooked rice
    Cilantro, slivered red
      onion, thin slices
      jalapeño or serrano
      peppers*, and sour
      cream

1 Rinse beans. Place beans and 8 cups water in a 6-quart Dutch oven. Cover and let soak 8 to 24 hours. Sprinkle chicken generously with salt and black pepper. Refrigerate, uncovered, overnight.

2 Drain and rinse beans; return to pan. Set aside. In a large nonstick skillet slowly cook salt pork until lightly browned. Add salt pork, pasilla peppers, if desired, and broth to Dutch oven. Sprinkle with salt; bring to a simmer. Simmer, partially covered, for 1¼ hours.

3 Meanwhile, in same large nonstick skillet cook chicken about 15 minutes or until brown, turning once. Remove chicken from skillet; set aside. Drain fat, reserving 2 tablespoons in skillet. Add onions; sprinkle with salt. Stir well, scraping up any browned bits from bottom of skillet.

4 Stir in Anaheim peppers, serrano peppers, and garlic; cook slowly for 5 to 10 minutes, stirring often. Stir in paprika, chili powder, and cocoa. Add tomato paste and honey; cook 3 to 5 minutes more.

5 If necessary, add more stock or water to cover beans. Ladle 1 cup of bean liquid into onion-pepper mixture. Bring to a simmer. Carefully add to bean mixture in Dutch oven. Season to taste with salt and black pepper.

6 Add chicken thighs. Simmer slowly, partially covered, for 10 to 15 minutes.

7 Add pumpkin; cook 15 minutes more or until chicken and pumpkin are tender. Remove and discard salt pork and pasilla peppers. Serve stew over rice with cilantro, red onion, sliced peppers, and sour cream.

nutrition facts per serving: 575 cal., 23 g total fat, 83 mg chol., 964 mg sodium, 56 g carb., 18 g dietary fiber, 37 g protein.

*note: See tip on handling chile peppers, page 31.

Bits of spinach and artichoke color this creamy chicken soup. Serve it as a main dish for four or as an elegant first course for eight.

chicken-artichoke-brie soup

prep: 30 minutes cook: 20 minutes
makes: 8 servings

¼ cup butter
1 cup chopped carrot
   (2 medium)
1 cup sliced celery
   (2 stalks)
1 cup chopped onion
   (1 large)
2 cloves garlic, minced
2 14-ounce cans
   chicken broth
½ teaspoon ground
   white pepper
¼ teaspoon salt
2 cups half-and-half,
   light cream,
   or whole milk
¼ cup all-purpose flour
1½ cups cubed cooked
   chicken or turkey
   (about 8 ounces)
1 cup whipping cream
½ of a 10-ounce
   package frozen
   chopped spinach,
   thawed and well
   drained
½ of an 8- to 9-ounce
   package frozen
   artichoke hearts,
   thawed and cut into
   bite-size pieces
1 4.5-ounce round
   Brie or Camembert
   cheese, rind
   removed, cut up
   Croutons (optional)

1 In a large saucepan melt butter over medium heat. Add carrot, celery, onion, and garlic; cook and stir until tender. Add broth, pepper, and salt. Bring to boiling; reduce heat. Simmer, uncovered, for 15 minutes.

2 In a large screw-top jar combine half-and-half and flour. Cover and shake until smooth. Stir into soup; cook and stir until thickened and bubbly.

3 Stir in chicken, whipping cream, spinach, artichoke hearts, and cheese; cook and stir over medium-low heat about 5 minutes more or until heated through and cheese is melted. (Stir often to make sure soup doesn't scorch on bottom of saucepan.) If desired, top each serving with croutons.

nutrition facts per serving: 393 cal., 31 g total fat, 119 mg chol., 760 mg sodium, 12 g carb., 2 g dietary fiber, 16 g protein.

Tangy tomatillos—small round green fruit—add a bright, almost citrusy flavor to this soup. Tomatillos are encased in a papery hull that often splits open as the fruit nears maturity. Find them in large supermarkets or at Mexican markets, especially during the summer and fall months.

southwest tomatillo-tortilla soup

prep: 25 minutes cook: 30 minutes
makes: 4 to 6 servings

1   tablespoon cumin
     seeds
1   tablespoon vegetable
     oil
3   6-inch corn tortillas,
     cut into thin strips
1   cup thinly sliced red
     onion
3   or 4 cloves garlic,
     thinly sliced
1   32-ounce carton
     chicken broth
12 ounces fresh
     tomatillos, husks
     removed and cut
     into wedges (about
     3 cups)
2   teaspoons finely
     shredded orange
     zest
⅓   cup orange juice
     Roasted red sweet
     peppers, cut into
     thin strips, and/or
     chopped tomatoes
     (optional)
     Salt
     Ground black pepper
     Baked Tortilla Strips
     (optional)
     Sour cream and/
     or snipped fresh
     cilantro (optional)

1 In a large dry saucepan cook and stir cumin seeds over medium heat for 3 to 5 minutes or until seeds are toasted and aromatic; remove seeds.

2 Add oil to saucepan and heat over medium heat. Add toasted cumin seeds, tortilla strips, red onion, and garlic; cook and stir for 5 to 6 minutes or until onion is tender.

3 Add broth, tomatillos, orange zest, and orange juice. Bring to boiling; reduce heat. Simmer, covered, for 30 minutes, stirring occasionally. If desired, stir in roasted peppers and/or tomatoes and heat through. Season to taste with salt and black pepper.

4 If desired, garnish each serving with Baked Tortilla Strips, sour cream, and/or cilantro.

nutrition facts per serving: 217 cal., 11 g total fat (3 g sat. fat), 6 mg chol., 691 mg sodium, 25 g carb., 4 g dietary fiber, 8 g protein.

baked tortilla strips: Preheat oven to 425°F. Cut desired amount of 6-inch corn tortillas into strips. Place in a 15×1×10-inch baking pan. Bake for 10 minutes or until light brown, tossing once.

Clams are the traditional seafood choice for this traditional tomato-based chowder. You can also use chunks of tilapia. Just add the fish during the final minutes of simmering.

manhattan clam chowder

prep: 30 minutes cook: 10 minutes
makes: 4 servings

1   pint shucked clams or
    two 6½-ounce cans
    minced clams
1   cup chopped celery
    (2 stalks)
⅓   cup chopped onion
    (1 small)
¼   cup chopped carrot
    (1 small)
2   tablespoons olive oil
    or vegetable oil
1   8-ounce bottle clam
    juice or 1 cup
    chicken broth
2   cups cubed red
    potato (2 medium)
1   teaspoon dried
    thyme, crushed
⅛   teaspoon cayenne
    pepper
⅛   teaspoon ground
    black pepper
1   14.5-ounce can
    diced tomatoes,
    undrained
2   tablespoons purchased
    cooked bacon pieces
    or cooked crumbled
    bacon*

1 Chop fresh clams (if using), reserving juice; set clams aside. Strain clam juice to remove bits of shell. (Or, drain canned clams, reserving the juice.) If necessary, add enough water to the reserved clam juice to equal 1½ cups. Set clam juice aside.

2 In a large saucepan cook celery, onion, and carrot in hot oil until tender. Stir in reserved 1½ cups clam juice and bottled clam juice. Stir in potato, thyme, cayenne pepper, and black pepper. Bring to boiling; reduce heat. Simmer, covered, for 10 minutes. Stir in clams, undrained tomatoes, and bacon. Return to boiling; reduce heat. Cook for 1 to 2 minutes more or until heated through.

nutrition facts per serving: 252 cal., 9 g total fat (1 g sat. fat), 41 mg chol., 503 mg sodium, 24 g carb., 3 g dietary fiber, 18 g protein.

*note: If you prefer to cook your own bacon, cook 2 slices, reserving 2 tablespoons drippings. Omit oil. Cook the celery, onion, and carrot in the reserved drippings.

Have your crackers ready for this thick and creamy eastern seaboard classic. Fresh clams, along with the briny clam juice, smoky bacon, and hints of thyme, add deep, rich flavors.

new england clam chowder

start to finish: 45 minutes
makes: 4 servings

1	pint shucked clams or two 6.5-ounce cans minced clams
2	slices bacon, halved
2½	cups chopped, peeled potato (3 medium)
1	cup chopped onion (1 large)
1	teaspoon instant chicken bouillon granules
1	teaspoon Worcestershire sauce
¼	teaspoon dried thyme, crushed
⅛	teaspoon ground black pepper
2	cups milk
1	cup half-and-half or light cream
2	tablespoons all-purpose flour

1 Chop fresh clams (if using), reserving juice; set clams aside. Strain clam juice to remove bits of shell. (Or, drain canned clams, reserving juice.) If necessary, add enough water to reserved clam juice to equal 1 cup. Set clam juice aside.

2 In a large saucepan cook bacon until crisp. Remove bacon, reserving 1 tablespoon drippings in pan. Drain bacon on paper towels; crumble bacon and set aside.

3 Stir reserved clam juice, potato, onion, bouillon granules, Worcestershire sauce, thyme, and pepper into saucepan. Bring to boiling; reduce heat. Simmer, covered, about 15 minutes or until potato is tender. With the back of a fork, mash potato slightly against the side of the pan.

4 Stir together milk, half-and-half, and flour. Add to potato mixture; cook and stir until slightly thickened and bubbly. Stir in clams. Return to boiling; reduce heat. Cook for 1 to 2 minutes more or until heated through. Sprinkle each serving with crumbled bacon.

nutrition facts per serving: 376 cal., 15 g total fat (8 g sat. fat), 76 mg chol., 495 mg sodium, 35 g carb., 2 g dietary fiber, 24 g protein.

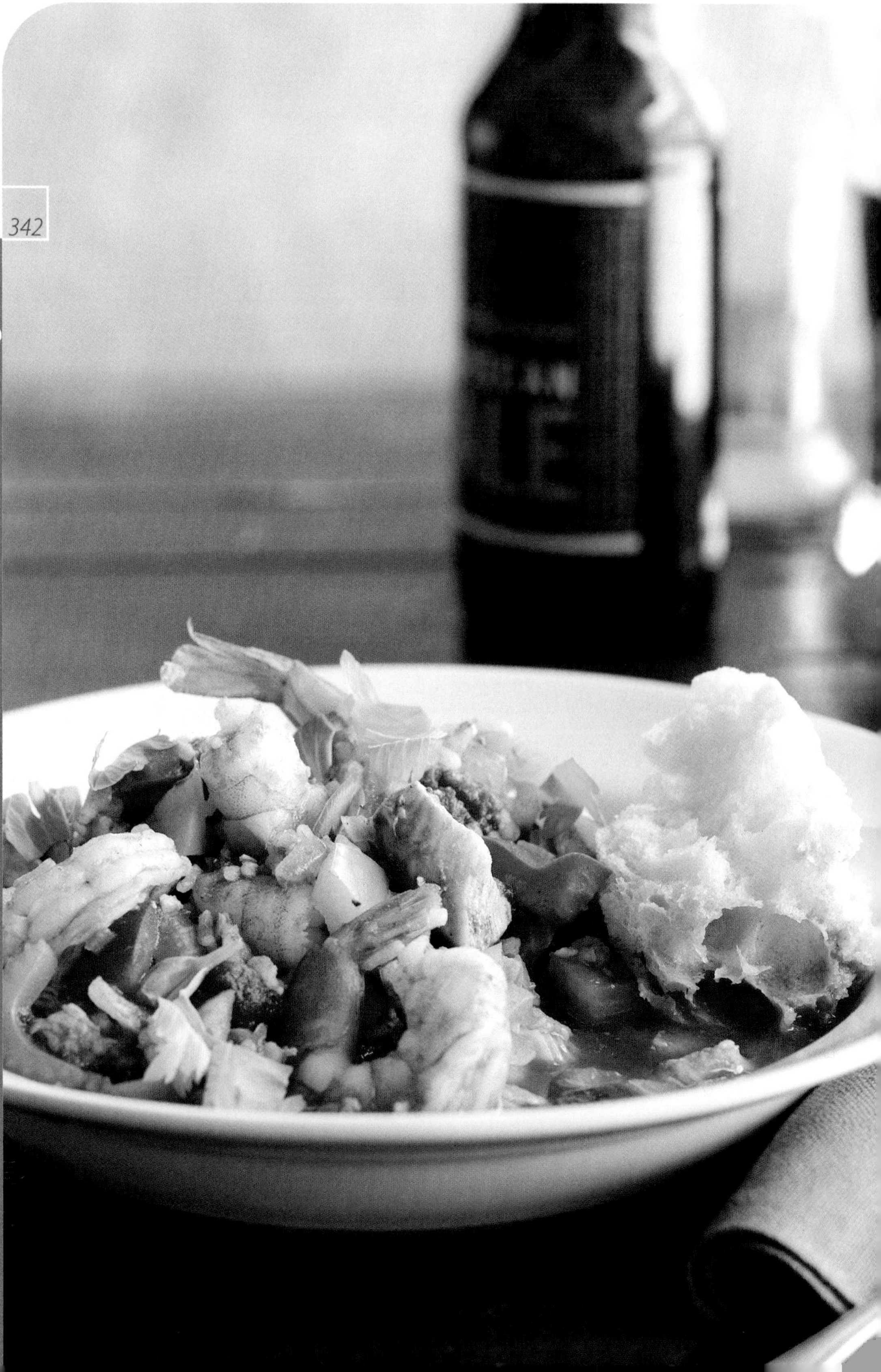

The three-pepper Homemade Salt-Free Cajun Seasoning adds lots of fiery flavor to this slow-cooked version of jambalaya.

chicken and shrimp jambalaya

prep: 20 minutes slow cook: 4 ½ to 5½ hours (low) or 2¼ to 2¾ hours (high) + 30 minutes (high)
makes: 8 servings

1 pound skinless, boneless chicken breast halves or thighs, cut into ¾-inch pieces
2 cups thinly sliced celery (4 stalks)
2 cups chopped onion (2 large)
1 14.5-ounce can no-salt-added diced tomatoes, undrained
1 14.5-ounce can reduced-sodium chicken broth
½ 6-ounce can no-salt-added tomato paste (⅓ cup)
1 recipe Homemade Salt-Free Cajun Seasoning or 1½ teaspoons salt-free Cajun seasoning
2 cloves garlic, minced
½ teaspoon salt
1½ cups instant brown rice
¾ cup chopped green, red, and/or yellow sweet pepper (1 medium)
8 ounces fresh or frozen peeled and deveined cooked shrimp (tails on, if desired)
2 tablespoons snipped fresh parsley
Celery leaves (optional)

1 In a 3½- or 4-quart slow cooker combine chicken, celery, onion, undrained tomatoes, broth, tomato paste, Homemade Salt-Free Cajun Seasoning, garlic, and salt.

2 Cover and cook on low-heat setting for 4½ to 5½ hours or on high-heat setting for 2¼ to 2¾ hours.

3 If using low-heat setting, turn to high-heat setting. Stir in rice and sweet pepper. Cover and cook about 30 minutes more or until most of the liquid is absorbed and rice is tender.

4 Thaw shrimp, if frozen. Stir shrimp and parsley into chicken mixture. If desired, garnish each serving with celery leaves.

nutrition facts per serving: 211 cal., 2 g total fat (0 g sat. fat), 88 mg chol., 415 mg sodium, 26 g carb., 4 g dietary fiber, 23 g protein.

homemade salt-free cajun seasoning: In a small bowl stir together ¼ teaspoon onion powder, ¼ teaspoon garlic powder, ¼ teaspoon ground white pepper, ¼ teaspoon paprika, ¼ teaspoon ground black pepper, and ⅛ to ¼ teaspoon cayenne pepper.

A Minnesota staple—nutty and chewy wild rice—stars in this creamy soup. Wild rice isn't truly rice as all. It is a long-grain marsh grass native to the northern Great Lakes region.

minnesota wild rice soup

prep: 35 minutes   cook: 50 minutes
makes: 4 servings

1	tablespoon butter
½	cup finely chopped carrot (1 medium)
½	cup finely chopped onion (1 medium)
½	cup finely chopped celery (1 stalk)
4	cups chicken broth
¾	cup wild rice, rinsed and drained
12	ounces skinless, boneless chicken breast halves, cut into ¾-inch pieces
2	tablespoons all-purpose flour
2	tablespoons butter, softened
2	cups half-and-half or light cream
	Salt
	Ground black pepper

1 In a large saucepan heat 1 tablespoon butter over medium heat until melted. Add carrot, onion, and celery; cook for 4 to 6 minutes or until tender, stirring occasionally. Add broth and wild rice. Bring to boiling; reduce heat. Simmer, covered, for 30 minutes. Add chicken. Simmer, covered, for 20 to 25 minutes more or until wild rice is tender.

2 In a small bowl combine flour and 2 tablespoons softened butter to make a smooth paste. Stir the flour mixture into rice mixture; cook and stir until thickened and bubbly. Cook and stir for 1 minute more. Add half-and-half; cook and stir over medium heat until heated through. Season to taste with salt and pepper.

nutrition facts per serving: 479 cal., 24 g total fat (14 g sat. fat), 119 mg chol., 1213 mg sodium, 36 g carb., 3 g dietary fiber, 30 g protein.

Savor a shellfish-rich stew where shrimp, cod, and mussels mingle in a mix of pungent garlic and savory seasonings. Serve with warm, crusty bread and lemon wedges for squeezing into the broth.

san francisco seafood stew

start to finish: 45 minutes
makes: 6 servings

8 ounces fresh or frozen cod or other white fish
8 ounces fresh or frozen shrimp
1 cup finely chopped leek (3 medium)*
1 medium fennel bulb, trimmed, cored, and chopped (1 cup)
½ cup chopped celery (1 stalk)
½ cup chopped carrot (1 medium)
12 cloves garlic, minced
1 tablespoon olive oil
1 tablespoon tomato paste
2 teaspoons dried Italian seasoning, crushed
¼ cup dry white wine or reduced-sodium chicken broth
1 28-ounce can no-salt-added diced tomatoes, undrained
1 14-ounce can reduced-sodium chicken broth
1½ cups water
½ cup clam juice
1 pound mussels, soaked, scrubbed, and beards removed**
½ cup snipped fresh parsley

1 Thaw fish and shrimp, if frozen. Rinse fish and shrimp; pat dry with paper towels. Cut fish into 1-inch pieces. Peel and devein shrimp; halve shrimp lengthwise. Set fish and shrimp aside.

2 In an 8-quart Dutch oven cook leek, fennel, celery, carrot, and garlic in hot oil about 5 minutes or until tender. Stir in tomato paste and Italian seasoning; cook for 1 minute. Carefully add wine; cook and stir until wine is nearly evaporated.

3 Stir in undrained tomatoes, broth, the water, and clam juice. Bring to boiling; reduce heat to medium-low. Simmer, uncovered, for 10 minutes.

4 Add mussels and fish. Cook, covered, about 5 minutes or until mussels open. Discard any unopened mussels. Add shrimp; cook for 1 to 2 minutes more or until shrimp are opaque. Stir in half of the parsley. Sprinkle each serving with the remaining parsley.

nutrition facts per serving: 214 cal., 5 g total fat (1 g sat. fat), 90 mg chol., 588 mg sodium, 17 g carb., 4 g dietary fiber, 26 g protein.

*note: See tip on cleaning leeks, page 464.

**note: Scrub mussels in shells under cold running water. Remove beards.

Two flavors of canned soup—asparagus and mushroom—come together to create an elegant soup that takes just 20 minutes to make. This version gains extra spark from the addition of a little dry sherry.

easy maryland crab bisque

start to finish: 20 minutes
makes: 6 servings

2¾   cups milk
1   10.75-ounce can
      condensed cream of
      asparagus soup
1   10.75-ounce can
      condensed cream of
      mushroom soup
1   cup half-and-half or
      light cream
5   to 6 ounces crabmeat,
      drained, flaked, and
      cartilage removed
3   tablespoons dry
      sherry or milk
      Fresh chives
      (optional)

In a 3-quart saucepan combine milk, asparagus soup, mushroom soup, and half-and-half. Bring just to boiling over medium heat, stirring frequently. Stir in crabmeat and dry sherry; heat through. If desired, garnish each serving with chives.

nutrition facts per serving: 225 cal., 12 g total fat (5 g sat. fat), 51 mg chol., 882 mg sodium, 15 g carb., 0 g dietary fiber, 12 g protein.

easy shrimp bisque: Prepare as above except substitute cream of shrimp soup for the cream of mushroom soup and 8 ounces cooked small shrimp for the crabmeat.

easy mushroom bisque: Prepare as above except cook and stir 2 cups sliced fresh button, shiitake, and/or portobello mushrooms in 2 tablespoons hot butter until tender. Continue as directed, omitting crabmeat. Omit chives. If desired, garnish each serving with additional sautéed mushrooms and caramelized onions.

Creole cooking is a fusion of Spanish, French, and African cuisines that came together in New Orleans. The robust tomato base and traditional spicy-hot seasonings make this a delightful stew.

shrimp creole

prep: 25 minutes slow cook: 5 to 6 hours (low) or 2½ to 3 hours (high)
makes: 6 to 8 servings

1   14.5-ounce can
     diced tomatoes,
     undrained
1   14-ounce can chicken
     broth
1½ cups chopped onion
     (3 medium)
1   cup chopped green
     sweet pepper
     (2 small)
1   cup sliced celery
     (2 stalks)
1   6-ounce can tomato
     paste
⅓   cup thinly sliced
     green onion (3)
1   bay leaf
1½ teaspoons paprika
½   teaspoon ground
     black pepper
¼   teaspoon salt
⅛   teaspoon bottled hot
     pepper sauce
2   cloves garlic, minced
1½ pounds peeled and
     deveined cooked
     medium shrimp
3   cups hot cooked rice

1 In a 3½- to 4-quart slow cooker combine undrained tomatoes, broth, onion, sweet pepper, celery, tomato paste, green onion, bay leaf, paprika, black pepper, salt, hot pepper sauce, and garlic.

2 Cover and cook on low-heat setting for 5 to 6 hours or on high-heat setting for 2½ to 3 hours.

3 Discard bay leaf. Stir shrimp into tomato mixture; heat through. Serve over rice.

nutrition facts per serving: 344 cal., 3 g total fat (1 g sat. fat), 227 mg chol., 673 mg sodium, 39 g carb., 3 g dietary fiber, 37 g protein.

The rich flavor of salmon is combined with sautéed mixed vegetables and fresh parsley to create an elegant cream-based soup. A fresh jalapeño chile pepper adds a touch of heat.

northwest salmon chowder

start to finish: 25 minutes
makes: 4 servings

1 tablespoon butter

2 cups assorted frozen vegetables, such as broccoli florets, sliced carrots, chopped sweet peppers, and/or corn kernels

2 tablespoons seeded and finely chopped jalapeño peppers* (optional)

2 tablespoons all-purpose flour

2 cups milk

1 cup half-and-half or light cream

2 cups frozen hash brown potatoes with onions and peppers, thawed

12 to 14 ounces cooked, skinned fresh salmon, flaked**; or 14.5-ounce can salmon, drained, flaked, and cartilage removed

¼ cup snipped fresh parsley

2 tablespoons lemon juice

½ teaspoon salt

½ teaspoon ground black pepper

1 In a large saucepan heat butter over medium heat until melted. Add frozen vegetables and, if desired, chile peppers; cook for 3 to 5 minutes or until tender. Stir in flour. Gradually stir in milk and half-and-half; cook and stir until slightly thickened and bubbly. Cook and stir for 1 minute more.

2 Stir in hash brown potatoes, salmon, parsley, lemon juice, salt, and black pepper; heat through.

nutrition facts per serving: 383 cal., 19 g total fat (9 g sat. fat), 98 mg chol., 1009 mg sodium, 23 g carb., 4 g dietary fiber, 30 g protein.

*note: See tip on handling chile peppers, page 31.

**note: To cook fresh salmon, place fish on the greased unheated rack of a broiler pan, tucking under thin edges. Broil 4 inches from the heat for 4 to 6 minutes per ½-inch thickness or just until fish flakes easily when tested with a fork.

Jazz up classic corn chowder for a memorable one-bowl meal. Here, sweet potatoes and andouille sausage make their way into the mix, along with cumin, chili powder, and Cajun spice for a little zing.

sweet potato–corn chowder

prep: 30 minutes cook: 35 minutes
makes: 8 to 10 servings

12 ounces andouille, kielbasa, or smoked pork sausage, halved lengthwise and cut into ½-inch slices
1 cup chopped onion (1 large)
1 cup chopped celery (2 stalks)
1 tablespoon minced garlic (6 cloves)
3 tablespoons all-purpose flour
1½ teaspoons ground cumin
1½ teaspoons chili powder
1 teaspoon Cajun or Creole seasoning
6 cups chicken broth
1 16-ounce package frozen whole-kernel corn or 3 cups fresh sweet corn kernels
2 cups ½-inch cubes peeled sweet potato (about 2 small)
12 ounces skinless, boneless chicken breast halves, cut into ¾-inch pieces
1 cup whipping cream
1 teaspoon ground black pepper

1 In a 6-quart Dutch oven brown sausage over medium heat for 5 minutes, stirring occasionally. Add onion, celery, and garlic; cook and stir for 5 minutes. Stir in flour, cumin, chili powder, and Cajun seasoning. Cook and stir for 2 minutes more. Stir in broth. Bring to boiling.

2 Add frozen corn, sweet potato, and chicken. Return to boiling; reduce heat. Simmer, covered, for about 20 minutes or until sweet potato is tender. Stir in whipping cream and pepper; heat through.

nutrition facts per serving: 408 cal., 25 g total fat (13 g sat. fat), 86 mg chol., 1161 mg sodium, 27 g carb., 3 g dietary fiber, 19 g protein.

This famous seafood soup (pronounced cha-PĒ-noh) is credited to San Francisco Italian immigrants. For added interest, use two different kinds of fish for this recipe.

california cioppino

start to finish: 35 minutes
makes: 8 servings

2 pounds skinless
    fresh salmon or cod
    fillets, and/or sea
    scallops
2 fennel bulbs, trimmed
    and thinly sliced
3 tablespoons olive oil
4 cloves garlic, minced
3 cups coarsely
    chopped tomato
    (3 large)
1 14- to 15-ounce can
    fish stock or chicken
    broth
1 teaspoon dried
    oregano, crushed,
    or 2 teaspoons
    snipped fresh
    oregano
½ teaspoon anise seeds,
    crushed (optional)
    Salt
    Ground black pepper
    Fennel leaves or
    shredded fresh basil

1 Rinse fish and/or scallops; pat dry with paper towels. If using fish, cut into 2-inch pieces. Set aside.

2 In a 4- to 6-quart Dutch oven cook sliced fennel in hot oil over medium heat about 10 minutes or until tender, stirring occasionally. Add garlic; cook and stir for 1 minute more.

3 Add tomato, stock, dried oregano (if using), and, if desired, anise seeds. Bring to boiling. Stir in fish and/or scallops. Return to boiling; reduce heat. Simmer, uncovered, for 6 to 8 minutes or until fish flakes easily when tested with a fork and/or scallops are opaque. Season to taste with salt and pepper. Stir in fresh oregano (if using). Garnish each serving with fennel leaves.

nutrition facts per serving: 178 cal., 6 g total fat (1 g sat. fat), 49 mg chol., 169 mg sodium, 9 g carb., 3 g dietary fiber, 22 g protein.

Celebrate Wisconsin's beer and cheese heritage with this hearty vegetable chowder. The tang of the beer and smokiness of the bacon hold up to the bold cheddar and Parmesan cheeses.

wisconsin beer and cheese soup

prep: 25 minutes stand: 30 minutes cook: 25 minutes
makes: 10 servings

1½ cups shredded sharp cheddar cheese (6 ounces)
1¼ cups shredded white cheddar cheese (5 ounces)
¼ cup butter
½ cup finely chopped onion (1 medium)
½ cup finely chopped carrot (1 medium)
¼ cup thinly sliced green onion (2)
2 cloves garlic, minced
½ cup all-purpose flour
½ teaspoon dry mustard
5 cups chicken broth
1 12-ounce bottle beer
1 cup whipping cream
1½ cups frozen diced hash brown potatoes
1½ cups small broccoli florets
10 slices bacon, crisp-cooked, drained, and chopped
⅓ cup grated Parmesan or Romano cheese
½ teaspoon bottled hot pepper sauce
½ teaspoon Worcestershire sauce

1 Allow sharp cheddar cheese and white cheddar cheese to stand at room temperature for 30 minutes. Meanwhile, in a 4-quart Dutch oven melt butter over medium heat. Add onion, carrot, green onion, and garlic; cook for 8 to 10 minutes or until vegetables are tender, stirring occasionally.

2 Stir in flour and dry mustard (mixture will be thick). Add broth all at once; cook and stir until bubbly. Add beer and cream. Stir in potatoes and broccoli. Bring to boiling; reduce heat. Simmer, uncovered, for 5 minutes, stirring occasionally.

3 Gradually stir in sharp cheddar and white cheddar, stirring after each addition until cheeses are melted. Stir in bacon, Parmesan, hot pepper sauce, and Worcestershire sauce. Serve immediately.

nutrition facts per serving: 390 cal., 29 g total fat (17 g sat. fat), 90 mg chol., 964 mg sodium, 16 g carb., 1 g dietary fiber, 15 g protein.

If there's a day made for savoring our favorite comforting soups, it has to be laid-back, lazy Sundays. The cozy concoctions here are truly food for the soul. These work wonderfully for making guests feel at home, especially when everyone gathers for a casual soup supper.

12

sunday

spe

cials

Cayenne pepper sauce, crushed red pepper flakes, and red sweet peppers add up to triple-good flavor in this zesty stew.

three-pepper beef stew

prep: 35 minutes cook: 1½ hours
makes: 6 servings

1 tablespoon canola oil
4 carrots, cut into
      1-inch pieces
2 stalks celery, cut into
      1-inch pieces
½ cup chopped onion
      (1 medium)
6 cloves garlic, minced
2 pounds beef chuck
      roast, trimmed of fat
      and cut into 1-inch
      cubes
1¾ cups dry red wine
      or one 14-ounce can
      beef broth
1 14-ounce can
      reduced-sodium
      beef broth
2 tablespoons tomato
      paste
1 tablespoon
      Worcestershire
      sauce
2 to 3 teaspoons
      bottled cayenne
      pepper sauce
¼ to ½ teaspoon crushed
      red pepper flakes
2 potatoes, cut into
      1-inch pieces
2 red sweet peppers,
      cut into 1-inch
      pieces
2 tablespoons cold
      water
1 tablespoon cornstarch

1 In a 4- to 6-quart Dutch oven heat oil over medium heat. Add carrots, celery, onion, and garlic; cook about 5 minutes or until onion is tender, stirring occasionally. Add beef; cook about 15 minutes or until brown, stirring occasionally. Drain fat.

2 Stir in wine, broth, tomato paste, Worcestershire sauce, pepper sauce, and red pepper flakes. Bring to boiling; reduce heat. Simmer, covered, for 1 hour, stirring occasionally.

3 Add potatoes and sweet peppers. Return to boiling; reduce heat. Simmer, covered, for 15 to 20 minutes or until meat and potatoes are tender.

4 In a small bowl stir together the cold water and cornstarch. Stir into beef mixture; cook and stir until thickened and bubbly. Cook and stir for 2 minutes more.

nutrition facts per serving: 401 cal., 10 g total fat (3 g sat. fat), 82 mg chol., 358 mg sodium, 25 g carb., 4 g dietary fiber, 36 g protein.

This is the kind of stew that makes you want to stay inside and curl up next to the fireplace. Chunks of beef, potatoes, squash, and green beans make this a hearty yet healthful stew.

fireside beef stew

prep: 25 minutes slow cook: 8 to 10 hours (low) or 4 to 5 hours (high) + 15 minutes (high)
makes: 6 servings

1½ pounds boneless beef chuck pot roast
2½ cups peeled, seeded butternut squash cut into 1-inch pieces (about 1 pound)
2 small onions, cut into wedges
2 cloves garlic, minced
1 14.5-ounce can reduced-sodium beef broth
1 8-ounce can tomato sauce
2 tablespoons Worcestershire sauce
1 teaspoon dry mustard
¼ teaspoon ground black pepper
⅛ teaspoon ground allspice
2 tablespoons cold water
4 teaspoons cornstarch
1 9-ounce package frozen Italian green beans

1 Trim fat from meat. Cut meat into 1-inch pieces. In a 3½- to 4½-quart slow cooker combine meat, squash, onions, and garlic. Stir in broth, tomato sauce, Worcestershire sauce, dry mustard, pepper, and allspice.

2 Cover and cook on low-heat setting for 8 to 10 hours or on high-heat setting for 4 to 5 hours.

3 If using low-heat setting, turn to high-heat setting. In a small bowl combine cold water and cornstarch. Stir into mixture in cooker. Stir in frozen green beans. Cover and cook about 15 minutes more or until thickened. If desired, sprinkle each serving with more pepper.

nutrition facts per serving: 206 cal., 4 g total fat (1 g sat. fat), 67 mg chol., 440 mg sodium, 15 g carb., 3 g dietary fiber, 27 g protein.

This hearty stew gets its distinctive flavor from Jerusalem artichokes, a root vegetable that resembles gingerroot and is often used as a potato substitute. It has a delicate flavor that is slightly sweet and nutlike, similar to jicama and water chestnuts.

beef stew with red wine gravy

prep: 30 minutes **slow cook:** 12 to 14 hours (low) or 6 to 7 hours (high)
makes: 6 servings

2 pounds boneless beef chuck roast
¼ cup all-purpose flour
2 teaspoons Italian seasoning
1 teaspoon salt
½ teaspoon ground black pepper
2 tablespoons olive oil
2 large onions, cut into thin wedges
8 ounces parsnips, quartered lengthwise and halved
8 ounces carrots, quartered lengthwise and halved
8 ounces Jerusalem artichokes (sunchokes), peeled and coarsely chopped
1 cup Cabernet Sauvignon or beef broth
½ cup beef broth
¼ cup tomato paste
   Chopped roma tomatoes, golden raisins, and/or red wine vinegar or balsamic vinegar
   Crusty French bread (optional)

1 Trim excess fat from beef; cut into 1-inch cubes. In a large resealable plastic bag combine flour, Italian seasoning, salt, and pepper. Add meat, shaking to coat. In a 12-inch skillet brown meat half at a time in hot oil, adding more oil, if necessary.

2 Meanwhile, in a 4½- to 6-quart slow cooker place onions, parsnips, carrots, and artichokes. Top with meat. Combine wine and beef broth; pour over all.

3 Cover and cook on low-heat setting for 12 to 14 hours or on high-heat setting for 6 to 7 hours. Stir in tomato paste. Pass tomatoes, raisins, and/or vinegar to sprinkle on each serving. If desired, serve with crusty bread.

nutrition facts per serving: 356 cal., 9 g total fat (2 g sat. fat), 90 mg chol., 601 mg sodium, 26 g carb., 4 g dietary fiber, 35 g protein.

If you have some ginger left over from this boldly flavored stew, wrap it loosely in a paper towel and refrigerate it for 2 to 3 weeks. For longer storage, place unpeeled ginger in a freezer bag and store in the freezer; you can grate or slice the ginger while it's frozen.

gingered beef and vegetable stew

prep: 25 minutes slow cook: 7 to 8 hours (low) or 3½ to 4 hours (high) + 15 minutes (high)
makes: 8 servings

2½ pounds boneless beef round steak
Nonstick cooking spray
1 tablespoon vegetable oil
2 medium carrots, bias-sliced into ½-inch pieces
¾ cup chopped red sweet pepper (1 medium)
⅔ cup sliced leek (2 medium)*
1¼ cups water
3 tablespoons soy sauce
1 tablespoon grated fresh ginger
3 cloves garlic, minced
1½ teaspoons instant beef bouillon granules
⅛ to ¼ teaspoon cayenne pepper
2 tablespoons cornstarch
2 tablespoons cold water
1 10-ounce package frozen sugar snap peapods, thawed
½ cup sliced green onion (4)

1 Trim fat from meat. Cut meat into 1-inch pieces. Coat the inside of a 3½- or 4-quart slow cooker with cooking spray; set aside. Coat a large skillet with cooking spray; heat skillet over medium-high heat. Add meat half at a time; cook until brown, adding oil if necessary. Transfer meat to the prepared cooker. Add carrots, sweet pepper, and leeks. For sauce, in a medium bowl combine the 1¼ cups water, soy sauce, ginger, garlic, bouillon granules, and cayenne pepper. Pour over mixture in cooker.

2 Cover and cook on low-heat setting for 7 to 8 hours or on high-heat setting for 3½ to 4 hours.

3 If using low-heat setting, turn to high-heat setting. In a small bowl combine cornstarch and the 2 tablespoons cold water. Stir into mixture in cooker. Stir in peapods. Cover and cook about 15 minutes more or until sauce is thickened and peapods are tender, stirring once. Stir in green onions.

*note: See tip on cleaning leeks, page 464.

nutrition facts per serving: 253 cal., 9 g total fat (2 g sat. fat), 82 mg chol., 448 mg sodium, 9 g carb., 2 g dietary fiber, 33 g protein.

Crusty pieces of French bread are perfect for soaking up the wonderful rosemary-seasoned broth in this bean-and-beef combo.

french country soup

prep: 20 minutes stand: 1 hour slow cook: 8 to 10 hours (low) or 4 to 5 hours (high)
makes: 6 servings

8   ounces dried navy,
      Great Northern,
      or cannellini (white
      kidney) beans
1   pound lean beef or
      lamb stew meat,
      cut into ¾- to 1-inch
      pieces
4   cups reduced-sodium
      chicken broth
2   medium carrots, cut
      into 1-inch pieces
2   stalks celery, cut into
      1-inch pieces
1   large onion, cut into
      thin wedges
1   cup dry white wine
6   cloves garlic, minced
3   bay leaves
1½ teaspoons dried
      rosemary, crushed
½   teaspoon salt
¼   teaspoon ground
      black pepper

1 Rinse beans; drain. Place beans in a 4-quart Dutch oven. Add enough water to cover beans by 2 inches. Bring to boiling; reduce heat. Simmer, uncovered, for 10 minutes. Remove from heat. Cover and let stand for 1 hour. Drain and rinse beans.

2 In a 3½- to 6-quart slow cooker combine beans, meat, broth, carrots, celery, onion, wine, garlic, bay leaves, rosemary, salt, and pepper.

3 Cover and cook on low-heat setting for 8 to 10 hours or on high-heat setting for 4 to 5 hours. Discard bay leaves.

nutrition facts per serving: 288 cal., 3 g total fat (1 g sat. fat), 45 mg chol., 652 mg sodium, 31 g carb., 11 g dietary fiber, 27 g protein.

Delicate biscuits top this saucy stew that's delicious with either store-bought or homemade marinara sauce. Cremini mushrooms, also known as brown or baby portobello mushrooms, heighten the flavor of the sauce.

pizza stew with biscuits

prep: 20 minutes slow cook: 3 hours (low) + 45 minutes (high)
makes: 5 servings

3	cups quartered or sliced fresh cremini mushrooms (8 ounces)
¾	cup chopped green sweet pepper (1 medium)
⅓	cup finely chopped onion (1 small)
1	teaspoon dried Italian seasoning, crushed
¼	teaspoon salt
¼	teaspoon ground black pepper
2	cups marinara sauce
1¼	pounds ground turkey breast
¾	cup low-fat pancake and baking mix
⅓	cup grated Parmesan cheese
¼	teaspoon dried oregano, crushed
¼	cup fat-free milk
½	cup shredded part-skim mozzarella cheese (2 ounces) (optional)

1 In a 3½- or 4-quart slow cooker combine mushrooms, sweet pepper, onion, Italian seasoning, salt, and black pepper. Pour marinara sauce over all. Using a wooden spoon, break up ground turkey into bite-size pieces. Add to cooker, stirring to combine. Cover and cook on low-heat setting for 3 hours.

2 For biscuits, in a small bowl combine baking mix, Parmesan, and oregano. Add milk; stir with a fork until combined.

3 Turn cooker to high-heat setting. Drop biscuit dough by the tablespoonful into stew to make 5 biscuits. Cover and cook for 45 to 60 minutes more. (Do not lift cover during cooking.)

4 If desired, sprinkle each serving with mozzarella cheese.

nutrition facts per serving: 323 cal., 7 g total fat (2 g sat. fat), 62 mg chol., 851 mg sodium, 32 g carb., 4 g dietary fiber, 33 g protein.

Burgundy wines are made from Pinot Noir grapes, so if you don't want to splurge for a real Burgundy wine from France, simply choose a good Pinot Noir from California or Oregon.

burgundy beef stew

prep: 20 minutes slow cook: 10 to 12 hours (low) or 5 to 6 hours (high)
makes: 6 servings

2   pounds boneless beef chuck pot roast
½   teaspoon salt
¼   teaspoon ground black pepper
2   tablespoons vegetable oil (optional)
6   medium carrots, cut into 1½-inch pieces
1   9-ounce package frozen cut green beans
2   cups frozen small whole onions
2   cloves garlic, minced
2   tablespoons quick-cooking tapioca
1   14.5-ounce can reduced-sodium beef broth
1   cup dry red wine
3   cups hot cooked egg noodles (optional)
4   slices bacon, crisp-cooked, drained, and crumbled
    Snipped fresh parsley (optional)

1 Trim fat from meat. Cut meat into 1-inch pieces. Sprinkle meat with salt and pepper. If desired, in a large skillet cook meat, one-third at a time, in hot oil over medium-high heat until brown. Drain fat.

2 In a 3½- or 4-quart slow cooker combine carrots, frozen green beans, frozen onions, and garlic. Add meat. Sprinkle with tapioca. Pour broth and wine over all.

3 Cover and cook on low-heat setting for 10 to 12 hours or on high-heat setting for 5 to 6 hours. If desired, serve over hot cooked noodles. Sprinkle each serving with bacon and, if desired, parsley.

nutrition facts per serving: 317 cal., 8 g total fat (3 g sat. fat), 95 mg chol., 977 mg sodium, 16 g carb., 3 g dietary fiber, 37 g protein.

Adding red wine and tomato paste to this hearty soup brings out the rich flavors of the beef and portobello mushrooms. A quick browning of the beef in the beginning helps concentrate its meaty taste as it simmers to fork-tender doneness in a slow cooker.

chunky pot roast–portobello soup

prep: 20 minutes slow cook: 7 to 8 hours (low) or 4 to 5 hours (high) + 30 minutes (high)
makes: 6 servings

1   2½-pound boneless
     beef chuck pot roast
¼   cup all-purpose flour
1   teaspoon dried
     thyme, crushed
½   teaspoon ground
     black pepper
2   tablespoons olive oil
1   cup chopped onion
     (1 large)
3   cloves garlic, minced
3   cups reduced-sodium
     beef broth
1   cup dry red wine,
     such as Burgundy
3   tablespoons tomato
     paste
½   teaspoon salt
1   pound fresh
     baby portobello
     mushrooms, halved
¾   cup coarsely chopped
     red sweet pepper
     (1 medium)
     Snipped fresh parsley

1 Trim fat from meat. Cut meat into 1½-inch pieces. In a plastic bag combine flour, thyme, and black pepper. Add meat, a few pieces at a time, shaking to coat. In a large skillet heat 1 tablespoon of the oil over medium-high heat. Add half the meat; cook about 5 minutes or until meat is brown. Transfer meat to a 4-quart slow cooker. Repeat with the remaining meat and the remaining 1 tablespoon oil, adding onion and garlic for the last 3 minutes of cooking. Transfer meat mixture to the cooker. Stir in broth, wine, tomato paste, and salt.

2 Cover and cook on low-heat setting for 7 to 8 hours or on high-heat setting for 4 to 5 hours.

3 If using low-heat setting, turn to high-heat setting. Stir in mushrooms and sweet pepper. Cover and cook for 30 minutes more. Sprinkle each serving with parsley.

nutrition facts per serving: 551 cal., 33 g total fat (12 g sat. fat), 166 mg chol., 606 mg sodium, 14 g carb., 3 g dietary fiber, 41 g protein.

Kale adds a bit of a cabbage-like flavor to this hearty soup. If your family likes spicy food, use hot Italian sausage links in place of the mild ones.

white bean soup with sausage and kale

start to finish: 30 minutes
makes: 5 servings

12 ounces mild Italian
sausage links,
sliced ½ inch thick
¼ cup water
½ cup chopped onion
(1 medium)
1 teaspoon bottled
minced garlic
1 tablespoon vegetable
oil
2 15-ounce cans
cannellini (white
kidney) beans,
rinsed and drained
2 14-ounce cans
reduced-sodium
chicken broth
1 14.5-ounce can diced
tomatoes with basil,
garlic, and oregano,
undrained
4 cups coarsely
chopped kale
or spinach
Ground black pepper

1 Combine sliced sausage and the water in a large skillet. Bring to boiling; reduce heat. Simmer, covered, about 10 minutes or until sausage is no longer pink. Uncover and cook about 5 minutes more or until sausage is brown, stirring frequently. Remove sausage with a slotted spoon; set aside.

2 Meanwhile, in a large saucepan cook onion and garlic in hot oil about 5 minutes or until onion is tender. Stir in beans, broth, and undrained tomatoes. Bring to boiling, covered; reduce heat. Simmer, covered, for 5 minutes.

3 Stir in cooked sausage and kale. Simmer, uncovered, about 3 minutes more or until kale is tender. Season to taste with pepper.

nutrition facts per serving: 394 cal., 19 g total fat (7 g sat. fat), 46 mg chol., 1510 mg sodium, 38 g carb., 10 g dietary fiber, 25 g protein.

Here's a stick-to-your ribs meal with a nifty twist. The sweetness of bottled plum or hoisin sauce takes the place of ordinary barbecue sauce.

simple short rib stew

prep: 35 minutes slow cook: 7 to 8 hours (low) or 3½ to 4 hours (high)
makes: 6 servings

2 pounds boneless beef short ribs
Nonstick cooking spray
1 pound tiny new potatoes, halved
5 medium carrots, cut into 1-inch pieces
1 12-ounce jar beef gravy
½ cup plum sauce or hoisin sauce

1 Trim fat from ribs. Cut ribs into 1½-inch pieces. Lightly coat a 12-inch skillet with cooking spray; heat skillet over medium-high heat. Add meat, half at a time; cook until brown. Drain fat.

2 In a 3½- or 4-quart slow cooker combine potatoes and carrots. Top with meat. In a medium bowl stir together gravy and plum sauce; pour over mixture in cooker.

3 Cover and cook on low-heat setting for 7 to 8 hours or on high-heat setting for 3½ to 4 hours. Skim fat.

nutrition facts per serving: 621 cal., 26 g total fat (11 g sat. fat), 173 mg chol., 670 mg sodium, 30 g carb., 3 g dietary fiber, 62 g protein.

Tender chunks of beef and hearty kale make up this light but filling main-dish soup. Serve with crusty whole-grain bread and a slice or two of cheese.

kale, beef, and white bean stew

prep: 25 minutes slow cook: 6 to 7 hours (low) or 3 to 3½ hours (high) + 30 minutes (high)
makes: 6 servings

1¼ pounds boneless beef top sirloin steak
1 14.5-ounce can stewed tomatoes, undrained
1 14.5-ounce can reduced-sodium beef broth
1 cup chopped onion (1 large)
1 tablespoon paprika
2 cloves garlic, minced
1 teaspoon dried thyme, crushed
½ teaspoon dried rosemary, crushed
¼ teaspoon ground black pepper
7 cups chopped, trimmed kale (about 1 bunch)
2 15-ounce cans no-salt-added cannellini (white kidney) beans, rinsed and drained
1 to 2 tablespoons balsamic vinegar

1 Trim fat from meat. Cut meat into 1-inch pieces. In a 4- to 5-quart slow cooker combine meat, undrained tomatoes, broth, onion, paprika, garlic, thyme, rosemary, and pepper.

2 Cover and cook on low-heat setting for 6 to 7 hours or on high-heat setting for 3 to 3½ hours.

3 If using low-heat setting, turn to high-heat setting. Stir in kale and beans. Cover and cook for 30 minutes more. Stir in vinegar.

nutrition facts per serving: 326 cal., 7 g total fat (2 g sat. fat), 29 mg chol., 562 mg sodium, 39 g carb., 9 g dietary fiber, 30 g protein.

The rich, creamy flavors in this colorful soup warmed the hearts of our taste panel judges. If you like, cut calories by substituting turkey kielbasa, fat-free milk, and low-fat cheese.

hot-stuff kielbasa-cheese soup

prep: 25 minutes cook: 20 minutes
makes: 6 to 8 servings

1 large onion, halved
   lengthwise and
   thinly sliced
1 cup sliced celery
   (2 stalks)
¼ cup butter
¼ cup all-purpose flour
2 teaspoons
   Worcestershire
   sauce
¾ teaspoon dry mustard
1 14.5-ounce can
   chicken broth
3 cups peeled and
   cubed potato
1 cup chopped carrot
   (2 medium)
8 ounces fully cooked
   kielbasa (Polish
   sausage), sliced
   ¼ inch thick
3¼ cups milk
3 cups shredded sharp
   cheddar cheese
   (12 ounces)
¼ teaspoon ground
   black pepper
   Shredded sharp
   cheddar cheese
   or coarsely ground
   black pepper
   (optional)

1 In a 4-quart Dutch oven cook onion and celery in hot butter until tender. Stir in flour, Worcestershire sauce, and mustard; cook and stir for 2 minutes. Carefully stir in broth.

2 Add potato, carrot, and kielbasa. Bring to boiling; reduce heat. Simmer, covered, for about 20 minutes or until potato is tender.

3 Stir in milk. Heat and stir until mixture almost comes to a boil; reduce heat. Add 3 cups cheese and ¼ teaspoon pepper; cook and stir until cheese is melted. If desired, sprinkle each serving with cheese or pepper.

nutrition facts per serving: 629 cal., 44 g total fat (24 g sat. fat), 129 mg chol., 1294 mg sodium, 31 g carb., 3 g dietary fiber, 29 g protein.

Sweet potatoes, parsnips, and apples are an intriguing combo in this autumn stew. A porter is a good brew to use in stews like this, because its toasted malt flavors work very well with slow-cooked meat.

hearty pork-beer stew

prep: 35 minutes **slow cook:** 7 to 8 hours (low) or 3½ to 4 hours (high)
makes: 8 servings

1   pound boneless pork shoulder roast
    Nonstick cooking spray
2   large sweet potatoes, peeled and cut into 1-inch pieces
3   medium parsnips, peeled and cut into ¾-inch slices
2   small green apples, cut into wedges
1   medium onion, cut into thin wedges
3   cups vegetable broth or chicken broth
1   tablespoon packed brown sugar
1   tablespoon Dijon-style mustard
1½ teaspoons dried thyme, crushed
2   cloves garlic, minced
½   teaspoon crushed red pepper flakes
1   12-ounce can beer or 1½ cups vegetable broth or chicken broth
4   large roma tomatoes, cut up

1 Trim fat from meat. Cut meat into ¾-inch pieces. Lightly coat a large skillet with cooking spray; heat skillet over medium-high heat. Add meat; cook until brown. Transfer meat to a 5- to 6-quart slow cooker.

2 Add sweet potatoes, parsnips, apples, and onion. In a medium bowl whisk together broth, brown sugar, mustard, thyme, garlic, and red pepper flakes. Pour broth mixture and beer over mixture in cooker.

3 Cover and cook on low-heat setting for 7 to 8 hours or on high-heat setting for 3½ to 4 hours. Stir in tomatoes.

nutrition facts per serving: 209 cal., 4 g total fat (1 g sat. fat), 37 mg chol., 471 mg sodium, 27 g carb., 5 g dietary fiber, 14 g protein.

This twist on traditional wild rice soup, simmered in a slow cooker, uses ground pork, Italian seasoning, and fresh spinach.

italian wild rice soup

prep: 25 minutes   slow cook: 7 to 8 hours (low) or 3½ to 4 hours (high)
makes: 8 servings

1	pound ground pork
4	cups water
2	14.5-ounce cans reduced-sodium beef broth
1	14.5-ounce can no-salt-added diced tomatoes with basil, garlic, and oregano, undrained
1	6-ounce can tomato paste
1	cup chopped onion (1 large)
¾	cup wild rice, rinsed and drained
6	cloves garlic, minced
2	tablespoons Italian seasoning, crushed
1½	teaspoons paprika
1	teaspoon fennel seeds
½	teaspoon ground black pepper
¼	teaspoon salt
¼	teaspoon crushed red pepper flakes
1	9-ounce package fresh spinach, chopped
½	cup finely shredded Parmesan cheese (2 ounces)

1 In a large skillet cook pork over medium heat until no longer pink, using a wooden spoon to break up meat as it cooks. Drain fat.

2 In a 4- to 6-quart slow cooker combine cooked pork, the water, broth, undrained tomatoes, tomato paste, onion, wild rice, garlic, Italian seasoning, paprika, fennel seeds, black pepper, salt, and red pepper flakes.

3 Cover and cook on low-heat setting for 7 to 8 hours or on high-heat setting for 3½ to 4 hours.

4 Top each serving with cheese. Stir spinach into soup.

nutrition facts per serving: 272 cal., 11 g total fat (5 g sat. fat), 45 mg chol., 632 mg sodium, 24 g carb., 6 g dietary fiber, 20 g protein.

Five-spice powder infuses distinctive flavor in this Oriental pork and shredded broccoli soup. The spice blend often includes star anise, cloves, Szechuan peppercorns, and either ginger or cardamom.

five-spice pork soup

prep: 35 minutes slow cook: 6 to 7 hours (low) or 3 to 3½ hours (high) + 20 minutes (high)
makes: 8 servings

1 2-pound boneless pork top loin roast (single loin)
1 teaspoon five-spice powder
¼ teaspoon ground black pepper
2 tablespoons vegetable oil
½ cup chopped onion (1 medium)
2 14.5-ounce cans reduced-sodium chicken broth
2½ cups water
¼ cup reduced-sodium soy sauce
¼ cup fish sauce
1 tablespoon rice vinegar
1 tablespoon grated fresh ginger
1 small jalapeño pepper, seeded and finely chopped*
2 ounces rice sticks, broken
3 cups packaged shredded broccoli (broccoli slaw mix)
Snipped fresh cilantro
Lime wedges

1 Trim fat from meat. Cut meat into 1-inch pieces. Sprinkle meat with five-spice powder and black pepper. In a large skillet cook meat, half at a time, in hot oil over medium-high heat until brown. Transfer meat to a 4- to 5-quart slow cooker, reserving drippings in skillet.

2 Add onion to the reserved drippings; cook and stir until tender. Transfer onion to cooker. Stir broth, the water, soy sauce, fish sauce, vinegar, ginger, and chile pepper into mixture in cooker.

3 Cover and cook on low-heat setting for 6 to 7 hours or on high-heat setting for 3 to 3½ hours.

4 Cook rice sticks according to package directions; drain.

5 Skim fat from cooking liquid. If using low-heat setting, turn to high-heat setting. Stir in cooked rice sticks and broccoli slaw. Cover and cook for 20 to 30 minutes more or until heated through. Sprinkle each serving with cilantro. Serve with lime wedges.

nutrition facts per serving: 272 cal., 12 g total fat (2 g sat. fat), 72 mg chol., 1335 mg sodium, 11 g carb., 1 g dietary fiber, 27 g protein.

✱note: See tip on handling chile peppers, page 31.

Aromatic spices and citrus punch up the flavor of this Southwestern-style stew, making it a new favorite one-pot meal for meatless nights. Serve it with corn bread.

sweet potato–black bean stew

prep: 25 minutes cook: 15 minutes
makes: 6 to 8 servings

1 tablespoon canola oil
2 medium sweet potatoes, peeled and cut into 1-inch pieces
1 medium red sweet pepper, seeded and cut into ½-inch pieces
½ cup coarsely chopped onion (1 medium)
1 jalapeño pepper, seeded and chopped*
1 clove garlic, minced
1 tablespoon chili powder
1 teaspoon ground cumin
1 teaspoon cayenne pepper
3 cups vegetable broth
1 14.5-ounce can black beans, rinsed and drained
1 14.5-ounce can diced tomatoes, undrained
1 cup frozen whole-kernel corn
¼ cup snipped fresh cilantro
¼ cup lime juice
Salt
Ground black pepper
Shredded cheddar cheese

1 In a large Dutch oven heat oil over medium-high heat. Add sweet potatoes, sweet pepper, onion, chile pepper, and garlic; cook about 4 minutes or until sweet pepper and onion are tender, stirring occasionally.

2 Stir in chili powder, cumin, and cayenne pepper. Reduce heat to medium. Cook, covered, for 7 to 8 minutes or until sweet potatoes are tender, stirring occasionally.

3 Add broth, beans, and undrained tomatoes. Bring to boiling, stirring occasionally. Stir in frozen corn; reduce heat. Simmer, uncovered, for 15 minutes.

4 Stir in cilantro and lime juice. Season to taste with salt and black pepper. Top each serving with cheese.

nutrition facts per serving: 231 cal., 8 g total fat (3 g sat. fat), 15 mg chol., 708 mg sodium, 34 g carb., 7 g dietary fiber, 11 g protein.

*note: See tip on handling chile peppers, page 31.

The peanut butter base of this Cajun-seasoned soup gives it a pleasantly nutty flavor.

red bean, chicken, and sweet potato stew

prep: 20 minutes slow cook: 10 to 12 hours (low) or 5 to 6 hours (high)
makes: 6 servings

2   15-ounce cans no-salt-added red beans, rinsed and drained
4   cups peeled, cubed sweet potatoes (about 1 pound)
8   ounces boneless chicken breasts, cut into bite-size pieces
8   ounces boneless chicken thighs, cut into bite-size pieces
2   14.5-ounce cans reduced-sodium chicken broth
2½ cups chopped green sweet pepper (2 large)
1   14.5-ounce can no-salt-added diced tomatoes, undrained
1   10-ounce can tomatoes with chopped green chiles, undrained
1   tablespoon Cajun seasoning
2   cloves garlic, minced
¼   cup creamy peanut butter
    Snipped fresh cilantro
    Chopped peanuts (optional)

1 In a 5- to 6-quart slow cooker combine beans, sweet potatoes, chicken, broth, sweet pepper, undrained diced tomatoes, undrained tomatoes and green chiles, Cajun seasoning, and garlic.

2 Cover and cook on low-heat setting for 10 to 12 hours or on high-heat setting for 5 to 6 hours.

3 Remove 1 cup hot liquid from cooker. Whisk in peanut butter. Stir mixture into cooker.

4 Top each serving with cilantro and, if desired, peanuts.

nutrition facts per serving: 366 cal., 7 g total fat (2 g sat. fat), 53 mg chol., 830 mg sodium, 46 g carb., 16 g dietary fiber, 32 g protein.

Matzo balls, also called knaidlach, *are traditionally served in chicken soup during Jewish Passover. For a nonkosher version of this soup, use softened butter in place of the chicken fat (schmaltz) in the matzo balls.*

chicken–matzo ball soup

prep: 1 hour cook: 2 hours
makes: 10 servings

1 4- to 5- pound
   roasting chicken
2½ cups water
1½ cups sliced celery
   (3 stalks)
1 cup chopped onion
   (1 large)
½ cup sliced leek*
1 tablespoon salt
¼ teaspoon ground
   black pepper
1 cup sliced carrot
   (2 medium)
1 cup peeled, sliced
   parsnip (2 medium)
1 tablespoon snipped
   fresh parsley
1 tablespoon snipped
   fresh dill or ¼
   teaspoon dried dill
   weed (optional)
1 recipe Matzo Balls

1 Place chicken in an 8- to 10-quart stockpot. Add the water, celery, onion, leek, salt, and pepper. Bring to boiling; reduce heat. Simmer, covered, for 1½ hours. Add carrot and parsnip. Simmer, covered, about 30 minutes more or until chicken is no longer pink (180°F on an instant-read thermometer inserted into the thickest part of thigh without touching bone) and vegetables are tender.

2 Remove chicken from pot. When cool enough to handle, remove and discard skin from chicken. Pull meat from bones; discard bones. Chop meat, reserving 3 cups (cover and chill or freeze any remaining chopped chicken for another use).

3 Using a slotted spoon, remove vegetables from broth; set aside. Strain broth through two layers of 100-percent-cotton cheesecloth placed in a colander; discard solids. Skim fat from broth. Return broth, vegetables, and reserved chicken to pot. Add parsley and, if desired, dill; heat through. Serve soup with Matzo Balls.

nutrition facts per serving: 276 cal., 14 g total fat (4 g sat. fat), 127 mg chol., 451 mg sodium, 16 g carb., 2 g dietary fiber, 20 g protein.

*note: See tip on cleaning leeks, page 464.

matzo balls: In a mixing bowl combine 1 cup matzo meal, 1 teaspoon salt, and pinch ground black pepper. Beat in 4 lightly beaten eggs and ¼ cup chicken fat (schmaltz) until well blended. Stir in ¼ cup carbonated water. Cover and chill for at least 2 hours. Using wet hands, shape dough into 1-inch balls. Carefully drop dough into a large pot of gently boiling salted water. Simmer, covered, about 30 minutes or until Matzo Balls are light and cooked all the way through. (Do not lift cover during cooking.) Using a slotted spoon, carefully remove matzo balls. Makes about 30 balls.

Fresh, aromatic basil pesto and Parmesan cheese add Italian flair to the crisp cheese toasts that accompany this simple, soul soothing soup.

parmesan-pesto chicken noodle soup

start to finish: 35 minutes
makes: 4 servings

4½ cups reduced-sodium
    chicken broth
1   cup chopped onion
    (1 large)
1   cup sliced carrot
    (2 medium)
2   cloves garlic, minced
1   bay leaf
2   teaspoons Italian
    seasoning
¼   teaspoon ground
    black pepper
1½ cups dried shell pasta
1   small zucchini, halved
    lengthwise and
    sliced
2   cups bite-size pieces
    cooked chicken
    or turkey
4   ½-inch-thick slices
    Italian bread
1   tablespoon basil
    pesto
1   tablespoon finely
    shredded Parmesan
    cheese

1 In a large saucepan combine broth, onion, carrot, garlic, bay leaf, Italian seasoning, and pepper. Bring to boiling; reduce heat. Simmer, covered, for 5 minutes.

2 Stir in pasta and zucchini. Return to boiling; reduce heat. Simmer, covered, for 8 to 10 minutes or until pasta is tender but still firm and vegetables are just tender. Discard bay leaf. Stir in chicken; heat through.

3 Meanwhile, preheat broiler. Spread bread slices with pesto. Sprinkle each slice with cheese. Place bread, spread sides up, on a baking sheet. Broil 3 to 4 inches from heat about 2 minutes or until cheese is melted. Serve soup with toasted bread.

nutrition facts per serving: 599 cal., 19 g total fat (5 g sat. fat), 75 mg chol., 2026 mg sodium, 59 g carb., 5 g dietary fiber, 46 g protein.

Warm your family with this delicious curry-seasoned soup. Oven-roasting the squash and onions contributes to the flavor richness. If your family prefers small pieces of chicken, remove meat from bone, chop in bite-size chunks, and stir into the soup.

chicken–butternut squash soup

start to finish: 45 minutes oven: at 425°F/350°F
makes: 6 servings

1¼	pounds butternut squash, seeded, peeled, and cut into ¾-inch pieces
1	red onion, cut into ½-inch wedges
1	tablespoon curry powder
1	tablespoon olive oil
3	14.5-ounce cans reduced-sodium chicken broth
1	15-ounce can garbanzo beans (chickpeas), rinsed and drained
⅓	cup dried apricots, snipped
½	cup chopped walnuts
1	teaspoon olive oil
¼	teaspoon grated or ground nutmeg
1	2- to 2½-pound deli-roasted chicken, cut up
	Fresh cilantro leaves

1 Preheat oven to 425°F. In a shallow roasting pan combine squash, red onion, and curry powder. Drizzle with 1 tablespoon oil; toss gently to coat. Spread vegetables in a single layer. Roast, uncovered, about 20 minutes or until squash is tender. Reduce oven temperature to 350°F.

2 In a 4-quart Dutch oven combine roasted vegetables, broth, beans, and dried apricots. Bring to boiling; reduce heat. Simmer, covered, for 10 minutes; cool slightly. Transfer vegetable mixture, half at a time, to a food processor or blender. Cover and process or blend until smooth. Return pureed mixture to Dutch oven; heat through.

3 Meanwhile, in a small bowl combine walnuts, 1 teaspoon oil, and nutmeg; toss gently to coat. Spread nuts on an ungreased baking sheet. Bake about 7 minutes or until golden and toasted. If chicken is not warm, reheat according to package directions.

4 Top each serving with chicken, walnuts, and cilantro.

nutrition facts per serving: 577 cal., 35 g total fat (9 g sat. fat), 167 mg chol., 1905 mg sodium, 30 g carb., 6 g dietary fiber, 44 g protein.

A medley of fresh, savory vegetables and fragrant herbs mingle in the slow cooker to create a quintessential springtime soup.

primavera chicken and vegetable soup

prep: 15 minutes   slow cook: 7 to 8 hours (low) or 3½ to 4 hours (high) + 30 minutes (high)
makes: 4 servings

2   whole chicken legs (drumstick and thigh) (1¼ pounds total), skinned
1   32-ounce carton chicken broth
1   cup coarsely chopped carrot (2 medium)
½   cup sliced celery (1 stalk)
½   cup dry white wine or chicken broth
3   cloves garlic, minced
½   teaspoon dried thyme, crushed
½   teaspoon ground sage
¼   teaspoon dried rosemary, crushed
¼   teaspoon ground black pepper
1   cup asparagus spears cut into 1-inch pieces (8 ounces)
½   cup frozen peas
¼   cup sliced green onion (2)
    Coarsely snipped fresh parsley (optional)

1 Place chicken in a 3½- or 4-quart slow cooker. Add broth, carrot, celery, wine, garlic, thyme, sage, rosemary, and pepper. Cover and cook on low-heat setting for 7 to 8 hours or on high-heat setting for 3½ to 4 hours.

2 Using tongs, transfer chicken to a platter. When chicken is cool enough to handle, remove meat from bones; discard bones. Shred chicken; return to cooker. If using low-heat setting, turn to high-heat setting.

3 Stir in asparagus, frozen peas, and green onion. Cover and cook for 30 minutes more or until heated through. If desired, sprinkle each serving with parsley.

nutrition facts per serving: 250 cal., 6 g total fat (1 g sat. fat), 113 mg chol., 1105 mg sodium, 11 g carb., 3 g dietary fiber, 33 g protein.

There's no need to head to a Mexican restaurant when you can have this classic soup on hand. Cilantro, an assertive herb used widely in Mexican recipes, brightens the flavors, while crisp oven-baked tortilla strips form a fun topper.

mexican chicken-tortilla soup

prep: 25 minutes bake: 10 minutes oven: 375°F cook: 40 minutes
makes: 4 servings

2   medium chicken breast halves (about 1¼ pounds total)
1   14-ounce can reduced-sodium chicken broth
1¾ cups water
½   cup chopped onion (1 medium)
1   clove garlic, minced
½   teaspoon ground cumin
1   tablespoon vegetable oil
1   14.5-ounce can no-salt-added diced tomatoes, undrained
1   8-ounce can tomato sauce
1   4-ounce can whole green chiles, rinsed, seeded, and cut into thin bite-size strips
¼   cup snipped fresh cilantro
1   tablespoon snipped fresh oregano or 1 teaspoon dried oregano, crushed
4   6-inch corn tortillas
½   cup shredded cheddar or Monterey Jack cheese (2 ounces)

1 In a large saucepan or pot combine chicken, broth, and the water. Bring to boiling; reduce heat. Simmer, covered, about 15 minutes or until chicken is tender and no longer pink. Remove chicken. Set aside to cool. When chicken is cool enough to handle, remove and discard skin and bones. Finely shred chicken; set aside. Strain broth. Skim fat from broth; set aside.

2 In the same saucepan cook onion, garlic, and cumin in hot oil until onion is tender. Stir in strained both, undrained tomatoes, tomato sauce, chiles, cilantro, and oregano. Bring to boiling; reduce heat. Simmer, covered, for 20 minutes. Stir in shredded chicken; heat through.

3 Meanwhile, preheat oven to 375°F. Cut tortillas in half. Cut each half crosswise into ½-inch-wide strips. Place tortilla strips on a baking sheet. Bake about 10 minutes or until crisp.

4 Sprinkle each serving with shredded cheese and top with tortilla strips. Serve immediately.

nutrition facts per serving: 313 cal., 11 g total fat (4 g sat. fat), 71 mg chol., 836 mg sodium, 24 g carb., 5 g dietary fiber, 30 g protein.

Because they hold their shape well, Golden Delicious, Granny Smith, Rome, Jonathan, or Newtown Pippin are good apple options for this soup.

chicken-and-apple curry soup

prep: 25 minutes slow cook: 6 to 7 hours (low) or 3 to 3½ hours (high) + 10 minutes (high)
makes: 6 servings

1½ cups chopped, unpeeled apples
1 cup chopped celery (2 stalks)
1 cup chopped carrot (2 medium)
½ cup chopped onion (1 medium)
2 14.5-ounce cans chicken broth
1 cup apple juice
2 tablespoons quick-cooking tapioca, crushed
2 teaspoons curry powder
½ teaspoon salt
½ teaspoon dried thyme, crushed
1 pound cubed cooked chicken breast
½ cup half-and-half or light cream
2 cups hot cooked rice
    Thinly sliced apple (optional)
    Fresh thyme sprigs (optional)

1 In a 3½- or 4-quart slow cooker combine chopped apples, celery, carrot, and onion. Stir in broth, apple juice, tapioca, curry powder, salt, and dried thyme.

2 Cover and cook on low-heat setting for 6 to 7 hours or on high-heat setting for 3 to 3½ hours.

3 If using low-heat setting, turn to high-heat setting. Stir in chicken and half-and-half. Cover and cook about 10 minutes more or until heated through.

4 Serve soup with rice. If desired, garnish each serving with apple slices and thyme sprigs.

nutrition facts per serving: 293 cal., 6 g total fat (2 g sat. fat), 73 mg chol., 817 mg sodium, 32 g carb., 2 g dietary fiber, 27 g protein.

Leeks and carrots add a fresh-from-the-garden note to chewy barley and tender chicken in this satisfying stew.

chicken, barley, and leek stew

prep: 25 minutes slow cook: 4 to 5 hours (low) or 2 to 2½ hours (high)
makes: 6 servings

1   pound skinless, boneless chicken thighs, trimmed and cut into 1-inch pieces
1   tablespoon olive oil
1   49-ounce can reduced-sodium chicken broth
1   cup regular barley (not quick-cooking)
1   cup sliced leek (3 medium)*
1   cup thinly sliced carrot (2 medium)
1½ teaspoons dried basil or Italian seasoning, crushed
¼   teaspoon cracked black pepper
    Slivered fresh basil or snipped fresh parsley (optional)

1 In a large skillet cook chicken in hot oil until brown on all sides. In a 4- to 5-quart slow cooker combine chicken, broth, barley, leek, carrot, dried basil, and pepper.

2 Cover and cook on low-heat setting for 4 to 5 hours or on high-heat setting for 2 to 2½ hours or until barley is tender. If desired, sprinkle with fresh basil or parsley before serving.

nutrition facts per serving: 253 cal., 6 g total fat (1 g sat. fat), 60 mg chol., 622 mg sodium, 28 g carb., 6 g dietary fiber, 22 g protein.

✳note: See tip on cleaning leeks, page 464.

herb math

What do you do if a recipe calls for fresh herbs and you have only dried on hand? As a general rule, use 1 teaspoon dried herb for 1 tablespoon fresh. To retain peak flavor, keep dried herbs in an airtight container in a cupboard away from the oven. Properly stored, they should keep up to a year.

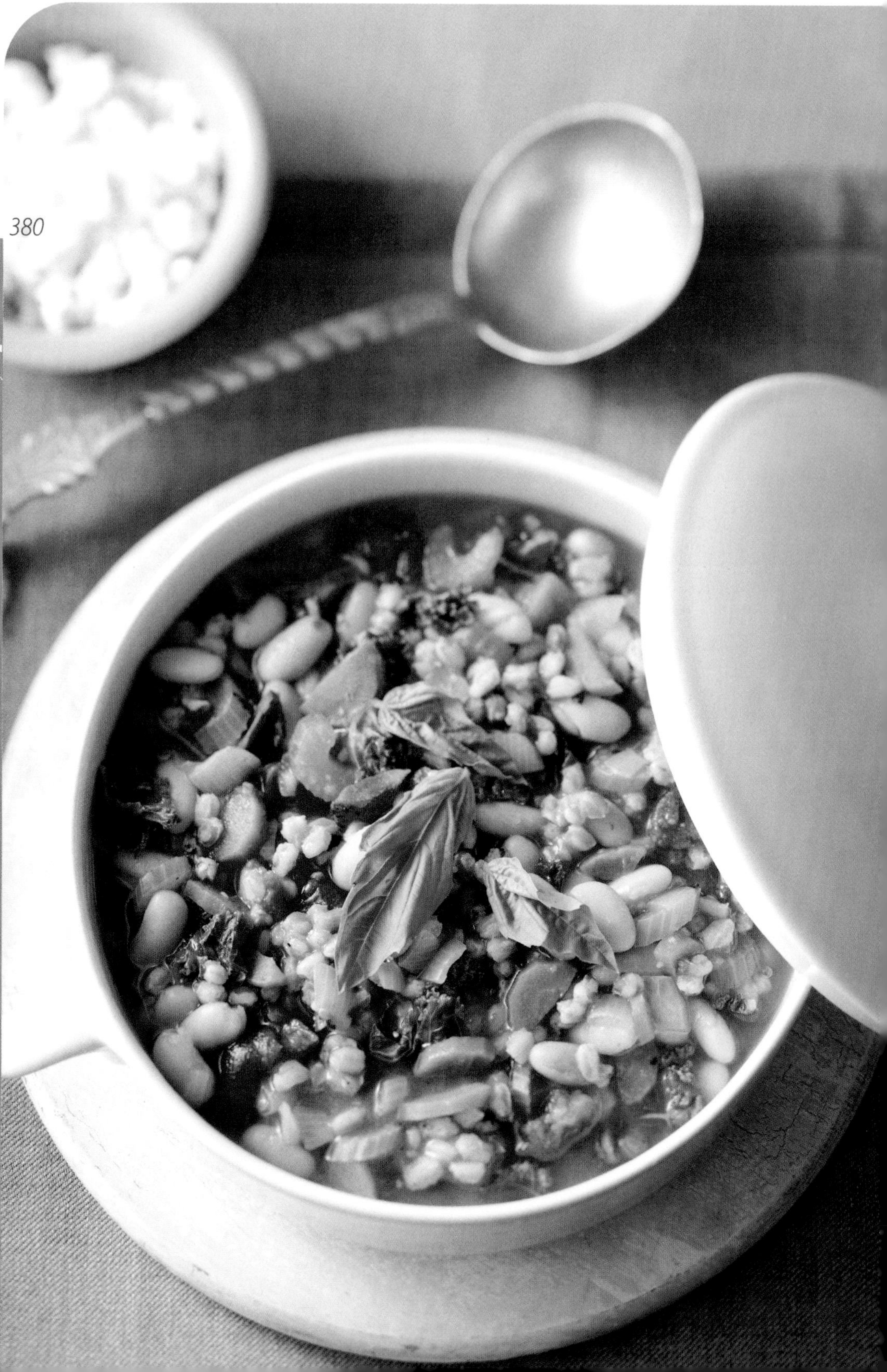

The fire-roasted tomatoes add a smoky undertone to this satisfying Italian soup, but if you can't find them, feel free to use regular.

mediterranean kale and cannellini stew with farro

prep: 20 minutes   slow cook: 2 hours (high) + 1 hour (high)

makes: 6 servings

4   cups reduced-sodium vegetable broth

1   14.5-ounce can no-salt-added fire-roasted tomatoes, undrained

1   cup farro, rinsed

1   cup coarsely chopped onion (1 large)

2   medium carrots, halved lengthwise and thinly sliced crosswise

1   cup coarsely chopped celery (2 stalks)

4   cloves garlic, minced

½   teaspoon crushed red pepper flakes

¼   teaspoon salt

4   cups coarsely chopped kale or Swiss chard

1   15-ounce can no-salt-added cannellini (white kidney) beans, rinsed and drained

3   tablespoons lemon juice

½   cup crumbled feta cheese (2 ounces) Snipped fresh basil or parsley

1 In a 3½- or 4-quart slow cooker combine broth, tomatoes, farro, onion, carrots, celery, garlic, red pepper flakes, and salt.

2 Cover and cook on high-heat setting about 2 hours or until farro is tender but still chewy. Stir in kale, beans, and lemon juice. Cover and cook for 1 hour more.

3 Serve with cheese and basil.

nutrition facts per serving: 274 cal., 4 g total fat (2 g sat. fat), 11 mg chol., 691 mg sodium, 46 g carb., 9 g dietary fiber, 14 g protein.

A hint of smokiness provided by the turkey breast adds an upscale touch to this creamy chowder.

smoked turkey and corn chowder

start to finish: 20 minutes
makes: 4 servings

In a medium saucepan, heat cream cheese over medium heat until softened. Add milk and corn, stirring until combined. Stir in turkey and peas; heat through. Season to taste with pepper.

1   8-ounce tub cream cheese spread with chives and onions
2   cups milk
1   14.75-ounce can cream-style corn
1½ cups chopped cooked smoked turkey breast (about 8 ounces)
1   cup frozen peas
    Ground black pepper

nutrition facts per serving: 397 cal., 23 g total fat (15 g sat. fat), 88 mg chol., 1159 mg sodium, 27 g carb., 3 g dietary fiber, 19 g protein.

A blend of crunchy vegetables—bean sprouts, broccoli, and straw mushrooms—pack flavor and texture in this easy-to-make and very addictive soup.

asian chicken and shrimp soup

start to finish: 45 minutes
makes: 6 to 8 servings

2   small chicken breast
      halves (12 ounces
      total)
2   cups water
4   cups chicken broth
1   tablespoon soy sauce
8   ounces small shrimp,
      peeled and deveined
8   ounces fresh bean
      sprouts
1   cup broccoli florets
½   15-ounce jar straw
      mushrooms or
      one 8-ounce can
      mushrooms,
      drained
½   cup chopped red and/
      or green sweet
      pepper
4   green onions,
      diagonally sliced in
      1-inch pieces
     Ground black pepper

1 In a 4-quart Dutch oven combine chicken and the water. Bring to boiling; reduce heat. Simmer, covered, for 20 to 25 minutes or until no longer pink. Remove chicken from pot. When cool enough to handle, remove and discard skin from chicken. Pull meat from bones; discard bones. Chop meat. Strain cooking liquid. Wipe out Dutch oven; add strained liquid. Add chicken broth.

2 Bring to boiling; add chicken, soy sauce, shrimp, bean sprouts, broccoli, mushrooms, sweet pepper, and green onions. Return to boiling. Cook, uncovered, 5 minutes. Season to taste with black pepper.

nutrition facts per serving: 152 cal., 3 g total fat (1 g sat. fat), 76 mg chol., 849 mg sodium, 7 g carb., 2 g dietary fiber, 26 g protein.

Every spoonful of this company-special soup is packed with colorful veggies, whole-grain pasta, and cannellini beans.

pasta e fagioli

prep: 35 minutes cook: 20 minutes
makes: 8 servings

1 tablespoon olive oil

2 ounces prosciutto
  or turkey bacon,
  chopped

2 cups chopped onion
  (2 large)

½ cup chopped celery
  (1 stalk)

½ cup chopped carrot
  (1 medium)

2 tablespoons bottled
  minced garlic

1 tablespoon dried
  oregano, crushed

1 teaspoon crushed
  red pepper flakes

2 14-ounce cans
  reduced-sodium
  chicken broth

1 28-ounce can
  no-salt-added
  diced tomatoes,
  undrained

1 cup medium whole-
  grain pasta shells

2 15-ounce cans
  no-salt-added
  cannellini (white
  kidney) beans,
  rinsed and drained

½ cup snipped fresh
  parsley

2 tablespoons lemon
  juice

¼ cup finely shredded
  Parmesan cheese
  (1 ounce)

1 In a Dutch oven heat oil over medium-high heat. Add prosciutto; cook for 2 to 3 minutes or until crisp. Using a slotted spoon, transfer prosciutto to paper towels; drain. Set aside.

2 Add onion, celery, carrot, and garlic to Dutch oven; cook over medium heat for 3 to 4 minutes or until softened, stirring frequently. Stir in oregano and red pepper flakes; cook and stir for 1 minute. Add broth, undrained tomatoes, and pasta shells. Bring to boiling; reduce heat. Simmer, uncovered, about 15 minutes or until pasta is tender.

3 Meanwhile, use a fork to mash one can of the beans. Stir all beans into pasta mixture. Simmer about 5 minutes or until heated through.

4 Stir in parsley and lemon juice. Sprinkle each serving with Parmesan and the prosciutto.

nutrition facts per serving: 235 cal., 5 g total fat (1 g sat. fat), 2 mg chol., 490 mg sodium, 35 g carb., 9 g dietary fiber, 13 g protein.

When purchasing pumpkin, check labels carefully, making sure you buy pure pumpkin—and not pumpkin pie filling.

pumpkin, barley, and sage soup

start to finish: 30 minutes
makes: 4 servings

1   tablespoon vegetable oil
8   ounces cooked andouille or smoked sausage links, chopped
⅓   cup chopped onion (1 small)
1   tablespoon snipped fresh sage
4   cups water
1   cup quick-cooking barley
1   teaspoon instant chicken bouillon granules
1   15-ounce can pumpkin
2   tablespoons maple syrup
1   tablespoon cider vinegar
    Salt
    Ground black pepper

1 In a 4-quart Dutch oven heat oil over medium heat. Add sausage, onion, and sage; cook for 3 minutes, stirring often. Add the water, barley, and bouillon granules. Bring to boiling; reduce heat. Simmer, covered, for 12 minutes, stirring occasionally.

2 Stir in pumpkin, maple syrup, and vinegar; heat through. Season to taste with salt and pepper.

nutrition facts per serving: 439 cal., 21 g total fat (6 g sat. fat), 35 mg chol., 832 mg sodium, 51 g carb., 11 g dietary fiber, 14 g protein.

all kinds of

13

vegg

Warmer weather brings bumper crops of veggies in all shapes and sizes—from asparagus to zucchini. In this collection of lighter soups, cooks will discover a bounty of fresh flavor in chunky broth soups, hearty purees, and elegant cream soups.

Pureed potatoes are the perfect backdrop for fennel's licorice-like character in this soup. Choose firm, greenish white fennel bulbs with no soft or brown spots. If the fronds are still attached to the bulbs, they should be bright green with no signs of wilting.

fennel and leek soup

prep: 25 minutes **cook:** 42 minutes
makes: 6 servings

1 tablespoon butter
1 tablespoon olive oil
3 fennel bulbs, trimmed, cored, and thinly sliced
2 leeks, sliced*
2 tablespoons dry sherry, vermouth, or white wine
3 14.5-ounce cans vegetable broth or chicken broth
1 pound russet potatoes, peeled and cut into 1-inch pieces
1 teaspoon snipped fresh thyme or ½ teaspoon dried thyme, crushed
Salt
Cracked black pepper
Sautéed sliced leek (optional)

1 In a 4-quart Dutch oven heat butter and oil over medium heat. Add fennel and 2 sliced leeks; cook about 10 minutes or until crisp-tender, stirring occasionally.

2 Carefully add sherry; cook and stir about 2 minutes or until sherry is nearly evaporated. Carefully add broth and potatoes. Bring to boiling; reduce heat. Simmer, covered, about 30 minutes or until vegetables are very tender; cool slightly.

3 Transfer fennel mixture in batches to a blender or food processor. Cover and blend or process until smooth. Return pureed mixture to Dutch oven. Stir in thyme; heat through. Season to taste with salt.

4 Sprinkle each sercing with pepper and, if desired, garnish with additional sautéed leeks.

nutrition facts per serving: 176 cal., 7 g total fat (3 g sat. fat), 8 mg chol., 979 mg sodium, 28 g carb., 7 g dietary fiber, 4 g protein.

*note: See tip on cleaning leeks, page 464.

Fire-roasted tomatoes give a toasty flavor to this mélange of fresh vegetables and cannellini beans. Aromatic oregano heightens the flavor of the broth.

roasted tomato and vegetable soup

prep: 30 minutes   cook: 25 minutes
makes: 8 servings

1 tablespoon olive oil
½ cup chopped onion
  (1 medium)
½ cup sliced celery
  (1 stalk)
½ cup chopped carrot
  (1 medium)
2 cloves garlic, minced
3 14-ounce cans
  reduced-sodium
  chicken broth
2 cups peeled, seeded,
  and chopped
  butternut squash
1 14.5-ounce can
  fire-roasted diced
  tomatoes or one
  14.5-ounce can diced
  tomatoes, undrained
1 15- to 19-ounce can
  cannellini (white
  kidney) beans,
  rinsed and drained
1 small zucchini,
  halved lengthwise
  and sliced
1 cup small broccoli
  and/or cauliflower
  florets
1 tablespoon snipped
  fresh oregano or
  2 teaspoons dried
  oregano, crushed
¼ teaspoon salt
¼ teaspoon ground
  black pepper
  Freshly shredded
  Parmesan cheese
  (optional)

1 In a 4-quart Dutch oven heat oil over medium heat. Add onion, celery, carrot, and garlic; cook for 5 minutes.

2 Stir in broth, squash, and undrained tomatoes. Bring to boiling; reduce heat. Simmer, covered, for 20 minutes. Add beans, zucchini, broccoli, oregano, salt, and pepper; cook for 5 minutes more. If desired, sprinkle each serving with Parmesan cheese.

nutrition facts per serving: 77 cal., 0 g total fat (0 g sat. fat), 0 mg chol., 641 mg sodium, 16 g carb., 4 g dietary fiber, 6 g protein.

slow cooker directions: Omit olive oil. In a 3½- or 4-quart slow cooker combine onion, celery, carrot, garlic, broth, squash, undrained tomatoes, beans, and dried oregano (if using). Cover and cook on low-heat setting for 7 to 8 hours or on high-heat setting for 3½ to 4 hours. If using low-heat setting, turn cooker to high-heat setting. Add zucchini, broccoli, fresh oregano (if using), salt, and pepper. Cover and cook 30 minutes more. Serve as directed.

Butternut squash has a delicately sweet flavor that marries nicely with carrots and oniony leeks. Top each serving of pureed soup with toasted pumpkin seeds for an added treat.

butternut squash and carrot soup

prep: 15 minutes **cook:** 35 minutes
makes: 6 servings

1 tablespoon butter
or margarine

3 cups peeled, seeded,
and diced butternut
squash (about 1
small squash)

2 cups thinly sliced
carrot (4 medium
carrots)

¾ cup thinly sliced leek
or chopped onion*

2 14.5-ounce cans
reduced-sodium
chicken broth

¼ teaspoon ground
white pepper

¼ teaspoon ground
nutmeg

¼ cup half-and-half
or light cream
Fresh tarragon sprigs
(optional)

1 Melt butter in a large saucepan over medium heat. Add squash, carrot, and leek; cook, covered, for 8 minutes, stirring occasionally. Add broth. Bring to boiling; reduce heat. Simmer, covered, for 25 minutes or until vegetables are very tender.

2 Transfer squash mixture, one-third at a time, to a food processor or blender. Cover and process or blend until almost smooth. Return pureed mixture to saucepan. Add white pepper and nutmeg. Bring just to boiling. Add half-and-half; heat through. If desired, garnish each serving with fresh tarragon.

nutrition facts per serving: 103 cal., 4 g total fat (2 g sat. fat), 9 mg chol., 447 mg sodium, 16 g carb., 4 g dietary fiber, 3 g protein.

*note: See tip on cleaning leeks, page 464.

The ultimate what's-on-hand recipe, vegetable soup adapts to Southwestern or Asian influences with equal ease.

versatile vegetable soup

prep: 40 minutes cook: 25 minutes
makes: 12 servings

2	leeks, thinly sliced (white part only)*
1½	teaspoons bottled minced garlic
1	teaspoon olive oil
8	cups water
1	14.5-ounce can stewed tomatoes, undrained
2	cups sliced celery (4 stalks)
1½	cups thinly sliced carrot (3 medium)
1	medium red apple, cored and coarsely chopped
1	medium sweet potato, peeled and cut into ½-inch cubes
4	teaspoons instant vegetable bouillon granules or vegetable bouillon cubes (to make 4 cups broth)
2	cups shredded cabbage
1	cup cut fresh green beans
¼	teaspoon salt
¼	teaspoon ground black pepper
½	cup snipped fresh parsley
2	tablespoons lemon juice

In a 4-quart Dutch oven cook leeks and garlic in hot oil about 3 minutes or until nearly tender. Carefully add the water, undrained tomatoes, celery, carrot, apple, sweet potato, and bouillon. Bring to boiling; reduce heat. Simmer, covered, for 15 minutes. Add cabbage, green beans, salt, and pepper. Return to boiling; reduce heat. Simmer, covered, about 10 minutes more or until vegetables are tender. Stir in parsley and lemon juice.

nutrition facts per serving: 62 cal., 1 g total fat (0 g sat. fat), 0 mg chol., 476 mg sodium, 13 g carb., 3 g dietary fiber, 1 g protein.

*note: See tip on cleaning leeks, page 464.

tex-mex chicken-vegetable soup: Prepare as directed, except add 1 teaspoon ground cumin with the leeks and garlic. Add 1 cup loose-pack frozen whole-kernel corn; 1 cup chopped cooked chicken; one 4-ounce can chopped green chiles, drained; and 3 tablespoons snipped fresh cilantro with the lemon juice. Heat through. If desired, garnish with lemon wedges and fresh cilantro sprigs.

nutrition facts per serving: 99 cal., 2 g total fat (1 g sat. fat), 10 mg chol., 514 mg sodium, 16 g carbo., 3 g dietary fiber, 5 g protein.

asian vegetable soup: Prepare as directed, except add ½ cup quick-cooking rice and ½ cup water with the cabbage. Substitute rice vinegar for the lemon juice. Add 1 cup thinly sliced fresh mushrooms and 2 green onions, thinly sliced, with the rice vinegar. Heat through. If desired, garnish with green onion slivers.

nutrition facts per serving: 80 cal., 1 g total fat (0 g sat. fat), 0 mg chol., 477 mg sodium, 17 g carbo., 3 g dietary fiber, 2 g protein.

Slow roasting of the garlic and sweet peppers in the oven adds natural sweetness to this pureed soup.

roasted garlic and red sweet pepper soup

prep: 1 hour roast: 20 minutes oven: at 425°F stand: 20 minutes
makes: 6 to 8 servings

2 whole heads garlic
1 large onion, sliced
1 tablespoon snipped
   fresh rosemary or
   1 teaspoon dried
   rosemary, crushed
1 tablespoon olive oil
4 large red sweet
   peppers, seeded
   and quartered
   lengthwise
⅓ cup firmly packed
   fresh parsley
   sprigs with stems
   removed
⅓ cup firmly packed
   fresh basil leaves
1 jalapeño pepper,
   seeded and
   chopped*
¼ teaspoon ground
   black pepper
¼ teaspoon crushed red
   pepper flakes
   Dash bottled hot
   pepper sauce
4 cups chicken broth or
   chicken stock
½ cup half-and-half or
   light cream
   Sour cream (optional)

1 Preheat oven to 425°F. Peel away the dry outer layers of skin from the garlic heads. Leave skins of the cloves intact. Cut ¼ inch off the pointed top portions to expose the individual cloves. Place the garlic heads, cut sides up, and onion slices in a small baking dish. Sprinkle rosemary over the onion and garlic; drizzle with olive oil. Place sweet pepper quarters, skin sides up, on a foil-lined baking sheet. Roast garlic, onion, and sweet peppers, uncovered, for 20 to 25 minutes or until garlic cloves feel soft when pressed and the pepper skins are bubbly and browned.

2 Wrap pepper quarters in foil; let stand for 20 to 30 minutes or until cool enough to handle. Using a paring knife, gently pull skins off pepper quarters; discard skins. When the garlic is cool enough to handle, press garlic paste from individual cloves. Discard skins.

3 In a blender or food processor combine the garlic paste, sweet peppers, onion, parsley, basil, chile pepper, black pepper, red pepper flakes, and hot pepper sauce. Blend or process until nearly smooth. Add 1 cup of the broth; blend or process until smooth. Transfer to a large saucepan. Stir in the remaining 3 cups broth and the half-and-half. Heat over medium-low heat until warm. If desired, serve with sour cream.

nutrition facts per serving: 117 cal., 6 g total fat (2 g sat. fat), 8 mg chol., 532 mg sodium, 12 g carb., 1 g dietary fiber, 6 g protein.

*note: See tip on handling chile peppers, page 31.

Quick and easy to prepare, this aromatic soup tastes light but is packed with flavor. When working with the fennel, use the inner layers of the bulb, which are the most tender.

tomato-garlic soup with fennel

prep: 45 minutes cook: 15 minutes
makes: 8 servings

1   fennel bulb
1   tablespoon olive oil
1   tablespoon butter
1   onion, quartered and
      thinly sliced
10 cloves garlic, minced
1   28-ounce can
      diced tomatoes,
      undrained
1   14.5-ounce can
      reduced-sodium
      chicken broth
1   8-ounce can tomato
      sauce
1   cup hot-style
      vegetable juice or
      regular vegetable
      juice
1   teaspoon dried basil
      or Italian seasoning,
      crushed

1 Reserve some of the feathery fennel tops to garnish the soup. Cut off and discard upper stalks of fennel. Remove any wilted outer layers; cut off and discard a thin slice from fennel base. Quarter the bulb lengthwise; remove and discard core. Chop fennel.

2 In a 4-quart Dutch oven heat oil and butter over medium-high heat. Add chopped fennel, onion, and garlic; reduce heat to medium-low. Cook, covered, about 25 minutes or until onion is tender, stirring occasionally. Cook, uncovered, over medium-high heat for 3 to 5 minutes or until onion is golden, stirring frequently.

3 Add undrained tomatoes, broth, tomato sauce, vegetable juice, and basil. Bring to boiling; reduce heat. Simmer, covered, for 15 minutes.

4 Garnish each serving with the reserved fennel tops.

nutrition facts per serving: 94 cal., 3 g total fat (1 g sat. fat), 4 mg chol., 546 mg sodium, 14 g carb., 2 g dietary fiber, 2 g protein.

The perfect balance of vegetable flavors in this creamy, rich soup (with just a hint of grapefruit) will have your guests positively swooning.

cream of roasted fennel soup

prep: 25 minutes **roast:** 25 minutes **oven:** at 375°F
makes: 8 servings

1 large fennel bulb
   (1½ to 2 pounds)
1 cup coarsely chopped
   onion (1 large)
2 teaspoons olive oil
½ teaspoon coarse salt
1 large russet potato,
   peeled and cut into
   ½-inch cubes
4 cups reduced-sodium
   chicken broth
1 cup fat-free half-and-
   half or evaporated
   fat-free milk
¾ teaspoon ground
   cumin
2 tablespoons
   grapefruit juice
   Ground white pepper
1 tablespoon fennel
   seeds

1 Preheat oven to 375°F. Cut off and discard tough upper stalks of fennel. Reserve feathery leaves. Remove any wilted outer layers; cut off and discard a thin slice from fennel base. Cut the bulb and tender stalks into ½-inch-thick slices.

2 Arrange fennel and onion in a 13×9×2-inch baking pan. Drizzle with olive oil and sprinkle with salt. Roast for 25 minutes or until the vegetables are just tender but not brown.

3 Transfer roasted fennel and onion to a large saucepan. Add potato and broth. Bring to boiling; reduce heat. Simmer, covered, for 10 minutes or until potatoes are tender. Cool slightly.

4 Transfer fennel mixture, one-third at a time, to a blender or food processor. Cover and blend or process until smooth. Return pureed mixture to saucepan. Stir in half-and-half, cumin, and grapefruit juice; heat through. Season to taste with white pepper.

5 Meanwhile, place fennel seeds in a small skillet over medium-high heat and toast for about 3 minutes or until lightly brown and fragrant, stirring frequently.

6 Top each serving with a length of fennel top, and sprinkle with toasted fennel seeds.

nutrition facts per serving: 77 cal., 1 g total fat (0 g sat. fat), 0 mg chol., 479 mg sodium, 12 g carb., 2 g dietary fiber, 3 g protein.

Adding a splash of vinegar just before serving boosts the flavor of this hearty white bean and vegetable stew.

provençal vegetable stew

prep: 25 minutes **slow cook:** 8 to 10 hours (low) or 4 to 5 hours (high)
bake: 6 minutes **oven:** at 400°F
makes: 4 servings

2   baby eggplants or
     1 very small eggplant
     (about 8 ounces)
1   large zucchini,
     quartered lengthwise
     and cut into ½-inch
     slices
1   large yellow summer
     squash, quartered
     lengthwise and cut
     into ½-inch slices
1   15- to 19-ounce can
     cannellini (white
     kidney) beans or
     Great Northern
     beans, rinsed and
     drained
1   large tomato, chopped
2   teaspoons bottled
     minced garlic
¼   teaspoon dried
     rosemary or thyme,
     crushed
¼   teaspoon ground
     black pepper
1   tablespoon snipped
     fresh basil or
     1 teaspoon dried
     basil, crushed
1½ cups low-sodium
     tomato juice
1   tablespoon white
     or regular balsamic
     vinegar
4   ½-inch slices
     baguette-style
     French bread
2   teaspoons olive oil
3   tablespoons finely
     shredded Parmesan
     cheese

1 If desired, peel eggplant. Cut eggplant into ¾-inch pieces (you should have about 3 cups).

2 In a 3½- or 4-quart slow cooker, combine eggplant, zucchini, yellow squash, beans, tomato, garlic, rosemary, pepper, and dried basil (if using). Add tomato juice.

3 Cover and cook on low-heat setting for 8 to 10 hours or on high-heat setting for 4 to 5 hours. Stir in fresh basil (if using), and balsamic vinegar.

4 Meanwhile, for croutons, preheat oven to 400°F. Lightly brush bread slices with olive oil. Sprinkle with 1 tablespoon of the cheese. Place bread slices on baking sheet. Bake for 6 to 8 minutes or until toasted.

5 Top each serving with croutons and sprinkle with remaining cheese.

nutrition facts per serving: 227 cal., 5 g total fat (1 g sat. fat), 4 mg chol., 424 mg sodium, 41 g carb., 10 g dietary fiber, 12 g protein.

Dried porcini mushrooms add a wonderful earthy flavor to this onion soup. Look for them near other dehydrated vegetables in your supermarket's produce section or at specialty food stores.

sweet onion soup with porcini mushrooms

prep: 30 minutes **stand:** 15 minutes **cook:** 30 minutes
makes: 6 servings

1	ounce dried porcini mushrooms
2	cups boiling water
4	ounces pancetta
1	tablespoon butter or olive oil
1½	pounds sweet onion, such as Vidalia or Maui, sliced
4	cloves garlic, minced
1	tablespoon packed brown sugar
1	teaspoon salt
¼	cup Marsala
4	cups reduced-sodium beef broth
1	sprig fresh thyme
1	sprig fresh rosemary
1	bay leaf

1 Place mushrooms in a medium bowl. Pour the boiling water over mushrooms. Cover and let stand for 15 minutes. Meanwhile, in a 4-quart Dutch oven cook pancetta in hot butter over medium heat until lightly browned. Using a slotted spoon, remove pancetta; drain on paper towels, reserving drippings in Dutch oven. Chop pancetta; set aside.

2 Add sweet onion, garlic, brown sugar, and salt to Dutch oven; cook and stir over medium-low heat until golden, stirring occasionally.

3 Meanwhile, using a slotted spoon, remove porcini mushrooms from the liquid (do not discard liquid). Chop mushrooms; set aside. Reserve all but about ¼ cup of the mushroom liquid (discard the liquid at the bottom of the bowl, which may be gritty).

4 When the onions are golden, stir in mushrooms and Marsala wine; cook until most of the liquid has evaporated. Add reserved mushroom liquid, broth, thyme, rosemary, and bay leaf. Bring to boiling; reduce heat. Simmer, uncovered, about 30 minutes. Discard thyme and rosemary sprigs and bay leaf.

5 Remove from heat; stir in pancetta. Serve with toasted baguette.

nutrition facts per serving: 158 cal., 8 g total fat (3 g sat. fat), 18 mg chol., 1118 mg sodium, 16 g carb., 2 g dietary fiber, 6 g protein.

Sweet and juicy caramelized onions, fresh ginger, and sweet potato create this flavorful soup. The best onions to use here are the sweet varieties, such as Vidalia or Walla Walla.

ginger-carrot soup

prep: 30 minutes cook: 50 minutes
makes: 12 servings

2 tablespoons vegetable oil
3 cups thinly sliced onion
2 tablespoons sugar
⅛ teaspoon ground black pepper
2 tablespoons grated fresh ginger
8 carrots (about 1¼ pounds)
1 sweet potato
6 cups chicken broth
1 cup half-and-half or light cream
Salt
Ground black pepper

1 In a large skillet heat oil over medium heat. Add onion, sugar, and pepper; reduce heat to low. Cook, covered, for 30 minutes, stirring twice. Add ginger. Cook, uncovered, 20 to 30 minutes more or until onion is golden brown, stirring occasionally.

2 Meanwhile, peel carrots and sweet potato and cut in 1-inch pieces. In a large saucepan or Dutch oven combine carrots, sweet potato, and broth. Bring to boiling; reduce heat. Simmer, covered, 40 minutes or until vegetables are very tender. Add half of the caramelized onions. Cool slightly. Transfer vegetable mixture, 2 cups at a time, to a blender or food processor. Cover and blend or process until smooth. Return mixture to saucepan. Add half-and-half; heat through. Season to taste with salt and pepper. Top each serving with remaining caramelized onions.

nutrition facts per serving: 105 cal., 5 g total fat (2 g sat. fat), 9 mg chol., 524 mg sodium, 13 g carb., 2 g dietary fiber, 2 g protein.

The flavor of this pureed potato soup is enhanced by licorice-flavored fennel and fresh snap peas. A spoonful of yogurt and fresh fennel frond adds a flavorful finish.

hearty
garlic and snap pea soup

prep: 30 minutes   **cook:** 19 minutes
makes: 8 servings

4	cloves garlic or 1 or 2 bulbs spring garlic, chopped
2	tablespoons olive oil
¼	cup chopped onion
1	pound Yukon Gold potatoes, quartered
2	14-ounce cans reduced-sodium chicken broth
1¾	cups water
1	medium fennel bulb, thinly slivered (feathery tops reserved)
1½	cups sugar snap peas, trimmed
½	teaspoon salt
¼	teaspoon ground black pepper
1	tablespoon snipped fresh fennel tops
	Plain yogurt (optional)
	Olive oil (optional)

1 In a large saucepan cook garlic in 2 tablespoons hot oil over medium heat for 1 minute. Add onion; cook until tender. Add potatoes, broth, and the water. Bring to boiling; reduce heat. Cook, covered, 15 to 18 minutes, or until potatoes are tender. Cool soup slightly.

2 Transfer soup in batches to a food processor or blender. Cover and process or blend until smooth. Return mixture to saucepan. Add fennel and peas. Bring to boiling; reduce heat. Simmer, uncovered, for 3 minutes.

3 Stir in salt and pepper. Top with fennel tops. Spoon yogurt over and drizzle with olive oil.

nutrition facts per serving: 102 cal., 3 g total fat (0 g sat. fat), 0 mg chol., 404 mg sodium, 15 g carb., 3 g dietary fiber, 3 g protein.

Curry powder adds a distinctly sweet and spicy flavor and intense color to this coconut milk–enriched soup. Sprinkling chopped fresh cilantro on top lends freshness to the soup.

curried vegetable soup

start to finish: 20 minutes
makes: 4 servings

3   cups cauliflower florets
1   14.5-ounce can vegetable broth or chicken broth
1   14-ounce can unsweetened coconut milk
¼   cup snipped fresh cilantro
1   tablespoon curry powder
¼   teaspoon salt
2   cups frozen baby peas and vegetables blend
    Crushed red pepper flakes (optional)
    Chopped fresh cilantro (optional)
    Curry Pita Crisps (optional)

1 In a 4-quart Dutch oven combine cauliflower, broth, coconut milk, snipped cilantro, curry powder, and salt over high heat. Bring to boiling; reduce heat. Simmer, covered, about 10 minutes or until cauliflower is tender. Stir in frozen vegetables; heat through.

2 If desired, sprinkle each serving with red pepper flakes and cilantro and serve with Curry Pita Crisps.

nutrition facts per serving: 138 cal., 6 g total fat (4 g sat. fat), 0 mg chol., 620 mg sodium, 19 g carb., 4 g dietary fiber, 3 g protein.

curry pita crisps: Preheat broiler. Cut 2 pita bread rounds into wedges. Place on a large baking sheet. Brush both sides of wedges with 1 tablespoon olive oil and sprinkle with ¼ teaspoon curry powder. Broil 3 to 4 inches from heat for about 4 minutes or until golden, turning once halfway through broiling.

To trim fresh asparagus, gently bend each stalk about 2 inches from the bottom and the stalk should snap right at the point where the tender and woody parts meet. Peel any thicker stems.

creamy potato and asparagus soup

start to finish: 30 minutes
makes: 4 servings

1¼ pounds fresh asparagus spears, trimmed
1¼ pounds potatoes, peeled and chopped
1 12-ounce can evaporated milk
1¼ cups water
½ teaspoon salt
½ teaspoon ground black pepper
6 slices bacon
1 tablespoon honey Toppings, such as finely shredded lemon zest, fresh parsley, coarse salt, and/or ground black pepper (optional)

1 Set aside about one-third of the asparagus. In a large saucepan combine remaining asparagus, potatoes, evaporated milk, the water, salt, and pepper. Bring to boiling; reduce heat. Simmer, covered, about 10 minutes or until potatoes are tender; cool slightly. Transfer potato mixture, half at a time, to a blender or food processor. Cover and blend or process until smooth.

2 Meanwhile, in a large skillet cook bacon over medium heat until crisp. Remove bacon; drain on paper towels, reserving 1 tablespoon drippings in skillet. Add the reserved asparagus to the reserved drippings. Cook for 5 to 6 minutes or until asparagus is crisp-tender, stirring occasionally.

3 Coarsely chop bacon; place on a microwave-safe pie plate. Drizzle bacon with honey; cover with vented plastic wrap. Before serving, microwave bacon on 100 percent power (high) for 30 seconds.

4 Top each serving with cooked asparagus, honeyed bacon, and, if desired, toppings.

nutrition facts per serving: 356 cal., 15 g total fat (7 g sat. fat), 41 mg chol., 673 mg sodium, 43 g carb., 4 g dietary fiber, 15 g protein.

Yukon Gold potatoes are sweeter and creamier than standard baking potatoes, making this chowder truly impressive. Reserve leftover bread from hollowing out the bread bowls for dipping in the soup.

potato and roasted corn chowder in bread bowls

prep: 25 minutes **bake:** 20 minutes **oven:** at 450°F **cook:** 20 minutes
makes: 8 servings

1   16-ounce package frozen whole-kernel corn
1   pound Yukon Gold potatoes, peeled and cut into ½-inch cubes
2   tablespoons olive oil
½   cup thinly sliced leek*
2   tablespoons finely chopped shallot
4   cups chicken broth
1   teaspoon dried marjoram, crushed
1   teaspoon kosher salt or ½ teaspoon table salt
½   teaspoon ground ginger
½   teaspoon ground white pepper
3   cups half-and-half or light cream
8   individual round loaves sourdough bread

1 Preheat oven to 450°F. Thaw frozen corn and pat dry with paper towels. Line a 15×10×1-inch baking pan with foil. Lightly grease the foil. Spread corn on half of the prepared pan. In a resealable plastic bag, combine potatoes and 1 tablespoon of the oil, shaking well to coat. Spread potatoes on the other half of the prepared pan. Roast, uncovered, for 10 minutes; stir, keeping corn and potatoes separate. Continue to roast for 10 minutes more, stirring once or twice. Remove pan from oven. Set aside.

2 Transfer half of the roasted corn, about ¾ cup, to a food processor or blender. Cover and process or blend until smooth (if necessary, add a small amount of chicken broth to help mixture blend).

3 In a 4-quart Dutch oven heat remaining 1 tablespoon oil over medium-high heat. Add leek and shallot; reduce heat to medium. Cook and stir for 6 to 8 minutes or until leek is very soft and golden. Add whole corn and pureed corn; cook and stir for 1 minute. Stir in roasted potatoes, broth, marjoram, salt, ginger and white pepper. Bring to boiling; reduce heat. Simmer, covered, for 10 to 12 minutes or until potatoes are tender.

4 Add half-and-half; cook and stir till heated through. Season to taste with more salt and white pepper.

5 Hollow out sourdough loaves. To serve, spoon chowder into bread bowls.

nutrition facts per serving: 588 cal., 15 g total fat (7 g sat. fat), 33 mg chol., 1342 mg sodium, 94 g carb., 2 g dietary fiber, 20 g protein.

*note: See tip on cleaning leeks, page 464.

The surprising use of a vanilla bean is just one of this soup's many pleasures. It also cooks in a mere 15 minutes. Store the unused half of the vanilla bean in plastic wrap, place in an airtight jar, and store in the refrigerator for up to 6 months.

green bean soup

prep: 25 minutes **cook:** 15 minutes
makes: 6 to 8 servings

2 14-ounce cans vegetable broth
½ cup chopped onion (1 medium)
½ vanilla bean, split lengthwise
3 tablespoons butter, softened
3 tablespoons all-purpose flour
1 pound thin green beans, trimmed and cut into bite-size pieces (3 to 3½ cups)
    Steamed Green Beans (optional)
    Herbed Sourdough Breadsticks (optional)

1 In a large saucepan bring broth, onion, and vanilla bean to boiling; reduce heat. Simmer, covered, for 10 minutes or until onion is tender. Discard vanilla bean.

2 In a small bowl stir together butter and flour. Whisk into broth mixture; cook and stir until slightly thickened and bubbly.

3 Add beans to broth mixture. Return to boiling; reduce heat. Simmer, covered, for 5 to 7 minutes more or until beans are crisp-tender. If desired, garnish each serving with Steamed Green Beans and serve with Herbed Sourdough Breadsticks.

nutrition facts per serving: 94 cal., 7 g total fat (4 g sat. fat), 16 mg chol., 607 mg sodium, 11 g carb., 3 g dietary fiber, 2 g protein.

steamed green beans: Place 8 ounces thin green beans in a steamer basket. Cover and steam over boiling water for 5 to 7 minutes or until tender.

herbed sourdough breadsticks: Preheat oven to 375°F. Cut ½ of a 12-inch sourdough baguette lengthwise into ½-inch slices. Cut into 1-inch-wide sticks. Brush cut surfaces evenly with 2 tablespoons olive oil and sprinkle with 1 teaspoon snipped fresh thyme. Place on a baking sheet. Bake for 16 minutes or until golden.

Baby vegetables have a milder flavor and more tender texture than their full-size counterparts. Be sure to cook them until just tender for best taste and texture.

baby vegetable minestrone

prep: 20 minutes cook: 25 minutes
makes: 6 servings

2   teaspoons olive oil
½   cup thinly sliced
    baby fennel
1   medium carrot,
    halved lengthwise
    and sliced (½ cup)
2   large cloves garlic,
    minced
¼   teaspoon lemon
    pepper
2   14-ounce cans
    reduced-sodium
    chicken broth or
    3½ cups homemade
    chicken stock
½   cup dried ditalini
    or other small dried
    pasta
6   ounces baby zucchini,
    halved lengthwise
6   ounces baby yellow
    squash, halved
    lengthwise
½   cup sliced green
    onion (4)
¼   cup fresh basil
    leaves, thinly sliced
6   ounces Parmigiano-
    Reggiano or
    Romano cheese,
    cut into 6 very thin
    wedges (optional)

1 In a very large saucepan heat oil over medium heat. Add fennel, carrot, garlic, and lemon pepper; cook and stir for 3 to 4 minutes or until carrot is slightly brown. Carefully stir in broth. Bring to boiling; reduce heat. Simmer, covered, about 8 minutes or until vegetables are just tender.

2 Add pasta. Simmer, covered, for 5 minutes. Add zucchini and yellow squash. Return to boiling; reduce heat. Simmer, covered, for 5 minutes more or until pasta is tender. Stir in green onion and basil.

3 If desired, place a wedge of cheese in each of six warmed bowls. Add hot soup. Let cheese soften slightly before serving.

nutrition facts per serving: 77 cal., 2 g total fat (0 g sat. fat), 0 mg chol., 376 mg sodium, 12 g carb., 2 g dietary fiber, 4 g protein.

This cream-based soup seasoned with thyme is wonderful with any holiday menu. The secret to making it quick is using canned pumpkin.

creamy pumpkin soup

prep: 15 minutes **cook:** 20 minutes
makes: 4 servings

1   teaspoon canola oil
⅔   cup sliced leek
     (2 medium)*
2   14-ounce cans
     reduced-sodium
     chicken broth
1   15-ounce can
     pumpkin
2   teaspoons snipped
     fresh thyme or
     1 teaspoon dried
     thyme, crushed
¼   teaspoon ground
     black pepper
1   8-ounce carton
     light sour cream
     Tiny sprigs fresh
     thyme (optional)

1 In a large saucepan heat oil over medium-high heat. Add leek; cook and stir until tender. Stir in broth, pumpkin, dried thyme (if using), and pepper. Bring to boiling; reduce heat. Simmer, covered, for 20 minutes. Cool slightly. Stir in snipped thyme (if using).

2 Transfer mixture to a blender or food processor. Cover and blend or process until smooth. Return pureed mixture to saucepan; heat through. Stir in half of the sour cream.

3 Swirl each serving with remaining sour cream. If desired, garnish with thyme sprigs.

nutrition facts per serving: 165 cal., 9 g total fat (4 g sat. fat), 20 mg chol., 108 mg sodium, 17 g carb., 3 g dietary fiber, 7 g protein.

∗note: See tip on cleaning leeks, page 464.

Alphabet pasta will make kids want to try this colorful soup featuring a medley of garden vegetables. Reserving half of the vegetables and stirring them into the soup just before serving creates a tantalizing contrast between tender and crisp.

a-to-z vegetable soup

start to finish: 30 minutes
makes: 4 servings

1 tablespoon vegetable oil or olive oil

2 cups mixed, cut-up fresh vegetables, such as sliced small zucchini, carrots, celery, and chopped red onions

2 14.5-ounce cans reduced-sodium chicken broth

2 cloves garlic, minced

1 15-ounce can cannellini (white kidney) beans or Great Northern beans, rinsed and drained

½ cup dried alphabet-shaped pasta or tiny shells

2 tablespoons small fresh oregano leaves

1 ounce Parmesan cheese, thinly sliced (optional)

1 In a large saucepan heat oil over medium-high heat. Add mixed vegetables. Cook, uncovered, about 10 minutes or until vegetables are crisp-tender, stirring occasionally. Remove half of the vegetables; set aside.

2 Stir broth and garlic into remaining vegetables in saucepan. Bring to boiling. Stir in beans and pasta. Return to boiling; reduce heat. Simmer, covered, about 10 minutes or until pasta is just tender. Stir in oregano.

3 Top each serving with reserved vegetables. If desired, top each serving with cheese.

nutrition facts per serving: 188 cal., 4 g total fat (1 g sat. fat), 0 mg chol., 717 mg sodium, 33 g carb., 6 g dietary fiber, 12 g protein.

Every ladleful of this colorful soup brims with onions, carrots, and celery in a soothing broth. Get a head start on preparation by purchasing preshredded carrots.

vegetable pasta soup

start to finish: 35 minutes
makes: 12 servings

2	teaspoons olive oil
6	cloves garlic, minced
1½	cups coarsely shredded carrot (3 medium)
1	cup chopped onion (2 medium)
1	cup thinly sliced celery (2 stalks)
1	32-ounce carton reduced-sodium chicken broth
4	cups water
1½	cups dried ditalini pasta
¼	cup shaved Parmesan cheese
2	tablespoons snipped fresh parsley

1 In a 5- to 6-quart Dutch oven heat oil over medium heat. Add garlic; cook for 15 seconds. Add carrot, onion, and celery; cook for 5 to 7 minutes or until tender, stirring occasionally. Add broth and the water. Bring to boiling. Add pasta. Cook, uncovered, for 7 to 8 minutes or until pasta is tender.

2 To serve, top each serving with cheese and parsley.

nutrition facts per serving: 86 cal., 2 g total fat (0 g sat. fat), 1 mg chol., 227 mg sodium, 14 g carb., 1 g dietary fiber, 4 g protein.

Oregano and rosemary are flavorful herbal complements to a naturally sweet potato, carrot, and celery combo. Pureeing half of the mixture gives this soup extra body and richness.

sweet potato and rosemary soup

prep: 30 minutes cook: 30 minutes
makes: 6 servings

1   tablespoon olive oil
⅓   cup chopped onion
     (1 small)
2   cloves garlic, minced
1   cup chopped carrot
     (2 medium)
½   cup chopped celery
     (1 stalk)
1   teaspoon dried
     thyme, crushed
1   teaspoon dried
     rosemary, crushed
2   pounds sweet
     potatoes, peeled
     and chopped
     (3½ cups)
10 ounces russet potato,
     peeled and chopped
     (1½ cups)
2   14-ounce cans
     reduced-sodium
     chicken broth

1 In a large saucepan heat oil over medium heat. Add onion and garlic; cook and stir about 5 minutes or until onion is tender. Add carrot, celery, thyme, and rosemary; cook and stir for 3 minutes more. Add potatoes and broth. Bring to boiling; reduce heat. Simmer, covered, for 25 minutes. Cool slightly.

2 Transfer half of the vegetable mixture (about 3½ cups) to a large heatproof bowl. Transfer vegetable mixture in the bowl in batches to a blender or food processor. Blend or process until smooth. Return pureed mixture to saucepan and heat through.

nutrition facts per serving: 118 cal., 2 g total fat (0 g sat. fat), 0 mg chol., 361 mg sodium, 21 g carb., 3 g dietary fiber, 3 g protein.

Golden, pungent, and warmly spiced, curry powder adds a heady aroma and lush taste to this pureed soup. Create a striking presentation by topping with baked cheese crisps.

sweet potato soup with curried cheese crisps

start to finish: 30 minutes
makes: 4 servings

2 pounds sweet potatoes
3 green onions, coarsely chopped
1 14-ounce can vegetable or chicken broth
1 cup whipping cream
1 teaspoon curry powder
¼ teaspoon salt
¼ teaspoon ground black pepper
  Nonstick cooking spray
½ cup shredded white cheddar cheese (2 ounces)
  Paprika (optional)

1 Preheat oven to 425°F. Scrub potatoes and pierce in several places. Place potatoes in microwave oven. Cook on 100 percent (high) power for 10 minutes or until tender, turning once halfway through cooking. Carefully halve potatoes lengthwise. Hold with an oven mitt, then scoop flesh into a food processor. Add onions and half of the broth to food processor. Cover and process until smooth.

2 Transfer pureed potatoes to a large saucepan. Add remaining broth and cream; cook over medium-high heat, stirring occasionally, until heated through. Stir in ¾ teaspoon of the curry powder, salt, and pepper.

3 Meanwhile, for cheese crisps, lightly coat a large baking sheet with cooking spray, or cover baking sheet with parchment paper. In a small bowl toss together cheese and remaining ¼ teaspoon curry powder. Evenly divide into 8 mounds, 2 inches apart, on baking sheet; flatten mounds slightly. Bake 4 to 5 minutes, until melted and beginning to brown around edges. Cool slightly. Remove from baking sheet with a metal spatula. If desired, sprinkle with paprika. Serve cheese crisps with soup.

nutrition facts per serving: 416 cal., 27 g total fat (17 g sat. fat), 97 mg chol., 737 mg sodium, 37 g carb., 5 g dietary fiber, 8 g protein.

This pleasing potage begins with oven-roasted cauliflower florets. The roasting process caramelizes the creamy white vegetable's natural sugars, resulting in intense, luxurious flavor.

roasted cauliflower soup

prep: 15 minutes **roast:** 30 minutes **oven:** at 400°F **cook:** 20 minutes
makes: 8 servings

1 large head cauliflower, cut into florets (10 cups)
1 onion, sliced
2 cloves garlic, halved
2 tablespoons olive oil
2 14.5-ounce cans chicken broth
1 cup water
1 bay leaf
1 teaspoon snipped fresh thyme or ¼ teaspoon dried thyme, crushed
1 cup half-and-half or light cream
1 teaspoon salt
⅛ teaspoon ground black pepper

1 Preheat oven to 400°F. In a large roasting pan combine cauliflower, onion, and garlic. Drizzle with oil; toss gently to coat. Spread vegetables in an even layer. Roast, uncovered, for 30 minutes, stirring once.

2 In a 4-quart Dutch oven combine roasted vegetables, broth, the water, bay leaf, and thyme. Bring to boiling; reduce heat. Simmer, covered, for 20 minutes; cool slightly. Discard bay leaf.

3 Transfer vegetable mixture in batches to a food processor or blender. Cover and process or blend until smooth. Return pureed mixture to saucepan. Stir in half-and-half, salt, and pepper; heat through (do not boil).

nutrition facts per serving: 125 cal., 7 g total fat (3 g sat. fat), 12 mg chol., 756 mg sodium, 13 g carb., 3 g dietary fiber, 4 g protein.

410

For the fullest flavor, choose the ripest fresh tomatoes you can find. If homegrown or farm-fresh tomatoes are available, they'll make the best soup. Serve with breadsticks or garlic croutons.

mixed tomato soup

prep: 45 minutes **stand:** 30 minutes **cook:** 1 hour 5 minutes
makes: 8 servings

3   ounces dried tomatoes
     (not oil-packed)
1   tablespoon olive oil
     or vegetable oil
½   cup chopped onion
     (1 medium)
¼   teaspoon coarsely
     ground black
     pepper
8   tomatoes, chopped
     (about 2½ pounds)
4   cups water
1   teaspoon salt
1   cup whipping cream

1 Place dried tomatoes in a small bowl. Add enough boiling water to cover; let stand for 30 minutes. Drain and rinse. Coarsely chop rehydrated tomatoes.

2 In a Dutch oven heat oil over medium heat. Add rehydrated tomatoes, onion, and pepper; cook until onion is tender. Reserve ¾ cup of fresh tomatoes. Add remaining chopped fresh tomatoes to onion mixture. Cook, covered, over low heat about 20 minutes or until tomatoes are soft. Add the water and salt. Cook, uncovered, over low heat for 40 minutes more, stirring often.

3 Transfer mixture in batches to a food processor or blender. Cover and process or blend until smooth. Return pureed mixture to Dutch oven; heat to simmering. Stir in whipping cream. Return just to simmering. Remove from heat.

4 Top each serving with the reserved chopped fresh tomatoes.

nutrition facts per serving: 176 cal., 14 g total fat (7 g sat. fat), 41 mg chol., 540 mg sodium, 13 g carb., 3 g dietary fiber, 3 g protein.

Cajun seasoning and Mexican-style stewed tomatoes add fresh, lively character to a tasty stew that incorporates eight colorful vegetables.

savory vegetable stew

prep: 30 minutes slow cook: 8 to 9 hours (low) or 4 to 4½ hours (high)
stand: 5 minutes
makes: 6 servings

2   cups cubed, peeled
      sweet potato
1   cup cubed, peeled
      red-skinned potato
      (1 medium)
1   cup chopped carrot
      (2 medium)
1   cup cubed, peeled
      rutabaga
6   boiling onions, peeled
½   cup sliced celery
      (1 stalk)
½   cup chopped red and/
      or green sweet
      pepper (1 small)
1   15-ounce can
      garbanzo beans
      (chickpeas), rinsed
      and drained
1   6-ounce jar sliced
      mushrooms, drained
1   14.5-ounce can
      Mexican-style
      stewed tomatoes,
      undrained and
      cut up
1   14.5-ounce can
      vegetable broth
      or chicken broth
½   cup water
1   tablespoon quick-
      cooking tapioca,
      crushed
1   teaspoon Cajun
      seasoning
½   cup frozen peas
½   cup frozen cut green
      beans

1 In a 5- to 6-quart slow cooker combine potatoes, carrot, rutabaga, onions, celery, and sweet pepper. Stir in beans and mushrooms. In a medium bowl combine undrained tomatoes, broth, the water, tapioca, and Cajun seasoning. Pour over mixture in cooker.

2 Cover and cook on low-heat setting for 8 to 9 hours or on high-heat setting for 4 to 4½ hours. Stir in frozen peas and green beans. Cover and let stand for 5 minutes before serving.

nutrition facts per serving: 219 cal., 1 g total fat (0 g sat. fat), 0 mg chol., 921 mg sodium, 46 g carb., 8 g dietary fiber, 7 g protein.

As summer gives way to fall, come home with a bumper crop of late-season vegetables at their freshest, in-season best, then simmer them slowly in this wonderfully varied soup.

farmer's market vegetable soup

prep: 30 minutes **slow cook:** 8 to 9 hours (low) or 4 to 4½ hours (high)
makes: 4 servings

½ of a small rutabaga, peeled and chopped (2 cups)
1½ cups chopped tomato (2 large)
1 cup chopped carrot or parsnip (2 medium)
1 large red-skinned potato, chopped
⅔ cup chopped leek (2 medium)*
3 14-ounce cans vegetable broth
1 teaspoon fennel seeds, crushed
½ teaspoon dried sage, crushed
¼ to ½ teaspoon ground black pepper
½ cup dried bow tie pasta
3 cups torn fresh spinach
Garlic Toasts (optional)

1 In a 3½- or 4-quart slow cooker combine rutabaga, tomato, carrot, potato, and leek. Add broth, fennel seeds, sage, and pepper.

2 Cover and cook on low-heat setting for 8 to 9 hours or on high-heat setting for 4 to 4½ hours.

3 Meanwhile, cook pasta according to package directions; drain. Stir cooked pasta and spinach into soup mixture. If desired, serve with Garlic Toasts.

nutrition facts per serving: 198 cal., 2 g total fat (0 g sat. fat), 0 mg chol., 1313 mg sodium, 41 g carb., 8 g dietary fiber, 8 g protein.

*note: See tip on cleaning leeks, page 464.

garlic toasts: Preheat broiler. Brush both sides of eight ½-inch baguette-style French bread slices with 1 tablespoon garlic-infused olive oil. Arrange on a baking sheet. Broil 3 to 4 inches from the heat for 1 minute. Turn; sprinkle with 2 teaspoons grated Parmesan cheese. Broil for 1 to 2 minutes more or until light brown.

Chipotle peppers add the perfect amount of heat to this slightly sweet soup.

butternut squash bisque

prep: 40 minutes **cook:** 35 minutes
makes: 8 servings

1   2½- to 3-pound
    butternut squash
    or three 12-ounce
    packages frozen
    cooked winter
    squash, thawed
¼   cup butter
½   cup coarsely chopped
    carrot (1 medium)
½   cup chopped onion
    (1 medium)
½   cup coarsely chopped
    celery (1 stalk)
2   cloves garlic, minced
2   Braeburn or Gala
    apples, peeled,
    cored, and chopped
1   48-ounce carton
    reduced-sodium
    chicken broth
1   cup apple cider
    or apple juice
2   canned chipotle
    peppers in adobo
    sauce, coarsely
    chopped*
½   cup sour cream
3   ounces smoked
    Gouda or smoked
    cheddar cheese,
    finely shredded
    Crumbled crisp-
    cooked bacon and/
    or shaved Gouda
    cheese (optional)

1 Peel, seed, and cube butternut squash. In a 6-quart Dutch oven melt butter over medium-high heat. Add fresh squash (if using), carrot, onion, celery, and garlic; cook about 10 minutes or until vegetables are tender, stirring frequently. Add frozen squash (if using), apples, broth, cider, and chile peppers. Bring to boiling; reduce heat. Simmer, covered, about 25 minutes or until vegetables and apples are tender. Remove from heat; cool slightly.

2 Transfer soup, half at a time, to a food processor or blender. Cover and process or blend. Return pureed soup to Dutch oven. Stir in sour cream. Gently reheat over low heat, stirring occasionally and making sure soup does not boil.

3 Remove from heat. Add shredded cheese, stirring until melted. If desired, top with bacon and/or shaved cheese.

nutrition facts per serving: 213 cal., 11 g total fat (7 g sat. fat), 30 mg chol., 655 mg sodium, 26 g carb., 3 g dietary fiber, 6 g protein.

∗note: See tip on handling chile peppers, page 31.

A basketful of fresh veggies pumps up this soup of fresh tomatoes. Take your choice of carrots, celery, sweet peppers, fennel, and onion or any other vegetable you please. A classic grilled cheese sandwich is the perfect accompaniment to complete your meal

garden bounty tomato soup

prep: 25 minutes **slow cook:** 6 to 8 hours (low) or 3 to 4 hours (high)
makes: 8 to 10 servings

2 pounds roma tomatoes, chopped

2 14-ounce cans beef broth

2 cups finely chopped assorted vegetables (such as carrot, celery, sweet pepper, fennel, and/ or onion)

1 6-ounce can tomato paste

1 to 2 teaspoons sugar

1 In a 3½- or 4-quart slow cooker combine tomatoes, broth, vegetables, tomato paste, and sugar.

2 Cover and cook on low-heat setting for 6 to 8 hours or on high-heat setting for 3 to 4 hours.

nutrition facts per serving: 61 cal., 1 g total fat (0 g sat. fat), 0 mg chol., 372 mg sodium, 12 g carb., 3 g dietary fiber, 3 g protein.

Thai cuisine masterfully combines seemingly incompatible ingredients—such as the odd company of pumpkin, peanut butter, and mango nectar called for in this soup—and melds them into complex concoctions layered with flavor after flavor.

pumpkin-ginger soup

prep: 20 minutes **cook:** 30 minutes
makes: 6 servings

1 15-ounce can pumpkin
1 14.5-ounce can vegetable broth
1½ cups mango nectar or apricot nectar
1 tablespoon grated fresh ginger
2 cloves garlic, minced
1 5-ounce can evaporated milk or ⅔ cup canned unsweetened coconut milk
¼ cup creamy peanut butter
2 tablespoons rice vinegar
   Dash bottled hot pepper sauce or ¼ teaspoon crushed red pepper flakes
¼ cup snipped fresh cilantro
   Sour cream or plain yogurt (optional)
   Dried Thai chile peppers (optional)

1 In a large saucepan combine pumpkin, broth, nectar, ginger, and garlic. Bring to boiling; reduce heat. Simmer, uncovered, for 30 minutes, stirring occasionally.

2 Whisk in evaporated milk, peanut butter, vinegar, and hot pepper sauce until smooth. Stir in cilantro.

3 If desired, top each serving with sour cream and garnish with Thai chile peppers.

nutrition facts per serving: 236 cal., 14 g total fat (4 g sat. fat), 7 mg chol., 402 mg sodium, 23 g carb., 4 g dietary fiber, 9 g protein.

Broccoli and cauliflower, both cabbage family members, combine to make a flavorful sidekick for your favorite entrées. Dijon mustard and Gruyère cheese add a delightful tang and richness.

creamy broccoli-cauliflower soup

prep: 25 minutes **cook:** 40 minutes
makes: 8 servings

1 tablespoon olive oil
¾ cup chopped sweet onion
2 14-ounce cans chicken broth
¾ cup water
2¼ cups cauliflower florets
2 potatoes, peeled and chopped
1 tablespoon Dijon-style mustard
Ground black pepper
2¼ cups cauliflower florets
2¼ cups broccoli florets
4 ounces Gruyère cheese or Gouda cheese, finely shredded

1 In a 4-quart Dutch oven heat oil over medium heat. Add onion; cook for 5 minutes or until tender. Stir in broth, the water, 2¼ cups cauliflower florets, and potato. Bring to boiling; reduce heat. Simmer, covered, for 20 minutes or until cauliflower is very tender.

2 Cool mixture slightly. Transfer mixture, half at a time, to blender or food processor. Blend or process until smooth. Return pureed mixture to Dutch oven. Stir in mustard and pepper. Stir in 2¼ cups cauliflower florets and broccoli. Bring to boiling; reduce heat. Simmer, covered, for 20 minutes or until cauliflower is tender. Stir in cheese; cook and stir until cheese is melted.

nutrition facts per serving: 126 cal., 7 g total fat (3 g sat. fat), 17 mg chol., 517 mg sodium, 10 g carb., 3 g dietary fiber, 7 g protein.

mix and mash

These ingredients perform exceptionally well in pureed soups:

- **potatoes:** *The starch in potatoes thickens soups for excellent body.*

- **legumes:** *Cooked split peas, lentils, and black or cannellini (white kidney) beans become velvety smooth when blended.*

- **winter squash:** *Most types of cooked winter squash and pumpkin can be blended until smooth.*

- **veggies:** *Many starchy root vegetables, such as sweet potatoes, parsnips, turnips, carrots, and beets, make great pureed soups. So do peas and sweet corn.*

Combining fresh beets and apple creates a mellow, slightly sweet soup. Pureeing in a food processor or with an immersion blender makes it smooth and luscious. If you use a standard blender, the soup may be slightly chunky.

beet and apple soup with horseradish cream

prep: 30 minutes   **cook:** 25 minutes
makes: 6 to 8 servings

8	large fresh beets
3	14.5-ounce cans reduced-sodium chicken broth
½	cup chopped sweet onion (1 medium)
½	cup peeled and chopped potato (1 medium)
1	cooking apple, peeled, cored, and chopped
2	tablespoons dry sherry or white balsamic vinegar
	Salt
	Ground black pepper
1	8-ounce carton sour cream
2	tablespoons prepared horseradish
¼	teaspoon cayenne pepper
	Skillet Beets (optional)

1 Peel the beets*; cut each into 1-inch pieces. In a 4-quart Dutch oven combine beets, broth, onion, potato, and apple. Bring to boiling; reduce heat. Simmer, covered, for 25 to 30 minutes or until tender; cool slightly.

2 Transfer beet mixture, half at a time, to a food processor. Cover and process until smooth. Return pureed mixture to Dutch oven. (Or blend with a handheld immersion blender in Dutch oven.) Stir in sherry. Season to taste with salt and black pepper; heat through.

3 For horseradish cream, in a small bowl combine sour cream, horseradish, and cayenne pepper. Stir about ½ cup of the horseradish cream into hot soup.

4 Top each serving with remaining horseradish cream and, if desired, Skillet Beets.

nutrition facts per serving: 222 cal., 9 g total fat (5 g sat. fat), 17 mg chol., 729 mg sodium, 31 g carb., 6 g dietary fiber, 7 g protein.

*note: Peel beets with a sharp vegetable peeler or paring knife. To avoid staining your hands, wear rubber gloves.

skillet beets: Trim tops from 2 large beets to leave 1 inch of stem. Peel and thinly slice beets lengthwise from top to bottom. In large skillet cook beet slices in 2 tablespoons hot oil over medium heat for 8 minutes or until tender, turning once.

The natural sweetness of the sweet potatoes combined with maple syrup in this soup contrasts nicely with the salty, savory bacon sprinkled on top.

new england sweet potato soup

prep: 25 minutes slow cook: 6 to 8 hours (low) or 3 to 4 hours (high)
makes: 6 servings

2½ to 3 pounds sweet
     potatoes, peeled
     and cut into 1-inch
     pieces
½   cup chopped onion
     (1 medium)
¼   cup maple syrup
1   clove garlic, minced
½   teaspoon dried sage,
     crushed
¼   teaspoon salt
⅛   teaspoon ground
     black pepper
2   14.5-ounce cans
     chicken broth
1   cup water
½   cup half-and-half,
     light cream,
     or whole milk
     Crisp-cooked,
     crumbled bacon
     (optional)
     Sliced green onion
     (optional)

1 In a 3½- or 4-quart slow cooker combine sweet potatoes, onion, maple syrup, garlic, sage, salt, and pepper. Pour broth and the water over all.

2 Cover and cook on low-heat setting for 6 to 8 hours or on high-heat setting for 3 to 4 hours.

3 Using a potato masher, mash sweet potatoes until desired consistency.* Stir in half-and-half. If desired, sprinkle each serving with bacon and green onion.

nutrition facts per serving: 192 cal., 3 g total fat (1 g sat. fat), 9 mg chol., 712 mg sodium, 39 g carb., 4 g dietary fiber, 3 g protein.

*note: For a smoother texture, use a blender or food processor to puree the soup.

small-bowl

star

Create a spectacular first course for a special-occasion dinner—small bowls of soup with bold, exciting flavors. Of course, these soups are also noted for their presentation with simple garnishes that offer an inviting range of fresh colors and textures. You'll even find a few worth adding to your holiday repertoire.

You'll love the simplicity of this exquisitely creamy soup. The superb combination of sherry, leeks, salmon, and cream makes this luscious soup worthy of any special occasion.

sherried salmon bisque

start to finish: 35 minutes

makes: 8 servings

12   ounces fresh or frozen salmon fillets or steaks, cut ¾ inch thick

3   cups sliced stemmed fresh shiitake or other mushrooms

¾   cup thinly sliced leek or ½ cup thinly sliced green onion*

2   tablespoons butter

1   14-ounce can chicken broth or vegetable broth

1½   teaspoons snipped fresh dill or ½ teaspoon dried dill

¼   teaspoon salt
      Pinch ground black pepper

2   cups half-and-half or light cream

2   tablespoons cornstarch

2   tablespoons dry sherry
      Fresh dill sprigs (optional)

1 Thaw salmon, if frozen. Rinse salmon; pat dry with paper towels. Discard salmon skin and bones. Cut salmon into ½-inch pieces; set aside. In a large saucepan cook mushrooms and leek in hot butter until tender. Stir in broth, dill, salt, and pepper. Bring to boiling.

2 In a medium bowl combine half-and-half and cornstarch. Stir into mushroom mixture; cook and stir over medium heat until thickened and bubbly. Add salmon. Simmer, covered, about 4 minutes or until salmon flakes easily when tested with a fork. Gently stir in sherry. If desired, garnish with dill.

nutrition facts per serving: 232 cal., 15 g total fat (7 g sat. fat), 55 mg chol., 345 mg sodium, 14 g carb., 1 g dietary fiber, 11 g protein.

*note: See tip on cleaning leeks, page 464.

Take your pick of meaty mushrooms. They all add up to a filling bowl of soup with an intensely earthy aroma and flavor.

mixed mushroom soup

prep: 25 minutes   cook: 30 minutes
makes: 6 servings

10   ounces fresh cremini, oyster, button, and/ or stemmed shiitake mushrooms, sliced
 2   ounces fresh portobello mushrooms, stemmed and sliced ½ inch thick
 ½   cup chopped onion (1 medium)
 3   cloves garlic, minced
 1   tablespoon olive oil
 3   14.5-ounce cans vegetable broth or chicken broth
 1   tablespoon snipped fresh thyme or ½ teaspoon dried thyme, crushed

1 In a large saucepan cook mushrooms, onion, and garlic in hot oil over medium heat about 10 minutes or until mushrooms are softened and most of the liquid is evaporated, stirring occasionally.

2 Add broth and dried thyme (if using). Bring to boiling; reduce heat. Simmer, covered, for 20 minutes. Stir in fresh thyme (if using).

nutrition facts per serving: 55 cal., 2 g total fat (0 g sat. fat), 0 mg chol., 693 mg sodium, 5 g carb., 1 g dietary fiber, 4 g protein.

Put your slow cooker to work for a shrimp soup that is every bit as good as what you'd get at a restaurant. Use a whisk to stir the soup as you add the beaten egg to ensure it forms delicate strands of cooked egg.

oriental hot-and-sour soup

prep: 20 minutes slow cook: 9 to 11 hours (low) or 3 to 4 hours (high)
+ 50 minutes (low or high)
makes: 8 servings

4	cups chicken broth
1	8-ounce can bamboo shoots, drained
1	8-ounce can sliced water chestnuts, drained
1	4-ounce can sliced mushrooms, drained
3	tablespoons quick-cooking tapioca
3	tablespoons rice wine vinegar or vinegar
1	tablespoon soy sauce
1	teaspoon sugar
½	teaspoon ground black pepper
1	8-ounce package frozen peeled and deveined shrimp
4	ounces firm tofu, (fresh bean curd), drained and cubed
1	egg, lightly beaten
2	tablespoons snipped fresh parsley or coriander

1 In a 3½- or 4-quart slow cooker combine broth, bamboo shoots, water chestnuts, mushrooms, tapioca, vinegar, soy sauce, sugar, and pepper.

2 Cover and cook on low-heat setting for 9 to 11 hours or on high-heat setting for 3 to 4 hours. Add shrimp and tofu. Cover and cook on low-heat setting or high-heat setting for 50 minutes more.

3 Pour the beaten egg slowly into the soup in a thin stream. Stir the soup gently so that the egg forms fine strands instead of clumps. Sprinkle with parsley.

nutrition facts per serving: 114 cal., 2 g total fat (1 g sat. fat), 83 mg chol., 664 mg sodium, 9 g carb., 1 g dietary fiber, 13 g protein.

So few ingredients, so much flavor! Even better, this soup freezes well, so make an extra batch.

butternut squash soup with ravioli

start to finish: 30 minutes
makes: 5 servings

1   2-pound butternut
    squash
2   14.5-ounce cans
    vegetable broth
½   cup water
⅛   teaspoon cayenne
    pepper
1   tablespoon butter
1   9-ounce package
    refrigerated cheese
    ravioli
1   tablespoon molasses
    (optional)

1 Peel squash. Halve lengthwise. Remove seeds and discard. Cut squash into ¾-inch pieces.

2 In a large saucepan combine squash, broth, the water, and cayenne pepper over medium heat. Cook, covered, for 20 minutes or until squash is tender. Cool slightly.

3 Transfer squash-broth mixture, one-fourth at a time, to a blender. Cover and blend until smooth. Return pureed mixture to saucepan. Bring to boiling; reduce heat. Simmer, uncovered, for 5 minutes. Add butter, stirring just until melted.

4 Meanwhile, prepare ravioli according to package directions; drain. Ladle hot squash mixture into bowls. Divide cooked ravioli among bowls. If desired, drizzle with molasses.

nutrition facts per serving: 259 cal., 10 g total fat (5 g sat. fat), 52 mg chol., 933 mg sodium, 36 g carb., 2 g dietary fiber, 10 g protein.

*Whirl tender peas in the blender to
thicken this Scandinavian-style soup.*

dilled buttermilk-pea soup

prep: 20 minutes   cook: 10 minutes
makes: 4 servings

1   14-ounce can
     reduced-sodium
     chicken broth
2   cups shelled fresh
     peas or one
     10-ounce package
     frozen peas
1   cup torn fresh
     spinach
¼   cup chopped onion
1   tablespoon snipped
     fresh dill or savory
     or ½ teaspoon
     dried dill or savory,
     crushed
¼   teaspoon salt
⅛   teaspoon ground
     black pepper
½   cup buttermilk
     Fresh dill sprigs with
     flowers (optional)

1 In a medium saucepan combine broth,
peas, spinach, onion, dill, salt, and
pepper. Bring to boiling; reduce heat. Simmer,
covered, for 10 to 15 minutes for fresh peas
(5 to 6 minutes for frozen peas) or until peas
are very tender. Cool mixture slightly.

2 Transfer pea mixture, half at a time, to a
blender. Cover and blend until smooth.
Return pureed mixture to saucepan. Stir in
buttermilk; heat through. If desired, garnish
with fresh dill sprigs.

nutrition facts per serving: 83 cal., 1 g total fat
(0 g sat. fat), 1 mg chol., 423 mg sodium, 14 g carb.,
4 g dietary fiber, 6 g protein.

Chunks of apples and potatoes make a surprising and satisfying addition to this cheese soup recipe.

apple-cheddar soup

prep: 20 minutes cook: 20 minutes
makes: 4 to 6 servings

½ cup finely chopped
  onion (1 medium)
1 tablespoon butter
2 medium baking
  potatoes, peeled
  and diced
2 cups apple cider
1 teaspoon snipped
  fresh thyme or
  ½ teaspoon dried
  thyme, crushed
½ teaspoon salt
  Pinch cayenne
  pepper
1 medium cooking
  apple, peeled and
  coarsely chopped
½ cup milk
2 tablespoons all-
  purpose flour
4 ounces sharp cheddar
  cheese, shredded
  (1 cup)
  Fresh apple slices
  Green peppercorns

1 In large saucepan cook onion in hot butter over medium heat until tender. Stir in potatoes, cider, thyme, salt, and cayenne pepper. Bring to boiling; reduce heat. Simmer, covered, 15 minutes. Add chopped apple. Simmer, covered, 5 minutes or until potatoes are tender. In small bowl combine milk and flour. Stir into soup; cook and stir until bubbly. Slowly add cheese, whisking until cheese is melted.

2 Top each serving with apple slices and peppercorns.

nutrition facts per serving: 352 cal., 16 g total fat (10 g sat. fat), 48 mg chol., 527 mg sodium, 32 g carb., 4 g dietary fiber, 12 g protein.

Carrot, leek, sweet pepper, and onion pack flavor into this pureed potato soup, elevating it to company-worthy status.

sweet potato soup with toasted pecans

prep: 20 minutes cook: 20 minutes
makes: 6 servings

2	teaspoons canola oil
¾	cup thinly sliced carrot
½	cup finely chopped leek*
⅓	cup chopped orange or yellow sweet pepper
⅓	cup finely chopped onion
1	clove garlic, minced
2	14-ounce cans reduced-sodium chicken broth
1	pound sweet potatoes, peeled, halved lengthwise, and thinly sliced crosswise
1	small potato (4 ounces), peeled, halved lengthwise, and thinly sliced crosswise
⅓	cup dry white wine or reduced-sodium chicken broth
⅛	teaspoon ground black pepper
1	bay leaf
¼	cup chopped pecans, toasted

1 In a large saucepan heat oil over medium-high heat. Add carrot, leek, sweet pepper, onion, and garlic; cook about 5 minutes or just until vegetables are tender, stirring occasionally.

2 Add broth, potatoes, wine, black pepper, and bay leaf. Bring to boiling; reduce heat. Simmer, covered, for 15 to 20 minutes or until the potatoes are tender. Discard the bay leaf. Remove from heat; cool soup slightly.

3 Transfer soup, half at a time, to a blender or food processor. Cover and blend or process until smooth. Return pureed soup to saucepan; heat through. Sprinkle each serving with toasted pecans.

nutrition facts per serving: 142 cal., 5 g total fat (0 g sat. fat), 0 mg chol., 358 mg sodium, 20 g carb., 3 g dietary fiber, 4 g protein.

*note: See tip on cleaning leeks, page 464.

Everyday cauliflower and carrots get a flavorful kick from cumin in this smooth and chunky soup. Fresh lime juice marries well with the garlic and spice.

cauliflower, carrot, and cumin soup

prep: 25 minutes cook: 25 minutes
makes: 6 servings

2 tablespoons olive oil
1 cup finely chopped onion (1 large)
2 cloves garlic, minced
3 cups small cauliflower florets
1½ cups coarsely shredded carrot (3 medium)
1 teaspoon ground cumin
2 14-ounce cans reduced-sodium chicken broth
1 cup half-and-half or light cream
1 tablespoon lime juice
   Salt
   Ground black pepper

1 In a large saucepan heat oil over medium heat. Add onion and garlic; cook about 5 minutes or until onion is tender. Stir in cauliflower, carrot, and cumin. Add broth. Bring to boiling; reduce heat. Simmer, covered about 20 minutes or until cauliflower is very tender. Remove from heat; cool slightly. Using a slotted spoon, set aside 1½ cups of the vegetables.

2 Transfer mixture, half at a time, to a blender or food processor. Cover and blend or process until smooth. Return pureed mixture to saucepan. Stir in reserved 1½ cups vegetables, half-and-half, and lime juice; heat through. Season to taste with salt and pepper.

nutrition facts per serving: 140 cal., 9 g total fat (4 g sat. fat), 15 mg chol., 466 mg sodium, 11 g carb., 3 g dietary fiber, 5 g protein.

perfectly pureed

Make your favorite soups thicker and creamier with a little blending action. Blenders and immersion blenders work great for tomato soup, vichyssoise, and other uniformly smooth soups. You can puree a portion of the beans or starchy root vegetables from your soup right in the pot with an immersion blender. To add luscious body, you can also use a blender. If you're pureeing warm soup in a blender, do small batches at a time, loosen the plug in the blender lid to let steam escape, and hold a towel firmly over the lid. Start on a low speed. Rising steam from the soup can create enough pressure to force the top off the blender, causing a mess and/or burns. Do not blend extremely hot soups.

If fresh shiitake mushrooms aren't available, soak dried ones in hot water. Two ounces of dried mushrooms equal 1 cup of the fresh.

shiitake mushroom–tomato bisque

prep: 20 minutes cook: 35 minutes
makes: 4 servings

2   tablespoons butter
½   cup sliced leek or
    chopped onion
    (1 medium)*
½   cup sliced celery
    (1 stalk)
2   cloves garlic, minced
1½ cups sliced, stemmed
    fresh shiitake or
    other mushrooms
1   14.5-ounce can
    diced tomatoes,
    undrained
1   14.5-ounce can
    chicken broth or
    vegetable broth
½   cup whipping cream
½   teaspoon dried dill
⅛   teaspoon ground
    black pepper
    Sautéed sliced
    mushrooms
    (optional)

1 In a large saucepan heat butter over medium heat until melted. Add leek, celery, and garlic; cook and stir until tender. Add mushrooms; cook and stir about 5 minutes or until mushrooms are tender. Stir in undrained tomatoes, broth, whipping cream, dill, and pepper. Bring to boiling; reduce heat. Simmer, covered, for 30 minutes; cool slightly.

2 Transfer mixture, half at a time, to a blender or food processor. Cover and blend or process until smooth. Return pureed mixture to saucepan; heat through.

3 If desired, garnish each serving with additional sautéed mushrooms.

nutrition facts per serving: 193 cal., 13 g total fat (8 g sat. fat), 47 mg chol., 607 mg sodium, 17 g carb., 2 g dietary fiber, 3 g protein.

*note: See tip on cleaning leeks, page 464.

Celebrate a most welcome hue of summer with creamy pureed soup flavored by green onions, watercress, and tarragon

tarragon-potato-watercress soup

prep: 30 minutes cook: 23 minutes cool: 15 minutes
makes: 8 servings

1¼ pounds russet potatoes, peeled, cut in 1-inch pieces (3 medium)

1½ cups sliced green onion (2 to 3 bunches)

2 tablespoons butter

6 cups reduced-sodium chicken broth

6 cups watercress, tough stems removed (about 3 bunches), or fresh baby spinach leaves

3 tablespoons snipped fresh tarragon

½ cup dry white wine or reduced-sodium chicken broth

Salt

Ground black pepper

½ cup sour cream (optional)

1 In 4- to 5-quart Dutch oven cook potatoes and onion in hot butter over medium heat for 3 to 5 minutes or until onions are tender but not brown, stirring occasionally. Add broth; bring to boiling. Reduce heat. Simmer, covered, for 20 minutes or until potatoes are tender.

2 Stir in watercress; return broth to simmering. Simmer, covered, for 3 to 5 minutes, until greens are tender. Remove soup from heat; cool 15 minutes. Stir in tarragon. Puree soup using immersion blender or in batches using a blender.

3 Stir wine into soup; season with salt and pepper. Heat through over low heat. If desired, top each serving with sour cream.

nutrition facts per serving: 125 cal., 6 g total fat (3 g sat. fat), 13 mg chol., 617 mg sodium, 13 g carb., 1 g dietary fiber, 5 g protein.

Basil brings out the delicate flavor of fresh asparagus in this springtime soup. You can also substitute regular milk for the soy or rice milk.

asparagus-basil soup

start to finish: 30 minutes
makes: 4 servings

1   pound fresh asparagus
1   14-ounce can vegetable broth
1½ cups loose-pack frozen chopped hash brown potatoes
1   cup water
1   cup regular soy milk or rice milk
½   cup chopped fresh basil
    Salt
    Ground black pepper
    Fresh basil leaves (optional)

1 Break off woody bases where asparagus spears snap easily. Cut off tips; set aside. Chop remaining asparagus stalks. In a medium saucepan, combine chopped asparagus stalks, broth, and potatoes. Bring to boiling; reduce heat. Cover and simmer about 5 minutes or just until asparagus is barely tender. Remove from heat. Cool for 5 minutes. Transfer mixture to a blender. Cover and blend until smooth. Return pureed mixture to saucepan.

2 Meanwhile, in a small saucepan combine the water and reserved asparagus tips. Bring to boiling; reduce heat. Simmer, uncovered, for 3 minutes. Drain; set aside. Add soy milk to pureed mixture; stir until well mixed. Stir in chopped basil; heat through. Stir in asparagus tips. Season to taste with salt and pepper. If desired, garnish each serving with basil leaves. Serve immediately.

nutrition facts per serving: 119 cal., 2 g total fat (0 g sat. fat), 0 mg chol., 515 mg sodium, 21 g carb., 3 g dietary fiber, 6 g protein.

Serve this fresh-tasting soup as a first course for a dinner party or a side dish at a luncheon.

tomato-basil soup with toasted cheese croutons

prep: 25 minutes cook: 10 minutes
makes: 6 servings

1 medium onion, chopped
2 cloves garlic, minced
2 teaspoons olive oil
2 14.5-ounce cans no-salt-added diced tomatoes
1½ cups reduced-sodium vegetable broth or reduced-sodium chicken broth
¾ cup jarred roasted red sweet peppers, drained and chopped
2 tablespoons snipped fresh basil or 2 teaspoons dried basil, crushed
2 teaspoons balsamic vinegar
1 recipe Toasted Cheese Croutons

1 In a medium nonstick saucepan cook onion and garlic in hot oil about 5 minutes or until tender, stirring occasionally. Add undrained tomatoes, broth, roasted sweet peppers, and dried basil (if using). Bring to boiling; reduce heat. Simmer, covered for 10 minutes to blend flavors. Cool slightly.

2 Transfer half of the tomato mixture to a blender or food processor. Cover and blend or process until smooth. Return pureed mixture to tomato mixture in saucepan; heat through. Stir in fresh basil (if using) and vinegar just before serving. Top each serving with a few Toasted Cheese Croutons.

nutrition facts per serving: 94 cal., 3 g total fat (1 g sat. fat), 3 mg chol., 267 mg sodium, 14 g carb., 3 g dietary fiber, 3 g protein.

toasted cheese croutons: Place four ¾-inch-thick slices whole-grain baguette-style bread on a small baking sheet. Broil 4 to 5 inches from the heat for 1 to 2 minutes or until lightly toasted. Turn bread slices over; sprinkle tops with ¼ cup shredded reduced-fat Italian cheese blend. Broil about 1 minute more or until cheese is melted. Cool bread slices slightly. Cut into irregular-shaped bite-size pieces.

*Both spinach and arugula—most often enjoyed fresh—
make wonderful, highly nutritious additions to hot soups.*

spring greens soup

prep: 20 minutes cook: 15 minutes
makes: 6 servings

1   medium onion,
      halved and sliced
1   tablespoon vegetable
      oil
3   cups reduced-sodium
      chicken broth or
      vegetable broth
¼   to ½ teaspoon ground
      black pepper
12 ounces Yukon Gold
      potatoes, quartered
3   cups sliced fresh
      mushrooms
      (optional)
2   tablespoons butter
3   cups fresh spinach
      leaves
3   cups fresh arugula
      leaves
2   cups fresh parsley
      leaves and tender
      stems
    Salt
    Fresh arugula

1 In 3-quart saucepan cook onion in hot oil over medium heat for 5 minutes. Add broth and pepper. Bring to boiling. Add potatoes. Return to boiling; reduce heat. Simmer, covered, for 10 minutes.

2 Meanwhile, in large skillet cook mushrooms in hot butter over medium heat for 6 to 8 minutes or until tender and liquid has evaporated; set aside.

3 Remove saucepan from heat. Using an immersion blender, blend onion-potato mixture until almost smooth. Add spinach, arugula, and parsley. Return to heat. Bring to boiling; remove from heat. Using an immersion blender, blend soup again until nearly smooth and flecks of green remain. Season to taste with salt. Serve immediately, topped with sautéed mushrooms and additional fresh arugula.

nutrition facts per serving: 92 cal., 3 g total fat (0 g sat. fat), 0 mg chol., 412 mg sodium, 14 g carb., 3 g dietary fiber, 4 g protein.

Carrots, sweet pepper, and onions are a terrific trio for adding flavor flair to pumpkin soup. Ginger and jalapeño pepper blend in perfectly, creating a starter soup with an assertive edge.

coconut-pumpkin soup

prep: 15 minutes cook: 15 minutes
makes: 5 servings

1 cup chopped carrot
   (2 medium)
¾ cup chopped green
   sweet pepper
   (1 medium)
½ cup chopped onion
   (1 medium)
1 tablespoon vegetable
   oil
1 15-ounce can
   pumpkin
1 14.5-ounce can
   vegetable broth
1 14-ounce can
   unsweetened light
   coconut milk
2 tablespoons packed
   brown sugar
1 jalapeño pepper,
   seeded and finely
   chopped*
¾ teaspoon salt
½ teaspoon ground
   ginger
2 tablespoons snipped
   fresh cilantro or
   parsley

1 In a large saucepan cook carrot, sweet pepper, and onion in hot oil over medium heat about 5 minutes or until vegetables are nearly tender. In a large bowl combine pumpkin, broth, and coconut milk. Stir in brown sugar, chile pepper, salt, and ginger. Stir pumpkin mixture into carrot mixture.

2 Bring to boiling; reduce heat. Simmer, uncovered, about 10 minutes or until heated through, stirring frequently. Before serving, stir in cilantro.

nutrition facts per serving: 151 cal., 7 g total fat (3 g sat. fat), 0 mg chol., 717 mg sodium, 21 g carb., 4 g dietary fiber, 2 g protein.

*note: See tip on handling chile peppers, page 31.

Coffee gives a deep, mellow flavor boost to this starter soup, which becomes even more pleasing topped with a spoonful of whipped cream at serving time.

tomato-joe soup

prep: 30 minutes cook: 25 minutes
makes: 6 to 8 servings

1 cup chopped onion
   (2 medium)
1 cup chopped celery
   (2 stalks)
1 cup chopped carrot
   (2 medium)
2 tablespoons butter
6 medium tomatoes
   (about 2 pounds),
   peeled and
   quartered, or two
   14.5-ounce cans
   diced tomatoes,
   drained
2 cups strong brewed
   coffee
½ cup water
1 6-ounce can tomato
   paste
2 teaspoons sugar
½ teaspoon salt
   Few dashes bottled
   hot pepper sauce
¾ cup whipping cream

1 In a saucepan cook onion, celery, and carrot in hot butter over medium heat about 5 minutes or until nearly tender, stirring occasionally. Add tomatoes, coffee, the water, tomato paste, sugar, salt, and hot pepper sauce. Bring to boiling; reduce heat. Simmer, covered, for 20 to 25 minutes, until vegetables are tender. Cool slightly.

2 Transfer tomato mixture, half at a time, to a blender or food processor. Cover and blend or process until smooth. Return pureed mixture to saucepan. Stir in ¼ cup of the whipping cream; heat through. In a mixing bowl beat remaining whipping cream with an electric mixer on low speed just until soft peaks form. Spoon some of the whipped cream on each serving.

nutrition facts per serving: 164 cal., 12 g total fat
(7 g sat. fat), 39 mg chol., 378 mg sodium, 14 g carb.,
3 g dietary fiber, 3 g protein.

Oven-roasting the garlic adds a sweet, mellow caramel flavor to this appetizer soup. When cleaning the mushrooms, wipe them with a clean, damp cloth. If you must rinse them, do it lightly, then dry them immediately—and gently—with paper towels. Never soak mushrooms in water because it ruins their texture.

portobello mushroom and roasted garlic soup

prep: 25 minutes roast: 45 minutes oven: at 325°F cook: 51 minutes
makes: 6 servings

1	whole head of garlic (10 to 12 cloves)
2	teaspoons olive oil
1	pound fresh portobello mushrooms
1	cup sliced celery (2 stalks)
1	cup chopped red or yellow sweet pepper (1 large)
2	tablespoons olive oil
1	tablespoon snipped fresh thyme or ½ teaspoon dried thyme, crushed
¼	teaspoon ground black pepper
2	14.5-ounce cans beef or vegetable broth
½	cup brown rice or pearl barley

1 Preheat oven to 325°F. To roast garlic, using a sharp knife cut off the pointed top portion from garlic head, leaving the bulb intact but exposing the individual cloves. Place in a small baking dish or custard cup; drizzle with 2 teaspoons olive oil. Bake, covered, for 45 to 60 minutes or until the cloves are very soft. Set aside until cool enough to handle. Squeeze garlic paste from individual cloves. Using a fork, mash garlic.

2 Cut off mushroom stems even with caps; discard stems and clean mushrooms. Thinly slice mushroom caps; cut slices into 2-inch pieces. Set aside.

3 In a large saucepan cook celery and sweet pepper in 2 tablespoons hot oil over medium-high heat for 3 minutes. Add mushrooms, dried thyme (if using), and pepper; cook for 3 to 4 minutes more or until vegetables are just tender, gently stirring occasionally.

4 Stir in broth; bring to boiling. Stir in brown rice and mashed garlic. Return to boiling; reduce heat. Simmer, covered, about 45 minutes or until rice is tender. Just before serving, stir in fresh thyme (if using).

nutrition facts per serving: 152 cal., 6 g total fat (1 g sat. fat), 3 mg chol., 375 mg sodium, 20 g carb., 4 g dietary fiber, 5 g protein.

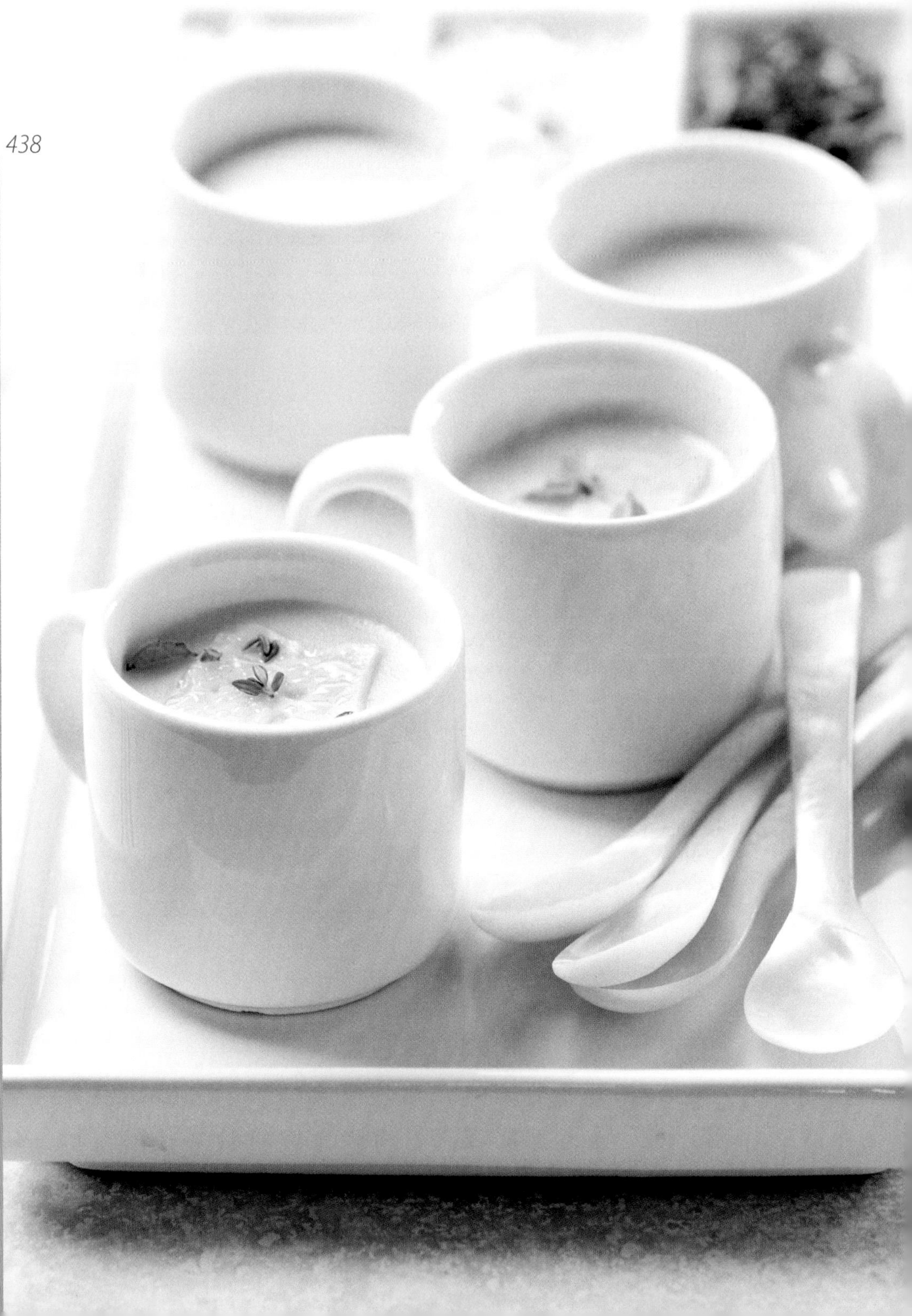

Yukon Gold potatoes have a beautiful golden color and a rich, creamy potato flavor, making soups like this extra delicious.

creamy potato soup

prep: 25 minutes   cook: 35 minutes
makes: 8 servings

2   cups thinly sliced
     onion or leek*
1   tablespoon olive oil
2   cups milk
3   tablespoons all-
     purpose flour
1   pound Yukon Gold
     potatoes, peeled
     and sliced
4   cups reduced-sodium
     chicken broth
8   ounces Swiss-style
     cheese, such as
     Gruyère or baby
     Swiss, shredded
     Salt
     Ground black pepper
     Snipped mixed fresh
     herbs
2   ounces baby Swiss
     cheese, thinly sliced
     (optional)

1 In a large saucepan or pot cook onions in hot oil over medium heat for 5 to 10 minutes or until tender. Whisk together milk and flour. Add to onions; cook and stir 5 minutes.

2 Add potatoes and broth. Bring to boiling; reduce heat. Cook, covered, for 20 minutes or until potatoes are tender. Remove from heat; cool slightly.

3 Transfer soup, half at a time, to a blender. Cover and blend until smooth. Return pureed mixture to saucepan. Add shredded cheese; cook and stir over medium heat just until cheese is melted. Season to taste with salt and pepper. Sprinkle with fresh herbs; garnish with sliced cheese. Serve at once.

nutrition facts per serving: 220 cal., 11 g total fat (6 g sat. fat), 31 mg chol., 441 mg sodium, 18 g carb., 1 g dietary fiber, 13 g protein.

*note: See tip on cleaning leeks, page 464.

make it easy

For smooth pureed soups, a handheld immersion blender is easy and safe to use. It lets you blend the soup right in the soup pot, so there's no need to bring out your blender or food processor.

Just the right amount of curry powder and pumpkin pie spice complements canned pumpkin puree for an easy, flavorful soup.

curried pumpkin soup

prep: 20 minutes   cook: 30 minutes
makes: 8 servings

2   tablespoons butter
2   medium onions,
      chopped (1 cup)
1   medium carrot,
      chopped (½ cup)
1   stalk celery, chopped
      (½ cup)
1   teaspoon curry
      powder
1   teaspoon pumpkin
      pie spice
2   15-ounce cans
      pumpkin
2   14-ounce cans
      reduced-sodium
      chicken broth
⅔   cup water
1   cup half-and-half
      or light cream
½   teaspoon salt
¼   teaspoon ground
      black pepper
1   recipe Orange-
      Cranberry Topper

1 In 4-quart Dutch oven melt butter over medium heat. Add onions, carrot, and celery; cook for 10 minutes until softened, stirring occasionally. Add curry powder and pumpkin pie spice; cook and stir 1 minute. Add pumpkin, broth, and the water. Increase heat to medium-high. Bring to boiling; reduce heat to medium-low. Simmer, covered, 15 minutes. Remove from heat; cool slightly.

2 Transfer pumpkin mixture, one-third at a time, to a food processor or blender. Cover and process or blend until smooth. Return pureed mixture to Dutch oven.

3 Stir half-and-half, salt, and pepper into pumpkin mixture; heat through. Sprinkle each serving with Orange-Cranberry Topper.

nutrition facts per serving: 145 cal., 7 g total fat (4 g sat. fat), 19 mg chol., 433 mg sodium, 20 g carb., 4 g dietary fiber, 4 g protein.

orange-cranberry topper: In small bowl combine ½ cup dried cranberries, 1 tablespoon finely shredded orange zest, and 2 tablespoons snipped fresh Italian parsley.

Saffron gives this garden-fresh chowder a bright orange-yellow color and a deliciously sophisticated flavor.

pepper-corn chowder

start to finish: 40 minutes
makes: 6 servings

Nonstick cooking
    spray
1   cup chopped onion
    (1 medium)
1   leek, chopped*
5   cups frozen whole-
    kernel corn
2   14-ounce cans
    reduced-sodium
    chicken broth
¾   cup chopped red
    sweet pepper
    (1 medium)
⅛   teaspoon ground
    black pepper
⅛   teaspoon cayenne
    pepper
3   threads saffron
    (optional)
    Snipped fresh chives
    and/or ground black
    pepper (optional)

1 Coat a 4-quart Dutch oven with nonstick cooking spray. Heat over medium heat for 1 minute. Add onion and leek; cook for 5 minutes or until tender, stirring occasionally.

2 Add frozen corn; cook for 5 minutes or until corn softens, stirring occasionally. Add 1 can of the broth. Bring to boiling; reduce heat. Simmer, covered, 20 minutes or until corn is very tender. Remove from heat; cool slightly.

3 Transfer half the corn mixture to a blender or food processor. Cover and blend or process until smooth. Return pureed corn mixture to Dutch oven.

4 Add the remaining can broth, sweet pepper, ⅛ teaspoon black pepper, cayenne pepper, and saffron; heat through. Top with snipped fresh chives and/or additional black pepper.

nutrition facts per serving: 155 cal., 1 g total fat (0 g sat. fat), 0 mg chol., 323 mg sodium, 35 g carb., 4 g dietary fiber, 7 g protein.

*note: See tip on cleaning leeks, page 464.

Lemongrass is a unique ingredient in Asian fare. As the name implies, the herb (which resembles a green onion) tastes like lemon. It's worth seeking out in an Asian market, but in a pinch, substitute 1 teaspoon finely shredded lemon zest for the 2 tablespoons lemongrass.

shiitake and lemongrass soup

prep: 20 minutes   cook: 20 minutes
makes: 4 servings

2   tablespoons butter
½   cup finely chopped onion (1 medium)
2   tablespoons finely chopped fresh lemongrass (2 stalks)
3   cups mushroom broth or vegetable broth
8   ounces fresh shiitake mushrooms, stemmed and sliced
1   tablespoon rice vinegar
⅛   teaspoon white pepper
1   cup coarsely chopped fresh spinach

1 In a large saucepan melt 1 tablespoon of the butter over medium-high heat. Add onion and lemongrass; cook about 5 minutes or until tender. Add broth. Bring to boiling; reduce heat. Simmer, uncovered, for 15 minutes. Pour through a fine-mesh sieve or a colander lined with 100-percent-cotton cheesecloth; discard onion and lemongrass.

2 Meanwhile, in a large skillet melt remaining 1 tablespoon butter over medium-high heat. Add mushrooms; cook about 5 minutes or until mushrooms are lightly browned on the edges. Remove from heat; set aside.

3 Stir in vinegar and pepper. Stir in spinach. Top each serving with cooked mushrooms.

nutrition facts per serving: 80 cal., 8 g total fat (4 g sat. fat), 16 mg chol., 770 mg sodium, 6 g carb., 2 g dietary fiber, 2 g protein.

Each bowl of this brothy soup holds a healthful portion of greens. In the produce aisle, look for peppery watercress with small dark green leaves. You can also use arugula.

italian spinach soup

start to finish: 35 minutes
makes: 6 servings

2   tablespoons butter
½   cup chopped onion
      (1 medium)
4   cloves garlic, minced
2   teaspoons dried
      Italian seasoning,
      crushed
2   tablespoons dry
      sherry (optional)
2   14.5-ounce cans
      chicken broth
1   cup peeled and
      chopped potato
      (1 large)
2   9-ounce packages
      fresh spinach
      Salt
2   cups watercress,
      tough stems
      removed
2   tomatoes, quartered,
      seeded, and thinly
      sliced
2   ounces Parmesan
      cheese, shaved

1 In a 4-quart Dutch oven heat butter over medium heat until melted. Add onion, garlic, and Italian seasoning; cook about 5 minutes or until onion is tender, stirring occasionally.

2 Carefully add sherry (if using); cook and stir for 1 minute. Add broth and potato. Bring to boiling; reduce heat. Simmer, covered, about 10 minutes or until potato is tender. Remove from heat.

3 Set aside 2 cups of the spinach. Stir remaining spinach, half at a time, into potato mixture just until wilted. Cook for 5 minutes.

4 Transfer potato mixture, half at a time, to a food processor or blender. Cover and process or blend until smooth. Return pureed mixture to Dutch oven; heat through. Season to taste with salt.

5 Top each serving with reserved 2 cups spinach, the watercress, tomatoes, and cheese.

nutrition facts per serving: 151 cal., 7 g total fat (4 g sat. fat), 18 mg chol., 881 mg sodium, 16 g carb., 4 g dietary fiber, 8 g protein.

Oven-roasting the carrots and parsnips for this pureed soup brings out their naturally sweet and nutty taste. For an elegant presentation, top each serving with mesclun, a mixture of young, tender greens with a range of colors and textures.

carrot-parsnip soup

prep: 30 minutes   roast: 35 minutes   oven: at 425°F
makes: 6 servings

8   carrots, cut into
      1-inch pieces
2   parsnips, peeled
      and cut into 1-inch
      pieces
1   onion, cut into thin
      wedges
1   tablespoon olive oil
3   14.5-ounce cans
      chicken broth
1   teaspoon smoked
      paprika
1   teaspoon lemon juice
      Ground black pepper
      Mesclun (optional)

1 Preheat oven to 425°F. In a shallow baking pan combine carrots, parsnips, and onion. Drizzle with oil; toss gently to coat. Spread vegetables in a single layer. Roast, uncovered, for 35 to 40 minutes or until tender.

2 In a large saucepan combine roasted vegetables, broth, and paprika. Bring to boiling; cool slightly.

3 Transfer vegetable mixture, half at a time, to a blender or food processor. Cover and blend or process until smooth. Return pureed mixture to saucepan. Stir in lemon juice; heat through. Season to taste with pepper. If desired, top each serving with mesclun.

nutrition facts per serving: 113 cal., 3 g total fat (0 g sat. fat), 0 mg chol., 903 mg sodium, 20 g carb., 6 g dietary fiber, 3 g protein.

Just five ingredients and about 15 minutes stack up to a terrific starter for a special meal.

curried shrimp and coconut soup

start to finish: 15 minutes
makes: 5 servings

8 ounces fresh or frozen peeled and deveined small shrimp
2 14-ounce cans chicken broth
4 ounces dried angel-hair pasta or vermicelli, broken into 2-inch pieces
1 tablespoon curry powder
1 cup unsweetened coconut milk
Sliced green onion or snipped fresh chives

1 Thaw shrimp, if frozen. Rinse shrimp; pat dry with paper towels. Set aside.

2 In a large saucepan bring broth to boiling. Add pasta and curry powder; return to boiling. Boil gently for 3 minutes. Add shrimp; cook for 2 to 3 minutes more or until shrimp are opaque and pasta is tender. Stir in coconut milk; heat through. Sprinkle each serving with green onion.

nutrition facts per serving: 268 cal., 14 g total fat (11 g sat. fat), 69 mg chol., 762 mg sodium, 22 g carb., 2 g dietary fiber, 15 g protein.

Edamame and carrots pair deliciously in this brothy soup. Crumb-coated and sautéed feta cheese cubes make up the tasty topper.

edamame soup with feta croutons

start to finish: 30 minutes
makes: 6 servings

¾ cup chopped sweet onion
4 teaspoons canola oil
1 cup thinly sliced carrot (2 medium)
2 cloves garlic, minced
2 14-ounce can reduced-sodium vegetable broth
1 12-ounce package frozen sweet soybeans (edamame)
1½ teaspoons snipped fresh thyme
1 egg white
1 tablespoon water
½ cup panko (Japanese-style) bread crumbs
4 ounces reduced-fat feta cheese, cut into ¾-inch cubes
Fresh thyme leaves (optional)

1 In a large saucepan cook onion in 2 teaspoons of the hot oil over medium heat about 5 minutes or until tender, stirring occasionally. Add carrot and garlic; cook and stir for 1 minute more. Add broth and edamame. Bring to boiling; reduce heat. Simmer, uncovered, about 5 minutes or until edamame and carrot are tender. Stir in thyme.

2 Meanwhile, for feta croutons, in a small bowl beat egg white and the water with a fork until frothy. Place bread crumbs in another small bowl. Dip feta cubes, one at a time, into egg white mixture to coat. Allow excess egg white mixture to drip off; coat feta cubes in bread crumbs.

3 In a large skillet heat the remaining 2 teaspoons oil over medium-high heat. Add feta cubes. Cook for 2 to 3 minutes or until brown but not softened, turning carefully to brown all sides of cubes. Drain feta croutons on paper towels.

4 Top each serving with feta croutons and, if desired, thyme leaves.

nutrition facts per serving: 193 cal., 9 g total fat (2 g sat. fat), 6 mg chol., 621 mg sodium, 15 g carb., 4 g dietary fiber, 14 g protein.

Curry and roasted sweet peppers—plus an aromatic pesto topper—deliver big color and flavor in this simple starter soup.

curried tomato–red pepper soup

start to finish: 25 minutes
makes: 6 servings

1   cup orzo
2   10.75-ounce cans condensed tomato soup
2½ cups milk
2   cups chopped cooked chicken
1   cup bottled roasted red sweet peppers, drained and chopped
1   teaspoon curry powder
    Pinch ground black pepper
2   tablespoons basil pesto

1 Cook pasta according to package directions. Drain; set aside.

2 Meanwhile, in a large saucepan stir together soup and milk. Heat over medium heat until soup simmers. Stir in cooked pasta, chicken, roasted sweet peppers, curry powder, and black pepper; heat through. Swirl 1 teaspoonful of basil pesto into each serving.

nutrition facts per serving: 362 cal., 9 g total fat (2 g sat. fat), 50 mg chol., 705 mg sodium, 45 g carb., 2 g dietary fiber, 23 g protein.

A Carolina favorite, this soup is usually made with crab roe. Since crab roe is only available for a short time, red caviar makes a tasty substitute that's available year-round. It gives the soup a delightful rosy hue.

she-crab soup

prep: 25 minutes   cook: 50 minutes
makes: 8 servings

1   tablespoon olive oil
1   cup chopped onion
     (2 medium)
½   cup sliced celery
     (1 stalk)
2   cloves garlic, minced
⅓   cup dry sherry
½   cup brown rice
1   recipe Fish Stock or
     3 cups reduced-
     sodium chicken
     broth
2   tablespoons crab roe
     or red caviar
2   cups fat-free half-
     and-half
8   ounces fresh or frozen
     cooked crabmeat,
     cartilage removed
     and flaked*
1   tablespoon snipped
     fresh chives

1 In a large saucepan heat oil over medium-high heat; add onion, celery, and garlic. Cook and stir until tender. Add sherry. Bring to boiling; reduce heat. Boil gently, uncovered, until liquid is nearly evaporated.

2 Stir in brown rice. Add Fish Stock and crab roe. Bring to boiling; reduce heat. Simmer, covered, about 40 minutes or until rice is very tender. Cool mixture slightly.

3 Transfer rice mixture, half at a time, to a blender or food processor. Cover and blend or process until almost smooth. Return pureed mixture to saucepan. Stir in half-and-half; heat through. Stir in crabmeat. Sprinkle each serving with snipped chives.

nutrition facts per serving: 160 cal., 3 g total fat (1 g sat. fat), 39 mg chol., 579 mg sodium, 19 g carb., 1 g dietary fiber, 9 g protein.

✳note: You can substitute canned lump crabmeat if fresh or frozen crabmeat is not available.

fish stock: Place the shells from 1 pound large shrimp in a large saucepan. Add 1 cup chopped carrot, ½ cup chopped celery with leaves, ⅓ cup chopped onion, 3 sprigs fresh parsley, 1 bay leaf, 3 whole black peppercorns, and ½ teaspoon salt. Add 3½ cups water and 1 tablespoon lemon juice. Bring to boiling; reduce heat. Simmer, covered, for 45 minutes. Strain mixture through 100-percent-cotton cheesecloth; discard solids. Store stock in the refrigerator for up to 3 days or in the freezer for up to 6 months. Makes 3 cups.

The subtle onion flavor of leeks blends sumptuously with the rich, nutty taste of Gruyère cheese in this velvety soup. Look for fresh looking leeks with crisp green leaves and stalks no greater than 1½ inches in diameter.

leek-gruyère cream soup

prep: 20 minutes cook: 15 minutes
makes: 8 servings

6 cups chicken broth
4 cups sliced leek*
1 cup sliced fresh mushrooms
1 teaspoon dried fines herbes, crushed
½ teaspoon ground white pepper
⅓ cup all-purpose flour
1½ cups shredded Gruyère cheese (6 ounces)
2 tablespoons snipped fresh parsley
1 cup whipping cream
 Thinly sliced leek (optional)

1 In a Dutch oven combine 4 cups of the broth, 4 cups leek, mushrooms, fines herbes, and pepper. Bring to boiling; reduce heat. Simmer, covered, for 10 to 15 minutes or until leek is tender. Cool slightly.

2 Transfer leek mixture, one-third at a time, to a blender or food processor. Cover and blend or process until smooth. Return pureed mixture to Dutch oven. Stir in 1 cup of the remaining broth.

3 In a small bowl stir together remaining 1 cup of broth and flour until smooth. Stir into leek mixture in Dutch oven. Stir in cheese and parsley; cook and stir over medium-low heat until slightly thickened and bubbly and cheese melts. Stir in whipping cream; heat through, but do not boil. If desired, garnish with additional sliced leeks.

nutrition facts per serving: 257 cal., 19 g total fat (11 g sat. fat), 60 mg chol., 768 mg sodium, 12 g carb., 1 g dietary fiber, 10 g protein.

*note: See tip on cleaning leeks, page 464.

15

cool summer

SO

Chilled soups made from fresh fruits and vegetables are a refreshing addition to warm-weather menus, whether it's a creamy vichyssoise for lunch or a tropical fruit soup for dessert. You may even be tempted to tote the savory or sweet bowlfuls in an ice-filled cooler for your next alfresco feast.

soups

Try something new by topping this chilled appetizer soup with queso fresco, a lightly salty Mexican cheese that has a mild, tangy taste. For the best overall flavor, be sure to use ripe avocados.

chilled avocado soup

prep: 15 minutes chill: 3 hours
makes: 6 servings

3 avocados, halved, pitted, and peeled
1 cup chicken broth
¼ cup water
1 cup half-and-half or light cream
¼ teaspoon salt
⅛ teaspoon onion powder
　 Pinch ground white pepper
1 tablespoon lemon juice
　 Lemon wedges (optional)
　 Crumbled queso fresco (optional)

1 Place avocados, broth, and the water in a blender or food processor. Cover and blend or process until smooth. Add half-and-half, salt, onion powder, and white pepper. Cover and blend or process until combined.

2 Transfer avocado mixture to a glass bowl. Stir in lemon juice. Cover and chill for 3 to 24 hours. Stir before serving. If desired, garnish with lemon wedges and queso fresco.

nutrition facts per serving: 167 cal., 15 g total fat (5 g sat. fat), 15 mg chol., 287 mg sodium, 7 g carb., 3 g dietary fiber, 3 g protein.

Sweet potatoes enhance our version of this classic soup, traditionally made with regular potatoes and leeks.

sweet potato vichyssoise

prep: 20 minutes   cook: 10 minutes   chill: 4 hours
makes: 6 to 8 servings

2   cups sliced leek
    (6 medium) or
    chopped onion
    (4 medium)*
2   tablespoons butter
2   cups cubed, peeled
    potato (2 medium)
2   cups chicken broth
1½ cups cubed, peeled
    sweet potato
    (1 large)
1   cup apple cider
    or apple juice
¼   teaspoon salt
    Pinch ground white
    pepper
2½ cups half-and-half,
    light cream,
    or whole milk
    Sour cream (optional)
    Snipped fresh chives
    (optional)

1 In a 3½- or 4-quart Dutch oven cook leek in hot butter until tender. Stir in potato, broth, sweet potato, apple cider, salt, and white pepper. Bring to boiling; reduce heat. Simmer, covered, for 10 to 15 minutes or until potatoes are tender.

2 Using an immersion blender, process until smooth**; transfer to a medium bowl. Stir half-and-half into potato mixture. If necessary, add more half-and-half to reach desired consistency. Chill for at least 4 hours. If desired, serve with sour cream and chives.

nutrition facts per serving: 270 cal., 16 g total fat (10 g sat. fat), 48 mg chol., 512 mg sodium, 25 g carb., 3 g dietary fiber, 5 g protein.

*note: See tip on cleaning leeks, page 464.

**note: If you don't have an immersion blender, cool potato mixture slightly. Transfer to a blender or food processor. Cover and blend or process until smooth. Return mixture to saucepan. (It is important to pulse when blending the soup to avoid overworking the potatoes.)

Canned tomatoes combine with fresh cucumber, green onions, and avocado for this simple summertime soup. For an added crunch and sweetness, the soup is topped with homemade corn bread croutons.

chilled tomato soup with corn bread croutons

start to finish: 25 minutes **oven:** at 400°F
makes: 4 servings

1   8.5-ounce package
    corn muffin mix
1   tablespoon olive oil
1   teaspoon chili
    powder
2   14.5-ounce cans
    diced tomatoes
    with green pepper,
    celery, and onion,
    undrained
½   of an English
    cucumber, seeded
    and coarsely
    chopped*
3   green onions,
    trimmed and
    coarsely chopped
1   cup ice cubes
1   medium avocado,
    halved, pitted,
    peeled, and sliced
    Assorted toppers
    (sliced green onion,
    chopped cucumber,
    and chili powder)
    (optional)
    Olive oil

1 Preheat oven to 400°F. Prepare corn muffin mix according to package directions. Spread in lightly greased 13×9×2-inch baking pan. Bake for 14 minutes or until golden and a toothpick inserted near the center comes out clean. Cool slightly. Cut in 1-inch cubes. Toss with oil and chili powder. Place on baking sheet and toast in oven for 5 minutes or until crisp.

2 In a blender combine undrained tomatoes, cucumber, onions, and ice. Cover and blend until nearly smooth. Pour soup in bowls; top with avocado and half the croutons (reserve remaining for another use). If desired, sprinkle with additional green onion, cucumber, and chili powder. Drizzle with olive oil.

nutrition facts per serving: 482 cal., 22 g total fat (2 g sat. fat), 40 mg chol., 1061 mg sodium, 66 g carb., 5 g dietary fiber, 9 g protein.

*note: Peel cucumber, if desired, for a lighter colored soup.

There is no cooking involved in creating this super-quick, refreshing summer soup. Serve it in small cups as a picnic appetizer.

garden-fresh gazpacho

prep: 40 minutes chill: 4 hours
makes: 12 servings

6   cups coarsely chopped tomato (6 medium)
1   cup peeled, seeded, and coarsely chopped cucumber (1 medium)
1   cup coarsely chopped green sweet pepper (1 medium)
1   cup tomato juice
¾   cup beef broth
¼   cup red wine
¼   cup red onion, finely chopped
1   jalapeño pepper, seeded and finely chopped*
2   tablespoons snipped fresh cilantro
1   tablespoon red wine vinegar
4   cloves garlic, minced
    Salt
    Ground black pepper
    Avocado pieces (optional)

1 In a very large bowl stir together tomato, cucumber, sweet pepper, tomato juice, broth, wine, onion, chile pepper, cilantro, vinegar, and garlic. Add salt and black pepper to taste. Cover and chill for at least 4 hours.

2 If desired, top each serving with avocado pieces.

nutrition facts per serving: 27 cal., 0 g total fat (0 g sat. fat), 0 mg chol., 115 mg sodium, 5 g carb., 1 g dietary fiber, 1 g protein.

*note: See tip on handling chile peppers, page 31.

seafood gazpacho: Prepare as directed, except before serving stir 8 ounces chopped cooked shrimp or 8 ounces lump crabmeat into the soup.

Ingredients found in hummus—chickpeas, tahini, lemon juice, and garlic—jazz up this pureed soup. Look for tahini (sesame seed paste) in the ethnic foods section of the supermarket.

cucumber-chickpea soup

start to finish: 25 minutes
makes: 4 to 6 servings

8   ounces peeled and
    deveined cooked
    cocktail shrimp,
    chopped
1   recipe Coriander-
    Paprika Spice Rub
2   medium cucumbers
1   15-ounce can
    garbanzo beans
    (chickpeas), rinsed
    and drained
¼   cup tahini (sesame
    seed paste)
¼   cup packed fresh
    mint leaves
2   tablespoons lemon
    juice
1   tablespoon olive oil
1   tablespoon honey
2   cloves garlic, smashed
1½ teaspoons ground
    coriander
¼   teaspoon salt
¼   teaspoon ground
    black pepper
¼   teaspoon cayenne
    pepper
3   cups ice cubes
½   cup cherry tomatoes,
    halved
4   green onions, cut into
    1-inch slivers

1 In a medium bowl toss shrimp with Coriander Paprika Spice Rub; set aside. Thinly slice enough cucumber to measure ⅓ cup; set aside. Peel, seed, and chop remaining cucumber.

2 In a blender combine chopped cucumber, chickpeas, tahini, mint, lemon juice, oil, honey, garlic, coriander, salt, black pepper, and cayenne pepper. Cover and blend until smooth, scraping sides of blender as needed.

3 Just before serving, with motor running, add ice cubes through lid opening a few at a time; process until smooth and thickened (blender will be full). Top each serving with shrimp, reserved sliced cucumber, tomatoes, and green onions.

nutrition facts per serving: 357 cal., 14 g total fat (2 g sat. fat), 111 mg chol., 752 mg sodium, 41 g carb., 7 g dietary fiber, 22 g protein.

coriander-paprika spice rub: In small bowl combine 1 teaspoon coriander, ½ teaspoon paprika, ¼ teaspoon salt, and ¼ teaspoon ground black pepper.

The jicama (HEE-kah-mah) *is a crisp, sweet edible root with a unique flavor that resembles a cross between an apple and the water chestnut. When choosing jicama, look for medium-size, firm tubers with dry roots.*

carrot-cucumber gazpacho

prep: 25 minutes chill: 1 hour
makes: 5 servings

2 large (about 1 pound) tomatoes, quartered and seeded
1½ cups carrot juice
2 tablespoons coarsely chopped fresh chives
1 medium cucumber, seeded and coarsely chopped (1½ cups)
1½ cups fresh corn kernels (3 ears) (optional)
¼ of a jicama, peeled and chopped (1 cup)
½ cup shredded arugula
1 to 2 tablespoons prepared horseradish
½ teaspoon salt
4 large or 6 small radishes, quartered or cut into chunks
Shredded arugula (optional)
Coarsely chopped radishes (optional)
Fresh corn (optional)
Lime wedges (optional)

1 In a blender or food processor combine tomatoes, carrot juice, and chives. Cover and blend or process until smooth. Transfer pureed mixture to a large bowl. Stir in cucumber, corn (if desired), jicama, ½ cup arugula, horseradish, and salt. Cover and refrigerate for at least 1 hour or up to 24 hours before serving.

2 Ladle soup into bowls or glasses. Top with the radishes. If desired, top with additional arugula, chopped radishes, and corn. Pass lime wedges.

nutrition facts per serving: 66 cal., 0 g total fat (0 g sat. fat), 0 mg chol., 270 mg sodium, 15 g carb., 2 g dietary fiber, 2 g protein.

This make-ahead soup is a great starter for a Mediterranean-inspired dinner featuring grilled lamb or chicken with roasted vegetables.

cucumber-yogurt-mint soup

prep: 20 minutes chill: 2 hours
makes: 4 servings

1   cucumber, peeled, seeded, and chopped
1   6-ounce carton plain low-fat yogurt
1   tablespoon lime juice
1   teaspoon honey
½   teaspoon ground cumin
¼   teaspoon salt
2   tablespoons milk (optional)
⅓   cup snipped fresh mint
     Snipped fresh mint

In a food processor or blender combine cucumber, yogurt, lime juice, honey, cumin, and salt. Cover and process or blend until smooth. If necessary, stir in milk to reach desired consistency. Stir in ⅓ cup mint. Cover and chill for 2 to 24 hours. Stir soup before serving. If desired, sprinkle each serving with additional snipped mint.

nutrition facts per serving: 56 cal., 1 g total fat (1 g sat. fat), 3 mg chol., 176 mg sodium, 8 g carb., 1 g dietary fiber, 4 g protein.

This make-ahead chilled soup is a colorful blend of tomatoes, tomatillos, cucumber, shrimp, and cilantro—it's as refreshing as it is easy.

red and green gazpacho

prep: 30 minutes chill: 1 hour
makes: 6 servings

3 cups chopped red and/or partially green tomatoes
½ cup chopped tomatillo
1 16-ounce can tomato juice (2 cups)
½ cup chopped cucumber
1 tablespoon seeded and finely chopped jalapeño pepper*
¼ cup finely chopped green onion
1 clove garlic, minced
¼ teaspoon bottled green hot pepper sauce
1 tablespoon olive oil
1 tablespoon lime juice
¼ cup finely snipped fresh cilantro
6 ounces peeled, cooked medium shrimp (12 to 15)

1 In a bowl combine tomatoes, tomatillo, tomato juice, cucumber, chile pepper, green onion, garlic, pepper sauce, oil, lime juice, and cilantro. Cover and chill for at least 1 hour and up to 8 hours.

2 To serve, reserve 6 shrimp. Coarsely chop remaining shrimp. Stir chopped shrimp into gazpacho. Spoon gazpacho into chilled bowls. Top each serving with reserved whole shrimp.

nutrition facts per serving: 90 cal., 3 g total fat (0 g sat. fat), 55 mg chol., 371 mg sodium, 10 g carb., 2 g dietary fiber, 8 g protein.

*note: See tip on handling chile peppers, page 31.

Ripe, creamy avocados, zesty lime juice, tomato salsa, and aromatic cumin give this soup a definite Southwestern appeal.

holy guacamole soup

prep: 25 minutes chill: 2 hours
makes: 6 to 8 servings

1 tablespoon vegetable oil
1 tablespoon butter
1 cup chopped red onion (1 large)
6 cloves garlic, minced
3 medium avocados, halved, pitted, peeled, and mashed (1¾ cups)
1 14-ounce can chicken broth or vegetable broth
1½ cups whipping cream
1 cup bottled salsa
2 tablespoons lime juice
2 tablespoons lemon juice
1 tablespoon ground cumin
 Assorted toppers (avocado slices, chopped red or yellow tomato, tortilla chips, lime slices, sour cream, and/or cooked shrimp) (optional)

In a 3-quart saucepan heat oil and butter over medium heat. Add onion and garlic; cook and stir about 5 minutes or until tender. Remove from heat; cool for 10 minutes. Stir in avocado, broth, whipping cream, salsa, lime juice, lemon juice, and cumin. Cover and chill for 2 to 4 hours. If desired, serve with assorted toppers.

nutrition facts per serving: 349 cal., 33 g total fat (16 g sat. fat), 88 mg chol., 436 mg sodium, 13 g carb., 4 g dietary fiber, 3 g protein.

The Spanish chilled soup gazpacho epitomizes the glory of the late summer garden's bounty. Honey, lime, and fresh ginger infuse this version with cool, refreshing character.

honey-lime gazpacho

start to finish: 20 minutes
makes: 4 servings

3   ripe red tomatoes, cored, seeded, and cut into chunks
2   cucumbers, seeded and cut into chunks
2   orange sweet peppers, seeded and cut into chunks
1   jalapeño pepper, seeded and chopped*
1   clove garlic, minced
⅓   cup lime juice
2   tablespoons honey
2   tablespoons fresh cilantro leaves
1½ teaspoons grated fresh ginger
¼   teaspoon sea salt
    Ice cubes
    Lime wedges and green onions (optional)

1 In a large bowl combine tomatoes, cucumbers, sweet peppers, chile pepper, and garlic. Transfer the tomato mixture, half at a time, to a food processor. Cover and process with several on/off pulses until you have large chunks. Return all of the mixture to the food processor. Add lime juice, honey, cilantro, ginger, and ¼ teaspoon sea salt. Cover and process with several on/off pulses until the mixture is just a little chunky. If desired, season to taste with additional sea salt.

2 To serve, place 2 or 3 ice cubes in each of four shallow bowls or glasses; ladle soup over ice. If desired, serve with lime wedges and green onions.

nutrition facts per serving: 114 cal., 1 g total fat (0 g sat. fat), 0 mg chol., 114 mg sodium, 28 g carb., 4 g dietary fiber, 3 g protein.

*note: See tip on handling chile peppers, page 31.

Choose the ripest tomatoes for the most luscious gazpacho. Sautéed in garlic and oil, whole wheat croutons add a delicious, satisfying crunch.

gazpacho
with garlic croutons

prep: 20 minutes **chill:** 2 hours
makes: 8 servings

2   cloves garlic
3   ripe tomatoes, peeled
      and cut into chunks
1   cucumber, peeled and
      cut into chunks
½   red sweet pepper,
      cut into chunks
½   sweet white or red
      onion, cut into
      chunks
1   cup tomato juice
1   tablespoon lemon
      juice
¼   teaspoon salt
⅛   teaspoon cayenne
      pepper
1   tablespoon olive oil
2   slices whole wheat
      bread, cut into
      ½-inch cubes

1 With a food processor running, drop
1 garlic clove through the feed tube and
process until finely chopped. Add tomatoes,
cucumber, sweet pepper, and onion to food
processor. Cover and process until smooth.
Transfer pureed mixture to a large bowl. Stir in
tomato juice, lemon juice, salt, and cayenne
pepper. Cover and chill for 2 to 24 hours.

2 Meanwhile, mince remaining 1 clove
garlic. In a large nonstick skillet cook garlic
in hot oil over medium-low heat until golden.
Add bread cubes; cook and stir 3 minutes or
until brown and crisp. Transfer croutons to a
bowl and let cool.

3 Stir gazpacho before serving. Top each
serving with croutons.

nutrition facts per serving: 61 cal., 2 g total fat
(0 g sat. fat), 0 mg chol., 189 mg sodium, 10 g carb.,
2 g dietary fiber, 2 g protein.

The Ancho Chile Tomato Sauce adds a smoky depth and a kick of spice to this tomato-based soup. You can make the sauce ahead and cover and refrigerate it for up to 1 week to use in this richly spiced soup.

chilled bloody mary soup

prep: 10 minutes   chill: 1 hour
makes: 4 servings

1	recipe Ancho Chile Tomato Sauce
1½	cups tomato juice
¼	cup lemon juice
1	tablespoon Worcestershire sauce
1	tablespoon prepared horseradish
½	teaspoon celery salt
	Prepared horseradish (optional)
	Bottled hot pepper sauce (optional)

In a blender combine Ancho Chile Tomato Sauce, tomato juice, lemon juice, Worcestershire sauce, horseradish, and celery salt. Cover and blend until smooth. Refrigerate, covered, for at least 1 hour or up to 3 days. If desired, add a dollop of horseradish or a few splashes of bottled hot pepper sauce to each serving.

nutrition facts per serving: 145 cal., 8 g total fat (1 g sat. fat), 0 mg chol., 973 mg sodium, 19 g carb., 4 g dietary fiber, 3 g protein.

ancho chile tomato sauce: Core 2¼ pounds tomatoes (5 or 6 medium) and cut in half; squeeze out and discard seeds. Cut tomatoes in chunks. Transfer tomato chunks, one-third at a time, to a food processor or blender. Cover and process or blend with several on/off turns; tomatoes should remain chunky. Transfer tomato mixture to a medium bowl. You should have about 3¼ cups tomatoes. Set aside. In a medium saucepan, heat 2 tablespoons olive oil over medium heat. Add ½ cup finely chopped onion; cook and stir until tender. Stir in 2 cloves garlic, minced, and 1 tablespoon ancho chile powder; cook and stir for 1 minute. Stir in tomatoes. Bring to boiling; reduce heat. Simmer gently, uncovered, about 15 minutes or until sauce is thickened. Stir in ¼ cup snipped fresh basil and ¾ teaspoon salt; heat through. Makes about 3 cups.

Buttermilk brings a pleasant tang to this classic French chilled potato soup. If you don't have room in your refrigerator to store a large container of the soup, add the buttermilk just before serving.

lemon-leek vichyssoise

prep: 35 minutes cook: 15 minutes chill: 8 hours
makes: 16 to 20 servings

6   medium leeks, thinly
    sliced*
2   tablespoons olive oil
    or vegetable oil
3   pounds potatoes,
    peeled and sliced
3   14-ounce cans
    reduced-sodium
    chicken broth
2   teaspoons finely
    shredded lemon zest
½   teaspoon salt
½   teaspoon ground
    white pepper
4   cups buttermilk
1   8-ounce carton fat-
    free or light sour
    cream
1   tablespoon lemon
    juice
    Lemon wedges
    (optional)

1 In a 4- to 5-quart Dutch oven cook leeks in hot oil until tender. Remove about half of the leeks with a slotted spoon. Transfer to a small container; cover and chill. Add potatoes, broth, lemon zest, salt, and white pepper to leeks in Dutch oven. Bring to boiling; reduce heat. Simmer, covered, about 15 minutes or until potatoes are tender. Cool slightly.

2 Transfer potato mixture in small batches to a blender or food processor. Cover and blend or process until smooth. Transfer pureed mixture to a very large container. Stir in buttermilk. Cover and chill for 8 to 48 hours.

3 Ladle into appetizer-size soup cups or bowls. In a small bowl, combine sour cream and lemon juice. Dollop a small spoonful of the sour cream mixture onto each serving. Top with chilled leek slices. If desired, serve with lemon wedges.

nutrition facts per serving: 115 cal., 2 g total fat (1 g sat. fat), 2 mg chol., 329 mg sodium, 19 g carb., 1 g dietary fiber, 5 g protein.

*note: To clean leeks, halve them lengthwise; rinse under cold running water, separating the layers to remove any dirt hidden inside.

The combination of chunky vegetables gives this refreshing soup a beautiful color. The garlic and lemon juice gives it a bit of zip.

chilled tomato-bean soup

prep: 40 minutes chill: 4 hours
makes: 8 to 10 servings

1 28-ounce can crushed tomatoes
1 15-ounce can garbanzo beans (chickpeas), rinsed and drained
1 14.5-ounce can diced tomatoes with basil, garlic, and oregano, undrained
1 11.5-ounce can hot-style vegetable juice
1 cup water
1 7-ounce jar roasted red sweet peppers, drained and chopped
1 medium cucumber, seeded and coarsely chopped
½ cup thinly sliced green onion (4)
½ cup snipped fresh parsley
¼ cup lemon or lime juice
4 cloves garlic, minced
   Whole green onions (optional)

1 In a large mixing bowl combine crushed tomatoes, garbanzo beans, undrained diced tomatoes, vegetable juice, the water, roasted sweet peppers, cucumber, ½ cup green onion, parsley, lemon juice, and garlic. Cover and chill for 4 to 24 hours

2 To serve, ladle soup into bowls or mugs. Garnish with whole green onions, if desired.

nutrition facts per serving: 116 cal., 1 g total fat, 0 mg chol., 797 mg sodium, 24 g carb., 5 g dietary fiber, 5 g protein.

If your watermelon is good and sweet, omit the sugar. Besides giving the soup a pretty presentation, the vegetable confetti adds flavor and crunch. Use a vegetable peeler to create the thin strips.

watermelon soup
with vegetables

prep: 25 minutes chill: up to 4 hours
makes: 6 servings

1 5- to 6-pound seedless
   watermelon
   Sugar (optional)
¾ cup finely julienned
   strips of carrot,
   zucchini, and/or
   yellow summer
   squash
1 tablespoon balsamic
   vinegar

1 Halve melon; scoop out pulp. Transfer pulp in batches to a blender or food processor. Cover and blend or process until smooth. Line a large colander with a double thickness of 100-percent-cotton cheesecloth. Strain pulp through cheesecloth, pressing out as much juice as possible. Discard pulp. Measure 6 cups watermelon juice. (Add water, if necessary, to equal 6 cups.)

2 Add sugar to taste. Cover and refrigerate soup until ready to serve.

3 Meanwhile, cook vegetables in a small amount of lightly salted boiling water for 2 minutes. Drain; transfer to a bowl of ice water to cool. Drain; wrap in plastic wrap. Chill in refrigerator until ready to serve.

4 To serve, stir balsamic vinegar into juice mixture. Ladle into bowls. Float strips of vegetables on top.

nutrition facts per serving: 69 cal., 0 g total fat (0 g sat. fat), 0 mg chol., 13 mg sodium, 17 g carb., 1 g dietary fiber, 1 g protein.

keep it cool

Serve your summer soup in chilled bowls so it stays refreshing longer. To chill soup bowls, place them in the refrigerator for 10 to 15 minutes before serving time.

Using a high oven temperature concentrates the mulled-fruit flavor of the pear, plums, cranberries, and apple in this gently spiced dessert.

spiced fruit soup

prep: 10 minutes   cook: 5 minutes   chill: 6 to 24 hours
makes: 6 servings

1   cup cranberries
      (4 ounces)
1   medium pear, cored
      and cut into bite-
      size pieces
1   medium cooking apple
      (such as Rome,
      Jonathan, or Fuji),
      cored and cut into
      bite-size pieces
3   plums, halved, pitted,
      and cut into thin
      slices
3   cups cranberry-apple
      juice
¼   cup packed brown
      sugar
1   tablespoon lemon
      juice
2   3-inch pieces stick
      cinnamon

In a large saucepan combine cranberries, pear, apple, and plums. Stir in cranberry-apple juice, brown sugar, lemon juice, and cinnamon sticks. Bring to boiling; reduce heat. Simmer, covered, for 5 to 6 minutes or until fruit is tender and skins on cranberries pop. Discard cinnamon sticks. Remove from heat; cool. Cover; chill 6 to 24 hours. Serve cold.

nutrition facts per serving: 174 cal., 0 g total fat (0 g sat. fat), 0 mg chol., 13 mg sodium, 45 g carb., 3 g dietary fiber, 1 g protein.

Enjoy this brisk, sweet soup best as a palate-refreshing chiller on a warm sunny day. To serve as a piping-hot comforter on a cold day, return the blended peas mixture to saucepan. Heat through and stir in the lemon juice.

chilled lemony pea soup

prep: 5 minutes   cook: 8 minutes   chill: 1 hour
makes: 4 servings

2   teaspoons olive oil
¼   cup sliced green
       onion (2)
1   14-ounce can
       reduced-sodium
       chicken broth
2   teaspoons cornstarch
2   cups shelled fresh
       peas or one
       10-ounce package
       frozen peas, thawed
1   tablespoon snipped
       fresh mint
1   tablespoon lemon
       juice
       Lemon slices

1 In a medium saucepan heat oil over medium heat. Add green onion; cook and stir for 30 seconds or until soft. Reserve 2 tablespoons of the chicken broth; add remaining broth to saucepan. Bring to boiling; reduce heat. Cook, covered, over medium-low heat for 5 minutes.

2 In a small bowl stir together cornstarch and reserved broth until smooth. Add cornstarch mixture to saucepan; cook and stir until slightly thickened and bubbly. Cook and stir for 2 minutes more. Remove from heat. Stir in peas and mint. Let mixture cool slightly.

3 Transfer pea mixture to a blender or food processor. Cover and blend or process until smooth. Transfer pureed mixture to a bowl. Cover and chill thoroughly, at least 1 hour. To serve, stir in lemon juice and garnish with lemon slices.

nutrition facts per serving: 93 cal., 3 g total fat (0 g sat. fat), 0 mg chol., 276 mg sodium, 13 g carb., 4 g dietary fiber, 5 g protein.

Reserve your ripest, juiciest melons for this tangy, sweet, and invigorating soup. Smell the melons when you shop for them at the market; they should make you want to close your eyes and drink in their fragrance.

strawberry-melon soup with gingered melon balls

prep: 40 minutes cook: 5 minutes chill: overnight
makes: 8 servings

1 small cantaloupe
½ of a small honeydew melon
½ cup unsweetened pineapple juice
⅓ cup sugar
1 tablespoon grated fresh ginger
1 8-ounce carton sour cream
1 6-ounce carton vanilla yogurt
4 cups fresh or frozen unsweetened strawberries
2 cups milk
   Fresh mint leaves (optional)

1 Using a small melon baller, scoop cantaloupe and honeydew into balls or use a knife to cut melons into cubes. You should have about 4 cups cantaloupe and 2 cups honeydew. Set melon pieces aside.

2 In a small saucepan combine pineapple juice, sugar, and ginger. Bring to boiling, stirring until sugar dissolves; reduce heat. Simmer, uncovered, over medium heat for 5 to 7 minutes or until mixture is the consistency of a thin syrup. Remove from heat; cool. Transfer syrup to a storage container. Add 2 cups of the cantaloupe pieces and all of the honeydew pieces. Cover and chill overnight.

3 Meanwhile, in a large bowl stir together sour cream and yogurt; set aside. In a blender or food processor, blend or process strawberries until smooth. Add pureed strawberries to sour cream mixture. Add remaining 2 cups cantaloupe pieces to blender or food processor. Cover and blend or process until smooth. Add pureed melon and milk to strawberry mixture; stir to combine. Cover and chill overnight.

4 To serve, drain melon balls, reserving syrup. Stir reserved syrup into the chilled soup. Ladle soup into bowls; top with melon balls. If desired, garnish with mint leaves.

nutrition facts per serving: 198 cal., 7 g total fat
(4 g sat. fat), 21 mg chol., 78 mg sodium, 30 g carb.,
2 g dietary fiber, 5 g protein.

note: Page numbers in *italics* indicate illustrations.

index

index

metric information

The charts on this page provide a guide for converting measurements from the U.S. customary system, which is used throughout this book, to the metric system.

Product Differences

Most of the ingredients called for in the recipes in this book are available in most countries. However, some are known by different names. Here are some common American ingredients and their possible counterparts:
- Sugar (white) is granulated, fine granulated, or castor sugar.
- Confectioners' sugar is icing sugar.
- All-purpose flour is enriched, bleached, or unbleached white household flour. When self-rising flour is used in place of all-purpose flour in a recipe that calls for leavening, omit the leavening agent (baking soda or baking powder) and salt.
- Light-colored corn syrup is golden syrup.
- Cornstarch is cornflour.
- Baking soda is bicarbonate of soda.
- Vanilla or vanilla extract is vanilla essence.
- Green, red, or yellow sweet peppers are capsicums or bell peppers.
- Golden raisins are sultanas.

Volume and Weight

The United States traditionally uses cup measures for liquid and solid ingredients. The chart below shows the approximate imperial and metric equivalents. If you are accustomed to weighing solid ingredients, the following approximate equivalents will be helpful.
- 1 cup butter, castor sugar, or rice = 8 ounces = ½ pound = 250 grams
- 1 cup flour = 4 ounces = ¼ pound = 125 grams
- 1 cup icing sugar = 5 ounces = 150 grams

Canadian and U.S. volume for a cup measure is 8 fluid ounces (237 ml), but the standard metric equivalent is 250 ml.

1 British imperial cup is 10 fluid ounces.

In Australia, 1 tablespoon equals 20 ml, and there are 4 teaspoons in the Australian tablespoon.

Spoon measures are used for smaller amounts of ingredients. Although the size of the tablespoon varies slightly in different countries, for practical purposes and for recipes in this book, a straight substitution is all that's necessary. Measurements made using cups or spoons always should be level unless stated otherwise.

Common Weight Range Replacements

Imperial / U.S.	Metric
½ ounce	15 g
1 ounce	25 g or 30 g
4 ounces (¼ pound)	115 g or 125 g
8 ounces (½ pound)	225 g or 250 g
16 ounces (1 pound)	450 g or 500 g
1¼ pounds	625 g
1½ pounds	750 g
2 pounds or 2¼ pounds	1,000 g or 1 Kg

Oven Temperature Equivalents

Fahrenheit Setting	Celsius Setting*	Gas Setting
300°F	150°C	Gas Mark 2 (very low)
325°F	160°C	Gas Mark 3 (low)
350°F	180°C	Gas Mark 4 (moderate)
375°F	190°C	Gas Mark 5 (moderate)
400°F	200°C	Gas Mark 6 (hot)
425°F	220°C	Gas Mark 7 (hot)
450°F	230°C	Gas Mark 8 (very hot)
475°F	240°C	Gas Mark 9 (very hot)
500°F	260°C	Gas Mark 10 (extremely hot)
Broil	Broil	Grill

*Electric and gas ovens may be calibrated using Celsius. However, for an electric oven, increase Celsius setting 10 to 20 degrees when cooking above 160°C. For convection or forced air ovens (gas or electric) lower the temperature setting 25°F/10°C when cooking at all heat levels.

Baking Pan Sizes

Imperial / U.S.	Metric
9×1½-inch round cake pan	22- or 23×4-cm (1.5 L)
9×1½-inch pie plate	22- or 23×4-cm (1 L)
8×8×2-inch square cake pan	20×5-cm (2 L)
9×9×2-inch square cake pan	22- or 23×4.5-cm (2.5 L)
11×7×1½-inch baking pan	28×17×4-cm (2 L)
2-quart rectangular baking pan	30×19×4.5-cm (3 L)
13×9×2-inch baking pan	34×22×4.5-cm (3.5 L)
15×10×1-inch jelly roll pan	40×25×2-cm
9×5×3-inch loaf pan	23×13×8-cm (2 L)
2-quart casserole	2 L

U.S. / Standard Metric Equivalents

⅛ teaspoon = 0.5 ml	
¼ teaspoon = 1 ml	
½ teaspoon = 2 ml	
1 teaspoon = 5 ml	
1 tablespoon = 15 ml	
2 tablespoons = 25 ml	
¼ cup = 2 fluid ounces = 50 ml	
⅓ cup = 3 fluid ounces = 75 ml	
½ cup = 4 fluid ounces = 125 ml	
⅔ cup = 5 fluid ounces = 150 ml	
¾ cup = 6 fluid ounces = 175 ml	
1 cup = 8 fluid ounces = 250 ml	
2 cups = 1 pint = 500 ml	
1 quart = 1 liter	

emergency substitutions

emergency **substitutions**

If you don't have:	Substitute:
Bacon, 1 slice, crisp-cooked, crumbled	1 tablespoon cooked bacon pieces
Baking powder, 1 teaspoon	½ teaspoon cream of tartar plus ¼ teaspoon baking soda
Balsamic vinegar, 1 tablespoon	1 tablespoon cider vinegar or red wine vinegar plus ½ teaspoon sugar
Bread crumbs, fine dry, ¼ cup	¾ cup soft bread crumbs, or ¼ cup cracker crumbs, or ¼ cup cornflake crumbs
Broth, beef or chicken, 1 cup	1 teaspoon or 1 cube instant beef or chicken bouillon plus 1 cup hot water
Butter, 1 cup	1 cup shortening plus ¼ teaspoon salt, if desired
Buttermilk, 1 cup	1 tablespoon lemon juice or vinegar plus enough milk to make 1 cup (let stand 5 minutes before using) or 1 cup plain yogurt
Chocolate, semisweet, 1 ounce	3 tablespoons semisweet chocolate pieces, or 1 ounce unsweetened chocolate plus 1 tablespoon granulated sugar, or 1 tablespoon unsweetened cocoa powder plus 2 teaspoons sugar and 2 teaspoons shortening
Chocolate, sweet baking, 4 ounces	¼ cup unsweetened cocoa powder plus ⅓ cup granulated sugar and 3 tablespoons shortening
Chocolate, unsweetened, 1 ounce	3 tablespoons unsweetened cocoa powder plus 1 tablespoon cooking oil or shortening, melted
Cornstarch, 1 tablespoon (for thickening)	2 tablespoons all-purpose flour
Corn syrup (light), 1 cup	1 cup granulated sugar plus ¼ cup water
Egg, 1 whole	2 egg whites, or 2 egg yolks, or ¼ cup refrigerated or frozen egg product, thawed
Flour, cake, 1 cup	1 cup minus 2 tablespoons all-purpose flour
Flour, self-rising, 1 cup	1 cup all-purpose flour plus 1 teaspoon baking powder, ½ teaspoon salt, and ¼ teaspoon baking soda
Garlic, 1 clove	½ teaspoon bottled minced garlic or ⅛ teaspoon garlic powder
Ginger, grated fresh, 1 teaspoon	¼ teaspoon ground ginger
Half-and-half or light cream, 1 cup	1 tablespoon melted butter or margarine plus enough whole milk to make 1 cup
Molasses, 1 cup	1 cup honey
Mustard, dry, 1 teaspoon	1 tablespoon prepared (in cooked mixtures)
Mustard, yellow, 1 tablespoon	½ teaspoon dry mustard plus 2 teaspoons vinegar
Onion, chopped, ½ cup	2 tablespoons dried minced onion or ½ teaspoon onion powder
Sour cream, dairy, 1 cup	1 cup plain yogurt
Sugar, granulated, 1 cup	1 cup packed brown sugar or 2 cups sifted confectioners' sugar
Sugar, brown, 1 cup packed	1 cup granulated sugar plus 2 tablespoons molasses
Tomato juice, 1 cup	½ cup tomato sauce plus ½ cup water
Tomato sauce, 2 cups	¾ cup tomato paste plus 1 cup water
Vanilla bean, 1 whole	2 teaspoons vanilla extract
Wine, red, 1 cup	1 cup beef or chicken broth in savory recipes; cranberry juice in desserts
Wine, white, 1 cup	1 cup chicken broth in savory recipes; apple juice or white grape juice in desserts
Yeast, active dry, 1 package	about 2¼ teaspoons active dry yeast
Seasonings	
Apple pie spice, 1 teaspoon	½ teaspoon ground cinnamon plus ¼ teaspoon ground nutmeg, ⅛ teaspoon ground allspice, and dash ground cloves or ginger
Cajun seasoning, 1 tablespoon	½ teaspoon white pepper, ½ teaspoon garlic powder, ½ teaspoon onion powder, ½ teaspoon ground red pepper, ½ teaspoon paprika, and ½ teaspoon black pepper
Herbs, snipped fresh, 1 tablespoon	½ to 1 teaspoon dried herb, crushed, or ½ teaspoon ground herb
Poultry seasoning, 1 teaspoon	¾ teaspoon dried sage, crushed, plus ¼ teaspoon dried thyme or marjoram, crushed
Pumpkin pie spice, 1 teaspoon	½ teaspoon ground cinnamon plus ¼ teaspoon ground ginger, ¼ teaspoon ground allspice, and ⅛ teaspoon ground nutmeg